WRITING GENDER
IN WOMEN'S LETTER COLLECTIONS
OF THE ITALIAN RENAISSANCE

MEREDITH K. RAY

Writing Gender in Women's Letter Collections of the Italian Renaissance

UNIVERSITY OF TORONTO PRESS
Toronto Buffalo London

©University of Toronto Press Incorporated 2009
Toronto Buffalo London
www.utppublishing.com
Printed in Canada

ISNB 978-0-8020-9704-0

Printed on acid-free paper

Library and Archives Canada Cataloguing in Publication

Ray, Meredith K., 1969–
Writing gender in women's letter collections of the Italian Renaissance / Meredith K. Ray.

(Toronto Italian studies)
Includes bibliographical references and index.
ISBN 978-0-8020-9704-0

1. Italian letters – Women authors – History and criticism.   2. Italian letters – Early modern, 1500–1700 – History and criticism.   3. Women and literature – Italy – History – 16th century.   4. Women and literature – Italy – History – 17th century.   5. Letter writing, Italian – History – 16th century.   6. Letter writing, Italian – History – 17th century.   7. Italian prose literature – To 1700 – History and criticism.   I. Title.   II. Series: Toronto Italian studies.

PQ4183.L4R39 2009   856'.4099287   C2009-901165-4

University of Toronto Press acknowledges the financial support for its publishing activities of the Government of Canada through the Book Publishing Industry Development Program (BPIDP).

University of Toronto Press acknowledges the financial assistance to its publishing program of the Canada Council for the Arts and Ontario Arts Council.

For my grandmother, Mary Gertrude Benante Wade, 1910–2008

Contents

Acknowledgments ix

PART ONE: THE VERNACULAR LETTER IN CONTEXT

Introduction: Reading the *Lettera familiare* 3

1 Women's Vernacular Letters in Context 19

PART TWO: THE EPISTOLARY CONSTRUCTION OF GENDER

2 Female Impersonations: Ortensio Lando's *Lettere di molte valorose donne* 45

3 '*A gloria del sesso feminile*': The *Lettere* of Lucrezia Gonzaga as Exemplary Narrative 81

PART THREE: EPISTOLARY SPACE AND FEMALE EXPERIENCE

4 The Courtesan's Voice: Veronica Franco's *Lettere familiari* 123

5 Between Stage and Page: The Letters of Isabella Andreini 156

6 The Pen for the Sword: Arcangela Tarabotti's *Lettere familiari e di complimento* 184

Epilogue: Writing Letters, Performing Gender 214

Notes 221
Bibliography 323
Index 355

Acknowledgments

In writing this book, I have benefited at every stage from the support of colleagues, friends, and family, who each contributed to it in their own fundamental ways. I am deeply grateful to Elissa Weaver, who read early versions of each chapter with her meticulous critical eye, and whose pioneering scholarship and passion for Italian literature and women's writing remain sources of great inspiration to me. I am fortunate to count her as my mentor and friend. I also thank Rebecca West and Paolo Cherchi, who offered valuable suggestions and insights early on, along with friendship and humour over the years. For their generosity in taking the time to read and comment on many drafts, I am grateful to Cristina Guardiola, Mark Jurdjevic, Dana Katz, Crennan Ray, Diana Robin, and, especially, Scott Johnson, who read more pages, more often, than anyone. Conversations with Virginia Cox, Barbara Fuchs, Daria Perocco, Laura Salsini, and many other colleagues here and in Italy kept me thinking and seeing things in new ways. The anonymous readers at the University of Toronto Press offered thoughtful comments on my manuscript for which I am also grateful; while the wonderful Ron Schoeffel guided me and my book through the publication process with the kindness, encouragement, and efficiency for which he is known. Many thanks to Anne Laughlin, Beth McAuley, and Shealah Stratton for their care and expertise in the preparation of the book.

Portions of chapter 3, section one, appear in my article 'Textual Collaboration and Spiritual Partnership in Sixteenth-Century Italy: The Case of Ortensio Lando and Lucrezia Gonzaga,' forthcoming in *Renaissance Quarterly*. Earlier versions of portions of chapter 6 appeared elsewhere as 'Letters From the Cloister: Defending the Literary Self in Arcangela Tarabotti's *Lettere familiari e di complimento*' published in

Italica 81, no. 1 (2004): 24–43, and 'Making the Private Public: Arcangela Tarabotti and the *Lettere familiari e di complimento*,' in *Arcangela Tarabotti: A Literary Nun in Baroque Venice*, edited by E. Weaver (Ravenna: Longo, 2006), 173–89. I am grateful for the suggestions of the anonymous readers at *Italica* and for the comments and lively discussion of the participants in the Tarabotti symposium at the University of Chicago back in 1997, all of which helped me better to shape my work.

The support of several institutions has been fundamental to the completion of this study. I gratefully acknowledge the Fulbright Foundation and the American Association of University Women for their financial support in 1999 and 2000 when I first began studying women's epistolary collections for my doctoral dissertation at the University of Chicago. I also thank my home institution, the University of Delaware, and especially Dr Richard Zipser, Chair of Foreign Languages and Literatures, for supporting and advocating for my project through research and travel funding and a crucial semester of research leave in 2007. A 2004–5 University of Delaware General Research Grant allowed me to complete new research that was essential to this book. I benefited greatly from the helpful and knowledgeable staff at the many libraries and archives I visited during the researching of this book, especially at the Biblioteca Nazionale of Florence, the Biblioteca Estense of Modena, the Biblioteca Marciana of Venice, the Vatican Library, and the state archives of Venice, Mantua, Modena, and Rovigo. In the United States, I was fortunate to have access to Special Collections at the University of Chicago and Newberry Libraries as well as at the University of Delaware. I am particularly indebted to John Pollack of the University of Pennsylvania's Rare Book and Manuscript Library for allowing me so freely to consult Penn's extensive holdings in early modern Italian letterbooks.

Finally, as my friends and family know, my life has taken some unexpected turns in the last few years. I want to thank each of them for their love and support in the hardest of times – especially my parents Crennan and David Ray, my sister Lauren Pollard, and John, Miranda, and Grace Pollard; Julie and Norman Johnson; my dear friends Dana Katz, Amy Chinn, and Natalia Bulgari, and, most of all, my husband Scott and my son Owen Johnson, who brings joy to me every day. I share with them the accomplishment of bringing this project, at long last, to a close.

PART ONE

The Vernacular Letter in Context

Introduction: Reading the *Lettera familiare*

I

In a letter published in her 1552 *epistolario,* Lucrezia Gonzaga da Gazuolo offers an apt definition of the *lettera familiare,* or personal letter, when she explains to Girolamo Parabosco that she enjoys his letters because they seem so natural: '... non sono vestite d'arte, né gonfiate di lusinghevole o vano studio, ma puramente favellano ...' ('they are not clothed in artifice, nor puffed up from excessive revision, but rather speak plainly ...').[1] Gonzaga's *epistolario* was printed at the height of the vernacular letter's popularity in Italy, and her comments to Parabosco reflect the common notion of what the vernacular, 'familiar' letter should be: a natural and spontaneous composition, rather than a studied, formal piece of writing.[2] The effect of spontaneity or artlessness – akin to what Castiglione termed *sprezzatura* – was much appreciated in the epistolary genre and lauded by its many theorists, but in reality published letters were not unmediated by literary artifice.[3] In fact, Parabosco's most successful published letters were those he wrote under a woman's name, while the authorship of Gonzaga's own letters has been questioned by critics who would identify the *poligrafo* Ortensio Lando as their composer, and her book derives part of its content from a repertory text. The familiar letters of the Venetian writer and courtesan Veronica Franco pay homage to classical models, and those of the Benedictine nun Arcangela Tarabotti are revised at points from earlier manuscript versions. Pietro Bembo famously reworked his vernacular letters for years (and died before he could see them published); other humanist letter writers were similarly obsessive revisers.[4] Self-fashioning, self-censorship, revision, masquerade – all are common to the epistolary genre.

4 The Vernacular Letter in Context

The familiar letterbook, a genre that flourished in Italy from the age of Petrarch to that of Marino, is a work of literary construction, one in which ostensibly personal correspondence is used to produce a carefully crafted epistolary self-representation. Under the guise of a 'private' communication between writer and addressee, the individual letters in a published *epistolario* provide readers with fragmentary sketches from which to reconstruct an image of the writer. When considered together, these fragments form the writer's public self. Following the enormous success of Pietro Aretino's first volume of letters in 1538, dozens of writers, grasping the genre's potential as both a commercial and literary endeavour, rushed to publish their correspondence, using it as a forum for self-representation, self-promotion, and even dissent.[5] Among this virtual flood of letter writers were a number of women, who brought to the genre a wide range of female experience, from discussions of marriage, motherhood, sexuality, and virtue to reflections on the challenges of being a woman writer. So marked was the audience for women's epistolary texts that even some male writers published letters under women's names. Such texts capitalized on the convergence of a broader cultural interest in defining social and gender roles (as evidenced, for example, in comportment literature or the *querelle des femmes*, or debate over women) with the conviction that letter-writing was, unlike other literary genres, an innately feminine form. This study focuses on epistolary representations of women, both authentic (written by women) and impersonated (male-authored), the dynamics and goals of which have never been fully examined and compared in the early modern Italian context. I argue that all such collections were a studied performance of pervasive ideas about gender as well as genre, a form of self-fashioning that variously reflected, manipulated, and subverted cultural and literary conventions regarding femininity and masculinity.[6]

Many of the women who wrote and published letters in early modern Italy are familiar to us through their other literary works. The courtesan Veronica Franco, for example, was also the author of a book of verse, as was the *petrarchista* Chiara Matraini. The *commedia dell'arte* actress Isabella Andreini was a poet and the author of a pastoral play, *La mirtilla*, as well as a book of letters; the Roman *virtuosa* Margherita Costa, who published a volume of *Lettere amorose*, was even more prolific. Suor Arcangela Tarabotti of Venice penned several protofeminist texts in addition to her *Lettere familiari e di complimento*. Still others, such as Lucrezia Gonzaga (whose Fratta *palazzo* served as a centre for literary gatherings), are known to us for their status as cultural figures. While the epistolary personae adopted by these women differ, all of these writers made an important contribution to the burgeoning epistolary genre by expanding its parameters to include the female voice.

Although these women were among the first to publish vernacular letter collections after Aretino, they were not the first to write letters for a public audience. The letters of Catherine of Siena, for example, a blend of spiritual and political counsel, were among the first printed books in Italy and indeed have been called 'the first great collection of letters in the vernacular.'[7] The fifteenth-century writers Isotta Nogarola, Laura Cereta, and Cassandra Fedele each made brilliant use of the genre in its pre-Aretinian, humanist incarnation, prefiguring in many ways the gendered self-portraiture of later women epistolarians.[8] Olimpia Morata of Ferrara wrote poems, dialogues and letters in Greek and Latin, published posthumously in her *Opera omnia*. Ceccarella, or Francesca Minutolo, enjoyed a measure of fame for her eclectic collection of letters that circulated in manuscript form around 1470.[9] In the first half of the sixteenth century, women contributed to many facets of the epistolary genre, producing not just familiar letters, but love letters, letters on religious themes, and didactic letters. The renowned poet Vittoria Colonna, for example, published a small but significant collection of spiritual letters in 1544. Letters by another important poet, Veronica Gambara, are included in several sixteenth-century anthologies and were finally collected and published in a single volume in the mid-eighteenth century.[10]

In addition, women – like men – engaged regularly in private correspondence that was not destined for publication, whether for personal or family business. Although it is beyond the scope of the present study to examine women's unpublished correspondence – that rich territory of actually exchanged letters intended only for a particular, specified reader, a subject worthy of a book in itself – it would be remiss not to recall the trove of material found in the letters exchanged between Vittoria Colonna and Michelangelo, for example, or Maria Savorgnan and Pietro Bembo, not to mention the family history laid out in the letters of Alessandra Macinghi Strozzi to her exiled sons.[11] Likewise, the letters of Suor Maria Celeste to her father, Galileo, paint an absorbing picture of seventeenth-century convent life, while also allowing us to see Galileo the scientist through the prism of his role as a father.[12] The archives are filled with countless such documents, most exchanged among far less well-known figures: letters penned by mothers, daughters, wives, and nuns to friends, relatives, husbands and patrons – they remain only to be discovered. Indeed, much of the important current work on women's letter-writing focuses on unpublished documents of this sort, which present a different set of interpretative and historical problems than their published counterparts.[13]

Published letter collections, however, take on characteristics beyond those found in correspondence not destined for so wide and so public a viewing.[14] As literary texts that aspired to the appearance of unmediated personal exchanges – yet were often revised, censored, or completely fabricated – collections of familiar letters were constructed at the intersection of private and public communication, a stand-in for intimate conversation made accessible to a broad audience. Demetrius, one of the earliest theorists of the letter, characterized the letter as one half of a spoken dialogue; Cicero, as a dialogue with an 'absent friend.'[15] Erasmus, one of the great epistolary theoreticians, echoed Turpilius' definition of the letter as a 'mutual conversation between absent friends';[16] and Francesco Sansovino wrote that 'famigliare è quella lettera che noi scriviamo all'amico delle nostre facende' ('a familiar [letter] ... is one we write to a friend with our news').[17] Integral to any letter is the participation of the reader, who provides the missing half of the 'conversation' necessary to complete its meaning. In the case of early modern letters, published or not, this missing piece might be supplied by more than one reader, or indeed by an entire epistolary community, for in many cases letters circulated as communal intellectual and social documents. As Gary Schneider points out in his recent study of the early modern English context, 'Letters ... were sociotexts: collective social forms designed, understood, and expected to circulate within designated epistolary circles.'[18]

All letters, then, depend upon a reader or readers, but a published letter collection requires at least two implicit and distinct readers to achieve its full interpretative significance. If, at one level, the published *epistolario* creates the illusion of a 'private' exchange between specific parties, it also establishes a second, equally important relationship between the letter writer and the reader of the entire collection. In a study of modern epistolary fiction, Janet Altman uses the terms 'internal' and 'external' readers to distinguish these levels of readership.[19] For a published letter collection, it is the external reader in particular who functions as the book's essential interpretive engine, organizing each individual letter into a narrative from which emerges an epistolary portrait of the writer. The letter writer is, in turn, influenced by both internal and external readers in the production of meaning: at the moment of writing, the writer's knowledge of a future audience (of the external as well as the internal reader, if the writer is aware that the letter will be published) influences the choice of linguistic and stylistic registers as well as content.[20] The letter writer may also, to a degree, influence the reader, setting out each individual letter as a piece of an epistolary puzzle, and anticipating the puzzle's consolidation in a future moment of interpretation by the external reader.[21] The epistolary personae that emerge from these letter collections can, in fact, mask a variety of hidden messages, agendas, and identities apparent to the external but not the internal reader: A wife writing letters on behalf of her husband, for example, may actually write to pursue her own place in the literary arena; a woman's letter may have been composed by a man (or vice versa).

In some cases the *epistolario* functions as a vehicle for controversial views, such as religious dissent or social criticism, which require the 'right' reader for retrieval.[22] The letter writer plants clues in a published collection; it is the external reader's job to extract the message contained in the text as a whole, completing the writer's process of epistolary self-construction. The process of constructing and publishing a letter, and thereby creating a public epistolary persona, involves writer, letter recipient(s), and outside reader in a multifaceted interpretative process, in which each plays a role in the manufacture of meaning. This process is never fully stable, however. As one recent study of early modern English letters notes, 'Acts of writing and reading the familiar letter involve making and inferring meanings that may be pertinent to a single reading only as well as constructing meanings that might shift with the circumstances in which the letter might be read.'[23] The complex layers of epistolary composition made it a useful and powerful tool as well as a creative instrument, one that offered exciting possibilities for self-construction and expression.

II. Women and the Epistolary Genre

If the published *epistolario* is a form of disguise, a pretense of intimate, one-to-one communication within the wider communicative network engendered by its circulation as a published document, it is also a public performance of identity and a declaration of literary authority unlike that found in other genres. Despite its aspirations to intimacy and spontaneity, the published collection of familiar letters is the product of a process of revision and self-construction that obscures boundaries between the writer's personal world (written exchanges with family, friends, and patrons) and the literary world (the audience for the collection). As Andrea Battistini notes, it took the 'corraggio' of Aretino to presume that his familiar letters (in Aretino's case, some 3,000 of them), from which his own personality and experience emerge as the clear protagonist, would be not only worthy of print, but of interest to the reading public.[24] If for male writers the publication of one's 'familiar' or personal correspondence constituted an act of public exposure and risked the accusation of narcissism, for women writers the act was still more audacious, performed in a cultural climate that seemed to discourage their participation in the public sphere.[25] That women were enjoined by cultural conventions to chaste silence in theory, if not in practice, is reiterated by numerous Renaissance treatises, including works such as Stefano Guazzo's *Civil conversazione*, which asserted, 'è sommamente lodato nella donna quel silenzio che tanto l'adorna e che tanto accresce l'opinione della sua prudenza' ('most highly prized in a woman is that silence which so suits her and augments her reputation for prudence'); and Castiglione's *Libro del cortegiano*, which similarly connected a woman's modest speech to her good reputation.[26] Dozens of others made the same point, including many works that were written in defence of women, such as Juan Luis Vives' *De institutione feminae Christianae*.[27] The humanist Isotta Nogarola, even as she circulated her own works, recalled Sophocles' characterization of silence as 'women's special adornment.'[28]

On a broader scale, cultural anxiety about woman's speech and her access to the written word were reflected in a number of early modern texts, many of which sought to limit women's education to the vernacular reading and writing skills that would make her a virtuous wife and mother. A woman's true education, according to Francesco Barbaro, lay in her comportment, including good manners, silence, and, of course, virginity.[29] By contrast, Barbaro characterized female speech as dangerous, equivalent to a public display of nakedness.[30] Even among defenders of women and their intellectual capabilities – more numerous, at least in literary debate, as the *querelle des femmes* continued to unfold over the course of the sixteenth century – such ideas about sex and speech persevered, even as women themselves began publishing in greater numbers. Vives linked women's education to chastity, stating, 'when this has been thoroughly elucidated, she may be considered to have received sufficient instruction,' while Agrippa's *Declamatio de nobilitate et praecellentia foeminei sexus* attributed women's superiority in part to their superior sense of shame.[31] Although Castiglione asserted that the *donna di palazzo* ought to be educated in letters as well as music and art, he maintained that one of her most important tasks was to refrain from gossip, lest she be considered unchaste. Likewise, she should not be remarked upon by others, lest her reputation suffer.[32] Part of women's *grazia*, that prized element of courtly interaction, lay in adeptly and imperceptibly navigating this paradox.

Historians such as Margaret L. King and Patricia LaBalme have argued that learned women were often viewed with hostility in early modern culture, their speech standing in opposition to the feminine virtues of silence and chastity. Hence erudite women might be perceived as 'intellectual transvestites' – a kind of third sex – or else sexually impure.[33] The humanist Laura Cereta complained that women themselves perpetuated this notion, and lambasted these 'veritable Megearas who can't stand to hear the epithet "learned women."'[34] They were tolerated, and even admired, primarily when seen to live lives of unquestionable chastity, or when they closely adhered to male literary norms, thus containing the destabilizing force that men seemed to fear in the female voice. Although recent work on women in early modern Italy has been most instructive in reasserting the degree to which women freely participated in literary culture, in many cases without evident opposition, such ideas about women intellectuals persisted in the sixteenth and seventeenth centuries, at least on the printed page.[35] This helps explain why a woman writer like Lucrezia Gonzaga could be praised for exemplary wifely fidelity even as she authorized a strikingly public as well as personal epistolary self-portrait, and Isabella Andreini's orthodox writings were widely lauded as paragons of masculine literary excellence; while outspoken protofeminist writers like Veronica Franco and Arcangela Tarabotti were, by contrast, the targets of great hostility throughout their careers.

If the female voice – both in its literal incarnation and in its reflection in women's learning and writing – was associated not only with unchecked speech but with physical accessibility, female silence (or not-writing) was the sign of chastity.[36] Letter-writing, described by theoreticians from Cicero to Erasmus as a substitute for conversation, makes concrete the connection between speech and writing. The letter, as Claudio Guillén points out, functions as a 'basic hinge between orality and writing.'[37] If a woman who speaks (or writes) becomes a 'public' figure, she is never more public or more available to her readers than within the very personal framework of the familiar letter. When the names of Lucrezia Gonzaga, Arcangela Tarabotti, or any other woman appeared on the frontispiece of her letters, the early modern reader was apt to connect that name to the experience and persona described in the text.[38] The act of publishing her familiar letters – or allowing someone else to publish them – thus made her vulnerable to accusations of lack of literary merit in comparison to men, as well as to speculation about her moral character.[39]

Given this cultural climate, the act of making public what was ostensibly private correspondence was an implicitly transgressive one for women writers, no matter how orthodox some of the resulting texts may have appeared. At the same time, as I show in this study, the gradual intersection of a growing literature concerned with defining the nature and role of women, together with the widely held perception that the letter was a 'natural,' even feminine medium, rather than an art (as implied by Gonzaga's comments to Parabosco), created a deep interest in women's epistolary collections – authentic or otherwise – by readers who sought them out as models of epistolary style and by editors and publishers eager to capitalize on a clear market demand for women's letters. Such texts, whether authored by women or the product of a form of literary ventriloquism on the part of male writers, engage in a kind of knowing construction (and deconstruction) of the conventions of gender identity, the epistolary genre, and literary persona.

III. The Feminization of Epistolary Writing

As the market for vernacular letterbooks continued to increase throughout the sixteenth century, so did readers' appetite for texts that reflected (or purported to reflect) the experience of women. Indeed, an interest in examining, defining, and appropriating female experience is apparent not just in epistolary texts, but across early modern literary genres. At one end of the spectrum were literary texts that inserted themselves into the *questione della donna* or 'woman question' (from Agrippa's *Declamatio* to Sperone Speroni's *Della dignità delle donne*), or that sought to codify female behaviour (for example Lodovico Dolce's *De la institution de le donne*). At the other end was a profusion of 'how-to' manuals, many of which addressed the experience or concerns of women. Male-authored medical treatises, for example, taught women how to conceive and give birth, while a barrage of less erudite *libri di segreti* added recipes for making soap or cosmetics and methods for removing stains from soiled clothing to discussions of pregnancy, childbirth, and lactation. What all such texts have in common is an interest in teaching women how to negotiate their world, in describing that world, and in making it accessible to an external audience. This interest speaks to the reality of a new female readership that emerged as vernacular texts began to replace Latin works, and the eagerness of writers and editors to take advantage of it; it also raises questions of literary authority and appropriation, as we will see in part two of this study.

If female experience attracted growing attention in dialogues, treatises, and how-to manuals, epistolary expressions of female experience were also increasingly embraced by an audience of both sexes, fuelled in large part by common perceptions of letter-writing as an innately 'feminine' activity. As scholars have pointed out, from the sixteenth through (at least) the eighteenth century, letter-writing was considered a natural and therefore innately feminine practice, distinct from more 'literary' forms of writing.[40] Letter-writing was merely the translation of experience onto paper, a practice requiring neither art nor training, but only spontaneity and feeling. This lack of 'art' did not detract from the enjoyment elicited in the reader. Indeed, a good letter was one that spoke simply but sincerely, with emotional force, as described by Gonzaga in her letter to Parabosco.[41] The best letters, therefore, were 'unliterary.' Although putatively devoid of rhetorical elaboration, they often and paradoxically were the result of heavy revision or direct literary imitation.

The construction of epistolary practice as natural and specifically feminine helps explain how women were able to navigate the gendered minefield of reputation and publication. On the one hand, women's *epistolari* constituted public expressions of self, implicit and explicit challenges to the cultural codes that privileged female silence. Indeed, the first-person narrative of epistolary writing and the association it encouraged between author and epistolary protagonist rendered the letter writer uniquely accessible to her audience. Therefore, as Elizabeth Goldsmith has noted, a conflict was staged when women published their letters and the 'new admiration for a "natural" feminine style' in the letter clashed with 'old arguments about female virtue,' for, Goldsmith continues, 'to be virtuous was to be modest, self-effacing, above all not talked about, and most certainly not published.'[42] On the other hand, when perceived as an emotional rather than an artistic outlet, letter-writing threatened no boundaries between the sexes, encroached upon no male literary space. In a sense, then, this gendering of genre may have contributed to the diffusion of women's letterbooks, obscuring the actual transgressive element of such texts. Of course, this effort to relegate women's writing to the realm of the non-literary was potentially limiting in its effects. Katharine Jensen investigates this problem with regard to French letterbooks, pointing to the circular reasoning set up by such 'gendered theories of letter-writing' as that of the seventeenth-century author La Bruyère, which claimed women were well-suited to epistolary writing but lacked the art necessary for other genres.[43] Men, according to such theories, did not come naturally by the emotion that women so effortlessly poured into their letters, but they could acquire it; in addition, they already possessed the requisite art. That is, although women could not satisfactorily compete in masculine genres, men could easily learn to participate in a feminine genre. By 'giving' epistolary writing to women, men saved the 'literary' realm for themselves (while at the same time reserving the right to engage in letter-writing). If letter-writing had the potential to threaten boundaries between public and private space by blurring the lines between the two, then the insistence on the non-literary quality of the letter was an attempt to preserve these divisions, to keep 'private' or feminine experience confined to its proper realm, a social function rather than a literary art.[44]

The construction of letter-writing as a social, feminine practice raises compelling questions about the concept of women's writing and about the literary construction of gender. What does it mean to write 'like a woman'? I don't mean to engage here in a critique of *l'écriture feminine*, but rather to stress that the idea of 'writing like a woman' evokes a concept of a writing that, in both its structural attributes and its content, reflects a specifically female experience. Yet ideas about what constitutes 'female' writing are the reflection of cultural concepts of male and female at any given time, constructs to be assumed, appropriated, or discarded. For early modern women writers, choosing a 'feminine' medium in which to express themselves – writing, that is, 'like women' – was, despite its apparent limitations, one way to circumvent restrictive attitudes towards female expression and presence in the public realm.[45] However – and we will return to this point throughout the subsequent chapters – many women writers went on to use epistolary space in transgressive ways, publicizing and valorizing their own experience and implicitly or explicitly commenting on the literary and cultural construction of gender. In some cases, like that of Andreini, a writer drew deliberate attention to such constructions by writing obviously fictionalized compositions in both male and female voices.

The conflict produced by the collision of cultural ideal and literary vogue forms an integral element of the *epistolari* authored by women in this period. But women were not the only writers who attempted to navigate this conflict and to use epistolary space as a forum for female experience. Some of the most frequently reprinted 'women's' letter collections of the second half of the sixteenth century were, in fact, 'female impersonations': texts written by men and published under women's names. Ortensio Lando's *Lettere di molte valorose donne*, an anthology of letters purportedly composed by nearly 200 women, was immediately reprinted following its initial publication in 1548; while Parabosco's phenomenally successful *Lettere amorose* included a section of love letters composed by the author in the 'female voice.'[46] The pseudonymous *Lettere amorose di Madonna Celia*, one of the most reprinted letter collections of the sixteenth century, has also been attributed to Parabosco.[47] Examples of epistolary ventriloquism abound in later centuries – the *Lettres portugaises*, Samuel Richardson's epistolary novels *Clarissa* and *Pamela*, as well as earlier examples that include Ovid's *Heroides* and Boccaccio's *Elegia di madama Fiammetta* (which drew upon Ovid).[48] At the heart of such cases of epistolary cross-dressing were issues of literary authority. If, on the one hand, these books could function as manuals of women's writing, teaching readers how to imitate the 'female' style, they were, on the other hand, demonstrations of the writers' own literary bravura in having mastered this style. The literary reconstruction of gender becomes the focal point of such texts and the core of their innovation, deliberately exposing what Linda S. Kauffman terms 'the literary artifice of gender.'[49] Stylistically, then, such female impersonations were a demonstration of skill – the successful literary imitation of gender the triumph of art over nature.

Female impersonations raise an important question about the literary construction of gender: if gender is itself a social construction, a kind of 'performance' (to follow Judith Butler's formulation), how is it represented in the epistolary context, which fashioned itself as a specifically feminine genre?[50] The efforts of male writers to master the female epistolary voice inevitably reflect perceptions about women and women writers as well as ideas about gender and genre, and differ to varying degrees from women's own self-constructions. Given not only the phenomenon of epistolary ventriloquism, but the wider, gendered theorization of epistolary writing, it is essential to interrogate how letter-writing came to be constructed as a feminine genre and how that construction was thought to be reflected in epistolary practice. As

Goldsmith contends, 'Any study of the female voice in epistolary literature ... must examine male ideas of what it means to write as a woman, along with the writings of real women.'[51] As we examine women's letters and male representations of women's letters, the literary and performative aspects of the epistolary construction of gender become ever more apparent.

Finally, writing 'like a woman' had commercial implications for both male and female authors. As recent studies have highlighted, the epistolary market was one in which literary production and the book market were beginning to come together, and in which editors took an active role in trying to create and meet reader demand.[52] Letters, as we will see in chapter 1, were a popular commodity – easily produced and quickly consumed, and publishing letters under one's own name granted immediate public status and recognition. Publishing letters under an assumed name, however, had its own benefits. An anonymous or pseudonymous book could be produced quickly and without fear of negative reflection on the author or accusations of literary narcissism, and some of the profits of a successful book would rebound to the writer, if only through future commissions. Thus, a Parabosco or Lando might simply have responded to a demand for women's letters that was not being fully met, given that women still published in far smaller numbers than men. Women's letters and pseudo-letters also fit into a growing interest among readers for books that could teach them how to do things. Epistolary manuals and repertories such as those published by Battista Ceci, Bartolommeo Miniatore, and Francesco Sansovino demonstrated a practical concern for promoting the kind of courtly culture and 'civil conversation' aspired to by Guazzo and Castiglione, and taught readers how to compose socially appropriate missives through the imitation of examples.[53] Some of these manuals included specific instruction on how to write 'like a woman,' often through the presentation of women's love letters, an epistolary typology that would continue to grow in popularity throughout the century. Many epistolary anthologies included women's letters as models as part of a broader project to promote the *volgare* as a literary language. Comportment literature, *libri di segreti*, and medical manuals exhibited a parallel concern with female experience via discussions of marriage, motherhood, pregnancy, childbirth, or household management. In female impersonations like that of Lando, for example, the didactic vein of texts like these merged with ideas about epistolary style and an almost voyeuristic interest in women's experience to produce the male-authored book of 'women's' letters.

Women's letter collections, those composed by women as well as female impersonations, thus evolved out of a literary and cultural climate that had a deep interest in women's experience and in feminine epistolary style, despite its broader ambivalence to women's participation in learning and the production of literature. Epistolary writing itself was theorized in gendered terms, and writers negotiated this framework in different ways. In all the cases considered in this study, the literary and epistolary construction of gender plays an increasingly central role.

The following chapters examine the ways in which early modern ideas about gender and women's social roles, and about literary activity in general and letter-writing in particular, converged in women's published *epistolari*. Chapter 1 situates women's epistolary production within the literary and cultural context of early modern Italy, focusing specifically on the development of the epistolary genre from its humanist origins (with particular attention to the work of women humanists such as Isotta Nogarola, Cassandra Fedele, and Laura Cereta), to its post-Aretinian form. It examines the literary tradition that gave rise to the new vernacular letterbook, and the expectations and concerns of letter writers and readers. I look at the models that existed for the kinds of gendered self-positioning found in later vernacular letters, and I investigate the gradual evolution of epistolary texts from Aretino's example to the highly stylized collections that characterize the later part of the century. My discussion here focuses on the letters of Aretino as well as on an important anthology published by Paolo Manuzio, both of which help provide a clear picture of the literary, cultural, and commercial aspects that fuelled the epistolary genre.

Part two of my study turns to the increasing sixteenth-century interest in women's letters, the accompanying assumptions of readers and writers regarding the female epistolary voice, and the problem of epistolary ventriloquism. How was gender constructed in male representations of the female voice within the space of the published vernacular letter? Chapter 2 focuses on Ortensio Lando's anthology of 'women's' letters, the *Lettere di molte valorose donne* (1548). I argue that Lando's collection, which addresses a range of issues pertaining to women, from the domestic (household chores, child-rearing, medical remedies, and cosmetics) to the literary (specifically the 'famous women' catalogue and the *querelle des femmes*), critiques humanist epistolary tradition by radically expanding the parameters of the epistolary genre and by doing so in the voices of women. At the same time, I question what it meant for Lando to write 'like a woman,' and what relationship his impersonation has to the epistolary self-representations of real women.

Chapter 3, by contrast, looks at the *Lettere ... a gloria del sesso feminile* (1552), a collection of letters by Lucrezia Gonzaga, a sixteenth-century woman who was widely acclaimed for her learning and her virtue, but which some critics have argued is actually another female impersonation by Lando (who made Gonzaga an interlocutor in many of his works, including the *Valorose donne*). Gonzaga claims to publish her *epistolario* in an effort to win support for her notoriously imprisoned husband, and indeed many of her letters are written to or about him; but other, equally important undercurrents run through her collection, from a desire for literary recognition to an increasing fascination with the heterodox religious views that were sweeping through Italy (and for which she would ultimately be tried by the Inquisition in Mantua). Gonzaga's collection thus performs multiple functions as a kind of true-crime narrative (through her husband's story), a model of exemplary womanhood (through her self-representation as a paragon of wifely loyalty), and as a literary self-portrait and a font of heterodox religious views. Although the complex literary relationship that existed between Gonzaga and Lando, along with certain stylistic similarities between the *Lettere ... a gloria del sesso feminile* and the *Lettere di molte valorose donne*, lends credence to his editorial intervention in her text, evidence for Gonzaga's involvement in this work published under her name can be found not only in the testimony of her contemporaries but also in Italian archives (specifically, a number of manuscript letters penned by Gonzaga to various correspondents). I argue, therefore, that a scenario of literary collaboration and partnership capitalizing on the market for women's epistolary collections is the more likely explanation for this text, which makes an interesting comparison to Lando's *Lettere*: the one choral in nature, the other strikingly individual.

Part three of this study continues to explore the wide range of women's published collections over the span of the genre's greatest popularity, turning now to three women who were known for their prolific literary activity. The letter collections of Veronica Franco (1580), Isabella Andreini (1607), and Arcangela Tarabotti (1650) – three women who occupied very different social roles – provide a panorama of female experience in the early modern period as well as of diverse approaches to epistolary writing. Franco, discussed in chapter 4, was a renowned courtesan, closely linked to Venetian literary society through her influential patron Domenico Venier. Her elegant missives recall classical and humanist models while also allowing her identity as a cultured courtesan to play a central role. Published as Franco's fortunes were on the wane, the collection was a last attempt at professional and artistic self-promotion, a literary performance that sought to capitalize on the particular popularity of women's epistolary texts. Andreini's letters, by contrast, the subject of chapter 5, reflect her experience as a *prima donna innamorata* on the commedia dell'arte stage. Essentially a collection of highly stylized discourses on love, Andreini's compositions engage in a knowing and overt performance of gender, as the author assumes both male and female voices to create what may be called a hermaphroditic epistolary text. Far removed from the narrative specificity of Gonzaga's letters, for example, Andreini's letters reflect an engagement with a late sixteenth-century trend towards increasingly generic, fictionalized letters, a movement informed by a growing body of epistolary manuals and repertories.

Finally, Tarabotti, whose *epistolario* is examined in chapter 6, was a *monaca forzata* – a nun forced to take vows without a religious vocation. Forbidden by the newly strengthened doctrine of *clausura* to leave her convent, yet determined to create a name for herself as a literary figure as well as to condemn the practice of forced enclosure, the letter had more practical importance for Tarabotti than for any of the other women discussed here. For her, letter-writing constituted a way – the only way – to transcend the convent of Sant'Anna and to establish and maintain relationships beyond its walls, especially in the literary world. As Tarabotti began to draw heated criticism for her other polemical works, including accusations of plagiarism, she used her letters to defend herself and promote her literary reputation. Her letters, in contrast to those of Andreini, constitute a distinct departure from the trend towards generic letters modelled on epistolary repertories, and instead recall Aretino's pointed use of the medium to punish his enemies and reward his supporters.

Studying women's letters and examining ideas about gender and epistolarity can contribute greatly to our understanding of the ways in which gender was constructed in the early modern period, yet this area has not been fully explored for early modern Italian letter collections. In negotiating the familiar letter's fundamental tension between public and private communication, between artifice and experience, women letter writers questioned the constructs of gender and genre. In all the cases considered here, the act of publication serves to assert the value of female experience, declaring it worthy of contemplation and imitation by a public that demanded that letters exhibit the qualities of *utilità* (usefulness) as well as *diletto* (entertainment), as we will see in the next chapter.

1 Women's Vernacular Letters in Context

I. Women and the Humanist Tradition

In 1552, the erudite noblewoman Lucrezia Gonzaga followed Aretino's epistolary example when she published her *Lettere ... a gloria del sesso feminile*, a collection of familiar letters composed in the vernacular. The writers Veronica Franco, Isabella Andreini, and Arcangela Tarabotti would soon follow suit. By the time these women were composing and publishing their *epistolari* in the sixteenth and seventeenth centuries, however, the letter had undergone significant linguistic, structural, and thematic transformations. The letterbooks of these late Renaissance women differed from their earlier, humanist predecessors in many respects, not only because they were written in Italian rather than Latin and therefore addressed a different public but also because of the central role that gender played in these volumes. This concern was largely absent from the male-authored humanist collections of the fifteenth and early sixteenth centuries. Only in the works of a small handful of early women humanists do we discern some precedents for the kind of gendered self-portraiture found in these later texts. Among vernacular letter writers of the sixteenth century, by contrast, gender was a frequent backdrop to letter-writing, due not only to the increased activity of women epistolarians but also to popular characterizations of letter-writing as a feminine activity, as we saw in the introduction. This chapter situates early modern women's epistolary writing in its historical and literary context by thinking about what the genre looked like in its Latin incarnation, when a *libro di lettere* was the hallmark of Italian humanists from Petrarch to Bembo – and what women were able to accomplish within its confines. It then examines the changes the letter underwent as a result of the vernacular renaissance set in motion by Pietro Aretino in the mid-sixteenth century, including the ways in which writers, editors, and readers approached and understood the published letterbook, both generally and with specific regard to women's epistolary production.

Undoubtedly, Aretino's experimentation with the letterbook helped pave the way for the women writers I examine in this study. Indeed, Aretino is widely recognized as the 'father' of the vernacular letterbook.[1] His letters (six volumes altogether) touched a chord among both readers and writers, who responded eagerly to this 'new' or at least reinvented genre. Aretino's first volume – by far his most successful – was reprinted twelve times within two years of its initial publication in 1538. Its impact was wide and enduring: by 1627 more than 500 such vernacular letter collections had been published in Italy.[2] The women who published epistolary collections in early modern Italy owed much to the vernacular bravado of Aretino's *Lettere,* but they also shared a genealogy with certain pre-Aretinian women who had sought to express the female voice within the parameters – or confines – of the humanist letterbook. In the mid-fifteenth century, well before Aretino made his appearance as Venice's 'secretario del mondo' (a self-designation that evoked the shift from the letter writer as a secretary in the service of a prince to one who served himself and his public) and inspired a revival of interest in the *lettera familiare,* the writers Isotta Nogarola, Cassandra Fedele, and Laura Cereta all sought to make their mark within humanist culture by composing and circulating letter collections.[3] Those of Nogarola (1418–66), one of the most learned women of the early Renaissance, circulated in Venice and Rome by the mid-1400s, and those of Fedele (1465–1558), considered by many of her contemporaries to have been the greatest woman writer of her century, were also read during her lifetime. Likewise, the letters of Laura Cereta (1469–99) were copied and distributed while the author was still alive, between 1488 and 1492. The fame attained by all three women during their lifetimes was due in great part to the compelling self-portraits they were able to paint in their letters, cementing their position as valid participants in humanist culture.[4]

In composing and circulating their letters, all three women participated in a genre with a history as old as literature itself, its models rooted in antiquity with the letters of Cicero, Pliny the Younger, and Seneca.[5] The fourteenth century had seen the felicitous discovery of Cicero's familiar letters by Petrarch (himself an epistolarian whose

Familiares would become a model for those who followed him) and Coluccio Salutati, marking the beginning of a gradual shift away from the medieval *ars dictaminis*.[6] In the fifteenth and early sixteenth centuries, as the humanists turned to the past for epistolary models, it was Cicero they strove to emulate (although letters continued to reflect a tension between the two traditions). Latin letters written by men such as Poggio Bracciolini, Antonio Beccadelli, Enea Silvio Piccolomini, and Pietro Bembo represented an attempt to recuperate the classical tradition, mediated through the example of Petrarch.[7] Although the humanists aspired to the 'familiar' quality of the Ciceronian model, their interest in rhetoric and their very imitation of classical models imbued their letters with a certain artificiality.[8] Fundamental to the humanist letter was its studied erudition, which truly set it apart from many of its vernacular descendants.[9] Because the humanists used letter-writing not only to prove their skill as writers but also to spread humanist principles, many of their letters were dissertations on issues of cultural or political import and intended for a wider audience than a single recipient.[10] According to one modern editor of Aretino's letters, 'la distanza cronologica e linguistica' of these learned letters transformed them into historical and literary documents, in which the author reigned as an 'unico testimone,' and from which the reader was, in a sense, excluded.[11] Often rendered abstract by the generality of the arguments they addressed, humanist letters were closer to treatises than private exchanges, and were intended primarily as a demonstration of the writer's abilities as well as a reflection of the epistolary networks in which he moved. A kind of intellectual autobiography, they highlighted the writer's relationships with other scholars and patrons, his reputation, and his accomplishments. Indeed, more than one critic has likened the humanist letterbook to today's scholarly dossier: it reflected the writer's credentials, his skill as a thinker and critic, and his position within the field.[12] To a certain extent these aspects persisted in the vernacular letterbooks of the sixteenth and seventeenth centuries – particularly the highlighting of important associations and literary accomplishments and the quest for public recognition – but they would come to exist alongside a new set of concerns relating to family, everyday life, and practical advice as quotidian as how to do one's laundry or swaddle a baby – a set of concerns that allowed ample room specifically to address the experience of women in domestic as well as literary life. The practical capacities of the letter would come to be emphasized over its rhetorical underpinnings, with Aretino demonstrating how to use the letter to navigate the myriad events and relationships that made up an individual's life.

Nogarola, Fedele, and Cereta used the letterbook to the same ends as did their male counterparts: to gain literary recognition and attain lasting fame. Structured like letters, the collections of Nogarola, Fedele, and Cereta are carefully constructed essays on a range of humanist themes, such as virtue, fortune, friendship, and other stock topics, and are aimed at displaying the authors' erudition. Despite the Ciceronian notion of the letter as a 'dialogue with an absent friend,' a definition that implicates (at least) two voices, these letters are, in effect, monologues rather than dialogues.[13] They are not 'personal letters' as we understand them today, but rather formalized discourses.[14] Diana Robin, for example, writes of Cereta's letters that they are 'little more than projections of her own ego – the entire letterbook is a soliloquy of sorts.'[15] Indeed, each of Cereta's letters is a self-contained work, complete in its own right. They do not require the participation of the reader to fill in blanks or silences, to supply the other half of the 'conversation,' to orient the letter in time and space. In contrast to many later vernacular letters, the humanist letter is meant to transcend time and space. Concrete details that might ground it to a specific place or moment are often absent (date, time, place, specific detail) and only occasionally do individual letters appear to respond to practical rather than literary exigencies. In this way, each letter can stand alone and the author can (attempt to) retain control over its meaning. Cereta's letter to 'Europa solitaria' on the theme of the virtues of solitude versus city life, for example, is so self-contained that it has been referred to as a true soliloquy, the addressee 'Europa' a stand-in for the writer herself.[16] Fedele's very formal letter of consolation to Duke Pietro d'Aragona follows humanist conventions and could be adapted easily to another correspondent, serving as it does first and foremost to highlight the writer's skill at the genre.[17] Similarly, Cereta's consolatory letter to Martha Marcella contains a variety of standard funerary tropes and resembles those of male humanists from Petrarch to Filelfo.[18] Such letters of consolation could be read, appreciated, and imitated by any reader basically familiar with the consolatory form. Compare these letters, by contrast, to Arcangela Tarabotti's much later letters of condolence regarding her friend, the French ambassador Nicolas Bretel de Grémonville (d. 1648). Tarabotti addresses this loss repeatedly in letters to his widow, his children, and his friends in a manner that assumes specific familiarity on the part of the reader with both the deceased and the circumstances of his death.[19] Although she makes use of some standard expressions of consolation, her letters require increased participation on the part of the reader to furnish the letter with its full context and meaning – something that can be difficult to do over the distance of time and space.

Humanist letters were composed in Latin rather than Italian, reflecting the education and authority of the author and showcasing his – or her – erudition, but also limiting their letters' audience in certain respects. The humanists wrote for an élite, male public of fellow humanists, capable of reading and responding to Latin works. The same names surface repeatedly in humanist letterbooks of the period, creating a kind of epistolary intertextuality defined by the experience of a specific network of men. Indeed, the very humanist education that was so hard-won for Nogarola, Fedele, and Cereta would have made their work less accessible to the many women whose knowledge of Latin was inferior or non-existent.[20] Certainly fewer women are the recipients of Latin humanist letters than of the later vernacular variety. Those to whom humanist letters are addressed tend to fall into three basic groups: women of high social status whose patronage the writer seeks, as in Erasmus' letter to Lady Anne of Veer; women who are objects of admiration for their 'exceptional' degree of learning and culture, as when Guarino Veronese writes to (or about) Nogarola; and women to whom the writer wishes to direct some piece of wisdom or advice, as in Bruni's well-known letter on women's education addressed to Battista da Montefeltro Malatesta.[21] Later vernacular letters continue to address women patrons, praise learned women, and teach female 'students,' yet they also make room for letters to and about women from many other parts of society, including mothers, sisters, courtesans, and servants.

Even among the women humanists, letters to men outnumber letters to women. Fedele addresses missives to royal women like Isabel of Spain, Eleanor of Aragon, and her daughter Beatrice of Aragon, but Nogarola writes to none at all. Both Fedele and Nogarola are concerned to replicate the humanist letterbook as closely as possible, and gender is not as underscored as much as patronage. Only Cereta addresses herself to a truly 'familiar' network of correspondents, many of them female, rather than focusing exclusively on *destinatari* of high status; thus, only in her letters do we see gender truly move to the forefront of epistolary expression.[22] By contrast, the sixteenth and seventeenth centuries saw a marked increase in the presence of women as both authors and addressees. Women make frequent appearances in such influential collections as that of Aretino, as well as in those of Bembo, Caro, and Tolomei (where the names of Veronica Gambara, Vittoria Colonna, and Giulia Gonzaga all recur regularly), and letters to and by women are anthologized in collections like Paolo Manuzio's *Lettere volgari di diversi nobilissimi uomini illustri* (1542), Lodovico Dolce's *Lettere di diversi eccellentissimi uomini* (1559), and the three volumes of *Lettere a Aretino* published in 1557.[23] Letter-writing manuals such as Bartolommeo Miniatore's *Formulario* (1568), Giovanni Antonio Taglienti's *Componimento di parlamenti* (1584), and Battista Ceci's *Compendio* (1618) included model letters formulated specifically for women.[24] Such a presence of female names and epistolary tools for women is indicative both of an increased female readership for the vernacular letter and of a growing interest in letters written by women.

Of the triad of letterbooks published by women humanists mentioned here, it is Cereta's that presages the gendered self-positioning of the later women writers discussed in this study. Cereta plays deliberately on gendered tropes – for example, juxtaposing her skill at embroidery with her literary bravura – to craft an intellectual autobiography that in many points transcends the masculine confines of the humanist model she imitates by highlighting female experience.[25] Her epistolary self is at once 'masculine' – competing with male humanists on their terms by displaying her knowledge of classical literature, philosophy, and the sacred texts – and 'feminine' – where she describes her role as a wife and daughter, recalls the obstacles she faces as a woman humanist, and defends women's right to education. Cereta's letters have been called a 'radical departure' from those of her contemporaries.[26] The merging of male and female aspects in her epistolary persona calls to mind the letters of Veronica Franco or Isabella Andreini more than those of Nogarola or Fedele; her focus on critiquing female experience prefigures the kind of commentary found in Lucrezia Gonzaga and, especially, in Arcangela Tarabotti. Whereas Fedele sticks closely to humanist themes, and Nogarola's catalogues of illustrious women are in many respects in keeping with traditional literary models (although she moves the figure of the learned woman to the forefront), Cereta rewrites the standard humanist autobiography by narrating the different stages specific to the woman writer's intellectual journey. Woven into this narrative is Cereta's uneasy relationship with her mother, her girlhood passed in the convent, a portrait of the father who encouraged her studies, and a memorial to the husband to whom she was married a brief eighteen months. None are subjects typically found in a humanist collection. Ever present is Cereta's inner conflict as a woman and writer, and the anxiety she experiences in trying to fulfill her duties as a daughter and wife – consuming roles she assumed with considerable resentment – and as a learned scholar. Cereta seems keenly aware of the gendered distinctions between public and private worlds, often referring to spatial imagery as she orients herself at the border of both. In her evocative autobiographical letter addressed to Nazaria Olimpica, for instance, Cereta describes how the rudiments of the education that would later allow her to become a public figure were first obtained in the private, female space of the convent, parceled out 'in the inner chambers of the convent, the doors to which were opened and shut with a hundred locks.'[27] The image is a gendered mirror of the male *studio* in Alberti's *Libri della famiglia*,[28] for Cereta's learning is acquired in a specifically female fortress, under conditions of great secrecy and security. The reader is left to imagine the force it must have required for Cereta to open those locks, break past the convent walls, and enter the public sphere through literary dialogue. In another letter, Cereta makes clear her desire and need to be recognized in this public sphere, writing that 'public acclaim has built a solid enough foundation for my immortality' and that such public acknowledgment is, 'in the order of things, quite important.'[29]

Cereta's focus on the feminine activity of embroidery as an expression of her artistic identity further suggests that she is integrating the territory of male and female space and even interrogating typical constructs of gender. She devotes ekphrastic pages to her skill at embroidery, a pursuit that she undertakes with the same dedication and art that she does her writing, and worries about finding the time to devote to her own intellectual and artistic expression. She describes the insomniac nights necessary for both her writing and sewing, and laments the time wasted in 'domestic leisure': 'I have no time for my own writing and studies unless I use the nights as productively as I can,' she writes. 'Time is a scarce commodity for those of us who spend our skills and labor equally on our families and our work.'[30] Certainly, such conflict does not appear in the letters of male humanists, who unlike Cereta, had the luxury of 'otium,' blank days to devote to study and composition.[31] Nor, needless to say, does such a portrait of women's experience occur in other humanist collections. Cereta is virtually alone in using this humanist medium as a vehicle for specifically female experience and the central role she allots to gender does not reappear until after Aretino.

This is not to say, however, that gender has *no* place in other humanist collections. Ann Rosalind Jones has argued that even when women adhere to the literary conventions of dominant culture, sex matters: 'When a member of the sex systematically excluded from literary performance takes a dominant/hegemonic position toward an approved discourse, she is, in fact, destabilizing the gender system that prohibits her claim to public language.'[32] By the very act of writing, the woman writer challenges male models. In some cases, gender is manipulated for specific purposes. Nogarola, for instance, makes a strategy of gender in certain of her letters, calling on stereotypes of female weakness, inferiority, and volubility to create a kind of defensive posture and disarm her male critics. Nogarola writes gender as vulnerability, while in actuality using it to her advantage. In a letter to the humanist Ermolao Barbaro, for example, she excuses her presumption by saying 'my sex itself will provide the greatest excuse for me among some men, since it may be very difficult to find a silent woman.'[33] In a letter to Guarino Veronese, she laments having been born female, since 'women are ridiculed by men in both word and deed.'[34] Nogarola's frequent apologies for her lack of skill or learning – typical of many humanist letters – take on gendered implications in the context of her position as a woman who feels herself vulnerable to attack, as, for example, when she attributes Guarino's initial rejection of her to her sex. Similarly, Fedele excuses herself to her correspondents as a 'bold little woman' and 'both a woman and a naïve young girl,' 'scarcely allowed ... to go out of my little schoolhouse'; while Cereta calls herself a 'small chattering woodpecker among poetic swans' – disingenuous statements meant to deflect criticism and highlight accomplishment.[35] Both the sentiment and the strategy are present in vernacular letters by women, many of which are constructed specifically to combat criticism directed at the authors' literary activity.

The defence of women's intellectual capabilities, a subject taken up by male humanists with varying degrees of conviction in the context of the *querelle des femmes* (and rooted in the 'women worthies' tradition from Boccaccio and Christine de Pizan to Renaissance treatises such as those of Castiglione and Firenzuola) is also given new weight and a new perspective in the texts of the women humanists.[36] Whereas male catalogues of illustrious women tend to highlight sexual licentiousness, almost as a consequence of women's intellectual accomplishment or their activity in the public sphere, or to explain women's achievements by likening them to men, Nogarola and Cereta approach this literary problem from a different angle. Nogarola, for instance, uses the recitation of famous women to highlight their virtue and her own, thereby writing herself into this group. She does not completely refute the stereotype of women as overly loquacious, allowing that the actions of a few cause this notion to be perpetuated, but she highlights women's tradition of eloquence and virtue, implicitly challenging the silence/chastity construct.[37] Cereta, too, defends women's intellect and delineates even more clearly a female genealogy of learned women of which she is now a part. An impassioned letter to Bibolo Semproni recalls a vast female lineage that has won glory in 'virtue and literature': it stretches from the Ethiopian Queen Saba, called upon by Solomon, to Nicostrata, Sappho, and Semiramis, and indeed extends to 'Isotta of Verona' (Nogarola) and 'Cassandra of Venice' (Fedele).[38] 'The possession of this lineage is legitimate and sure,' Cereta writes, 'and it has come all the way down to me from the perpetual continuance of a more enduring race.'[39] Cereta thus sees herself as part of a community of learned women. Hers is a complex position, however. Although she writes in defence of learned women, she feels very much an outsider to her sex and to traditional feminine culture, which she views quite negatively. In this, she appears to have internalized much of the misogynist tradition regarding women's nature and behaviour. She ridicules most women as vain, empty-headed gossips ('gabbing and babbling women') content in the pleasurable confines of their own subjection.[40] All women should have the freedom to learn, Cereta says, but they must choose it, and most do not:

> And here choice alone, since it is the arbiter of character, is the distinguishing factor. For some women worry about the styling of their hair, the elegance of their clothes, and the pearls and other jewelry they wear on their fingers. Others love to say cute little things, to hide their feelings ... to indulge in dancing, and lead pet dogs around on a leash ... or they can yearn to deface with paint the pretty face they see reflected in mirrors. But those women for whom the quest for the good represents a higher value restrain their young spirits and ponder better plans ... For knowledge is not given as a gift but by study.[41]

Scornfully, emphasizing her own exceptionality, Cereta concludes that 'deep down we women are content with our lot.'[42] The use of catalogues and exempla is widespread in humanist letters and even picked up in some post-humanist collections (most pointedly by Ortensio Lando in the *Lettere di molte valorose donne*, discussed in chapter 2) as a tool to showcase the writer's erudition. However, Cereta's questioning of what it requires to be learned and why more women do not attempt to attain that for which they have a natural gift is unique. Cereta's pervasive focus on what it means to be a woman writer in a world of men, along with her ability to intertwine standard humanist epistolary rhetoric with an individualistic and gendered epistolary self-portrait make her an important example for early modern women writers of vernacular letters. In Cereta, the boundaries of the humanist letter are stretched and redrawn to include female experience, and it is in this sense most of all that her work prefigures that of the post-Aretinian women writers studied in chapters 3 through 6.

II. Aretino and After: The Vernacular Tradition

If the world of humanist letters to which Cereta, Nogarola, and Fedele sought access was an exclusive club, its doors were flung open when Pietro Aretino published his enormously influential first volume of letters in 1538. Aretino's most important divergence from the humanist tradition was, of course, his use of Italian rather than Latin in his letters, an innovation legitimized by the rising respectability of the vernacular. For Aretino, who had little proficiency in Latin, this was more a necessity than a choice.[43] Aretino's use of the *volgare* ensured that his letters would be accessible to a wider audience than their classical and humanist predecessors had been, including many more women. In his seminal essay, 'La letteratura italiana all'epoca del concilio di Trento,' Carlo Dionisotti argued that the linguistic openness of the period between 1545 and 1563 engendered by the emerging primacy of the vernacular in Italy fostered the entry into the literary arena of marginalized groups with limited access to formal, humanist education (such as Aretino himself).[44] Thus, a humanist education was no longer a prerequisite for authorship; similarly, readers were not required to read Latin or to be conversant with complex rhetorical formulas in order to appreciate the new vernacular *epistolario*. The wider diffusion of Aretino's letters, moreover, was aided by the increasing expansion of the printing industry, which rendered the publication (and acquisition) of books more economically feasible.[45] Dionisotti's analysis of the rise of the vernacular, when considered along with the impact of printing on authors and readers, is useful for contextualizing the huge success not only of Aretino's *Lettere* but also of the vernacular *epistolario* in general, and particularly the participation in the new genre by writers such as the so-called *poligrafi* (professional writers who wrote for the literary market, such as Nicolò Franco, Ortensio Lando, and Lodovico Dolce), and women.[46] The rapid development of print culture is also an important aspect to consider with regard to the passage of letters from the 'private' status of personal documents to the 'public' status of published text, for it undoubtedly affected the way letter writers thought about letter-writing.[47]

The success of Aretino's letters must be seen in the context of the debates over the *questione della lingua* that were pivotal in the shaping of Italian literature in the first half of the Cinquecento. Vernacular Italian was steadily replacing Latin as the literary language of Italy, and in the wake of Bembo's *Prose della volgar lingua* (1525) and the intense debate it provoked arose the need to demonstrate the merit of the vernacular in the classical genres, including letters. In the wake of Aretino's experiment with the vernacular, the letter was, for a time, largely freed of the thematic and rhetorical constraints that governed its humanistic predecessors, but traces of those precursors remained. Individual letters, for example, often retained the rhetorical distinctions of oratory.[48] They might reflect the traditional division into *salutatio, exordio, narratio, petitio,* and *conclusio,* although these distinctions might collapse into one another or be partially dispensed with. Some letter writers continued to imitate classical models intentionally and cast themselves as abstract epistolary models for others to follow, reflecting a culture that, in many ways, sought to promote and disseminate the art of 'civil conversation.'[49] A literature of compendia flourished in the sixteenth and early seventeenth centuries that promised to teach readers the art of 'ben parlare volgare' and 'correttamente scrivere' (speaking and writing properly in the vernacular) and offered vast collections of letters for readers to imitate (including, as noted above, models for women writers and readers). Such collections were highly concerned with the social relations imbedded in the letter and offered detailed guides to navigating them.[50] On the whole, however, the vernacular familiar letter – the least canonical of the letter 'types' described in classical theory – was a fluid medium, difficult to codify (as evidenced by the dozens of widely varying attempts to define it).[51] It therefore lacked rigid rules governing structure and style and could address almost any subject, as it did most spectacularly at the hands of Aretino.[52] This lack of precise guidelines provoked some debate over the function as well as the boundaries of the new genre, as we will see further on in our discussion of an important early anthology, Paolo Manuzio's *Lettere volgari di diversi nobilissimi huomini*. Nevertheless, such flexibility is an important factor in explaining the popularity of the letter collection in the sixteenth and seventeenth centuries and its appeal to both writers and readers.

Aretino's letters also departed from the traditional themes of their epistolary ancestors. Rather than focus on the heroes or examples of the past or concern themselves with abstract intellectual problems, Aretino's familiar letters were rooted firmly in the present, their attention turned toward the self in the modern world. As Francesco Erspamer points out, much of Aretino's impact and innovation lay in his 'modernity,' his ability to paint the world around him, and himself in it, in brief epistolary fragments directed at a readership of his contemporaries.[53] Aretino's letters depicted the epistolary web of his relationships and chronicled the events of his day-to-day life.[54] A detail as small as the view from his window could constitute the basis for a letter, as could a good meal or a description of the seasons.[55] Broader concerns could also be represented, as may be seen in letters to Charles V, Francis I, and Pope Clement VIII. Aretino included letters to prominent cultural figures, such as Michelangelo and Titian, to underline his own standing. Yet he also addressed letters to people further down in the social hierarchy, including courtesans like Angela del Moro of Venice, the hermaphroditic Zufolina of Pistoia, and his own servants. In an oft-cited letter to Nicolò Franco, Aretino characterized himself as a kind of protojournalist who observes and describes the world around him in order to convey it to his readers. He explains, 'La natura istessa, de la cui semplicità son secretario, mi detta ciò che io compongo' ('Nature herself, whose simple pleasures I record, dictates to me that which I compose').[56] He was conscious of his own innovation and described his style in a letter to Bembo, highlighting the down-to-earth, accessible quality of his letters with a metaphor that emphasized practicality:

> Io con lo stile de la pratica naturale faccio d'ogni cosa istoria, et èmmi forza secondare l'alterezza de i grandi con le gran lodi ... A me bisogna trasformare digressioni, metafore, e pedagogarie, in argani che movano e in tanaglie che aprano.[57]

With the stylus of my natural practicality, I make a story of everything, and force myself to address my superiors with great praise ... My duty is to transform digressions, metaphors, and everything else one is taught into windlasses that move and pliers that pry open.

Aretino's attention to day-to-day impressions and his concentration on personal experience renders him the protagonist of his letters: his letters tell a story, or rather stories, about Aretino himself. Thus, the writer becomes a forceful epistolary personality, as integral to the letters as the incidents described in them. Many letterbooks of the mid-sixteenth to mid-seventeenth century, including those of women, exhibit a similar narrative quality. Although such letters are not necessarily joined in a conventional narrative sequence, they often have a sense of character and event, anchoring the reader to specific moments in the writer's experience.[58] These moments may not be of any obvious significance: vernacular collections are full of brief notes narrating not much at all – a greeting, a complaint, a description. Often the events and incidents to which such letters refer are so oblique as to be nearly impenetrable for the modern reader. Many of Tarabotti's letters, for example, require a broad understanding of Seicento Venetian culture to adequately decipher their meaning.[59] Unlike the humanist letter, written to preserve an image of the writer for posterity, Aretino's letters and those of the men and women who followed his example were written to advertise and promote the writer to an audience of contemporaries.

Aretino, known as the 'scourge of princes,' was instrumental in understanding the power of the letter as a weapon or a means to an end.[60] Particularly adept at exploiting this aspect of epistolary discourse, he used his letters to punish, reward, cajole, and threaten, to win allies and to embarrass enemies. His letters are full of references to favors promised, fulfilled, or left unsatisfied, and praise for his admirers and patrons or bitter diatribe for his competitors.[61] Many of Aretino's letters acknowledge gifts of money, favours, clothes or food and often make explicit the reciprocal dynamic of the patronage relationship. He thanks Guidobaldo II della Rovere, for example, for 'accepting' his gift of a literary work, the *Ipocrito*, and for making him a gift of money in return.[62] He reassures Barbara Pallavicini that her generous gift of clothing ('la veste di dobletto lionato tessuto d'oro, le maniche di velluto pavonazzo ricamate d'argento, e la cuffia di seta verde dorata' ['the doublet vest woven in gold, the sleeves of purple velvet embroidered in silver, and the cap of gilded green silk']), will not go unacknowledged: 'Ma credete voi ... ch'io sia così villano che non vi restituisca cortesia per cortesia? Ben trovarò io modo di darvi un cambio, che se non sarà trappunto in drappi, sarà scritto in carta col suo nome dentro' ('But can you really believe ... that I am such a villain as to not repay your favour with a favour? I will surely find a way to repay you; which, if it is not embroidered on cloth, will be written on paper with your name within').[63] Aretino repays Pallavicini with a letter, a literary artifact with an almost economic value in terms of its social significance, a form of currency to be treasured, exchanged, and displayed as a sign of status.[64]

Aretino's famous letter to Lodovico Dolce regarding the writer Nicolò Franco, by contrast, shows how Aretino used the letter to address what he saw as Franco's betrayal. Franco, who had assisted with the preparation of the *Lettere*, earned Aretino's enduring wrath by daring to publish his own book of letters shortly thereafter. Aretino describes him as the worst kind of dog, ungrateful and despised by all:

> Il meschino simiglia un cane da ogniuno scacciato, e a tutti odioso ... Io per me ho visto de i pazzi, de gli insolenti, de gli invidiosi, de i maligni, de gli iniqui, de i frappatori, de gli ostinati, de gli arroganti, de i villani, e de gli ingrati; ma de la spezie di cui è la pazzia, la insolenzia, la invidia, la malignità, la iniquità, la vanitade, la ostinazione, l'arroganza, la villania, e la ingratitudine sua non mai.[65]

> That sorry fellow resembles a dog that no one wants, and everyone hates ... For my part, I've seen men who are mad, insolent, envious, spiteful, wicked, destructive, stubborn, arrogant, villainous, and ungrateful; but I've never known anyone with his degree of madness, insolence, envy, spitefulness, wickedness, vanity, stubbornness, arrogance, villainy, and ingratitude.

Aretino's personal vendettas, along with his triumphs and good fortune, are thus given public valence in his *epistolario*, put to use in the process of epistolary self-construction.[66] The letters of such women as Lucrezia Gonzaga, Veronica Franco, and Arcangela Tarabotti demonstrate that this lesson, too, was thoroughly acquired and absorbed after the publication of Aretino's letters.

Positive or negative, Aretino's letters addressed a wide swath of society. He meant to capture each detail of the world in which he lived, and this meant that, in contrast to the humanist example, Aretino addressed letters not just to other men of literary or political stature, or even women of cultural renown, but also to men and women of lower social status and lesser education, an interest that was not limited to his epistolary production. Women were frequent interlocutors for Aretino, who wrote to noblewomen and to courtesans, in high style and low, and they would become a constant presence in the female-authored collections that followed his. Aretino's letter to Marguerite Hapsburg, natural daughter of Charles V, makes use of traditional praise techniques in referring to her as 'bella, onesta, illustre, nobile, prudente, gentile, benigna, e magnanima' ('beautiful, honest, illustrious, noble, prudent, gentle, kind, and magnanimous').[67] Less traditional but typical of Aretino is his directness in linking this encomium of Marguerite to the favours he wishes to procure: first, the amity of her father the Emperor ('ho pensato di laudarlo col tenervi laudata' ['I thought to praise him by praising you']); and second, mentioned in a postscript as if an afterthought, her assistance in procuring a gift promised him by the Duke of Camerino.[68] Again, Aretino makes clear his use of the letter as a tool to procure favour and to embarrass those who fail to furnish it. Aretino's praise of women also extends in some cases to courtesans: he writes favourably of a certain Franceschina, for example, lauding her musical ability (although he then goes on to compare her to a 'bevanda avelenata,' or poisoned drink – sweet but toxic).[69]

Aretino also addressed servants, at least for show. His comic letter to the unfortunate Lucietta is another example of the breadth of his epistolary network, and also reveals much about the levels on which the published letter functions. Lucietta has fled after having carelessly broken her master's possessions, and Aretino revels in his description of her clumsiness: '... tu piagni, ti acori e ti scusi, che ti sei fuggita di casa per la paura ch'io non ti ammazzasse, per avermi con bestialissima trascuraggine rotto, isfracassato, e mandato in mal'ora, vetri, vasa, e roba, per tuo salaro in due anni' ('... you weep, plead, and make excuses for having fled the house for fear I might kill you for having, with incredible carelessness, broken, wrecked, and shattered glasses, vases and belongings worth two years of your wages').[70] He rebukes Lucietta for fleeing, not because she has been careless, but because she seems to fear his temper. The letter becomes a pretext for Aretino to paint himself as a liberal employer, one whose anger is 'più corta che un fume di paglia' ('burns more quickly than a fire of straw') and whose household is known to be generous and comfortable: 'la mia è una stanza di quelle ..., volendo concludere in tuo linguaggio che qui non si serra il pane, che qui non si adacqua il vino, e che qui non si dorme in la paglia, né si va iscalza se non in letto ...' ('mine is one of those houses in which, to speak your language, the bread is not rationed, the wine is not watered, and one doesn't sleep on straw, nor go barefoot, unless to bed ...').[71] Lucietta's crime is not her mishap, but the shadow she casts on her employer's reputation, which he must rehabilitate through this letter. It is a good example of how any single letter in a published *epistolario* becomes an integral part of the author's self-construction. While Aretino has shown that he moves in the higher circles of court and politics, corresponding with kings and dukes, he now also shows his ability to communicate just as appropriately with members of an entirely different social stratum.

The letter to Lucietta is also an example of the way in which familiar letters exist at the intersection of public and private intercourse. Although this letter ostensibly addresses a domestic drama, it becomes part of a published collection, and even as he writes it, Aretino ponders this dynamic. The letter is obviously intended for a general audience, not for his likely illiterate servant, and indeed assumes a meta-epistolary quality as Aretino muses to Lucietta about including it in the collection he is thinking of assembling:

> ... mi è venuto in fantasia di fare un dì una leggenda di chiacchiare iscritta non pure a massare e gentaglie, ma a ogni sorte di famigli e briganti ancora, e forse anche tu ci sarai intabaccata da senno.[72]

> ... the idea came to me to one day make a collection of idle conversations, written not just to maidservants and ruffians, but to every sort of servant, and brigands too, and perhaps you will find yourself remembered in it.

Aretino makes several things explicit: first, his intention to create an *epistolario* that has space for a wide range of interlocutors ('ogni sorte di famigli e briganti'), not just the highly placed, taking the prized concept of epistolary *variatio* to a new level. Second, even as he addresses Lucietta, he is imagining a wide audience for his letter. Finally, he understands that there is great appeal in being memorialized in a published letter. Thus, in reading the letter to Lucietta, the general reader understands that the letter is also addressed directly to him (or her), and is placed in the curious position of moving between past, present, and future, and between public and private realms, participating, along with Aretino, in the construction of the collection.

Aretino's letters required the active participation of the reader for completion; yet by choosing which letters to include in the collection, he guided his readers' interpretation of the situations he described.[73] By casting himself as the protagonist of his letter collection and narrating every situation to reflect positively on himself and negatively on his detractors, Aretino elicited the reader's trust. His exceptional ability for self-construction and self-presentation would be imitated, with widely varying degrees of success, in dozens of collections after him. Luigi Matt emphasizes the complete change in the world of epistolary writing once Aretino came along, noting that his 'disinvolta capacità di sfruttare, anche commercialmente, le nuove possibilità messe a disposizione dall'editoria cinquecentesca ha creato un orrizzonte di attese riguardo all'epistolografia ... del tutto imprevedibile.'[74] Indeed, the intersection of Aretino's epistolary experiment with a growing literary market and a rising interest in books written in the *volgare* created the conditions for a literary trend that would continue for over a century.

III. Defining the Genre: Paolo Manuzio's *Lettere volgari*

The vast success of Aretino's letters can thus be situated both in a specific historical moment – within the context of the debate over the *questione della lingua* – and in the more elusive theoretical realm of epistolary self-fashioning and self-promotion so central to Aretino's letters. His reinvention of the letter as a vernacular genre, stylistically flexible and adaptable to all manner of content, rendered the medium extremely appealing to those who wished to construct themselves within the public sphere of literary discourse. Yet, as we have seen, Aretino's project was a significant departure from previous models of epistolography. Did writers agree on the merits of this new vernacular genre? How did writers, editors, and, indeed, readers feel the letter might be best employed? How were questions of gender addressed, if at all? A lesser known but important text which sheds light on these questions is Paolo Manuzio's *Lettere volgari di diversi nobilissimi huomini*, an anthology of vernacular letters published in 1542 that contains letters to and from a wide range of people, adhering to the promise made in the *dedicatoria* to show 'la vera forma del ben scrivere' ('the true form of good writing') in a variety of registers.[75] Indeed, the letters in this anthology range from the solemn (for example, letters of condolence), to the literary (letters on letter writing), to the burlesque (a letter to Aretino from an oenophilic priest), reinforcing the conception of the vernacular letter as lacking in rigid rules and capable of addressing any number of subjects. Among the *epistolografi* represented are such prominent figures as Annibal Caro, Pietro Bembo, Claudio Tolomei, Sperone Speroni, Lodovico Dolce, and Aretino himself; women writers are fewer, with four letters by Vittoria Colonna and one by Veronica Gambara in Book I, and a second letter by Gambara in Book II. Important for its position early in the epistolary 'boom' of the second half of the Cinquecento, the letters in Manuzio's anthology, a number of which focus on the vernacular letter itself, can give us some idea of the reception afforded the new genre by writers and readers. Was the vernacular familiar letter considered suitable for 'serious' (i.e., publishable) epistolary discourse? How did writers feel about seeing their letters in print? Several letters in the anthology also shed light on the process by which letters became published documents, including practical problems such as the way in which letter collections were assembled and the revisions to which they were subjected prior to publication.

Manuzio sets forth the objectives of his anthology in the dedicatory letter to Federico Badoero and Dominico Veniero, both important figures in the Venetian cultural milieu and defenders of the *volgare*.[76] Although the collection, riding the wave of the popularity of vernacular letters, surely had a raison d'être in reader demand alone, Manuzio casts his project in a more noble light, explaining that he intends to show that the Italian vernacular is a graceful, worthy language as suited to important topics as to the mundane: the collection is to be the manifesto of the vernacular familiar letter. In defence of the *volgare*, Manuzio states that 'questa lingua è bella, e nobile, e nostra, e questa parte di scrivere cade ogni dí in uso' ('this language is beautiful, and noble, and it is ours, and this sort of writing is used every day'), drawing an important connection between the beauty and nobility of the vernacular and its practicality: aesthetic and day-to-day utility are made to coincide.[77] The anthology, moreover, performs a service not only by demonstrating the capacities of the vernacular but also by functioning as a sort of writer's manual. The letters should inspire those who already know how to write, and teach those who do not: the writers represented 'porgeranno ardire alla industria di quei che sanno, e quei che non sanno gli averanno obligo, potendo da questi essempi ritrar la vera forma del ben scrivere' ('will inspire those who know how, and those who do not will be obliged to learn, as they can find in these examples the true form of good writing').[78] This didactic intent is echoed in letter-writing manuals such as that of Taglienti, which presents itself as a tool for those 'uomini communevoli, i quali non hanno troppo frequentato le scuole di grammatica' ('common men who haven't had much formal schooling').[79]

Evident in Manuzio's opening letter are the tenets of the new epistolary genre, the twin qualities of 'utilità' and 'diletto' by which writers might justify the appearance in print of their familiar letters and avoid implications of literary narcissism.[80] Ideally, a writer publishes his letters first and foremost as a 'service' to his readers, rather than as a demonstration of his own talents or of the singularity of the personal experience he recounts in print. Bernardo Tasso, for example, is typical in his insistence that he publishes his letters to please his friends rather than to seek praise; by contrast Guazzo's refusal to adhere to this common trope is quite striking.[81] Manuzio's dedication downplays the role of the author in publication, explaining, 'mi persuado che gli auttori di queste lettere non avranno a male ch'io dimostri al mondo i fiori dell'ingegno loro con *utilità comune*' ('I am convinced that the authors of these letters will not mind that I display the fruits of their intellect to the world, for the *common good*').[82] Such distancing of authors from the act of publication may be helpful in explaining the popularity of epistolary anthologies in sixteenth- and seventeenth-century Italy, where works like Lodovico Dolce's *Lettere di diversi eccellentissimi uomini* (1554) and Dionigi Atanagi's *Lettere di tredici uomini illustri* (1554) existed, with much success, alongside the *libro d'autore*, or collection of letters by a single author.[83] A book of letters by various writers, compiled by an editor rather than an author, could evade the problem of narcissism raised in a one-author collection depicting the experience of a single epistolary 'I.' Something else emerges from Manuzio's words, however. Although he assures readers that the writers included in the anthology will not object to this public appearance because their letters serve the greater good, the extent to which he has procured their consent is unclear. This is a potentially significant problem, particularly for an anthology: to what degree does the letter writer participate in or indeed condone the publication of his or her letters? The editor lends authority to the epistolary text but can also be a source of anxiety for the writer, especially if their objectives do not coincide.[84] It also highlights the delicate balance entailed in the publication of personal correspondence: some kind of justification is required for revealing one's 'private' self in print. Here, the authors are justified both by the premise of the anthology, to prove the worth of the vernacular, and by their distance from the act of publication, a responsibility assumed by Manuzio. These problems are more difficult to avoid in the *libro d'autore*, in which such justification and distancing are more difficult. These issues, as we will see further on, are particularly tricky for women writers, already forced to justify less transparently 'personal' forms of writing such as poetry or treatises.

Unlike a *libro d'autore*, which strives for the illusion of a real and spontaneous epistolary exchange, Manuzio's anthology makes no effort to convince its readers that they have happened upon a genuine correspondence. The anthology lays bare its inner framework to the reader, who is thus allowed access to both its purpose (to defend the vernacular) and the way in which it has been assembled. Contributing to this structural transparency are the explanatory lines that accompany the names of some *destinatari*. The first letter in the anthology, for example, is addressed to Cardinal Giovanni de' Medici, 'che fu poi Papa Leone' ('who then became Pope Leo').[85] Dolce's anthology *Lettere di diversi eccellentissimi huomini* takes this tactic even further, prefacing each letter with a detailed 'argomento' that sums up the letter's content (and listing each one in an index at the back), a device later used in Isabella Andreini's *Lettere*. Such extra-epistolary notations, which become increasingly commonplace throughout the century, immediately break the illusion that we are about to enter into a real correspondence, and call our attention to the fact that we are peering in on an already-completed epistolary cycle, now recycled for public consumption. Another element that differentiates Manuzio's anthology from many *libri d'autore* is the typographical presentation of the letters, in which the name of the addressee appears in bold relief at the beginning of each letter, and that of the author only at the end, in some cases several pages later. Thus, the reader's interpretative processes, so essential to the completion of the epistolary cycle, are initially based on the internal reader, the recipient of the letter, rather than on its author, whose name appears only later. Like Manuzio's dedicatory letter, this format serves to de-emphasize the role of the author and to work against the construction of that epistolary persona, which instead is both the primary focus and raison d'être of the *libro d'autore*.

Manuzio's concern to demonstrate the merit of the vernacular familiar letter suggests that not everyone agreed with him on this point. In an interesting tactic, Manuzio introduces both supporting and opposing opinions with the letters he selects for the volume, thus making his case more effectively by addressing the arguments against it and demonstrating that even in an anthology, which lacks the sort of narrative cohesion and self-constructive aspect of the *libro d'autore*, the letter, and the reader along with it, can be adroitly manipulated. This creates a meta-textual effect, for the letters included in a volume meant to celebrate their existence are engaged in a self-conscious debate over that existence. This debate tends to emerge in brief 'narrative' cycles; as, for example, in a pair of letters involving Speroni, Molza, and Manuzio himself. In the first of these, Speroni calls the vernacular familiar letter unfit for publication, adding that it does the *volgare* no honour to publish familiar letters, which are written in a low style and deal with the mundane matters of everyday life.[86] In the next letter, however, Molza praises Manuzio for undertaking the project, thereby offsetting Speroni's negative comments.[87]

An effusive letter by Iacopo Bonfadio, also addressed directly to Manuzio, praises the editor's efforts on behalf of the new language and the new genre, while acknowledging the surrounding debate.[88] Bonfadio recognizes that anthologies such as this one are necessary to develop and establish both the *volgare* and the familiar letter in the literary arena. His lively letter goes on to condemn the overly constructed nature of Latin discourse and to praise the simplicity of the vernacular familiar letter (calling to mind Lucrezia Gonzaga's compliment to Parabosco):

> Quei lunghi periodi hanno troppo campo, e l'uom ci si pere dentro; oltre che in lettere famigliari par che non convenghino. È molto più bello e più sicuro quel breve giro, ove voi cosí felicemente v'aggira, senza punto mai aggirarvi, e volteggiate lo scriver vostro con una leggiadria mirabile, senza mai cadere. Seguirò dunque voi ...[89]

> Those long clauses take too much space, and a man could get lost in them; moreover, they do not seem suited to familiar letters. Far more pleasing, and sure, is your own felicitously brief turn of phrase, in which you never get turned around, and you guide your writing with an admirable grace, never falling. Therefore, I will follow your example ...

Bonfadio praises the ease and natural quality of the vernacular letter, contrasting it to the artificiality and complexity of the Latin letter.

In addition to such pro-vernacular, pro-*lettera familiare* texts as Bonfadio's, and in response to those who, like Speroni, deem the vernacular letter unworthy of publication, Manuzio tucks two unusual letters into his anthology that further undermine any pretence of immediacy the external reader might feel in reading the anthology. These are the two letters by Petrarch and Boccaccio, the founding fathers (with Dante) of the vernacular, found in the middle of the anthology. By including their letters in his collection, Manuzio invokes the authority of these vernacular giants in the matter of the dignity of the *volgare*. Moreover, the presence of Petrarch and Boccaccio (as opposed to Dante) would have evoked an inevitable association with the epistolary genre: Petrarch through the Latin *Familiares*, which revived the Ciceronian model, and Boccaccio through the *Elegia di Madonna Fiammetta*, a precursor to epistolary discourse (and epistolary fiction) written in the vernacular, as described in the previous chapter (Boccaccio's letter, moreover, is addressed here to 'Fiammetta,' rendering the association still more apparent).

A final point of interest that emerges from the *Lettere volgari* concerns the compilation of the anthology and the revision of the letters included in it. In a letter to Benedetto Ramberti, Speroni, who, as we saw above, was opposed to the publication of vernacular familiar letters, explains that he hasn't responded to his correspondent's letters because he was afraid his reply would be published against his wishes: 'non volendo che si stampassero le mie lettere, le quali scrivo famigliarmente sempre-mai nel medesimo stile ... ch'io compongo le quetanze de' debitori' ('not wishing that my letters, which I write familiarly and in the same style I use for business matters, be published ...').[90] Speroni, who, as Giacomo Moro points out, never edited or authorized an edition of his own letters, although they appeared in anthologies like Manuzio's, did not feel his – or others' – familiar letters were worthy of public display, and feared they would be published without his consent, a not-uncommon practice, as editors rushed to take advantage of demand.[91] Such haste to publish anthologies even led editors to publish substandard letters: the same Ramberti, for example, tells Manuzio that '... per empiere il libro, raccogliamo lettere in quel modo che si fanno i fiori l'autunno, che la penuria fa che ciascuno par bello ...' ('... in order to fill up the book, we are collecting letters as one collects flowers in autumn, when their scarcity makes each one seem beautiful ...').[92] Not all the letters contained in the *Lettere volgari* appeared with the blessing of their authors (although many did), and Manuzio and others probably published letters that were not the best examples of the genre in order to flesh out their collections. In some cases, an author at first resisted publication but consented when given the opportunity to revise the letters prior to publication. Tolomei, for example, expresses his displeasure in hearing that his letters might be printed, then relents: 'Di grazia, M[esser] Paolo, s'egli è possibile, non mi fate ingiuria di stamparle. Et se pur non ve ne potete tenere, rimandatemele, vi prego, prima perch'io le rivegga e le ricorregga un poco' ('I beg you, M[esser] Paolo, if it is possible, do not do me the injury of publishing them. And if you really can't help yourself, I beg you to return them to me first so that I may look over them and revise them a bit').[93] It is interesting to note that Manuzio himself, upon publishing his own *Lettere volgari* some ten years after his anthology, claimed rather disingenuously to do so only because he feared they would otherwise be published anyway, without benefit of revision.[94] The revisions referred to by Tolomei were by no means unusual; rather, they were the norm – especially for those *libri d'autore* in which the author planned and controlled the publication process to a greater extent. In the flurry to publish letters, writers frequently struggled to retrieve letters previously sent to correspondents in order to revise them. Moro individuates three aspects of revision with regard to letters written originally for private communication and retrieved for publication: *taglio*, cutting out parts of the original letter prior to publication; *mascheramento*, concealing or changing identifying factors such as names (or dates); and *riscrittura*, a broad term for any other changes (both in style and content).[95] Many writers composed new letters with an eye to publication. All correspondence, however, underwent some degree of revision, for it was ultimately to form part of a published whole which would present a public picture of the writer, whether in an anthology or a *libro d'autore*. What is interesting for us, however, is the way these issues are clearly put forth in Manuzio's anthology. The *Lettere volgari* function as a meta-epistolary study of the merits of the new vernacular epistolary discourse, the arguments against it, and the issues involved in bringing a 'private' text to publication. Manuzio's collection of seemingly private letters, each part of a discrete correspondence, situate themselves in a self-conscious realm of public exposure and assume new meanings from their relationships to other letters in the collection and to the general reader (the public). The anthology thus occupies a transitional space in the epistolary realm as writers and editors react to Aretino's example and try to absorb it, defending the merit of both the vernacular and the new genre.

While anthologies like Manuzio's *Lettere volgari* remained popular throughout the sixteenth century, aided by the relative ease with which publishers could assemble them and the appeal of their variety to readers, the *libro d'autore* enjoyed increasing success, at least up until the end of the century.[96] Such single-author collections took a number of forms. Not all were books of familiar letters: some dealt specifically with love letters, for example, others with *lettere di complimento* (polite letters of greeting or congratulations), comic letters, letters of consolation, and so on. One steadily increasing trend was towards manuals that taught epistolary writing through explanation and imitation. Indeed, towards the end of the Cinquecento and the early Seicento, *segretari* and letter-writing guides began to overtake the more individualistic branch of the 'libro d'autore,' following the example of Sansovino's *Del secretario*, a practical handbook to the art that included sections on folding and sealing letters.[97] While presenting oneself as a teacher of epistolary style required a certain amount of confidence, the abstraction of such model epistles also circumvented the potential problems of a more personal collection chronicling specifics aspects of the author's experience, like that of Aretino. Writers such as Sansovino, Capaccio, and Pucci are representative of this trend towards epistolary abstraction, as are women writers such as Chiara Matraini, whose letters on subjects such as the depiction of virtue in art or the debate over arms versus letters aim to display her humanistic skill in addressing a wide variety of topics rather than present a deeply personalized portrait of the writer.[98] Isabella Andreini's highly stylized *Lettere*, discussed in chapter 5, is another example of this kind of epistolary text. The more self-reflective *libro d'autore*, however, continued to develop in collections by both men and women. In such collections the writer figures prominently as the subject of his or her narrative, confronting the risks entailed by such public exposure of the 'private' self, from the appearance of narcissism to poor reviews of one's writing abilities to, in the case of women, suggestions of unchastity or, at the very least, behaviour inappropriate to a woman. Unlike the more impersonal *segretario* collections, in which the author was distanced and protected by the generality or universality of the model letters he proposed, the author of this second type of collection was immediately identifiable with the more specific, particular experience described within. At the same time, however, even these *libri d'autore* played into the broader trend towards didactic texts, offering up epistolary self-portraits to admire and imitate, to learn from and reproduce. For women writers, both aspects of epistolary writing – its capacity as a vehicle for self-construction and its function as a literary and social model – presented challenges as well as rewards. On the one hand, to make their letters public meant that women were required to negotiate the cultural minefield of gender ideology that prized female silence and invisibility, at least in theory. On the other hand, the characterization of epistolary writing as a feminine genre, along with a broader interest in describing and defining women's experience, ensured that there was an audience for women's letter collections, both genuine and impersonated, as discussed in part two of this study.

PART TWO

The Epistolary Construction of Gender

2 Female Impersonations: Ortensio Lando's *Lettere di molte valorose donne*

I. Landian Signs in the *Lettere di molte valorose donne*

If sixteenth-century theorizations of epistolary writing prized the 'feminine' qualities of naturalness and spontaneity in letters, in the years immediately following Aretino's success both male and female writers sought to produce texts that would fulfill these requirements. As noted in the introduction, not only did women writers publish correspondence but male writers also composed and published letters under women's names, seeking to capitalize on the interests of their audience in a climate of increased scrutiny of the female experience. Perhaps the most unique – and problematic – case of female impersonation among sixteenth-century letterbooks is the *Lettere di molte valorose donne, nelle quali chiaramente appare non esser né di eloquenza né di dottrina alli uomini inferiori*, an anthology of women's letters published anonymously by Ortensio Lando in 1548. The first book of 'women's' letters (either genuine or male-authored) to follow in the wake of Aretino's groundbreaking *epistolario*, the *Valorose donne* were also the only anthology of the period to consist entirely of letters exchanged between women.[1] Comprising 253 letters on subjects from marriage and children to literature and religion, the *Valorose donne* are unconventional in another sense as well, for they constitute a particularly flamboyant case of epistolary ventriloquism in which Lando, a lover of masquerade and paradox, disguises himself in the supposed letters of 181 different women. Varyingly polemic, reproving, instructive, playful, and even comic, the *Valorose donne* are a seemingly unrelated melange of epistles threaded with citations from classical and modern authorities, on a range of subjects from the serious to the absurd. The majority of letters bear the names of women who really existed, but some women are almost certainly invented by Lando, creating a juxtaposition of real and imagined epistolary characters that adds to the anthology's illusionary, deceptive structure. Dates, as well as references to specific places or events, are vague, and most of the letters appear to exist more for the sake of making a point than as part of any actual epistolary exchange, a facet intensified by the apparent lack of an internal logic to the letters. No one thematic thread recurs with enough frequency to offer an immediate key for interpretation or a unifying framework for the anthology. Rather, it is difficult to discern a dominant point of view, for, in typical Landian fashion, one letter's argument is contested by another's. The complicated issue of authorship raised by this extensive impersonation, along with the seemingly unorganized and often contradictory content of the letters themselves, render the *Valorose donne* a text that defies easy categorization or analysis. Not surprisingly, perhaps, critics have never quite come to grips with the anthology and, rather than fully address either the problems of authorship or those of content, have remained largely content to dismiss the *Valorose donne* as an oddity, a minor project thrown together by Lando in response to market demand for women's letters.[2]

Yet Lando's impersonation of female epistolary discourse makes the anthology a valuable resource for the study of the literary construction of gender in the published *epistolario* and the use of women as vehicles for epistolary discourse. It permits us to investigate the material Lando deems appropriate for the women who function as his epistolary mouthpieces, as well as his efforts to reconcile conceptions of the letter as a feminine genre with the actual discourse he attributes to women. Moreover, not only is there abundant textual evidence to demonstrate Lando's authorship of the *Valorose donne*, but the anthology does possess an internal logic beyond its claim to defend women against their detractors. Beneath Lando's flamboyant manipulation of female epistolary discourse lies a larger project, one closely linked to that played out in many of his other works: a critique of the humanist culture that Lando had come to find vastly irrelevant for modern society. This chapter uses close textual analysis and comparisons to other works by Lando to explore the levels on which this curious and multifaceted text operates.

Sources of a 'Dottrina Femminile' in the Lettere di molte valorose donne

Although critics agree that Lando was involved in the production of the *Valorose donne*, questions remain as to the scope of that involvement.

Did Lando write some of the letters, or all of them? Was he primarily an editor or an author? It is important to establish with as much precision as possible Lando's role in the production of the anthology, for a letter written by a man and attributed to a woman is not the same thing as a letter written by a woman, or a letter written by a woman and subsequently edited by a man.[3] A male-authored representation of female discourse is different from a woman's, at the very least because it is constructed through an additional filter, through the distancing mechanism of fiction and projection. If the concept of 'gender' is itself a construction, affecting both men and women by pinning specific sociocultural characteristics to their biological sex, we can speak of the 'construction of gender' in women's writing as well as in that of men writing as women.[4] Yet when a male writer decides to 'write like a woman,' the artifice of gender is made overt, as in Ovid's *Heroides* or Boccaccio's *Fiammetta*, both of which furnished important models for the male-authored female letter writer. The conscious impersonation of a female letter writer by a male in the desire to appropriate the female-gendered epistolary genre not only makes concrete the links between femininity and letter writing but also necessarily reflects certain cultural ideas and biases about (female) sex and gender.

Although the *Valorose donne* were published 'anonymously,' they were recognized as Lando's work by contemporaries such as Anton Francesco Doni, who in his *Libraria* of 1550 listed them under Lando's name.[5] This attribution has been accepted by most critics over the centuries who, in spite of their differences regarding the extent or quality of Lando's role, agree that the overall stylistic uniformity of this lengthy volume attests to Lando's hand in its production.[6] It would indeed be unusual, if not impossible, to find such a degree of stylistic similarity in the diverse letters of nearly 200 women of varying social and geographic provenance without the extensive intervention of an editor. Moreover, the content of the letters – which in addition to discussions of 'women's issues' such as marriage and children includes evaluations of various professions, recipes for miraculous remedies, letters of consolation, stories of bizarre deaths, and sexual double entendres – suggests Lando's presence, echoing themes addressed in his other works. Many of the arguments taken up in the *Valorose donne's* numerous moral letters, for example, such as the perils of avarice, lust, or unrestrained speech, reappear in other Landian texts, such as the *Ragionamenti familiari* (1550); while the letters of consolation contained in the *Valorose donne*, with their unsentimental approach to misfortune and death (accusing the bereaved of envying the departed's new closeness to God or doubting in the hereafter), echo sentiments expressed in works such as the *Paradossi* (1543) and the *Consolatorie* (1550).[7] Finally, the frequent use of the paradox, a technique that juxtaposes letters arguing for and against a particular position, and the 'dubbio,' which employs long lists of rhetorical questions, further suggests Lando's presence, recalling the structural characteristics he employs elsewhere.[8] A letter by Ottavia Baiarda, for example, which consists entirely of a series of questions about love, is not just a stereotypical example of a female epistolarian writing about love, but a rhetorical exercise, and is based on Equicola's *Libro de natura d'amore,* as Serena Pezzini points out.[9] The passage (reproduced nearly verbatim in a later work by Lando, the *Quesiti amorosi* [1552]), is just one of many examples of the thematic and stylistic links between parts of the *Valorose donne* and other works by Lando.[10]

The most concrete evidence of Lando's role not just as an editor of the *Valorose donne,* but as an author with a vision for the anthology as a whole, however, lies in the constant recourse by these women epistolarians to examples, citations, and *detti* gleaned from classical sources in order to shore up their arguments, in a clear nod to their humanist predecessors. The text's most striking characteristic is the consistent use in nearly every letter of classical authorities, from Aristotle to Martial, from Virgil to Pliny, from Tacitus to Statius (or of material drawn from, but not attributed to, such sources) to illustrate or validate a point, whether it concerns the dignity of women or the proper way to launder linens. Not only does this technique attribute a remarkably high and consistent degree of erudition to a large group of women, it also lends a further stylistic constancy to the letters. These ubiquitous references furnish the final piece of our authorial puzzle, convincingly demonstrating that Lando was indeed the author of the *Valorose donne.*[11] Not only are the citations and exempla used so consistently by the *valorose donne* fully in keeping with Lando's own literary style, but – also in keeping with Lando's common practice – they are gleaned almost entirely from a sixteenth-century repertory compiled by the humanist Jean Tixier de Ravisy (often referred to as Ravisius or Textor), the *Officina,* as I have shown elsewhere.[12] This work was, in fact, one of Lando's preferred sources: he had turned to it in earlier works such as the *Paradossi,* and would do so again later, most evidently in the *Sette libri di cataloghi* of 1552.[13] Not only does the consistent sacking of a single encyclopedic text in order to illustrate a variety of points of view provide a unifying structure and authorial project for the *Valorose donne,* but it also points unmistakably to that project being Lando's and not that of the women to whom the collection is attributed. The systematic presence of the *Officina* points to the hand of a single author who constructed the majority of the letters according to an identical structural principle, in which an argument is presented and subsequently bolstered by the evidence of classical authority gleaned from – but never attributed to – the *Officina*. Often, it seems that it is the material from the *Officina* that determines the content of the letter, rather than the contrary.

No matter the content, the constant presence of the *Officina* in the *Valorose donne* imbues the letters with a patina of broad erudition. The attribution of such erudition to women paints them as the bearers of considerable learning, squaring nicely with the intent expressed by the anthology's frontispiece. There we read that these letters are meant to demonstrate women's capacity for learning and expression, showing that women are 'né di eloquenza né di dottrina alli uomini inferiori' ('inferior to men in neither eloquence nor learning'). According to the title, then, the primary purpose of the *Valorose donne* is to demonstrate women's parity with men in letters. In this sense, Lando's anthology sets itself apart from standard conceptions of female epistolarians, later epitomized by the figure of Madonna Celia, whose passionate *Lettere amorose* would become one of the most popular collections of the sixteenth century. Lando's women writers are, by contrast, specifically characterized as the equals of men not only in (letter) writing (*eloquenza*), but also in learning (*dottrina*), breaking away from the restrictive 'superiority' granted to women in the theorization of the epistolary medium as a natural rather than a literary genre. The *Valorose donne* suggest that these women letter writers possess not only the natural ease and sincerity women are thought to bring to the letter genre, but also a degree of learning and literary sophistication that will force the reader to expand his conceptions of the woman writer's literary abilities (the *dedicatoria* to Celia's letters, by contrast, characterizes that text as having been written 'frettalosamente,' in a time of passion and travail, and completely lacking in 'dottrina' – indeed, Celia, we are told, was not schooled in 'buoni studi').[14]

To this end, a number of letters in the *Valorose donne* are specifically concerned with women's literary and intellectual capacities, and many of these are backed up by the *Officina*. A letter from Ippolita Crema to Fulvia Rulla listing examples of literary women, for example, draws heavily on the *Officina*, Book I, 'Mulieres Doctae':[15]

Lando, *Valorose donne*	*Officina* I, 'Mulieres Doctae'
Strana cosa mi pare che gli uomini si vantino tanto di esser soli nati alle lettere, essendoci tante e tante femine non meno di loro alli buoni studi atte: *Aspasia Milesia* fu pur maestra di Pericle avanti che le fusse moglie. Fa pur onorata menzione Gellio della dottrina di Pamphila, la quale scrisse tanti belli commentari nella Grammatica; fassi pur menzione di *Phemonoe*, di *Sosipatra*, di *Theano*, di *Alpaida*, di *Demophila*, e di altre infinite ...[16]	*Aspasia, mulier Milesia*, magna doctrinae fama clarvit: in studiis philosophicis abundè promovit; rhetoricen exercuit. Fuit Periclis magistra, et tandem uxor. Plutarchus in Pericle ... *Damophila*, Graeca, uxor Pamphili, socia Sapphus poëtriae, poemata scripsit amatoria, et Dianae laudes. Theoprastus in vita Apollonii.
It seems strange to me that men should boast so of being the only ones born to letters, since there are many, many women no less adept at study than they: *Aspasia Milesia* was the teacher of Pericles before she was his wife. Gellius makes honorable mention of the erudition of *Pamphila*, who wrote many excellent commentaries on Grammar; he also mentions *Phemonoe, Sosipatra, Theano, Alpaida, Demophila*, and infinite others ...	*Phemonoë* prima Apollinis Delphici vates fuisse, carmenque heroicum invenisse dicitur. Suidas apud Volat. *Sosipatra*, vates fuit Lyda, multis disciplinis cumulatissima, quam propterea creditum est à numinibus quibusdam fuisse educatam, Eugapius apud Volat. *Theano*, mulier fuit apud Locros in Lyricis præcellens ... *Alpaides* virgo, quum religionem magno cultu amplecteretur, coelitus meruit, scripturae sacrae bibliorumque sensum percipere.

Further on, when Lucietta Soranza reprimands Lucrezia Masippa for doubting women's literary abilities, she uses more examples from the same section of the *Officina*.[17] The technique of introducing a review of classical examples by linking them to a contemporary conversation, person, or event is typical of the *Valorose donne*. Here, Lucrezia Masippa's lack of faith in her sex provides the pretext for Lucietta's display of erudition; in other letters such displays are prompted by the death of a relative, an upcoming marriage, a friend's poor conduct.[18]

The *Officina* thus serves to lend the weight and dignity of classical authority to such subjects as the defence of women's intellect and literary skill. When the same technique is used in a letter of less elevated content, on the other hand, the effect is somewhat different. By using classical examples to bolster less weighty arguments, a satirical effect is created: the style seems not to fit the content, as when one writer laments the death of a pet parrot, comparing her situation to a host of examples listed in the *Officina*.[19] Finally, the *Officina* provides the key to an otherwise inexplicable cycle of letters focusing on strange, fatal accidents: Virginia Gambera's litany of those who have died from falling off horses; the Contessa da Gambera's letter about people killed while boar-hunting; and Tadea Centana's list of those who have died of laughter – to name just a few cases.[20] Although these letters, composed as they are of classical examples, function as showcases for *dottrina*, they seem to be isolated and superficial displays, mere lists of names, rather than actual correspondence or evidence of real learning. When seen against the backdrop of the *Officina's* silent participation in the *Valorose donne*, however, such compositions make sense, for they exist as another manifestation of Lando's epistolary rewriting of Textor's humanist anthology. Finally, within the confines of the *Valorose donne*, these odd consolatory letters subvert the trope of the sentimental, feminine *consolatoria* by replacing emotion with a register of exaggerated erudition that verges at times on parody.

Lando was not the only writer of his period to engage in extensive 'riscrittura,' or what we might today even term plagiarism (although the negative connotations of the modern term need not be applied to early modern literary practice) to fill out and elaborate his work.[21] He may well have expected, even intended, informed readers to recognize what he was doing with his incorporation of Textor's repertory.[22] What, then, is the significance of recasting a humanist repertory as an epistolary exchange among women, and what is the effect of this elaborate masquerade on the anthology's supposed celebratory intent? In a study of another female impersonation, the *Elegia di Madonna Fiammetta*, Janet Smarr notes that Boccaccio uses classical allusions throughout the text as a distancing mechanism, a way of distinguishing Boccaccio the writer, who is fully aware of the context of these allusions, from Boccaccio/Fiammetta the narrator, who is unaware of their cautionary implications even as she cites them.[23] The allusions in the *Valorose donne* have a similar function: they distinguish author from protagonist, and Lando's broader cultural critique throughout the collection from the content of each individual letter.

Lando uses his source to attribute an impressive breadth of learning to his epistolarians that is ultimately superficial and ornamental. The use of the *Officina* in the *Valorose donne* suggests that the explanation for the anthology may lie not in the simple motives expressed in the frontispiece – to celebrate and defend women – but rather in the more murky territory of literary critique and vague dissent. Always a virulent critic of humanist learning as a system irretrievably out of touch with the current social and political reality, Lando was perhaps more concerned with advancing a satirical critique of humanism as irrelevant for contemporary life than with mounting a defence of women. The fact remains, however, that Lando chose the 'difesa della donna' as a cover for his cultural commentary and women's letters as the vehicle. In order to evaluate the celebratory claims of the *Valorose donne*, therefore, it is well worth investigating where Lando stood on the *questione della donna* in general and what he suggests in the *Valorose donne* about women's epistolary discourse in particular.

Lando and the 'Difesa della donna'

Echoing the laudatory tone of the title, the anthology's dedicatory letter to Sigismondo Rovello, the English ambassador to Venice, claims that these letters of 'savie donne' ('wise women') have been collected and published to protect women from 'le maligne lingue nemiche degli onori feminili' ('the malicious tongues that are the enemies of feminine honour'), so that their detractors might instead learn to 'riverire et onorare questo nobilissimo sesso' ('revere and honor this noblest of sexes').[24] The anthology thus situates itself squarely within the genre of the *difesa della donna*, in a period in which the debate over the capacities and merit of women flourished in Europe. Although the anthology presents itself as a defence of women, however, the ambiguous and inconsistent content of the letters themselves requires that the reader approach this alleged motive with reservations. More a demonstration of women's writing ability (mediated through the *Officina*) than a defense of their sex in general, the *Valorose donne* offset letters praising women's virtue with others reprimanding women who eat, drink, or spend excessively, seeming rather to reinforce these negative images. Even defences of women's intelligence and capacity for learning are rebutted by letters that relegate women to the domestic realm, claiming that they have neither the aptitude nor need for learning, and by others that claim women talk and generally think too much. Letters celebrating the dignity of women are undermined by still others that seem to mock or parody women's intellectual aspirations and moral authority. Because Lando uses women as his mouthpiece for both sides of these issues, it becomes almost impossible for the reader to discern an all-encompassing point of view: all arguments are equally attributed to the female perspective, women are pitted against women. Lando's 'defence' of women, therefore, is built around a structure of paradox.

While in other of Lando's works, the use of the paradox actually strengthens a point by approaching it from both sides, ultimately reinforcing a moral point (as, for example, in the *Paradossi* or its *Confutazione*), this is not the case with the *Valorose donne*.[25] Here the paradox serves not as a means to advance a moral point, but as a structural device with which to mimic the fundamental multiplicity of epistolary exchange. The *Valorose donne*, after all, fictional though they are, are supposed to represent a variety of epistolary positions. In this way they 'justify' their inconsistency. Rather than achieve any ultimate conjunction in which paradox is transformed into message, the *Valorose donne's* myriad viewpoints merely reflect, often with a heavy dose of parody, arguments that were being discussed – often more seriously – in the literature of the defence of women, especially women's capacity for learning and their moral character. Ultimately, the *varietas* of the *Valorose donne* and their lack of a firm ideological foundation turn the anthology into what is primarily a showcase for Lando's literary talents, a demonstration of his ability to argue any subject and any point of view, all in the 'female' voice.

Because the anthology's ideological instability makes it difficult to evaluate its initial claim to defend women – and because so many letters seem to run counter to this claim – we must first examine the position of the letters in relation to Lando's broader literary production. Does a defence of women represent a natural continuation of Lando's work, or a departure? Lando, who has been characterized for centuries by critics as a *poligrafo*, or a professional writer who produced works in accordance with demand, experimented with numerous genres, including the catalogue, the paradox, the treatise, and the novel, in addition to the letter.[26] He was clearly conscious of emerging literary trends and aware of the demands of the literary market. In examining the *Valorose donne*, then, we should keep in mind the larger context of the literary milieu from (or for) which the anthology was produced. The *difesa della donna* literature with which the anthology purports to identify itself flourished in the Cinquecento, particularly in the editorial and cultural centre of Venice, where the *Valorose donne* were published. Works such as Galeazzo Flavio Capella's *Della eccellenza e dignità della donna* (1525), Sperone Speroni's *Dialogo della dignità delle donne* (1542), and Henricus Cornelius Agrippa's *Declamatio de nobilitate et praeccellentia foeminae* (1544) furnished some early examples of the genre and provided its literary parameters. Faced with so many examples of the genre and the continuing interest of readers in this subject matter, it is easy to imagine that Lando would have wanted to exercise his skills in this genre, too – and that using the letter as a vehicle for a discussion of women would have been equally attractive to him, given the epistolary genre's soaring popularity after 1538. Lando, moreover, was quick to praise women in many of his other works, both prior to and following the *Valorose donne*, frequently referring to the learning or virtue of those women who were likely his more generous patrons, such as Lucrezia Gonzaga da Gazzuolo (of whom we will hear more in the next chapter), her sister Isabella Gonzaga da Puvino, and Isabella Sforza. Given the positive attitude towards women's intelligence displayed, for example, in the *Forcinaes Quaestiones* (1535), the *Paradossi,* and, later, the *Cataloghi,* the *Valorose donne* do not initially appear out of character for Lando in terms of their laudatory intent.

An indication of the slippery nature of Lando's own attitude towards the subject, however, can be found in his *Sferza de scrittori* (1550), a tongue-in-cheek denunciation of writers from the Ancients to the Moderns in which Lando likely refers to the *Valorose donne* when, reflecting on his own literary career, he writes '... mi occorse occasione di far parer illustri fra molte onorate donne alcune pettegolette che si tengono da più che se fossero degli Reali di Francia o di quei di Baviera ...' ('... I had occasion to elevate, among many honourable women, a few gossips who think themselves superior to French or Bavarian royalty ...'), indicating that his anthology was not an uncomplicated praise of women.[27] And before imagining Lando as a staunch defender of the female sex, we might look at his language in the following passage from the same text, in which he bitterly denounces the lack of gratitude with which another attempt to celebrate women was met:

> ... fui de primi che mostrarono al mondo essere le donne di maggior eccellenza e dignità degli uomini, e molte ne lodai d'ogni parte d'Italia; et donde sperai riportarne relazione de grazie (ch'altro non ne aspettava) già io della lor spilorcheria, vi fu una Palavicina che me ne disse male, e meco fieramente turbossi; allora dissi io fra me stesso, deh venga la quartana

febre a chi ha voglia di lodar giamai questo diabolico sesso, queste velenose serpi, e queste crudelissime tigri ...[28]

... I was among the first to show the world that women are of greater worth and dignity than men, and I praised many of them from every part of Italy; and where I hoped to reap a relationship of gratitude (for I expected no less), instead – there was a certain Palavicina woman who spoke ill of me – I was very upset. So I said to myself, may the quartan fever strike him who wishes to praise this diabolical sex, these poisonous snakes, and these cruelest tigers ...

Evidently, Lando's celebratory instincts were motivated at least in part by the desire to establish a relationship of obligation with certain female patrons.

We might also recall a lesser-known work attributed to Lando, the *Brieve essortatione agli huomini perché non si lascino superar dalle donne* of 1545, bound and published with a treatise in praise of women, Vincenzo Maggi's *Brieve trattato dell'eccellentia delle donne*.[29] Lando's quasi-misogynist *Essortatione* warned men that, if they did not reverse their own decadence and return to study, learning, and virtue, they would be surpassed by women, who had begun to prove themselves in these arenas. If men did not reform, Lando warned, women would assert their superiority and rule men cruelly, seeking vengeance for their own mistreatment.[30] That Lando should have composed a treatise warning against women's superiority actually serves to strengthen the argument that the *Valorose donne* were composed as a contribution to the defence of women genre, and helps illuminate the way in which Lando worked. First of all, as Conor Fahy points out, the *Essortatione* is not strictly misogynistic in nature, for it does not deny that women have the capacity to learn and even to govern. Rather, it highlights the threat to men represented by this capacity and urges that women be restricted to the domestic sphere in order to avoid a reversal of roles. It is not, therefore, a shift for Lando to proclaim women's excellence in learning and writing in the *Valorose donne*. Furthermore, just as the *Essortatione* fits into the defence of women genre, albeit from the other side of the debate, so too the *Valorose donne* present themselves as a contribution to this genre. Lando has merely – apparently – switched positions. Rather than representing an interpretive problem, this switch does much to explain the *Valorose donne*. The anthology exists less as an effort to support women's cause than as a contribution to a literary genre: the side taken by the author is of less importance than the rhetorical act of taking a side.[31] Just as Fahy insists that the *Essortatione* was intended primarily to amuse, and argues, '... dobbiamo vedere nella *Brieve essortatione*, non tanto la reazione di un misogino contro un pericolo sentito come reale ed imminente, quanto una variazione arguta sul tema della superiorità femminile,'[32] so too the *Valorose donne* can be seen as, first and foremost, a rhetorical exercise.

That Lando should have conceived the *Valorose donne* in order to try his hand in yet another literary genre is not, however, to say the letters should be dismissed as a technical exercise and nothing more. Regardless of the motives behind its creation, this text claims to speak in the voice of women and to represent female epistolary discourse. Moreover, if, as critics such as Francine Daenens and Simonetta Adorni Braccesi suggest, the collection functions as an epistolary disguise in which to promote heterodox viewpoints, the anthology demonstrates an engagement with religious and social issues.[33] If the *Valorose donne* were, in fact, born as an experiment in rhetoric and genre, as a means by which the writer could test and exhibit his skills by arguing both sides of a problem in a newly popular medium, the motives underlying Lando's female impersonation remain to be examined.

II. Writing Women's Letters: Female Experience in the *Lettere di molte valorose donne*

In an article on textual impersonations, Nancy Miller asks, 'What secondary gains accrue to a male writer who supplies first-person feminine fictions ...?'[34] Why should Lando choose to impersonate female letter writers? Female impersonation is not out of character for Lando. Isabella Sforza's 1544 spiritual treatise, *Della vera tranquillità dell'animo*, has been attributed to Lando, suggesting that at least once prior to the *Valorose donne* he had chosen to publish under the name of a female patron.[35] In the dedicatory letter to *Della vera tranquillità dell'animo* – signed, with one of Lando's pseudonyms, 'il Tranquillo' – the text is framed, as in the *Valorose donne*, as a demonstration of women's literary (and moral) merit. 'Il Tranquillo' explains that although he, too, had been working on a book similar to this, he thought Isabella's superior and decided to publish it.[36] The *Valorose donne* also share similarities with the *Consolatorie*, a collection of epistles that includes several letters attributed to women.[37] Here, too, Lando positions himself within the cultural and literary controversy over women: a letter from Benedetto

Agnello urges Susanna Valente, '… se alcuno vi rinfaccia la debolezza et imperfezione del sesso feminile, armatevi con le belle diffese che per cotal sesso ha fatto Cornelio Agrippa, Galeazzo Capra, Ortensio Lando …' ('… if anyone should taunt you with the weakness and imperfection of the female sex, arm yourself with the excellent defences of that sex made by Cornelio Agrippa, Galeazzo Capra, Ortensio Lando …').[38] In the *Ragionamenti familiari,* Lando is absent as an authorial voice and speaks through a variety of both men and women, including some who appear in the *Valorose donne,* while the *Oracoli de' moderni ingegni* (1550) feature sayings attributed to such Landian muses as Lucrezia and Isabella Gonzaga, Emilia Rangona, and Susanna Valente.

The *Valorose donne* are not, therefore, unique in Lando's work in terms of their use of the female voice and their desire to situate themselves within the genre of the *difesa della donna.* Yet the question remains as to the purpose behind the assumption of numerous female voices in the *Valorose donne.* There are (at least) three possible answers to this question. First, by framing a debate over women's intellectual capacities and moral qualities in the voices of women, Lando seeks authenticity. While in many instances it is the woman writer who seeks a man's support to lend validity to her literary project, here the situation is reversed. By speaking in the diverse voices of 'real' women, Lando can claim a 'genuine' understanding of the issues at stake and approach them from a number of angles. Second, and most practically, many of the women who appear in the *Valorose donne* were acquaintances and patrons of Lando. Presenting them as models of female eloquence and learning could have functioned simply as a means of earning continued support or as a form of repayment for their generosity (as intimated in his comments in the *Sferza de scrittori,* cited above). Third and finally, if the letters contain controversial heterodox viewpoints, then the assumption of a variety of female personae functions as protective mechanism, distancing the real author as much as possible from the content of the letters – not only through the use of pseudonym, but through a gender switch and the fragmentation of the author into multiple identities. Lando's works were, with the exception of the *Dialogo sopra la sacra scrittura* and the *Vari componimenti,* published anonymously or pseudonymously, and some were placed on the *Index.*[39] Disguise was hardly foreign to him; in the *Valorose donne* he merely takes it to a new degree.

In assuming such a variety of female epistolary voices, Lando invites us to question his conception of what it means to 'write like a woman.' What, according to Lando, do women write about, and how do they write about it? To approach these problems I will examine some of the more clearly discernible thematic threads which run through the *Valorose donne*: distinct groups of letters that focus on learning, virtue, the 'female sphere' (including marriage, pregnancy and childbirth, and household government), and finally, vices presented as specifically 'female.' I will begin, however, with a group of letters characterized by their attention to religious and spiritual problems and which, as mentioned above, provide one possible key to understanding the anthology.

Religion

For at least one modern critic, the key to the *Valorose donne* lies in the women named in its pages, some of whom are historical figures known for their heterodox religious beliefs. Echoing Amedeo Quondam, Francine Daenens reminds us that the recourse to the epistolary format 'è sempre rivelatrice di una ragnetela di rapporti;' that is, the 'internal readers' represented in an *epistolario* communicate something to the external reader about the author.[40] The female protagonists of the *Valorose donne*, according to Daenens, are deliberately chosen for their relevance to the heterodox sensibility the letters want to convey.[41] If this is the case, how might the *Valorose donne* function as a facade for religious dissent?

The very first letter in the collection, an exchange between two prominent Sforza women, Isabella and Bona, Queen of Poland, constitutes a good key for reading the anthology as a whole. It is significant that the first woman to be addressed in the collection is a queen reigning after her husband's death, immediately establishing these letters in a space between the 'female' practice of letter-writing and the 'male' one of public self-representation. Isabella reminds Bona that she is now a role model for all women: 'tutte le donne del regno vostro e de' vicini stati si specchiaranno ora in voi, e da voi torranno l'essempio e la norma di santamente governar le lor giuridizioni' ('all the women of your realm and the nearby states will see themselves reflected in you, and from you they will draw the example and the model with which to honourably govern their own realms'). She offers this advice: 'Converavi, Signora, molte cose prudentemente dissimulare, e il tutto però sapere' ('It will behoove you, my lady, to prudently dissimulate many things, and to know everything').[42] That single verb, 'dissimulare, stands as a Nicodemitic clue to the text's hidden core of religious dissent, a reminder that one's outer appearance need not correspond to one's true beliefs.[43] For Daenens, this signifies that while the *Valorose Donne* may masquerade as an anthology of women's letters, this is merely a protective device to obfuscate their true, religious message.

Heterodoxy is without question an important element in the *Valorose donne*, most obviously and frequently apparent in letters regarding scripture. Although there was no codified 'heterodox' position – the term connotes a general questioning of orthodox tenets in sixteenth-century Italy – heterodox views were influenced by Erasmus and Luther, particularly with regard to such issues as the reform of abuses within the Church, justification by faith alone, and the reading of scripture.[44] This last is a common theme for Lando – indeed, he later devotes an entire book to it – and is taken up in the *Valorose donne* in several points.[45] For Lando, scripture, freed of the complications and distortions of interpretation, commentary and allegory, is at the base of religion, an 'antidote for the ills of the Church.'[46] Giovanna Cavalleria, for example, in a lengthy letter to Clara Gualanda, praises scripture over all other forms of writing. In true Landian fashion, Giovanna resorts to extensive lists to make her point, arguing that having read widely herself, she regrets it. Fervently, she asserts her devotion to scripture, the only true book: 'non vorrei da che appresi la santa Croce aver mai letto altra cosa che la divina scrittura; vorrei aver mangiato questo sacro volume come per il profeta Iddio comandò; vorrei avermelo convertito in succo et in sangue perché egli sarebbe stato come una lucerna a' piedi miei ...' ('Ever since I came to know the holy Cross, I have wished never to have read anything but the divine scripture; I wish I had consumed this holy book as God commanded through the prophet; I wish I had turned it into nectar and blood because it would have been as a lantern at my feet ...').[47] Similarly, Francesca Ruvissa urges a simple, straightforward approach to scripture as the true path to God: 'se con umiltà trattarete la sacra scrittura, e non ambiziosamente (come oggidí molti fanno) avrete per vostro maestro lo Spirito Santo' ('if you treat the holy scripture with humility, not ambition [as many do these days], you will have the Holy Spirit for your teacher').[48] Isabella Sforza commends Fulvia Colonna for having begun to study scripture and encourages her not to be overwhelmed by commentators who distort and corrupt it; elsewhere she complains to Isabetta Castigliona that priests stray too far from scripture in their sermons:

> ... questi nostri predicatori mi paiono non predicatori e ministri della parola d'Iddio, ma istrioni; certamente parrebbemi di commettere minor peccato andando a vedere i giuochi Circensi o li Nemei, se ora si usassero,

che ad udir questi parabalani che ci contano i lor sogni con le lor cabalistiche fizioni, et lasciano star i sacri misteri della scrittura.[49]

... these preachers of ours seem to me not preachers and ministers of the word of God, but performers; it would certainly seem to me less of a sin to go to see the Circean or Nemean games, if they still existed, than to listen to these charlatans who recount their dreams with cabbalistic fictions, and ignore the holy mysteries of scripture.

A letter from Apollonia Rovella to Leonora da Vertema, by contrast, praises a priest who interprets scripture faithfully: 'Non è gonfio, non è pettoruto, non sputa parole sesquipedali, non si vendica spirito di profezia, usa parcamente le allegorie conoscendo per il lor mezo non potersi efficacemente insegnar i dogmi della fede ...' ('He is not puffed up, nor pompous, he doesn't spout sesquipedalian words, he doesn't claim to be a prophet, he is sparing with allegory knowing that it is not an effective means for teaching the dogma of the faith').[50]

For Lando, the misuse of religion verges on superstition, and superstition in all forms is anathema to him. Lando's opinions are certainly provocative: it is perhaps largely to the credit of the elaborate disguise he enacts in the *Valorose donne* that they have passed largely unnoticed over the centuries. Daenens makes an important contribution by pointing out the element of religious dissent in the *Valorose donne*. She takes it even further by suggesting an interaction between religious dissent and the text's other concerns, such as the intellectual and social status of women, which would represent a range of dissent from social to religious. In this epistolary world, the male/female opposition is transposed upon that of Christian/heretic: 'il conflitto uomo/donna si dissolve anche nel significato traslato vir catholicus/mulier haeretica, e ... la "questione femminile" si innesta sulle dispute sacramentarie.'[51]

While an element of dissent undoubtedly characterizes the text in its religious content, however, it does not suffice to explain the anthology. First of all, Lando's emphasis on scripture constitutes not only a heterodox position of religious dissent but also a more general manifestation of Lando's rejection of humanist learning. If the Bible represents the true source of all learning, then humanist erudition is unnecessary.[52] Lando's religious stance thus becomes intertwined with his parody of humanism in the pointed recourse to the *Officina* in the *Valorose donne*. Second, although Daenens reads much of the *Valorose donne* as the expression of a 'mondo radicale' characterized by religious and social dissent,⁵³ the anthology advances a more complicated and finally less progressive depiction of women in terms of the debate over women's education, intellectual abilities, and morality. The significance of Isabella Sforza's advice to Bona of Poland to learn the art of dissimulation goes beyond its religious/heterodox connotations, constituting a reference to the illusionary nature of the *Valorose donne* as a whole, and to the fact that the anthology is not what it seems.

Learning

Keeping in mind Isabella Sforza's comments to Bona about dissimulation, but recalling that the *Valorose donne* purport to argue for women's *dottrina* and *eloquenza* and that this, at least superficially, constitutes the text's primary raison d'être, let us turn to some of the letters on this subject. What, exactly, does the anthology say about women and learning? Where does it fit into the corpus of *querelle des femmes* texts? A letter by Ippolita Crema, for example, wonders at men's ability to ignore women's capacity for learning and urges her young correspondent to continue in her studies.⁵⁴ Similarly, a letter from the Duchess of Amalfi to Clarizia B is prompted by the Duchess' delight in Clarizia's studiousness.⁵⁵ Lucietta Soranza reproaches Lucrezia Masippa for speaking disparagingly of learned women, reminding her that 'le lettere sono invenzione delle donne' ('letters are women's invention') and furnishing a long list of literary women to prove her point.⁵⁶ Lucietta closes her letter by noting that those 'valorose donne' who have given up their embroidery needles ('lasciato l'ago') for literature would be furious if they knew of Lucrezia's comments. She explains that only by educating themselves can women reestablish their honour and escape male oppression. Lucietta's feminist stance is echoed in a letter from Livia D'Arco reprimanding Laura Pestalossa for wishing she had been born a man. Livia reminds Laura of all the areas in which women have equalled or surpassed men, including tolerance, beauty, generosity, and even war, as well as learning. While Livia's examples of female excellence derive from the *Officina*, her impassioned praise of women is introduced with a reference to modern defenders of women, among whom, significantly, she numbers Ortensio Lando.⁵⁷ Interestingly, while Livia's litany of the areas in which women have distinguished themselves is introduced by *dottrina*, the last category is reserved for chastity, as if to emphasize that women can be both learned and chaste, in spite of cultural tropes equating virtue with silence and implicitly with circumscribed learning for women ('Qual uomo ritroverete voi più di castità amico che già fusser Sulpizia, Marcia, Eugenia, Sophronia, Etelfrida, Drias, Rodoguna, Daphne ...?' ['What man will you find who is a better friend of chastity than ever were Sulpizia, Marcia, Eugenia, Sophronia, Etelfrida, Drias, Rodoguna, Daphne ...?']).[58]

We have discussed the problems encountered in trying to pull any single, straightforward message from the *Valorose donne*. What is argued in one letter can be subtly undermined or even blatantly contradicted in another, a technique typical of many of Lando's works. Grendler suggests that Lando sometimes argued both sides of an issue in order to ridicule rhetoric itself, and that his purpose in doing so 'was not to prove that the skilled orator could defend both sides but *to cast doubt on the importance of the question*' (emphasis added).[59] With this in mind, I turn now to a group of letters that demonstrate the unsteady dynamics of epistolary viewpoint in the *Valorose donne* when it comes to women's capacity for learning and the debate over their proper role.

In keeping with the anthology's claim to celebrate women's intellectual capacities, a letter by Paula Treccia praises Livia Portia's dedication to her studies and, in contrast to common views regarding learned women, draws a link between women's education and honourable actions: 'preseverate (vi supplico) come avete incominciato perché si comprenda un giorno non esser le donne men atte all'onorate imprese degli uomini ...' ('perservere [I beseech you] as you have begun, so that one day it will be known that women are no less capable of honourable deeds than men ...').[60] Paula's letter, however, is followed by another that focuses entirely on traditional feminine pastimes such as embroidery, as if to establish an opposition between these activities and study. Similarly, a letter reprimanding Margherita Pobbia for having abandoned 'female' duties for poetry is juxtaposed with another letter, also addressed to Margherita, that takes up the defence of poetry.[61] Thus a paradoxical pro/contra structure is set up, complicating any attempt to discern the *Valorose donne's* 'real' message. Learning or embroidery? In which lies the worth of women?

This oscillation is compacted into a single letter in the case of Lucrezia Gambera's complaint that she can find nothing worth reading: '... non trovo scrittore alcuno o in la greca o in latina lingua che pienamente sodisfar mi possa ...' ('... I can find no writer in Greek or Latin that fully satisfies me').[62] Listing a number of erudite works which have left her dissatisfied, Lucrezia decides to embrace traditional, 'natural' female pursuits over literature and urges her correspondent to respect her decision: '... lasciatemi più tosto attender all'aco, alla qual cosa sentomi dalla natura più inchinata e più disposta' ('... leave me instead to my needle, to which I feel naturally more inclined and disposed').[63] On the surface, Lucrezia's letter depicts a woman who rejects an alternative path for a traditional one. The erudition Lucrezia displays in explaining herself, however, complicates this message in two important ways: first, because her decision is clearly made on the basis of her own *dottrina*, for her numerous references to both Greek and Latin authors demonstrate that she is familiar with them and finds them (not herself) lacking; and second, because she makes a free choice to renounce one world for the other. Text and subtext are at odds, education for women neither promoted nor condemned. Ultimately, and perhaps paradoxically, the letter falls back on traditional tropes by arguing that a woman intelligent enough to be as educated as Lucrezia is also smart enough to realize her true calling lies not in the literary but in the domestic arena.

A letter from Aurelia Magia to Laura Ceruta picks up on the theme of the inadequacy of literature alluded to by Lucrezia. Aurelia explains that she declines to dedicate herself to study as 'tante nobili madonne e tante illustre signore' have done because she finds fault with everything she reads.[64] Aurelia's missive uses the debate over women's learning as a pretext to target the pretentiousness and uselessness of learning and literature in general, a theme that characterizes Lando's later *Sferza de scrittori*. Aurelia fears theology will cause her to fall into 'qualche mala sospizione' ('some wrong belief') while she calls grammarians 'poverelli' ('poor things') who can neither 'ragionare né giudicar d'altro che de' nomi e verbi ...' ('reason nor judge anything but nouns and verbs'). She finds similar fault with poets, sophists, and logicians, finally determining, like Lucrezia, that it is more sensible to devote herself to traditional women's duties: 'L'è adunque meglio che io li lasci star in pace, e mi trattenga nelli esercizi dalle donne sinora usitati ... io non voglio doventar poetessa perché veggo che quelle che si danno alle lettere non si sanno ... rassettar un paio di calze o lavarsi un moccichino' ('Therefore it is better for me to leave them in peace, and to devote myself to the customary work of women ... I do not wish to become a poetess, because I see that those women who devote themselves to letters do not know how ... to mend a pair of stockings or wash a rag'). Like that of Lucrezia, Aurelia's decision to forsake *dottrina* for traditional feminine skills like sewing cannot be taken completely seriously. First of all, even to make such assertions about literature requires a high degree of learning, which Aurelia shows she has acquired.

Second, her declaration that a woman's true fulfilment lies in the limiting role traditionally assigned to her rings hollow, coming as it does from a woman who has accessed the world of learning. When Aurelia writes, 'Io non so la più bella via di farmi stimare e onorare al mondo che con l'esser casta, modesta, taciturna, e umile, senza tante lettere e senza tante filosofie' ('I know no better way to earn respect and honour in the world than through being chaste, modest, silent, and humble, without all this learning and without all this philosophizing'), she seems merely to parrot the feminine virtues so often praised by writers of comportment literature.

The letters of both Aurelia and Lucrezia, while ostensibly focusing on women's learning, fit into the larger scheme of Lando's negative judgment of the Renaissance literary world. They thus raise important themes for reading the *Valorose donne*: nothing is as it seems, arguments made in favour of one position will always be contradicted elsewhere in the anthology, and many letters are less the result of a wish to praise and support women than the manifestation of a more general agenda of cultural critique.

Virtue

Like the letters on learning, those praising and defending women's virtue and dignity encompass a range of approaches. Alongside sober *apologia* for women's 'antico valore' are exaggerated claims of women's superiority and men's immense inferiority that are difficult to take seriously. On the one hand, for example, Beatrice Pia laments that women, forgetting their illustrious collective past, have come to accept their subjection to men: 'per certo che ad altro non ci riputiamo nate che a servire e ad ubidire gli uomini: abbiamo pur l'essempio di molte grandi et valorose femine, le quai regnarno et signoreggiarno altri, più che virilmente' ('clearly we deem ourselves born only to serve and obey men, and yet we have the example of many great and valorous women, who reigned and governed others, with even more manly heart').[65] Similarly, Caterina Visconte Landessa, in response to a misogynist dialogue she has read that targets women as 'cosa di poco ingegno, di niuna prudenzia, di niuno giudicio, e di minor invenzione (salvo l'oprar male)' ('a thing of little intelligence, no prudence, no judgment, and less imagination [but for mischief]'), lists the great inventions of women.[66] Letters like these echo arguments and techniques common to the texts of the *querelle des femmes*. On the other hand, however, Lando's satirical force becomes increasingly evident in letters like that of Isabella Sforza, who lambastes the pretensions of educated men in her opening lines: 'Sempre, da che il mondo è mondo, gli uomini litterati o furono superbi, arroganti, e ambiziosi ...' ('Always, since the world came to be, lettered men were proud, arrogant, and ambitious ...').[67] She goes on to deride male writers who threaten women with ruining them in print if they are not generous with their patronage and accuses them of trying to make their living at the expense of women.[68] If all women were above reproach, Isabella argues ('caste, forti, modeste, giuste, magnanime, discrete, prudenti, grate, dotte, bellicose, liberali' ['chaste, strong, modest, just, magnanimous, discreet, prudent, grateful, learned, courageous, generous']), men would have nothing negative to write about. Not only should women aspire to perfection, Isabella writes, but when they have acquired it, they should also turn their own pens upon the failings of men: 'scriviamo ancora noi in biasimo e vituperio degli uomini, sí come essi longo tempo hanno fatto contra di noi' ('let us then write of men with condemnation and scorn, as they have written against us for so long') – perhaps confirming the fears of female retribution expressed in Lando's *Brieve essortatione*. At this point, Isabella's letter strays into a realm of exaggeration in which it is impossible not to read her words as the result of a Landian delight in mockery and hyperbole. In a list of adjectives nearly a page long, she catalogues the defects of men: they are 'temerari, litigiosi, fraudolenti, protervi, ingrati, loquaci, importuni, perfidi, pergiuri, traditori, ingiusti, vani, bugiardi, volubili, inconstanti, paurosi nelle oneste impresi e audaci nelle ingiuste azioni ...' ('audacious, argumentative, deceitful, insolent, ungrateful, talkative, bothersome, traitorous, untrustworthy, unjust, vain, liars, fickle, inconstant, fearful in honest endeavours and audacious in unjust actions ...'), to name just a few of their faults.

The solemn dignity of such letters as those of Beatrice Pia and Catherina Visconte are further undermined by the exaggerated, antimale declarations made in still other letters. The language of Contessa Aurelia's letter to Sulpizia Biraga, for example, is especially strong. The letter, a bizarre *consolatoria* written upon the death of Sulpizia's father, reprimands Sulpizia for taking her father's death too hard and attributes her grief to women's dependence on men: 'L'è pur gran cosa la pusilanimità delle donne moderne, perché non potiamo far nulla senza l'agiutto degli uomini, e pur si può far senza essi in molte cose ...' ('The cowardice of today's women is truly astonishing, for we can do nothing without the help of men, and yet we could do without them in many things ...').[69] Aurelia herself, by contrast, has no need of men and indeed would prefer never to lay eyes on one again, were they not necessary for the continuation of the human race: 'cosí si potesse senza la lor opra mantener l'umana schiatta, io per me ne sarei molto ben contenta, tanto m'ho recato in odio questo sesso diabolico' ('were it possible to perpetuate the human race without their help, I for one would be quite content, so much do I despise this diabolical sex'). Aurelia's hatred stems from her belief that men exist solely to render women's lives a misery. She proposes the radical solution of a world peopled only by women, in which she and Sulpizia will live together: 'm'ho deliberato di far mia vita con esso voi ... Vi prometto la mia nuda fé che vorrei più tosto veder la faccia di Satanasso che veder un uomo ...' ('I have decided to make my life with you ... I swear to you that I would rather see the face of Satan than see a man'). Not only does she urge Sulpizia not to remarry, but she tries to convince her to abandon her son in order to rid her house entirely of the male sex: '... disponetevi voi di non ripigliar marito, e di sgombrar la casa d'uomini, lasciate Monsignor vostro figlio nella sua badia. E del resto non vi curate' ('... prepare yourself not to remarry, and to rid the house of men; leave Monsignor your son in the abbey. And don't worry about the rest').[70]

The extreme rhetoric of such a diatribe makes it difficult to read the letter as a true evaluation of women's social role or as a proposal for an alternative solution. Does Lando take his argument seriously, or does he mock women by exaggerating their grievances? Ultimately, the solution has little to do with women specifically and much to do with Lando's general social criticism and with his interest in the utopian literature that circulated in early modern Europe. Thomas More's *Utopia* was read with great interest by those in Lando's circle, and Lando himself was behind its Italian translation.[71] Doni's *Mondo savio e pazzo* took up the problem, followed by others.[72] The utopia, workable or not, sincere or satirical, was a response to social inequalities and oppression. Utopias did not necessarily provide solutions, but they did point out problems by presenting them in new and arresting ways. In similar fashion, as Grendler writes, Lando uses humour and satire in his works to launch fierce social critiques, but fails to propose any practical solution for the renewal of society.[73] Aurelia's plea for retreat to a perfect, wholly female world that she and Sulpizia will create for themselves is neither a call for female solidarity nor a parody of it, but rather an acknowledgment of the problem of women's subjection in contemporary culture.

The 'Female' Sphere

Lando's letters concerning women's dignity and education thus seem to function primarily as vehicles for the more general themes he expresses elsewhere: social discontent, disillusionment, and contempt for the humanist system of learning. To discover what Lando thought about women's epistolary discourse specifically, we may do better to examine another thematic grouping in the *Valorose donne* which concerns issues the writer deems specifically 'female' and to which he imagines women might devote their epistolary exchanges: choosing a husband (or attenuating the bad qualities of the husband one already has), deciding on marriage or the convent, enduring childbirth and rearing children, suggestions for running a household and for getting one's laundry perfectly clean. Like the letters on *dottrina* and virtue, these letters are often contradictory, frequently bolstered by the *Officina*, and reflect Lando's general social criticisms in addition to his ideas about female epistolary discourse. Moreover, they reflect a broader literary trend towards producing informal, popular texts aimed at women, which focused on many of these same subjects. *Libri di segreti* – or 'books of secrets' – like those of Alessio Piemontese, Pietro Bairo, Leonardo Fioravanti, and many others focused on a vast array of medical ailments and their cures and included extensive sections that specifically treated women's concerns; while beauty books like Giovanni Marinello's *Gli ornamenti delle donne* (1562) were a more practical incarnation of Neoplatonic treatises like Firenzuola's *Dialogo della bellezza delle donne* (1548). Learned texts as well as popular ones sought to define the relationship between husband and wife, as Lando's writers also do: It is perhaps significant that Erasmus' *Declamatio* in support of marriage, for example, was included in a letter writing manual (followed by a letter that expressed the opposite point of view).[74] The letterbook, as we saw in chapter 1, was beginning to function as the site of a whole range of didactic purposes. It had become a tool not only for teaching how to write letters, but also for disseminating ideas about social roles, customs, and religious beliefs.

Lando's *Valorose donne*, therefore, reflect a confluence of literary trends. They constitute the intersection of attempts to codify female epistolarity with comportment literature and 'how-to' manuals for women, including the 'books of secrets' that would continue to gain popularity throughout the century. The *Valorose donne* actually precede by several years the most well-known of the *libri di segreti* they closely resemble, and stand practically alone in their use of the female voice to confer added authenticity to this didactic discourse.[75] Whereas manuals like Bairo's *Secreti medicinali*, with its extensive sections on menstruation, pregnancy, childbirth, and lactation, or beauty books such as Marinello's *Gli ornamenti delle donne*, with its fetishistic attention to each part of the female body, can be read as efforts to exert control over specifically feminine realms of power, the female impersonation of the *Valorose donne* constitutes an even more complex appropriation of women's experience. The result is at once a voyeuristic glimpse of the 'real' world of women (as Lando imagines it), and an inversion of traditional constructions of male literary authority: here it is the female voice that confers it.

One omnipresent theme debated in the *Valorose donne* is marriage, certainly a central issue for early modern women (as well as for Protestant reformers, who supported marriage over the cloister).[76] Lando presents women as the primary movers of the marriage negotiation, granting them a certain agency and allowing them to choose between marriage and the convent. Ever irreverent, Lando pokes fun at the entire negotiation process by furnishing exaggerated descriptions of the physical and moral defects of the husbands proposed. Virginia Trotta, for example, warns of a suitor's unpleasant qualities, including the 'puzzolente sudore che dal corpo le n'esce,' the 'fetore della bocca' ('the stink of his breath'), his malodorous feet, and so on.[77] Although Lando's tone is humourous, serious discussions of such problems – which could interfere with marital relations – are found in many *libri di segreti*, along with recipes for cures that correspond to those described by Virginia.[78] A letter from Susanna Valente about a friend's learned fiancé turns into a comic mockery not only of the marriage process but of studious men when Susanna laments that a *dottore* will make a terrible husband: '... che diavolo volete voi far di dottori? Non sapete che sono questi litterati per la maggior parte tisichi, gelosi e franetichi?' ('... what the devil do you want with doctors? Don't you kow that these learned men are for the most part consumptive, jealous, and frantic?').[79] Although Lando, who is thought to have studied medicine in his youth, was surely quite learned himself, this did not stop him launching similar diatribes against the medical and other 'learned' professions in other works as part of a general rejection of contemporary learning.[80] Once again, Lando appears to use a subject of specific concern to women to frame a larger social criticism.

Like the marriage negotiation, the decision whether to marry or enter a convent is granted much space in the *Valorose donne*, and elicits letters arguing in favour of each. Giulia Rosa, for example, preempts her correspondent's intention to become a nun by finding her the perfect husband: 'Acciò non vi facciate monaca v'ho proveduto d'un marito il quale, da che nacque, non fu mai udito né mentire, né giurare, né adirarsi, né ociosamente favellare, col quale spero averete vita giocondissima ...' ('To keep you from becoming a nun, I have found you a husband who, since the day he was born, has not been heard to lie, swear, rage, nor chatter idly, with whom I hope you will share the happiest of lives ...').[81] This specimen sounds too perfect: the litany of his good qualities seems to suggest that most men are, in fact, guilty of the negative attributes of which this one is free. The convent, however, is equally problematic. Caterina Visconte describes the convent not as a place of spiritual retreat but rather a hotbed of secular intrigue, while Lavinia Sforza's description of convent life does not condemn nuns but characterizes them as subject, like everyone else, to human passions.[82] The general view of the convent is a negative one, although even these depictions of corruption are offset by one unequivocally positive example, that of Suor Diana de Contrari, lauded for her 'vita angelica.'[83] Suor Diana, however, is the exception to the rule. Lando presents marriage as preferable to convent, a position that has perhaps less to do with its value as an institution than with his broader views on the corruption of the Church. Lando himself was an apostate monk and many of his works are streaked with anticlericalism.[84] His negative view of the convent stems from his general disgust with religious corruption and the divorce of religious life from the world rather than a specific concern with the choices available to women.

Marriage provides fodder for a number of letters on women's comportment as well, many of which offer very specific suggestions for their behaviour within the marital union. Lucrezia Agnella, for example, explains that marriages should take place when both parties are most ready to have children: 'far debbonsi i matrimoni quando l'uomo è atto a generare e la donna a concepire; altrimenti, liti e discordie per la casa tutta via s'odono' ('marriages should take place when the man is able to generate and the woman to conceive; otherwise, arguments and disagreements will fill the house').[85] She concludes that a woman should be about eighteen and a man thirty-six to marry.[86] A letter from Lucrezia Martinenga to M. Lucistella dal Pozzo repeats classic Albertian views on a wife's duties, interrogating the future bride:

> Saprete voi conservare in casa stando quel che il marito guadagnerà fuor di casa andando? Che questo è una de principali uffici della buona madre

di famiglia? Saprete voi discretamente commandare a' servidori e allevare i figliuoli come alle buone madri si conviene?[87]

Will you know how to conserve in the home that which your husband earns by going outside it? For this is one of the principle duties of a good mother? Will you know how to discreetly command the servants and raise your children as a good mother should?

Again, such letters reformulate in epistolary form themes that are common in comportment and didactic literature. In some cases, Lando's views on women's role within marriage are staunchly conservative and even misogynist. Catherina, for example, tells Lucietta she must always submit to her husband, rather than imitate the 'sfacciate femine che ad altro non aspirano che a tiranneggiare ... a rubare le maritali facultà ...' ('shameless females who aspire to nothing else but to tyrannize ... to steal their husbands' wealth ...'), and that when her husband is away she should stay out of public sight.[88] Maria de Benedetti tells a correspondent that it is her own fault if her husband beats her; similarly Paula Castigliona writes to Leonora Forteguerra: 'Se vostro marito vi dà alle volte delle busse, non è che voi non lo meritate, poscia che non avete alcuna considerazione di provocarlo a sdegno' ('If your husband beats you once in a while, it's not that you don't deserve it, as you think nothing of disdainfully provoking him').[89] Here Lando's parodic intent seems evident: few marriage manuals endorse domestic abuse so enthusiastically, preferring to promote the idea of marriage as a loving partnership.[90]

A letter by Lucrezia Martinenga, finally, congratulates the newly married Laura Gonzaga and offers a variety of suggestions for leading a happy married life. Lucrezia advises Laura to keep peace in her house, retain loyal servants and entertain generously, give to the poor, and be humble and malleable in conversation. Lucrezia's advice extends to details such as the tablecloths and linens Laura should use, and she frames her advice in terms of utility, explaining, 'l'utile sempre più mi piacque che il diletto' ('I have always preferred the useful over the enjoyable').[91] These lines recall Paolo Manuzio's declaration in the *Lettere volgari* of the tenets of the vernacular epistolary genre: it should be entertaining, but it should most of all be useful.[92] In this sense, we can argue that Lando uses the *Valorose donne* as a vehicle for a specifically feminine discourse of 'utilità'– as a kind of manual for women's duties. Of course, the parodic vein that runs through so many of these letters makes us question his motives. Does he actually mean to propose a useful manual for women? Let us examine Lando's treatment of some of the other topics this 'manual' covers.

Like marriage, pregnancy and childrearing receive a variety of treatments in the *Valorose donne*. A number of letters on these subjects are congratulatory notes on the birth of a son or daughter, generally accompanied by comparisons to classical examples, as when Lucrezia Masippa tells Camilla Palavicina that neither 'Diagora Rodiotto ... Chilone Lacedemonio ... Policrata nobile romana' could have felt more happiness than she about the birth of Camilla's child.[93] Some of the more interesting letters on pregnancy and childbirth deal with issues like breastfeeding or hiring a good wetnurse, topics discussed at length by male writers in a variety of venues. Matteo Palmieri's treatise on civic life located breastfeeding in the context of creating and moulding future citizens; similarly, Dolce's *Della institutione delle donne* and Agrippa's *Declamatio* praised the special properties of mothers' milk,[94] while remedies for common problems with lactation abound in the *libri di segreti*.[95] Isabella Lonardi follows the general view of most discussions of the subject when she urges Maddalena Peverella to breastfeed her son herself and adds a prescription for 'toughening up' the newborn's tender skin by spreading salt in his swaddling.[96] Caterina Fregosa, on the other hand, obtains a wet nurse for Lucia Spinella, 'la quale fa più latte, e migliore, che non faceva Philix nodrice di Domiziano ...' ('who makes more and better milk than Philix, Domitian's nurse'), and Nicola Trotta writes Luigia Biraga about a potential *balia* who has recently given birth herself and is physically perfect for the job: 'non è pettiginosa e ha le mamelle né troppo grosse, né troppo piccine; il petto ha largo ...' ('she is not freckled and her breasts are neither too large nor too small; her chest is broad ...').[97] Just as Lando looked to the *Officina* when treating the *querelle* topic of women's intellect (making a point, as I argued above, more about the devolution of learning into rote citation than about women's potential), so too he draws on *libri di segreti* in discussing issues pertaining to the female body, again critiquing the tradition itself as much as women's relation to the subject. The advice of 'Mamma Riminalda' regarding her sister's pregnancy, for example, recalls that offered by numerous manuals. Because her sister is prone to miscarriages, Riminalda gives her a recipe for a powder of cardamom, mint, and other herbs to protect her, and a coral amulet to wear while giving birth.[98] Riminalda's recipe, which is striking in its detail, may seem an odd note in an anthology of letters, but makes perfect sense when seen in relation to similar prescriptions for warding off miscarriage and facilitating labour and birth found in many *libri di segreti* and pamphlets.[99] Lando's ventriloquism continues to be twofold, exercised at the level not only of gender (his use of female voices) but that of intertexuality (his constant referencing of *libri di segreti*, in addition to the *Officina*), as we will see in the remainder of this section.

In these letters, Lando grants the reader a seemingly intimate glimpse into the private world of women, a female network of mothers, sisters, and friends in which advice, comfort, and support are passed from one to the other. Repeatedly, he indicates that women's knowledge, which comes from direct experience, is superior to that of men, which is indirect and derived from study. Clara de Nobili highlights this dichotomy in a letter to Alessandra Nossona, a doctor's wife, regarding Alessandra's infertility. On the one hand, Clara hesitates to offer advice in an area that is surely the territory of learned men, not women. Out of friendship, however, she agrees to help, and launches into an extensive discussion of both causes and cures that, in fact, mirrors common medical opinion. When Clara suggests that Alessandra drink a potion derived from the dried uterus of a hare, she is echoing remedies found in the 'books of secrets.'[100] Her assurances that the problem may just as easily lay with the husband as with the wife are also found in these texts, although her sensititivy towards her friend is perhaps less common ('Non ve ne tribolate adunque poi che l'esser sterile, po' cosí accadere per mancamento degli uomini, come per mancamento delle donne' ['Do not worry, for infertility can stem from a problem with the man as well the woman']). This letter suggests that women are as capable as men of advising on matters of the female body; indeed, the advice they offer may be similar, but women have the added authority of direct experience.[101] Lando makes the point more directly in a letter by 'Madama la Grande' on the possible causes and cures for disorders of the uterus, considered a major element of female illness and therefore afforded much attention in the pages of medical texts for all audiences.[102] Hypothesizing that her friend's problem is linked to a dislocation of the 'matrix' due to an imbalance of bodily humours, Madama la Grande suggests a detailed remedy, some of which she gives in Latin.[103] If this doesn't work, she assures her friend, there is any number of learned women as knowledgable as Galen who can provide advice: 'contadinelle da star al paragone con i piú dotti phisici ch'oggidí sieno in Padova, o nella dotta Bologna ...' ('country girls who are as learned as any physician found today in Padua or in learned Bologna ...').[104]

This attitude is, once again, in keeping with Lando's overall position with regard to established culture (literary, cultural, medical): experience trumps study.[105]

Another category of letters pertaining to a specifically 'female' realm regards the running of the household. These are generally brief, although numerous, compositions concerning the hiring or treatment of servants. Giulia Gelminia, for example, sings the praises of a particularly good maid to Camilla P, while Caterina Visconte takes her unnamed correspondent to task for working her 'damigelle' too hard when, like plants, they will flourish if treated with care.[106] In some instances, letters are addressed directly to servants, perhaps with Aretino's example in mind.[107] Caterina Bonvisi, for example, writes to a servant she has placed with Lucrezia d'Este that she must be courteous and discreet, and that her duties will include making bread, washing clothes, and helping in the kitchen. Caterina gives the servant specific instructions on how to do the laundry – how much to wash at once, how to let it dry – and making bread.[108] Such letters, like those on childbirth, are filled with interesting details and advice – again, much of it common to the 'how-to' tradition – but raise the inevitable question of whether a servant could have read them.[109] As I am not arguing that the *Valorose donne* were ever part of any real epistolary exchange, the fact that these letters must be fictional is not a surprise. Lando wants to create an intimate portrait of 'real' women's lives, to penetrate the domestic sphere and expose its mysteries to the public eye within the framework and the fiction of the anthology's 'utility' as a domestic manual for women.

A final thematic grouping in the *Valorose donne* supports a reading of the anthology as a manual for women, but also raises the question of Lando's parodic intent. A series of letters concerning the production of various remedies and potions to cure illness, enhance beauty, or preserve youth is again clearly linked to the *libri di segreti* tradition. Although the *libri di segreti* offered advice in all seriousness, at least for the most part, Lando was making a comment on the extremes it went to. Rudolph Bell, who reads 'how-to' manuals as serious texts that were read seriously, singles out another work by Lando, the *Paradossi*, as a particular 'spoof' of such manuals.[110] The *Valorose donne* have a similar function, although the satire is not always overt. Take, for example, Isabella Sforza's description of a miraculous distilled potion that cures leprosy, removes spots from laundry, clears the vision, and keeps one eternally young:

Pigliate limatura d'argento, ferro, ramo, piombo, acciaio, oro, schiuma d'argento e schiuma d'oro ... Porrete dette cose per il primo giorno nell'urina di un fanciullo vergine, il secondo giorno in vino bianco caldo, il terzo nel succhio di fenocchio, il quarto giorno nel bianco dell'uova, il quinto giorno nel latte di femina che allatti un fanciullo ...[111]

Take filings of silver, iron, twigs, lead, steel, gold, (along with) foam of silver and gold ... on the first day soak these things in the urine of a virgin youth, on the second in warm white wine, on the third in fennel juice, on the fourth in egg white, and on the fifth in the milk of a woman who is nursing a son ...

Libri di segreti did offer similar remedies, often for potions that could do a host of things at once.[112] As William Eamon notes, 'changing medical fashions' had created a market for new kinds of drugs, and '"Paracelsian" remedies, distilled products, and various medical "secrets" became increasingly popular.'[113] The ingredients required for such remedies could run to several pages and lacked specific indications for proportions and measurements. As Eamon points out, it could not have been easy to procure all these materials.[114] So while Lando attributes to Isabella a recipe that could easily be found in the pages of any how-to manual, he highlights the elaborate nature of the ingredients and preparation it requires. That this is indeed a gentle parody at the expense of Isabella (the same woman who advises the Queen of Poland earlier in the anthology) is made clear by the scepticism of Isabella's correspondent, who chides her for spending all her time distilling such potions.[115] It is as if Lando undermines Isabella's intellectual authority by making her a mouthpiece for such practices. Maddalena Delli Alberti's letter to Cassandra Lanfreducci, mocking her for the excessive time she spends attending to her skin, supports this reading of Lando's parodic intent. So intent is Cassandra on keeping her face smooth (with mixtures of egg yolks, dried hare's blood, and horse's urine), that she completely neglects her household, leaving her husband and children to go about in rags.[116] Certainly, there is no doubt here regarding Lando's opinion of such remedies as a waste of time. Finally, mixed in with Lando's commentary is a satire of the alchemical vein that runs through many *libri di segreti*. Isabella Cortese's book, for example, bills itself as a book of alchemy (its subtitle claims it contains *cose minerali, medicinali, arteficiose, et alchimiche*).

Other *libri di segreti* like those of Alessio Piemontese and Timotheo Rossello also devoted sections to alchemy. Alchemy was embraced by learned figures such as Agrippa and Paracelsus, but many others reacted with scorn to what they considered mere quackery.[117] Erasmus' colloquy *Alcumistica,* for example, mocks alchemy as pure folly; Lando, a follower of Erasmus in many areas, would seem to follow him here, too.[118] Giulia Gonzaga's letter to Livia Negri lambastes alchemists as charlatans and derides the greed of those who suscribe to their theories, while part of the satirical subtext of Isabella Sforza's letter is its reliance on alchemical ingredients like the foam of silver and gold.[119] Gold foam, we learn in another letter, can be made through a complex operation wherein a distillation of wine, sulphur, salt, white tartar, and other ingredients over a series of days yields progressively more potent substances, each capable of curing various complaints.[120] A mere drop of the substance produced on the tenth day, when dropped into a gilded goblet, will create a *schiuma d'oro* that will turn anything it touches to gold.[121] When discussing remedies and potions, Lando's women frequently emphasize the extreme secrecy of the knowledge they are imparting. The writer who explains how to produce golden foam, for example, is at pains to reiterate the secret nature of the process, which she reveals only in recompense for a secret previously divulged to her by her correspondent. This, too, is a theme throughout the *libri di segreti* tradition, where it is often linked to the mysteries of alchemy. In Lando, this secrecy is almost competitive, the remedies a kind of currency among women, who race to outdo one another with potions that are ever more complex but ultimately ineffective.[122]

Letters such as these, which in many cases play on misogynist tropes such as female vanity, stand in opposition to the erudite demonstration of knowledge found in other letters that argue for women's literary skills and aptitude for study. As Novella Bellucci points out, Lando targets in these compositions 'le pratiche contemporanee, la degenerazione popolare ed il suo inquinamento con la magia, di cui dovevano apparirgli in gran parte responsabili gli stravolgimenti e la credulità femminili.'[123] In Lando's view, these practices exist alongside misguided religious ostentation as deviations from what should be the true focus of virtuous people, that is to say, scripture. These letters seem to cast doubt not only on the anthology's utility as a manual for women, but even on the vernacular letter's merit as a forum for intellectual discourse, an outlet in which *utilità* and *diletto* meet to the benefit of the reader. They suggest, rather, that the vernacular letter is an unserious medium, requiring neither *dottrina* nor *eloquenza*, suited not for intellectual exchange or literary models, but for the mundane, the trivial, and even the absurd.

Supporting a reading of the anthology as, ultimately, a satire of the letterbook genre itself, is a last grouping of letters which also works to negate the promotion of female dignity promised by the *dedicatoria*. These letters reinforce stereotypes of women as frivolous gossips who spread rumors about one another and cannot keep secrets – characterizations common in comportment literature and often used as justification for the limitations placed on the female voice. At the same time, they suggest that the letter itself is merely a new tool for the circulation of such gossip: a vehicle of misinformation rather than useful communication. In fact, close to half the letters in the anthology are introduced by a reference to what has been said about someone else or what the speakers have heard said about themselves. Letters open with reprimands: 'Mai mi ricordo d'aver sentito la maggior molestia di quella ch'io sentì l'altro giorno' ('I have never heard such an insult as I did the other day'); 'Mala fama si sparge di voi per bocca et de vicini e de servidori ...' ('Your neighbours and servants are spreading ugly rumours about you'); 'Brutta fama (se nol sapete) si sparge per ogni luogo de' vostri figliuoli' ('Your children [in case you don't know] are gaining a bad reputation all over').[124] In some cases the tone is quite hostile, as in Claudia Glizeria's opening lines to Tullia Castriccia: 'Io intendo, sfacciata meretrice, che tu hai ardimento di violar con la tua maledica e fracida lingua l'onore che m'ho aquistato ...' ('I hear, you shameless hussy, that you dare violate, with your malicious and rotten tongue, the honour I have earned').[125] If, as Goldsmith writes, women's virtue lies both in keeping silent and in not being talked about, here we have the reflection in print of this virtue's antithesis.[126] Not only do these women write about their private affairs, they publicize and make concrete a network of information in which all women are talked about and analysed, by one another.

In spite of occasional letters in which this network of rumour and hearsay is constructed more positively, as when it permits truly virtuous women to connect with one another, the characterization of women as frivolous gossips is extensive: in fact, among the letters on 'female' vices excessive loquaciousness is a prominent target.[127] The frequency with which Lando's epistolarians accuse one another of talking too much and too freely serves to reinforce stereotypes of woman as gossip (thus dismissing her words as mere *pettegolezze*) and echoes Albertian ideas about the danger of unregulated female speech. Lodovica Gavarda, for example, warns of the negative consequences of unrestrained speech, reproving her friend: 'La vostra importuna loquacità molti n'ha condotti a liti et a dure controversie, et ora più che mai perturba la vicinanza' ('Your importune loquaciousness has led many to arguments and bitter debates, and now it disturbs the neighbourhood more than ever').[128] One woman is looked upon with suspicion by her husband for having spoken with a relative in secret; another reprimands a friend who is deemed 'troppo loquace' and unable to keep secrets ('di non poter contenere alcun segreto che communicato vi sia'). Ippolita Sanseverina's criticism of Calandra Gariboldi's loquaciousness is a clearly gendered one. Calandra lacks the 'vergogna e la taciturnità che furono sempre virtú della donna' ('shame and reserve that have always been women's virtue').[129]

On the other hand, Lucrezia Masippa seems to mock the stereotypical criticism of women as talkative and unconstrained when she accuses Tadea Centana of taking silence to an extreme. Tadea is so quiet, writes Lucrezia, that a certain 'M. Ortensio' was quite taken aback upon meeting her: 'Io vi ricordo … ancora che il silenzio sia l'ornamento delle donne, disdirsi però l'esser totalmente mutola: si deve favellare alla presenza de valent'uomini con modestia e essaminando prima le parole' ('I remind you … that, while silence is the ornament of women, [a lady] should not be completely mute: she must speak up in the presence of worthy men, modestly and choosing her words with care').[130] A decorous silence is desirable, but not to the point of unnaturalness. Perhaps it is Livia Beltrama, in a letter reproving Adria della Rovere for her inability to keep quiet, who offers a key to reading these letters on speech, and indeed the anthology itself. Livia writes that speech, when kept private, has an essential integrity and unity. As soon as it is rendered public, however, it becomes not one, but many, no longer private, but public domain: 'l'è veramente la parola simile all'unità, la quale finché la non esce fuori de suoi confini, sempre rimane una, ma come l'esce e entra nella dualità, incontanente moltiplicasi in infinito' ('the word is truly similar to unity, which, as long as it does not escape its confines, remains intact, but once it escapes and enters into duality, it immediately multiplies itself infinitely').[131] Made public, words cannot be controlled, but rather are subject to an infinite number of interpretations by all who encounter them. In a sense, Livia's comment is a good metaphor for the anthology itself, which lends itself to so many readings.

Although the *Valorose donne* profess to defend women's literary merits and moral dignity, the best explanation for this unusual text lies in the arena of literary experimentation. Lando, a writer who explores virtually all literary genres, with the exception of poetry, and excels at the art of paradox, here tries his hand at a new genre – the vernacular letter – while constructing a complex and often contradictory approach to a current topic of debate: women. The project has a touch of literary exhibitionism: the author proves his skill by passing as not one, but 181 women letter writers, and in doing so tackles the notion that women are more naturally gifted at epistolary practice than men. Through his art, Lando demonstrates that he can 'learn' to write like a woman, appropriating not only a feminine genre, but also – among other things – the subjects he perceives to be the very foundation of female discourse: home and family, the private and the domestic. By staking a claim to this feminine genre, Lando attempts to demonstrate his literary authority, showing that he can improve upon women's own self-representations.

At a deeper level, however, the *Valorose donne* gain complexity from the persistent subtext of Textor's *Officina*, which serves as a barely disguised commentary on that humanist learning that Lando finds hollow and irrelevant.[132] Grendler notes the 'general mockery of learning' that occurs in all of Lando's texts, which, while 'neither analytical nor profound ... was extensive.'[133] The classical citations reeled off in the *Valorose donne* – pages and pages of names and references devoid of explication – reflect this contempt for sixteenth-century humanist ideals and the belief that humanist learning had become an empty art, divorced from reality. It had taken on the function of a social attribute, and become part of the art of conversation elaborated so vividly by Castiglione. The examples dropped so freely in the *Valorose donne* constitute a facile erudition which provides no real possibility for communication, renewal, or change. Lando's parody of humanism through the use of the *Officina* also works as part of the religious message concealed in the anthology. Lando was convinced that the Christian need not be erudite, but rather rely on the simple reading of scripture.[134] His parody thus functions to emphasize his religious convictions as well as advance a social criticism.

If Lando's main project was literary exhibitionism and his main target humanism, this does not mean we can discount his choice of women protagonists and women's issues as the vehicle for his project. Lando, like Ovid in the *Heroides*, assumes multiple female identities. What did he hope to gain by his multiform epistolary *travestimento*? Kauffman's analysis of the *Heroides* suggests that Ovid delighted in the artificial, yet powerful illusion he created and argues that the 'Ovidian rhetorical ideal challenges the concepts of unity, fixity, and consistency: instead, it celebrates the fluid, the multiple, the capricious.'[135] In some senses, this observation can be applied to the *Valorose donne*. Certainly, these are adjectives easily applied to Lando, a writer ready to challenge official notions of culture and literature, and one who often hid behind textual tricks of pseudonymity and anonymity. They are also applicable to the text itself, with its many voices and quickly shifting point of view. The use of multiple female identities, which functions at certain points as a mask for religious dissent, also serves to call up and address a myriad of arguments about women's intellect, role, and moral character.

It is also likely that Lando saw in the *Valorose donne* not only the chance to repay the generosity of some of his female patrons by memorializing them in his work but also to perpetuate a cycle of mutual obligation. This hypothesis is supported by his comment in the *Sferza de scrittori* that he was one of the first in Italy to praise women in print, a passage that makes it clear that he expected gratitude for his mention of particular women, and that he was disappointed by the reception with which his gesture was met.[136] If, in fact, Lando's decision to use women protagonists stemmed in part from the desire to repay his female patrons, as well as to ensure their continued support, this could help explain the vast discrepancies between the viewpoints portrayed in the book. By attributing great erudition and moral or religious authority to certain women, Lando makes them stand out next to those who gossip idly or reprimand one another for their faults. Thus, the inconsistent approach to women's learning could have a primarily strategic purpose: by highlighting the shortcomings of most women and depicting a brave few as unusually erudite, serious, and moral, Lando pays a compliment to his patrons or to women he admires. Of course, by painting 'most' women as gossips or other stereotypes, Lando reinforces misogynist tropes. Moreover, writing at a time when the new vernacular genre of letter-writing was just taking off (Manuzio's defence of it, the *Lettere volgari*, had been published only six years before), Lando's attention to such trivialities seem to satirize the genre itself. In spite of an outward appearance of erudition fostered by the heavy reliance on the *Officina*, women are the unfortunate vehicle of Lando's satirization, resulting in an inevitable association of the lack of seriousness of the genre with the lack of seriousness of women.

While the *Valorose donne* may constitute a literary/rhetorical experiment and a commercial/strategic project, its intense concern with the details of women's lives reflects a deep curiosity about them. The *Valorose donne* is extremely concerned with what it perceives as 'women's' issues and what it imagines women talk about: marriage, children, running a household, the proper female role. What constituted the 'real' female experience? Could it be found in the epistolary exchanges of women? By focusing on themes such as family and household, in addition to broader problems like learning and religion, the *Valorose donne* allowed specifically feminine aspects of women's experience to become part of the public literary realm.

On one level, this publicization of women's private experience expanded the parameters of epistolary discourse for women. The protagonists of the *Valorose donne* are women, not men, and the anthology's content is specific to women and the domestic realm. Whether we read them as serious compositions or not, the *Valorose donne* bring these issues to the forefront in a literary forum. In spite of the frequent element of satire, this focus on the private sphere does lend, at times, a certain dignity to a wholly female culture.[137] For all its contradictions, impersonations, and idiosyncrasies, the *Valorose donne* are a valuable example of a male author's representation of the female epistolary realm.

On the other hand, as will become clear in the following chapters, it is significant that no other collection approaches the *Valorose donne* in terms of this detailed, intimate attention to so-called 'women's issues.' The *epistolari* of Lucrezia Gonzaga, Veronica Franco, Isabella Andreini, and Arcangela Tarabotti, while differing from one another in many aspects, uniformly avoid such detailed considerations on childbirth, laundry, cosmetics, and home remedies, concentrating rather on careful literary self-presentation. Female experience is always at the forefront of these epistolary self-representations, but they avoid the kind of voyeuristic glimpse into the intimate details of women's lives so eagerly supplied in the *Valorose donne*. Yet Lando's experiment with the female epistolary voice may not have ended with *Valorose donne*. In the next chapter, we will look at the letters of Lucrezia Gonzaga da Gazzuolo, the Mantuan noblewoman whose friendship with Lando has led some literary critics to suggest his intervention in her *epistolario*. Gonzaga's letterbook, which focuses on the image of one particular woman, rather than attempt to address the range of female experience, provides a telling contrast to the *Valorose donne* while raising many of the same questions regarding the epistolary construction of gender.

3 'A gloria del sesso feminile': The *Lettere* of Lucrezia Gonzaga as Exemplary Narrative

I. The *Lettere* in Literary and Historical Context

Like Ortensio Lando's *Lettere di molte valorose donne*, the *Lettere della ... donna Lucrezia Gonzaga* seem initially to locate themselves within the defence of women genre. As in the *Valorose donne*, this laudatory intent is made evident on the frontispiece, which declares that the letters have been published for the glory of all women: '*a gloria del sesso feminile ... in luce poste.*'[1] In this case, however, it is the collected letters of a single, celebrated woman that are to reflect and promote women's literary skills. The unsigned dedicatory letter to Pietro Paulo Manfrone, the governor of Verona and Gonzaga's relative by marriage, specifically highlights the 'prontezza dell'ingegno' and 'tenace memoria' ('quick mind' and 'formidable memory') of the writer and compares her letters favourably to other contemporary examples, urging that they be read 'con quella istessa attenzione che solete leggere le cose di importanze ... chiaramente vedrete che elle meritano di essere anteposte a molte scritte a' nostri tempi da letterati e accorti ingegni' ('with the same attention you give to important things ... you will clearly see that they outshine many works produced today by learned and clever minds').[2] If publishing personal correspondence implied a faith in one's own prestige and a confidence that one's letters had exemplary value for readers, the audacity of epistolary publication was intensified when undertaken by a woman, as I have discussed in the preceding chapters. Accordingly, the *dedicatoria* is quick to underscore the seriousness of Gonzaga's *Lettere* as 'cose d'importanza,' a contribution to the new vernacular letter genre as worthy of attention as that of any male writer.

Yet, like the *Valorose donne*, Gonzaga's collection raises complex issues regarding the epistolary construction of gender and notions of the woman letter writer. If the *Valorose donne* provide an often paradoxical epistolary portrait of women that borders at points on parody, Gonzaga's *Lettere* function as a serious response to that ambiguous portrait of women's epistolary discourse. Although some of Lando's epistolarians, as we saw in chapter 2, are depicted as dignified and learned, their erudition is called into question by the silent presence of the *Officina* and the burlesque conjunction of 'high' learning and 'low' content throughout the anthology. Gonzaga's letters, by contrast, are devoid of parody (although not of humour), and showcase her reflections on literary, moral, and spiritual matters. While the letters are expected to redound to the 'glory of the female sex,' it is Gonzaga herself who takes centre stage as a model of exemplary womanhood. Drawing on the sensational circumstances of her life, particularly her marriage to the notorious *condottiere* Giampaolo Manfrone, the letters sketch a detailed epistolary portrait not of the many facets of women's experience, as in the *Valorose donne*, but of the complexities of one woman's life. The principal elements of this portrait are drawn from the dramatic narrative of the arrest and imprisonment of Manfrone for attempting to murder Duke Ercole II D'Este of Ferrara, and the effect of these events on Gonzaga herself. The story was well known in northern Italy. Chronicles like Filippo Rodi's *Annuali di Ferrara* recounted how, enraged over the duke's designs on his married sister, Manfrone attempted first to poison and later to ambush Ercole II.[3] Compositions like Bartolommeo Ricci's *Deprecatio*, in turn, described Lucrezia's tearful intervention on behalf of her husband, and suggested that it was she who persuaded the duke to commute Manfrone's sentence from death to life in prison.[4] The *Lettere* themselves, which petition everyone from minor officials to the king of France and the duke himself on Manfrone's behalf, reinforce the characterization of Gonzaga as a tireless advocate for her unworthy husband, an image that has endured through the centuries, threatening to eclipse her significance as a literary figure.[5] If Gonzaga's loyalty to her husband constituted an admirable model of female virtue, the scandal also had currency in terms of the literary market. That there was an audience for Manfrone's story is evident from the various prose and poetry accounts devoted to it, including a 'Petrarchan' *canzoniere*.[6] What was missing was the other side of the story. Gonzaga's letters provided this alternate perspective, capitalizing on public fascination with this 'true-crime' drama in the immediate aftermath of

Manfrone's death in 1552, while also playing to a broader cultural interest in women's writing and female epistolarity.

In addition to her fame as Manfrone's wife, Gonzaga was widely admired for her erudition. As a girl, she had studied the classics with Matteo Bandello; as a young woman she participated in the *ridotto*, or salon, culture that flourished in the cities of Renaissance Italy. Gonzaga's admirers repeatedly remarked on her eloquence and learning, composing verse in her honour and urging her to publish her own works. When Gonzaga's letter collection was printed in 1552, her contemporaries naturally accepted it as authentic, that is, written by Gonzaga herself. In Anton Francesco Doni's *Libraria*, for example, the *epistolario* is catalogued under her name.[7] Some modern critics, however, pointing to textual similarities between Gonzaga's *Lettere* and the *Valorose donne* anthology of 1548, have argued that Ortensio Lando, with whom Gonzaga had a close association, was in fact the author of both texts. The suggestion raises the intriguing but also problematic possibility of an even more extensive project of ventriloquism on Lando's part than that undertaken in the *Valorose donne*. Could he have been behind Gonzaga's letters as well? The two were well acquainted. Lando frequented the informal *cenacolo* that arose at Gonzaga's Fratta palace, while she, for her part, makes frequent cameos in Lando's texts between 1548 and 1552.[8] Indeed, Lando devoted an entire *Panegirico* to Gonzaga, in which, significantly, he claims she was born to be 'la gloria del sesso feminile, e insegnare all'altre donne ...' ('the glory of the female sex, and to teach other women ...') – echoing, of course, the frontispiece of Gonzaga's *epistolario*, although the expression is not uncommon.[9]

As this chapter shows, it is plausible that Lando, a friend and an experienced author and editor with a demonstrated interest in women's letters, assisted the novice writer with the publication and perhaps even the composition of the *Lettere*. At the very least, he played the role alluded to in the unsigned *dedicatoria* of having gathered and edited the letters for publication.[10] However, a wholesale attribution of Gonzaga's letters to Lando overreaches, for several reasons. First, the *Lettere* correspond closely to the historical events of Gonzaga's life, particularly with regard to her husband's imprisonment, and surviving autograph letters by Gonzaga demonstrate that she actively composed and exchanged letters on this subject as well as others treated in the collection.[11] Second, as we will see, the testimony of her contemporaries shows that she was recognized to be a learned woman and writer in her own right. Finally, it is unlikely that Lando could have made such flagrant use of Gonzaga's name and persona without her collaboration and cooperation. It is therefore inaccurate to discount Gonzaga as the author of her own letters. We might better characterize this work as the product of a kind of literary partnership, one that meshed Lando's editorial expertise and knowledge of the literary market with the literary talent, reputation, and gripping story of Gonzaga. She generated the core material; he helped shape it into a form that capitalized on current literary tastes, addressing readers' interest in female epistolarity, the *questione della donna*, and current events all at once. The resulting epistolary portrait demonstrates how gender could be constructed and manipulated in the epistolary forum. The question of authorship takes a secondary position to the work's primary goal of promoting Lucrezia Gonzaga's public persona and cementing her celebrity.

Biographical Sketch

Before delving into the critical debate over the *Lettere* or indeed the dynamics of Gonzaga's epistolario itself, it may be useful to briefly review what we know about Gonzaga. Although she has been largely ignored by literary historians, she was celebrated in her own day. Matteo Bandello, Girolamo Ruscelli, Giulio Cesare Scaligero, and, of course, Lando, all praised her eloquence, erudition, and virtue. A volume of poems in her honour was published in 1565.[12] She even appears in a catalogue of virtuous women in a 1553 chivalric romance by Vincenzo Brusantino.[13] Born in Gazzuolo (near Mantua) circa 1521 to Pirro Gonzaga and Camilla Bentivoglio, Gonzaga was taken in by Luigi Gonzaga of Castelgoffredo (or Castel Giuffrè) after the deaths of both parents in 1529.[14] Her letters tell us that Gonzaga was educated by Bandello himself, who taught her Latin and Greek during his sojourn at the court of Castelgoffredo as secretary to Cesare Fregoso, Luigi's brother-in-law.[15] At a young age, arrangements were made for Gonzaga to marry Giampaolo 'Fortebraccio' Manfrone, a *condottiere* for the Venetian Republic known for his volatile temper.[16] Gonzaga followed her new husband first to Verona and then to Fratta, enduring, by all accounts, much humiliation as the object of his violent outbursts, but dutifully attempting to secure his release following his arrest in 1546.[17]

Less is known of Gonzaga's life following her husband's death in 1552. We know from Manfrone's will that her dowry was returned to her, although her husband left her nothing else.[18] Not long after Manfrone's death, Gonzaga was sent, probably under the authority of her cousin Vespasiano Gonzaga, to a convent in Bozzolo where she remained for at least three years. Five letters written by Gonzaga from the convent and conserved today in the Biblioteca Estense in Modena attest to her evidently unwilling and uncomfortable stay among the sisters. In all of them, Gonzaga implores that she be sent money for food and clothes.[19] In a letter to her cousin dated 9 October 1555, Gonzaga reminds him that three years have passed since she entered the convent and begs him to free her from its confines: 'già sonno tre anni che io son confinata in questo loco, et ormai saria tempo che Vostra Eccellenza me ne liberasse' ('I have already been confined here for three years, and it is time that you released me').[20]

Eventually, Gonzaga's pleas must have been heard. By the mid-1560s she was back in Mantua, having seen at least one of her two daughters, Isabella, married (to Fabio Pepoli of Bologna, in 1561). Caught up in the undercurrents of religious dissent that swept through Mantua in the late sixteenth century, Gonzaga appeared at the periphery of several Inquisition trials, and in June 1567 was herself tried on suspicion of heresy. Because of her social status and family connections, however, arrangements were made for the trial and her subsequent abjuration to be conducted quickly and in secrecy.[21] Two months later, in a letter to her sister Isabella, Gonzaga expressed amazement and dismay that she could have come under suspicion: '... io restavo meraviliata et stupefata ch'io fosse stata nominata in cosa talle essendo come in fatti sono tanto lontana da questi pensieri e da queste pratiche' ('... I was amazed and astounded to be named in such a matter, since I am in fact quite far from such thoughts and practices'); she insisted that any doctrinal irregularities attributed to her were due solely to a natural 'abondanza di parole' ('verbosity') that may have led her inadvertently to say something that was later misconstrued.[22] Yet, as we will see further on, Gonzaga did touch upon sensitive religious themes in her *Lettere* of 1552, particularly with regard to scripture and in her veiled references to the Lutheran tenet of justification by faith alone. Gonzaga died in Mantua in 1576, twenty-four years after the publication of her only book and nine years after her Inquisition trial.[23]

In spite of her difficult marriage, Gonzaga knew long periods of autonomy, spending much of her married life alone with her children and servants in her husband's formidable *palazzo* in the small village of Fratta. According to Lando's account of these years in the *Panegirico*, the young wife lived in a state of isolation, '... in somma solitudine, chiusa quasi che del continuo in una squalida torre' ('... in the greatest solitude, almost constantly confined to a squalid tower').[24] While Fratta may have been geographically isolated, however, it lay on the route from Mantua to Venice, and in reality Gonzaga often had visitors on their way from one city to the next.[25] Through the constant flow of friends and visitors to Fratta, Gonzaga established contacts with figures from the Venetian literary world, including the editors Dolce and Domenichi, the writer Luigi Groto (the 'Cieco dell'Adria'), and, of course, Lando. By the early 1550s, a *cenacolo* had sprung up around Gonzaga's palazzo in Fratta, organized by Giovan Maria Bonardo and by Gonzaga herself.[26] Although Gonzaga was not an official member of the *Accademia dei pastori frattegiani*, she was an integral part of this loosely knit literary society that, in addition to Dolce, Domenichi, and Groto, included such figures as Ruscelli, Parabosco, and Orazio Toscanella.[27] Even Lando, although not a member of the *Pastori*, participated in the group's meetings.[28] These contacts were important for Gonzaga's literary formation: according to her *Lettere*, she read their works avidly and often requested their latest publications. Her relationship with these literary figures was central to her own positioning as a literary and cultural figure as well, for just as she singled out and praised the *Pastori* in her *Lettere*, so they applauded her by dedicating many of their works to her. It is probable, moreover, that the *Pastori* – wishing, perhaps, to lend support to the participation of women in culture or to weigh in on the *questione della donna* – played a role in encouraging the publication of Gonzaga's *Lettere*.

It was likely that during this same period, in which Gonzaga's contact with writers from all over northern Italy was at its most intense, she was introduced to the religious debates and discussions that flourished in Italy in the years before the Counter-Reformation reached the peak of its repressive influence. As her letters – not to mention her later Inquisition trial – reflect, Gonzaga was influenced by many aspects of evangelist and reform thought, and may have been introduced to some of the views she espouses in the *Lettere* by members of the *Pastori frattegiani*. Groto, for example, had previously been involved with the *Accademia degli Addormentati* in Rovigo, which was forced to disband under suspicion of heresy.[29] Dolce and Domenichi both had heterodox sympathies and were associated with Andrea Arrivabene, a printer warned in 1549 by the Holy Office against selling heretical books.[30] Lando, as noted in chapter 2, expressed heterodox views in the *Valorose donne* and other works. The print diffusion of heterodox ideas in the mid-sixteenth century (from justification by faith alone to intense emphasis on scripture) was vast and affected the entire peninsula.[31] Not surprisingly, Gonzaga, like many other men and women, was exposed to these ideas and incorporated some of them into her own religious beliefs and her writing.

The relative autonomy experienced by Gonzaga during Manfrone's imprisonment seems to have diminished upon his death, when Gonzaga, much reduced in means, entered the convent in Bozzolo. Nevertheless, as the publication of Bonardo's *Rime* in 1565 and his *Madrigali* (which contain a dedication by Toscanella to Gonzaga) in 1571 would seem to indicate, Gonzaga retained links to the old literary circle long after the *Pastori frattegiani* had ceased to gather at her Fratta residence.

Agency and Authorship: The Debate over Lucrezia Gonzaga's Lettere

As in the case of Lando's *Valorose donne*, the questions raised by critics regarding the authorship of Gonzaga's *Lettere* must be addressed in order to talk about the process of epistolary self-construction undertaken within them.[32] The attribution to Lando stems, certainly, from the close relationship between the two – documented by Gonzaga's frequent presence in Lando's works, particularly in his *Dialogo* on scripture (1552) in which she appears as a principal interlocutor, and in the *Panegirico* (1552) of which she is the protagonist, and by his appearance in her *Lettere*, thirty-one of which are addressed to Lando.[33] Together with Lando's prior appropriation of women's epistolary voices in the *Valorose donne*, the literary association of Lando and Gonzaga has caused critics to turn to him instinctively as Gonzaga's 'ghostwriter,' her letters thereby constituting the culmination of a long process of appropriation on Lando's part. Some assertions of Lando's authorship have been fuelled by critical bias. Ireneo Sanesi, for example, argued that certain, unspecified, stylistic similarities between the *Valorose donne* and the *Lettere* constituted proof of their common authorship (seemingly ignoring that Gonzaga's letters are almost entirely lacking in the exempla and detti that characterize many of Lando's works and the *Valorose donne* in particular). At the same time, however, Sanesi accepted similar correspondences between the *Valorose donne* and a male-authored text, Pietro Lauro's *Lettere*, as a valid example of direct literary imitation.[34] Sanesi further claimed the 'contradictory' nature of Gonzaga's *Lettere* as proof of their inauthenticity, citing Gonzaga's characterizations of her husband (which indeed vary dramatically depending on her audience), and a pair of letters concerning Lando's *Panegirico*. In one of these, Gonzaga thanks Lando, while in the second she professes ignorance of the book's author.[35] According to Sanesi, these 'numerose contradizioni' were 'inesplicabili quando vogliansi ritenere scritte da Gonzaga, spiegabilissime invece ove se ne ammetta autore il Lando.'[36] This explanation ignores the dynamic and evolving nature of epistolary exchange, which when captured in a printed *epistolario* can and usually does reflect changes in knowledge or point of view over time, not to mention the varying demands raised by the expectations of the internal reader to whom a letter is directed. By describing Manfrone differently to different readers, Gonzaga could expect to elicit various reactions. Her letters regarding the *Panegirico* show a natural progression from an earlier state of ignorance to a later one of knowledge, suggesting that the letters were written at different times.[37] Rather than indicate a 'Landian' element of epistolary paradox, the contradictions noted by Sanesi are in fact integral to real, or realistic, epistolary exchange.

Finally, although many of Gonzaga's letters are prompted by historical events, such as the arrest and imprisonment of Manfrone – events which she, as a literate woman, might reasonably have been moved to describe in letters – Sanesi was unwilling to accept that Gonzaga might have written about her own life. He argued, rather, that Lando, as Gonzaga's contemporary and friend, was equally up to date with general current events and with Gonzaga's own familial drama, and therefore similarly qualified to compose fictional letters about those subjects.[38] Yet there is no reason to suspect that Lando would be more likely to write about these events than the woman to whom they had actually happened – particularly when archival evidence shows that Gonzaga was indeed a writer of letters, did write letters to some of the people she addresses in her *epistolario*, and did, in fact, lobby for Manfrone's release from prison.[39] The letters exchanged between Gonzaga and her husband conserved in the Archivio di Stato di Modena, for example, are proof that the epistolary relationship so central to the structure of Gonzaga's *epistolario* did, in fact, exist. The surviving letters from Gonzaga to Manfrone are dated 1546 and 1548, while his to her cover the entire period of his incarceration, from his arrest in 1546 to his death in 1552. Much like her published letters to Manfrone, Gonzaga's brief, to-the-point manuscript missives briskly urge the prisoner to put his faith in God and bear his lot patiently.[40] Suggesting that Gonzaga did attempt to garner support for Manfrone's case as indicated in the *Lettere*, both these letters refer to journeys undertaken by Gonzaga on his behalf.[41] Moreover, Manfrone's own manuscript letters contain pleas for just the sort of help his wife purports to offer in the *Lettere*. In one case, for example, he begs her to 'placate' the Duke of Ferrara.[42] The published *epistolario* contains a number of letters seeking Manfrone's release, including two letters to Ercole II D'Este, just as Manfrone asks in his missive from prison. Moreover, the one manuscript letter we possess from Gonzaga to Ercole II D'Este, although it is a request for the duke's intervention in a land dispute arisen as a result of Manfrone's absence rather than a direct request for Manfrone's release, demonstrates that she was prepared to approach the duke for help.[43] Finally, Manfrone's repeated requests that his wife write to him in prison (in one letter he pleads: 'mi avisi due rige almeno et spesso del ben star suo, per l'amor di Dio' ['write me a few lines – often – telling me how you are doing, for the love of God'])[44] suggest that it would have been likely, even necessary, that Gonzaga correspond regularly with her imprisoned spouse, just as she appears to do in the *Lettere*. Not all of Gonzaga's published letters were pieces of genuine correspondence reproduced for publication, of course. On the contrary, many were certainly composed expressly for publication or at least revised before going to print. But many of the published letters are based on epistolary exchanges Gonzaga had, could have had, or wished to have. Regardless of whether her published letters to Ercole II D'Este were actually sent, for example, it is entirely plausible that Gonzaga might have composed such letters, especially when expressly asked by her husband to do so.

The only valid argument for Lando's intervention in Gonzaga's text must be a textual one, and there are, in fact, some suggestive correspondences between Lando's works and Gonzaga's text that are worth examining. In each case, however, the evidence is ambiguous, calling into question issues of textual practice and literary imitation that were widespread in sixteenth-century culture. Various forms of literary collaboration were common in Gonzaga's time: writers enlisted one another to edit or revise their work before publication, and the widespread practice of *riscrittura*, a form of literary 'plagiarism,' created complex intertextual links between writers.[45] Such practices tend to conflict with modern ideas about individual authorship. Yet a scenario of collaboration and intertextuality could account for certain overlaps between the *Lettere* and Lando's works. Salvatore Bongi, for example, cites a pair of similar passages from Lando's *Vari Componimenti* (1552) and Gonzaga's *Lettere*:[46]

Lando, *Vari componimenti*
Venne già gran desiderio all'oricalco di voler doventare oro, et mosso da questa voglia andossenne ad un orafo il più eccellente che ritrovar si potesse, e si gli disse: Maestro fammi (ti prego) per lo tuo Dio doventare oro, a te sia cosa molto agevole, poiché tanto me gli rassimiglio, e a me sara d'un estremo piacere. Sorrise l'orafo a sí pazza richiesta e a lui rivolto, con severo viso disse: Potrai tu sofferire que' duri colpi di fuoco che dar si sogliono all'oro per affinarlo? Strinsesi nelle rimase, e allor s'apprese che a grandezza pervenir non si può senza sostener travaglio.

A great desire came over orichalc to turn himself into gold, and spurred by this wish he went to the best goldsmith he could find, and he said to him: Master, ask your god (I beg you) to make me into gold; it is easy to do since I so closely resemble it already, and it will make me very happy. The goldsmith smiled at so mad a request, and turning a stern face to him said: Will you be able to withstand the hard blows of fire that we use to refine gold? Orichalc shrugged, and resigned himself to his state, and understood that greatness cannot be achieved without toil.

Gonzaga, *Lettere*
... venne (dico) desiderio all'ottone di voler doventare oro, et andossene ad un orafo, e si gli disse: Vedi Maestro, dall'oro a me vi è poca differenza, sí che agevolmente mi potreste far doventar oro se tu volessi; guardollo l'orafo pieno di ira et di giusto sdegno, e finalmente gli disse: potrai tu sofferire que' duri colpi di fuoco che si danno all'oro per raffinarlo? Strinsesi l'ottone nelle spalle, e isbigotito dal travaglio che l'orafo gli ricordò, andossene contento di rimanersi ottone, e non piú cercando di divenir oro ...

... a desire (I say) came over brass to become gold, and he went to the goldsmith and said to him: Look, Master, there is not much difference between me and gold, and you could easily turn me into gold if you wished; the goldsmith looked at him with anger and righteous scorn, and finally he said: will you be able to withstand those hard blows of fire we use to refine gold? Brass shrugged and, speechless upon hearing of the toil of which the goldsmith spoke, went away resigned to remaining brass, and never again sought to become gold ...

No one could dispute the similarity between the two renderings of the fable. Naturally, it is possible that Lando inserted the passage himself. Yet Gonzaga makes it clear that she is repeating a story she has heard and applying it to the discussion at hand.⁴⁷ We know that Lando himself borrowed liberally, and often literally, from Textor's *Officina* and other texts to compose the *Valorose donne*; Sanesi notes with approval Pietro Lauro's borrowing from Lando in his *Lettere*. Gonzaga, like Lauro, would have been familiar with Lando's work. Perhaps, in analogous fashion, she too borrowed from it.

A similar question arises with respect to Dieter Steland's recent discovery that the content of some of Gonzaga's letters can be traced to a repertory collection called the *Concetti di Ieronimo Garimberto*, published in 1551.⁴⁸ Steland's description of the corresponding passages is clearly important for the light it sheds on the way Gonzaga's text was constructed with material from a repertory. Yet an attribution of the collection as a whole to Lando based solely on similar textual strategy is not convincing. As shown throughout this study, letter writers often turned to repertories and manuals for guidance. More indicative of a Landian hand in Gonzaga's *Lettere* is less the use of the *Concetti* in and of itself, but rather the appearance of the same lines from Garimberto in Lando's own works as well as in Gonzaga's letters. A letter from Gonzaga to Pietro Paolo Manfrone asserting that unjust imprisonment is preferable to undeserved liberty, for example, can be traced to the *Concetti*, but could also have reached Gonzaga via Lando's *Oracoli de moderni ingegni* (1550).⁴⁹ Lando could have added this internal reference himself; on the other hand, Gonzaga may have simply borrowed the phrase from either Lando or Garimberto. Similarly, a consolatory letter from Gonzaga to a grieving mother, warning her not to mourn excessively nor doubt in the resurrection of the body, closely echoes a sentiment expressed in Lando's *Consolatorie*.⁵⁰ Does the thematic and even linguistic link between the two texts negate literary agency? Or does it merely demonstrate that Gonzaga and Lando shared similar views? The idea that we ought to rejoice in, rather than lament, the death of a loved one is unremarkable in consolatory letters of this period. Pietro Lauro, for example, uses similar reasoning in his *Lettere* in a consolatory letter addressed to Gonzaga herself, while a manuscript letter of consolation written by Gonzaga echoes the same sentiment.⁵¹ Framing death as a welcome return to the Creator is a concept particular neither to Lando nor Gonzaga. The brief (and similarly phrased) flirtation with a heretical view, on the other hand – the denial of the resurrection of the body – would seem to denote a more specific point of contact. Again, this textual overlap might indicate Lando's influence on the passage. Alternatively, Gonzaga may have borrowed some of the elegant wording of Lando's *Consolatorie* for her own discussion of the concepts of death and resurrection.

A final area of textual intersection is pointed out by historian Silvana Seidel Menchi, whose attribution of Gonzaga's *Lettere* to Lando is based on several letters that espouse Erasmian (and, by 1552, suspect) themes taken up by Lando in his own work. Seidel Menchi notes, for example, that a letter from Gonzaga to Elena Vigonza urging her to make Christ's teachings of simplicity, charity, and patience her life's principal aspiration closely echoes an Italian translation of Erasmus' *Enchiridion*, a text used by Lando on other occasions.[52] On the other hand, Lando was not the only writer to make use of Erasmus in his works, as Seidel Menchi herself points out.[53] Furthermore, Seidel Menchi notes that the insertion of passages from Erasmus, Luther, and other philo-protestant thinkers into otherwise 'orthodox' texts was a common method for attempting to elicit thought or doubt about traditional theology and teachings on the reader's part.[54] While it is possible that Lando was responsible for the insertion of these particular passages as he edited Gonzaga's letters, it is also possible that Gonzaga shared the religious views of Lando and others in the heterodox circles of which she was a part, and was familiar with the practice of inserting heterodox passages into new texts.[55]

Finally, Lando is more present than any other *destinatario* in Gonzaga's collection. Many letters chronicle the gossip and 'mal dire' that periodically endanger Gonzaga's relationship with Lando, calling to mind Lando's own *Valorose donne*, in which his female epistolarians constantly accuse one another of similar offenses.[56] Gonzaga, however, attempts to distance herself from the mechanisms of gossip, rarely repeating the rumours in any detail and pointing out that such superficial discourse is beneath her.[57] Perhaps more significant are those letters to Lando that touch on literary matters. Rather than necessarily suggest an attempt by Lando to insert himself into the book, however, these missives might be interpreted as a repayment for Lando's lavish praise of Gonzaga in his works, coupled with an effort by Gonzaga to solidify her own standing in the literary realm. In one instance, for example, Gonzaga thanks Lando for immortalizing her in 'libretti dove si chiudono le mie poche meritate lodi' ('little books which contain my ill-deserved praise') and expresses regret that she is unable to do the same for him: 'ma io misera ... che farò per voi?' ('but, poor me ... what shall I do for you?').[58] Elsewhere, Gonzaga tells Lando that she loves him not only for his virtue, but for his support of her ('per le vostre virtú, e per i molti uffici fatti in onor mio …' ['for your virtue, and the many things you do in my honour …']).⁵⁹ These 'uffici' might well refer to Lando's public praise of Gonzaga in such texts as the *Panegirico* or the *Cataloghi*. Through warm references to Lando and his works, Gonzaga manages simultaneously to praise and thank him while also reminding readers of her own stature as a literary figure honoured by others in print. Similarly, another letter that refers to Gonzaga's indebtedness towards Lando also draws attention to her own generosity as a literary patron. Gonzaga declares her willingness to materially support Lando, asking in return only that he share his work with her:

> … chiedete pur liberamente quanto vi va per la fantasia … se vi pare che io abbia cosa alcuna che sia per risultare in onore e commodo vostro, come sono danari o qualche altra cosa che io possa, che vi prometto che tanto mi sarà caro che ve ne vagliate, quanto si ricerca agli obblighi che io ho che ve ne debbiate valere … state sano e lieto, parte facendomi dei vostri dolcissimi componimenti quando avviene che il vostro divino e fecondo ingegno alcuno ne partorisca.⁶⁰

> … ask freely for anything that strikes your fancy … if you think I might have anything at all that could result in your honour or comfort, such as money or anything else I can provide, I promise you that my sincere wish that you will avail yourself of it corresponds to the obligation I have that you should avail yourself of it … be healthy and well, and share with me any works that your divine and fertile mind might produce.

In the *Cataloghi* Lando praises Gonzaga's generosity; here she returns the favour not only by behaving generously but also by praising Lando's literary gifts and 'divine' mind (if the sentiment appears spontaneous, it is worth noting that this passage derives directly from the *Concetti*).⁶¹ By asking to read his works, moreover, Gonzaga appears learned as well as generous.

This constant invocation is certainly not coincidental. These letters have a dual function. They promote Lando and call attention to his relationship with Gonzaga, while simultaneously presenting Gonzaga as an admired member of literary society, capable of reading and appreciating the works of her contemporaries. The publicity benefits both Lando and Gonzaga, and the elaborate intertwining of their personae here and in Lando's other works, along with their similar intertextual practice, does suggest that Gonzaga's *Lettere* were the product of some degree of literary collaboration.⁶² Rather than diminish Gonzaga's literary agency, such a collaboration can help us to refine our ideas about authorship and book production in the sixteenth century. Literary collaboration, imitation, and *riscrittura* were common elements of early modern literary practice, and did not detract from the works in which they were employed. As the nineteenth-century critic Pietro Ferri judiciously pointed out, it is unlikely that the precise degree of Lando's intervention – or lack thereof – can ever be definitively divined.⁶³ There is little reason to doubt, however, Gonzaga's own contribution to a book constructed around events in her own life and upon themes of wide interest to both writers and readers in this period, such as virtue, vice, and religion. Given her educated background and her participation in literary culture, it is quite conceivable that she should have undertaken to publish her letters, especially as the market for epistolary texts continued to grow. As Dionisotti noted, the period from 1545 to 1563 was one of linguistic and cultural openness, and one in which women participated in greater numbers than they did in the years preceding or following the Council of Trent.⁶⁴ Moreover, the thirteen surviving manuscript letters by Gonzaga further demonstrate that she was a writer of letters and support her authorship of the published letters. Finally, it is surely significant that Gonzaga's contemporaries harboured no suspicions about the *Lettere* and publicly recognized Gonzaga as a literary figure. Doni lists Gonzaga as the author of the *epistolario* in his *Libraria*, and many of the contributors to Bonardo's *Rime* refer admiringly to her literary talents, even describing her as a new Vittoria Colonna, implicitly suggesting a link to Colonna's own epistolary activity as the author of a 1544 volume of spiritual letters, as well as to Colonna's poetic production.⁶⁵ Even Apostolo Zeno, one of the first to suggest that Lando composed the *Lettere*, had no convincing proof to this effect. 'Le lettere impresse sotto nome di Lugrezia Gonzaga sono, a mio credere, di Ortensio Lando,' Zeno wrote in 1740, but admitted he had no evidence: 'Non ho per altro scrittore, che dichiari esser le dette Lettere componimento dell'amico della Gonzaga ...'⁶⁶

II. Modelling Exemplary Womanhood in the *Lettere* ... *a gloria del sesso feminile*

In the very first letter of her *epistolario*, Gonzaga confesses that her husband's disgrace motivates her to write as a form of self-consolation.

Only through study, she tells her sister-in-law Emilia, can she forget her unhappiness; writing itself is a defence against the blows of Fortune:

> ... cerco di consumare buona parte del tempo nelle lettere ... per ingannare il dolore che duramente mi preme ... ma se la fortuna mia né per se stessa, né per altri si muterà, la muterò io sola conoscendo ormai per lunga prova che non si può contrastare con essa e se non potrò valermi contro di lei co' fatti; me ne risentirò almeno con le parole e sfogherò in parte il mio dolore, col dolermi di lei ...[67]

> ... I try to spend a great deal of time in study ... to outwit the pain that cruelly oppresses me ... but if my fortune cannot be changed on its own or through others, I will change it myself; knowing from long experience, however, that one cannot fight it; and if I can't overcome it with actions, I will at least condemn it in words and express some of my despair in despairing of it ...

The literary trope of writing as consolation is enlisted to explain Gonzaga's act of authorial self-assertion, with Manfrone's plight the justification for publishing a book of *lettere familiari*. His story and her role in it frame the collection, the epistolary narration of Manfrone's imprisonment transforming an episode that greatly affected Gonzaga's private life into the narrative thread that informs her public persona.

Manfrone was arrested in 1546. He would die in prison in 1552, having descended, according to popular legend, into insanity (a theory supported by the increasingly incoherent letters he penned from prison).[68] When Manfrone was eventually arrested for the attempted murder of the duke, even the Venetian Republic, which had so long employed him, declined to come to his aid. Largely datable to this six-year period, Gonzaga's letters to and about Manfrone form several distinct groups, some recounting his arrest, others his imprisonment and death. The saga of Manfrone's arrest, imprisonment, and eventual death in a Ferrarese prison[69] provides a sense of character, chronology, and narrative coherence amid more general, humanistic letters on virtue, vice, and religion. What is perhaps most interesting about these narrative letters is the variety of angles from which Gonzaga presents both her husband and herself. The same 'contradictions' that Sanesi found so suspicious in the *Lettere* are not only a natural facet of epistolary discourse – by nature a mutable discursive medium – but also a strategic device that allows the reader to see Gonzaga in both traditional and unexpected roles, as a devoted – and unthreatening – wife, and as an adept literary and moral figure.

Depending on her internal audience, Gonzaga alternately condemns or excuses her husband, speaks of him in loving or censorious terms, and presents herself as distraught over his plight or boldly forging a new existence freed from the shackles of marriage. In a letter to her sister Isabella, for example, written just before Manfrone's arrest in 1546, Gonzaga affectionately describes her husband as 'la miglior parte dell'anima mia' ('the best part of my soul').[70] To another relative, Emilia Manfrona, Gonzaga paints him as a paragon of virtue, in the most enthusiastic terms we will find in the *Lettere*. Given Manfrone's reputation, her words are certainly satirical: 'niuno vive oggidí di maggior valore di lui, di miglior nerbo, di più ardito core, di più fermo volontà, di più candida fede, di più cristiana intenzione, di più fervente zelo, di maggior cortesia e di maggior onestà...' ('there is no one alive today more worthy than he, possessed of more nerve, braver heart, stronger will, purer faith, more Christian belief, stronger zeal, greater courtesy, and greater honesty').[71] When Manfrone is arrested, however, Gonzaga tells one correspondent that her husband has brought his disgrace upon himself, explaining: '... cosí piacesse pur a Dio di permettere un giorno che al ribaldone cadesse a dosso tutta quella disgrazia che merita la sua ingratitudine ...' ('... so may it please God that one day all the disgrace merited by that ruffian's ingratitude should befall him ...').[72] A letter to Manfrone's jailor provides a still less sympathetic portrait of a man overcome by his own cruelty, pride, ambition, and inability to accept authority – qualities that have rendered him hateful, writes Gonzaga, to friends, relatives, and the world at large:

> ... il poverello, accecato dal fumo dell'ambizione, era divenuto insupportabile a parenti, odioso a vicini, e dal resto degli uomini prima odiato che conosciuto, a tale che non si vide mai natura simile alla sua, poiché odiando i suoi maggiori, né potendo tolerare i pari suoi et sprezzando gli inferiori, mostrato ha sempre non aver manco del bestiale, che del superbo ...[73]

> ... the poor man, blinded by the fog of ambition, had become unbearable to his relatives, hateful to his neighbours, and hated by everyone else even before they met him, such that a character like his was never seen before, since by hating his superiors, and being unable to tolerate his peers, and despising his inferiors, he showed himself to be brutish as well as arrogant ...

Emphasizing her own (failed) attempts to set her husband right, Gonzaga places herself in a position of moral superiority. In contrast to conventional depictions of the woman (letter) writer, here she is the voice of reason, he that of passion:

> Ho più volte supplicato mio marito ch'ei si volesse astenere di andar dietro alle follie, volesse lasciar quella tanta fierezza che gli aveva occupato il core; ma non ci è mai stato ordine che egli abbia voluto non solo acconsentire alle mie umili e amorevoli prieghere, ma neanche pur tantino mollificare la rigidezza del suo protervo animo. Possono i cuori delle fiere farsi mansueti, ma quello dell'infelice mio marito è sempre stato implacabilissimo, per aver congiunta la crudeltà con una incomparabil superbia ...[74]

> Many times I begged my husband to stop chasing follies, that he should abandon the pride that had taken over his heart; but there was no way that he would deign either to agree to my humble and loving requests, or even to mollify the hardness of his proud soul the littlest bit. The hearts of beasts can be tamed, but that of my unhappy husband has always been most implacable, having combined cruelty with an unbelievable arrogance ...

Gonzaga, the wife, takes on the role of moral guide and counsellor, attempting to steer her husband onto the right path.

While Gonzaga may have believed that Manfrone's arrest was inevitable, she devotes many of her published letters to pleas for his release, attempting to win over her audiences through a number of strategies. Many of her appeals to public figures call on the familial or class ties that bind the Manfrone and Gonzaga families to the nobility she addresses, or on the glory that redounds to merciful princes. She urges the Duke of Parma, for example, to intercede with Ercole II D'Este by arguing that clemency and mercy increase a prince's power; while in a letter to Ercole himself, she reminds him of the bonds between the houses of Este and Gonzaga.[75] Similarly, a letter to the King of France pledges the eternal support of the Gonzaga and Manfrone families in exchange for aid in bringing about Manfrone's release: '... tarda (vi prometto) non sarà mai né la casa Gonzaga, né la famiglia Manfrona a ringraziarvene ... acquistatevi la servitù di casa Manfrona, della quale, per lo suo marital valore, tanta stima ne fa il senato viniziano, che le dà in governo le più forti città' ('... neither the house of Gonzaga nor the Manfrone family will delay [I promise you] in thanking you for it ... you will gain the allegiance of the house of Manfrone, which, because of the valour of [my husband], is held in such esteem by the Venetian senate that it has been entrusted with the government of the most powerful cities').[76] Finally, in a letter to Emperor Charles V, she argues that his intervention of behalf of her husband, now in his fifth year of prison, would be the emperor's crowning glory.[77]

In contrast to her letters to secular and political figures, Gonzaga's appeals to religious figures tend to cast her as a much weaker figure, a distraught wife barely able to survive her husband's absence. To Pope Paul III, Gonzaga presents herself as a grief-stricken wife whose letter is written in tears and begs for help on behalf of herself and her children ('... né sola io ve ne prego ... ve ne priegano parimenti quattro figliuoline, che paiono quattro agnoletti di paradise ...' ['... it is not only I who begs you ... four little children, like four little angels from heaven, also beseech you').[78] A letter to the monks of San Bartolommeo begs them to pray for the return of her beloved husband: 'sospirate ora, e tanto pregate, e tanto sospirate, finché riabbia lo sposo mio, vera metà dell'anima mia, senza la cui grata e dolce compagnia, amara mi è la vita ...' ('sigh now, and pray and sigh until I have my husband back, the true other half of my soul, without whose gracious and sweet company, life is bitter to me'). It declares piteously: 'Se non veggo il mio consorte, parmi d'esser ceca, se favellar non l'odo, parmi d'esser sorda, se non lo abbraccio, parmi che nulla stringa ...' ("If I don't see my spouse, I feel I am blind, if I don't hear him speak, I feel I am deaf, if I don't embrace him, it is as if I hold onto nothing').[79] Another letter to a nun lists additional physical manifestations of Gonzaga's distress: '... giorno e notte per la prigionia del mio consorte mi bagno il viso di lagrime, il petto mi percuoto, i capei rompo, e facciomi il viso tutto nero con quelle percosse che la disperazione mi insegna ...' ('... day and night I bathe my face in tears for the imprisonment of my spouse, I beat my chest, I pull my hair, and I blacken my face with those blows that my desperation inspires').[80] While such sentiments seem at odds with those expressed by Gonzaga to Manfrone's jailor, for example, these letters function on two levels. First, they constitute a reasoned attempt to garner support from a particular corner by performing the role of the distraught wife. An astute epistolarian realizes that different audiences will respond to different approaches. An informed audience familiar with Manfrone's reputation for violence and brutality, however, recognizes and admires the epistolary performance at work here, along with its underlying element of satire.

Gonzaga's lobbying, however, did not pay off. While Duke Ercole did commute Manfrone's sentence, he refused to release him.[81] At one point, Gonzaga claims to have lost hope of obtaining her goal. Listing

'A gloria del sesso feminile' 99

all those to whom she has turned for help, Gonzaga concludes that the duke will not be moved:

> ... pare che il core del signor Duca ... si vada di giorno in giorno facendosi più aspro e più rigido ... Io per me non so più che mi fare, non so più dove rivolgermi per soccorso. Ho scritto a papi e a cardinali, ho supplicato l'Imperadore, il re di Francia, il re di Boemia, principi, duchi, duchesse e marchesane; ho fatto istancare tutta la corte celeste con assidue orazioni, et holla fatta stancare da patriarchi, da arcivescovi, vescovi, arcimandriti, abbati, priori, proposti, decani, primiceri, arcipreti, arcidiaconi, diaconi, canonici, alcoliti, monaci, monache, beguine, romiti, murate e convertite. Che mi resta più a fare ...?[82]

> ... it seems that the Duke's heart ... becomes more bitter and hard each day ... For my part, I don't know what else to do, I don't know where to turn for help. I've written to popes and cardinals, I've implored the emperor, the king of France, the king of Bohemia, princes, dukes, duchesses and marquesses; I've wearied the whole of the heavenly court with constant prayers, and I've caused it to be bothered by patriarchs, archbishops, bishops, archimandrites, abbots, priors, provosts, deans, primiceri, archpriests, archdeacons, deacons, canons, acolytes, monks, nuns, beguines, hermits, cloistered nuns, and *convertite*. What else is there for me to do ...?

She is so desperate, she threatens, that she is thinking of turning to the Turks for help: 'Sono ... piena di disperazione; né so più dove rivolgermi se non mi rivolgo alla potenza invitta dell'Ottomano, se non chiamo le arme turchesche; non so più che sperare ...' ('I am ... full of despair; nor do I know where else to turn if not to the unvanquished power of the Ottoman; if I don't call on the weapons of the Turks, I don't know what else to hope for ...').[83] This letter has a rhetorical polish that is absent from many of Gonzaga's other compositions, suggesting that it, at least, was almost certainly composed for publication. While Gonzaga might have petitioned dukes and princes on the Italian peninsula as well as religious figures, that she should consider asking for aid from the Turks, the enemies of Christianity, seems improbable. Moreover, the constructed, rhetorical quality of the list of *potenti* Gonzaga has petitioned rings false, clearly a literary device.[84] At the same time, however, the letter serves to encapsulate the writer's admirable and exhaustive efforts on behalf of her husband. True to her word,

Gonzaga composes a letter to the Turks, a curious missive elaborately addressed to: 'Solimano Imperadore di Constantinopoli e di Trapesonda, S[ignor] della Soria, Egitto, Phrigia, Cilicia, Capadozia, Giudea, Panfilia e d'altri regni e ampissime provincie.' In it, she begs Suliman to free her husband through military intervention:

> Poscia che non truovo pietà, né misericordia presso de' cristiani, ch'esser ne dovrebbono la vera fontana, io Lucrezia Gonzaga, piena di giusto sdegno e tutta colma di ragionevol ira, a te, o Re potentissimo e Imperadore invittissimo, umilmente ne vengo, e priegoti ... che adoperar ti piaccia ancho le tue armi debellatrici del mondo in favore e beneficio dell'infelice mio consorte, che si sta prigione nelle mani di un duca ferrarese, il quale di potenza ti è di gran lunga inferiore, et quando anche ti fusse eguale, tale e tanta è però la tua virtú che tosto te lo faresti inferiore. Manda adunque a Ferrara il tuo diletto genero Rustan Basciah, e se egli fosse occupato nelle guerre persiane, basterà che tu ci mandi Sciala Rays o Dorgut Rays, i quali sono sí arditi e sí coraggiosi che basterebbono a molto maggiore impresa ...[85]

> Since I can find neither pity nor mercy among Christians, who should be the true font of such things, I, Lucrezia Gonzaga, filled with just disgust and overcome with righteous anger, address you, O most powerful King and unvanquished Emperor, humbly I come to you and beg ... that you agree to adopt the arms with which you make war on the world in favour of and for the benefit of my poor husband, who is imprisoned by the Duke of Ferrara, whose power is greatly inferior to yours, and even if it were equal, your virtue is such that you would quickly make it inferior ... Therefore send your adored son-in-law Rustan Basciah to Ferrara, or if he is occupied in the Persian wars, it would suffice to send Sciala Rays or Dorgut Rays, who are so daring and brave that they would be capable of a far greater enterprise ...

This letter, too, betrays its apocryphal nature. Certainly, such flattery of Suliman at the duke's expense (not to mention the invitation to military action) could not have advanced Gonzaga's cause at Ferrara. Rather, this letter epitomizes the use of Manfrone's plight as literary pretext, for it can be read in the context of an epistolary sub-genre that enjoyed some success in the second half of the sixteenth century, that of apocryphal (and sometimes genuine) correspondence with the Turks.[86] Gonzaga's careful roll call of Suliman's soldiers, and her request itself, seem to function as an internal reference to this minor genre. The sheer implausibility of such a letter renders its literary component all the more evident.

Real or fictional, Gonzaga's letters continue to lament the lack of success with which her epistolary efforts on Manfrone's behalf are met and express concern for her husband's fate. In a letter to Giberto da Sassuolo, for example, Gonzaga considers approaching the emperor for help but admits that, after six years, she has little hope of success.[87] She expresses concern about her husband's physical and mental condition in a letter to his relative Pietro Paolo Manfrone, while her letters to Manfrone himself also begin to reflect a fatalistic acceptance of his plight.[88]

If much attention is granted to Manfrone in life, a number of letters report his death. Although Gonzaga asks her sister Isabella to spread the news, as she is too overwrought to do so herself, her reactions to Manfrone's passing differ significantly in her various letters.[89] In some, she presents herself as a grieving widow, 'meschina, piena di lagrime, e tutta colma di cordoglio ...' ('distraught, full of tears, overcome by grief'), while in others she is resigned to fate and comforted by Manfrone's release from earthly misery, as in a letter to the Cardinal of Mantua: 'Scrivo ... per darle avviso della morte dello sfortunato signor Gioan Paulo, non perché ve ne abbiate a dolere, ma più tosto perché vi rallegriate ch'egli sia uscito da tanta miseria ...' ('I write ... to give you news of the death of the unfortunate signor Gioan Paulo, not so that you should mourn, but rather that you should rejoice that he has been released from such pain ...').[90] To Violante Trotta, however, Gonzaga explains that Manfrone's death comes as little surprise, given his actions in life:

> La nuova che mi date della morte di mio marito non mi è stata nuova, non perché l'abbia prima risaputa per altra via, ma perché sempre il tenni per morto da che egli fu fatto con tanta solicitudine prigione. Egli volle cosí, e in effetto da pazzo si portò a non uddibire i suoi signori che tante volte il consigliarono di rappaceficarsi col Duca ...[91]

> The news you give me of the death of my husband was not new to me, not because I had already heard from someone else, but because I gave him up for dead once he was so carefully made prisoner. He wished it so, and in effect he acted like a mad person by not obeying his masters, who so often advised him to make peace with the duke ...

Once again, the multifaceted representation of her husband allows Gonzaga to nuance her own epistolary self-portrait, portraying herself as a moral figure in contrast to Manfrone without appearing disloyal.

If some letters express grief at the loss of Manfrone, others pragmatically suggest that Gonzaga is well prepared for life without him. In fact, she looks forward to it eagerly, as is evident in several of her letters concerning marriage and remarriage. As the imprisonment and death of Manfrone provide Gonzaga with a 'reason' to write, so the tumultuous years of marriage to the ill-fated *condottiere* underlie her assertions on this institution in the *Lettere*.[92] Gonzaga devotes several letters to her refusal to remarry, contending that second marriages are unchaste. It is on this basis, for example, that she reprimands Orsola Pellegrini for suggesting she even consider such an action: '... neanche è compiuto il mese che l'infelice mio consorte è stato sepolto, e voi già mi parlate di rimaritare? Non sapete voi che casta non esser mai stata istimata chi due fiate si è maritata ... no, no, io non voglio più sentire de sí fatti cordogli, né altro marito intendo più di volere che Giesù Cristo ...' ('... not even a month has passed since my unhappy spouse was buried, and already you speak to me of remarriage? Don't you know that a twice-married woman is never thought chaste ... no, no, I don't wish to hear any more of such troubles, nor do I wish for any other husband than Jesus Christ').[93] This virtuous attitude is recalled admiringly in accounts of Gonzaga's life from Lando's *Panegirico* and Bonardo's *Rime* to the *Imprese illustri* of Ruscelli, who suggests the Latin phrase 'Noli me tangere' as the chaste widow's motto.[94]

While such letters cemented the idea of a chaste Gonzaga in readers' minds, functioning as a counterbalance to the linking of female speech with 'accessibility' discussed in chapter 1, Gonzaga had other grounds for refusing to remarry.[95] Having weathered some ten years of Manfrone's violent behaviour and its consequences without wavering (according to the *Lettere*) in dutiful support of her husband, Gonzaga had earned the authority to speak – longingly – of the unmarried state as one of autonomy and tranquility. Her refusal to remarry is based not only on a desire to live chastely but also, she tells us, on a desire to spend the remainder of her life in a state of freedom rather than subject to what she twice refers to as the 'yoke' of matrimony. In a letter to Andriana Trivulza, Gonzaga explains that one unhappy marriage is enough; she has no intention of giving up her newfound independence: 'Iddio finalmente mi ha restituito quella libertà che m'era stata occupata dalla fraterna voluntà, dandomi marito contra mia voglia, e voi, non so da quale spirito guidata, cercate di condurmi un'altra fiata sotto 'l marital giogo' ('God has finally returned to me that liberty usurped by fraternal will in giving me a husband against my own will, and you, guided I know not by what spirit, try to lead me once again to the marital yoke').[96] Rather than remarry, Gonzaga explains in several letters, she longs to join her sister Camilla in the cloister. Gonzaga's wish to live as a nun appears to be equally informed by a longing to be closer to God and a wish to avoid the burdens and limitations of marriage, as is evident in this letter to Camilla, which intertwines the two themes:

> O quanta invidia cara sorella porto io allo stato vostro, poiché aliena dai maritali incommodi avete nel munistero trovato quella santa quiete alla quale, sospirando con tutto 'l core, desperomi di poter io giamai pervenire, salvo se voi non pregate per me il padre eterno che mi faccia gustare del suo santo amore, per lo cui mezo a lui pervenga, il mondo abbandoni, et la vera pace trovi. O beata voi, che stando in questi sacri chiostri non vi è dato travaglio dalle tumultuose cogitazioni ...[97]

> Oh, how envious I am, dear sister, of your state since, untouched by marital difficulties, you have found in the convent that holy quietitude which I, sighing with my whole heart, despair of ever attaining, unless you pray to the eternal father for me that he allow me to taste of his holy love, that I might abandon the world and find true peace. Oh, how fortunate you are that in this holy cloister you are not worried by tumultuous reflection ...

A letter to Camilla written even before Manfrone's death expresses a similar longing to join her sister at her convent in Mantua.[98] Gonzaga did, in fact, enter a convent upon Manfrone's death, as her own manuscript letters tell us, although it was not the one in which Camilla resided. And although Gonzaga repeatedly expresses her desire to live a cloistered life in the *Lettere*, her manuscript letters tell us that after three years in a Bozzolo convent, she was desperate to leave.

Having refused to resubmit to the 'marital giogo,' Gonzaga cannot understand why anyone else would want to do so. She attempts to dissuade Constanza da Campi from a second marriage by pointing out the shortcomings of Constanza's suitor and inviting her friend to visit at Gonzaga's Fratta *palazzo* before committing herself:

... mi fu detto per cosa certa che voi eravate per rimaritarvi, ma non mi fu già detto con cui, se non ch'egli era un uomo sgarbato, inetto ... prodotto dalla natura al mondo per dispetto. Ma perché volete voi far sí gran torto alle gentilissime maniere vostre ...? Deh non vogliate correr sí infretta; parlatene prima alquanto meco. Trasferitevi sino alla Fratta prima che pogniate di nuovo il collo sotto 'l giogo maritale ...[99]

... I was told that it was certain that you were going to remarry, but I was not told who, except that he was a graceless, inept man ... produced by nature out of spite. But why do you want to commit such a wrong against your gentle ways ...? Come, don't hurry so; talk about it with me first. Come to Fratta before you place your neck under the marital yoke again ...

By offering a temporary refuge to Costanza, Gonzaga sets herself up as a champion of women's right to remain unmarried, or at least to choose their husbands carefully.[100] Gonzaga's attitudes concerning marriage, remarriage, and the cloister have in common an emphasis on women's need for autonomy and right to a say in their destiny, and revisit some of the same issues raised in the *Valorose donne*. By establishing her own opposition to remarriage as a commitment to maintaining her chastity, as in her letter to Orsola Pellegrini, Gonzaga gains room to oppose marriage in order to retain autonomy, as in her letter to Constanza.

The figure of Manfrone thus functions in the *Lettere* as a justification for Gonzaga's writing in general (undertaken as both consolation and activism on behalf of her husband), and more specifically for her views on social institutions such as marriage and the convent. At the same time, the literary retelling of Mafrone's dramatic saga creates a firm identification in the reader's mind between the epistolary persona and the woman, crossing the distance that separates writers from their literary personae in other genres. Gonzaga uses her husband's story to talk about herself, to position herself as the exemplary protagonist of her *epistolario*. Her epistolary self-portrait is painted in contrasts. She becomes the moral figure to her husband's immoral specter, preaching patience, acceptance, and responsibility as well as forgiveness. Yet, no passive victim of circumstance, she is also the active force who strives to garner support for Manfrone. Distancing herself from her husband's disgrace, yet refusing to abandon him to his fate, Gonzaga presents herself as an irreproachable moral figure and a model of female loyalty.

Gonzaga as Writer and Reader

We have examined how Gonzaga uses the narrative element in her *epistolario* to identify herself as the protagonist of her letters while offering a socially acceptable justification for their composition and publication in her steadfast efforts to obtain Manfrone's release. That narrative thread helps offset a second, more transgressive element of Gonzaga's epistolary project: her attention to constructing herself, through her letters, as a literary figure.

The full title of the *Lettere*, as we noted earlier, suggests that – like Lando's *Valorose donne* – they are somehow representative and celebratory of women in general (*'a gloria del sesso feminile ... in luce poste'*). Yet Gonzaga mounts no general defence of women's literary skills (although her own skills reflect positively on women). Rather, she specifically and adroitly highlights her own as both reader and writer. On the one hand, she solicits books from her literary contacts and offers her own informed comments and suggestions, praise and criticism. In doing so, she establishes herself as a participant in literary debate and proclaims her authority to judge the work of others. At the same time, well-placed references to her own literary undertakings underscore her status as a writer, while references to her appearances in the works of others function as a public declaration of the authorization conferred on her by the writers who admire and praise her in their work.

As a reader, Gonzaga seems equally familiar with classic and modern literature. A letter to Bandello, for example, recalls her girlhood study of Greek with her former tutor; while another concerning Francesco Robortello's commentaries on Aristotle and Aeschylus simultaneously manages to praise Robortello's work and highlight Gonzaga's own interest in the Greeks.[101] Gonzaga is also careful to reveal her mastery of rhetoric, which she praises to Zenobio Lanfranchi with the words of personal experience. Rhetoric, writes Gonzaga, is the 'ornamento delle altre scienze' ('the ornament of the other disciplines') and teaches us to 'favellare con eleganza ...' ('speak with elegance').[102] Although she herself composes her sole literary work in the newly respectable vernacular, Gonzaga emphasizes the importance of studying Latin in a letter to her friend Bonardo. Although the Latin authors are dense and use difficult rhetorical devices, she writes, there is nothing the human mind cannot master through effort.[103]

Above all, however, Gonzaga is an avid reader of vernacular texts. She is an admirer of many women poets, including Gaspara Stampa,

Vittoria Colonna, and Veronica Gambara, all of whom she praises in a letter to Lando:

> Ho letto più di mille fiate il sonetto composto dalla virtuosa Madonna Gaspra [sic] Stampa in lode vostra,[104] il quale mi è paruto sí maraviglioso e da sí bella vena procedere che io sono stata in forse se dovea credere da alcuna donna fusse stato composto, poiché la Marchesana di Pescara e la signora Veronica da Gambera se n'erano volate al cielo ...[105]

> I read more than a thousand times the sonnet composed by the virtuous Madonna Gaspra [sic] Stampa in your honour, which seemed to me so marvellous and to proceed in such a lovely vein that I was uncertain if I should believe that a woman had composed it, since the Marchesana of Pescara and the signora Veronica da Gambera had flown to heaven ...

To the tutor of her nephew Luigi Gonzaga, Gonzaga writes that the verses of Laura Terracina 'avanzino ogni lode che dar si possa ...' ('surpass every possible praise').[106] The presence of Stampa, Colonna, Gambara, and Terracina in the *Lettere* establishes Gonzaga within a community of women writers. By evoking these admired women, Gonzaga implicitly positions herself alongside them in the eyes of her readers.

Not suprisingly, Gonzaga reveals herself to be an enthusiastic reader of letters with firm opinions on what constitutes a good example of the genre, praising those of Girolamo Muzio, Bernardo Tasso, and Girolamo Parabosco in letters addressed to the authors themselves. Her judgments echo those that would be found in epistolary manuals throughout the century. She writes, for example, that Muzio's letters interest her because they speak 'purely,' yet wisely and gracefully, and she asks to be sent a copy of his collection.[107] A letter to Bernardo Tasso is generous with praise for his writing in general, and for his letters in particular.[108] In spite of her appreciation of rhetoric, expressed in her letter to Lanfranchi, Gonzaga showers Parabosco – a member of the *Pastori frattegiani* – with compliments for the natural, untutored quality of his familiar letters, which are neither 'vestite d'arte' ('clothed in artifice') nor 'gonfiate di lusinghevole o vano studio' ('puffed up from excessive revision') – essential qualities of the vernacular familiar letter. Her visceral description of his letters' effect on her is less conventional, however, and is infused with sensual imagery. She writes, 'Io non ne ricevo mai alcuna, che non mi senta tutta intenerire, anzi liquefare le viscere di dolcezza con una rapina di tutti i sensi miei …' ('I never receive one of them, but that I feel myself soften, that is my insides liquefy sweetly and I lose all my senses …'). At the same time, his letters fill her with envy and despair, for she fears she could never equal them: 'quando fie mai che io doppo lungo studio di imitazione, aggiugner possa a un cotal segno? Ma perché mentre parlo dell'eccellenza del vostro ingegno trafigger mi sento l'anima dagli stimoli dell'invidia, più oltre non intendo parlarne …' ('when could I ever match such mastery, even after long study [of the model]? But since I feel my soul pierced by the prods of envy when I speak of your skill, I don't wish to say anything more …').[109] Of note here is Gonzaga's reference to the way in which letters are composed. Although the effect should be one of ease and spontaneity, it is achieved through careful study and imitation of models ('lungo studio di imitazione') of the very sort that had begun to proliferate. Gonzaga's marked interest in the new epistolary genre is clear from the way she singles out these collections for praise. Her words to Parabosco, moreover, seem to reflect her own epistolary endeavour: her envy of his skill betrays her own aspirations to mastery of the vernacular letter.

Gonzaga often requests texts from her literary acquaintances, many of whom she may have met through the *Pastori frattegiani*. She praises Dolce's *Trasformazioni*, for example, and begs him to send her the final copy.[110] She thanks Torquato Bembo for his 'ornatissime e amorevolissime lettere' ('most ornate and lovable letters') and for the books he sends her, writing admiringly of the elegance with which they are bound.[111] In a letter to Alessandro Nugarola, Gonzaga reminds him of his promise to compose a biography of the valorous Queen Mary and asks him to send it to her when it is finished. A letter to Lando not only requests to read more of her friend's work, but ventures still further into the territory of the literary sphere by volunteering to be his patron.[112] Finally, Gonzaga was also called upon occasionally to procure books for others, evidence of her stature as a reader and someone with the connections to fill such requests. A letter to her sister Isabella, for example, refers to Isabella's request for books from Venice: 'È possibile che di negligenza non cessiate mai accusarmi per non aver io sí tosto mandato per quei libri che erano in Vinegia?' ('Can it be possible that you never cease to accuse me of negligence for not having sent you those books from Venice?').[113] This letter is most likely genuine, for autograph letters written by Isabella show that she was an avid reader and begged her family to send her new books.[114]

The network of *destinatari* who appear in an *epistolario* tells us something about the writer's own position within that epistolary circle. Here, the establishment of epistolary relationships with such important and diverse literary figures as Robortello, Muzio, Tasso, Parabosco, and Lando positions Gonzaga within the contemporary literary community. The authority of these figures is reflected back upon Gonzaga through these epistolary exchanges, validating her participation in the literary realm. Similarly, Gonzaga's references to such prominent women poets as Stampa and Terracina, Colonna and Gambara are not casual. Rather, her familiarity with and admiration for the work of these women functions to set up a kind of continuity of women's writing, a lineage into which she is placed through her own literary endeavour.

Equally central to the process of literary self-construction is Gonzaga's representation of herself as a very serious literary figure: not just a reader, but a writer and a woman whose erudition is widely recognized. To this end, Gonzaga carefully includes references to virtually all the works in which she has been lauded by others, both for her learnedness and for her steadfastness during Manfrone's imprisonment. In doing so, she walks a fine line between modesty and self-promotion, calling attention to the relevant texts while professing her unworthiness to be their subject. She devotes several letters, for example, to Lando's *Panegirico*, a celebration of both Gonzaga and Maria de Cardona Marchesa di Padulla. Gonzaga is clearly pleased and flattered by Lando's representation of her, although she modestly shifts her praise to the artistry of his pen and insists that all his kind words would have been better applied to the Marchesa:

> Avete veramente mostrato al mondo quel che sa fare la vostra dotta penna, ma non avete avuto riguardo a quanto si conveniva a me, che non se le conviene nulla per non valer io nulla. Molto meglio avreste voi fatto trapportando nel *Panegirico* della Signora Marchesana tutti i bei concetti e tutte le scelte parole che destinaste al *Panegirico* composto per illustrare il mio nome oscuro e appena dai familiari conosciuto ...[115]

> You have truly shown the world what your learned pen can do, but you did not think whether it suited me, for it does not suit me at all since I am utterly unworthy. You would have done much better to have used in the *Panegyric* of the Signora Marchesana all those pretty conceits and choice words you reserved for the *Panegyric* composed to praise my obscure name, barely known to those closest to me ...

Although Gonzaga is obviously aware here that Lando is behind the anonymous *Panegirico*, she professes ignorance of its author (thus creating one of the 'contradictions' that led Sanesi to declare the *Lettere* a forgery) in a letter to Girolamo Ruscelli, who added a letter in praise of Gonzaga to Lando's book. She guesses, however, at Lando's involvement: 'Sentomi ancora aver grand'obligo a chi di ciò ne fu instromento, ch'altri certo non puote esser stato che il nostro comune amico messer Ortensio Lando ...' ('I feel a great obligation to its author, who surely can be none other than our mutual friend Messer Ortensio Lando').[116] Gonzaga's initial profession of ignorance is almost coy: while wishing to appear properly modest and uncomfortable with such public exposure, she is nevertheless careful to make sure her readers know of this very flattering account of her life. In fact, she refers to the *Panegirico* yet again in a letter thanking Alfonso Nunnez for composing the *canzone* for her included at the end of that text. Again, Gonzaga modestly insists that she is unworthy of such praise and wishes Nunnez would bestow his verses on 'donna che ne fusse più degna di me' ('a woman who was more worthy than me').[117]

Like Lando, Girolamo Ruscelli was a great admirer of Gonzaga. In addition to the letter he contributed to the *Panegirico*, Ruscelli dedicated a section to Gonzaga in his *Imprese illustri* and later composed a dedicatory letter to her for Federico Luigini da Udine's *Libro della bella donna*.[118] Although Gonzaga often professes to be unworthy of the literary attentions bestowed upon her, as in the case of the *Panegirico*, she occasionally drops this modest facade to reveal a fervent desire to be memorialized. In one letter, probably concerning the *Imprese illustri*, Gonzaga specifically grants Ruscelli permission to write about her, explaining that rather than fear such public exposure, she yearns for it, especially at the hands of so gifted a writer. Her words here are in contrast to the retiring tone of her letters regarding the *Panegirico*:

> Per le vostre scritte alli IXI [sic] di dicembre, mi fate sapere quanto desiderate di farmi illustre e famosa di venire al mondo con i vostri scritti, ma che ciò non ardite voi di fare se prima da me non ne impetrate la licenza, temendo che come troppo nemica dell'umana gloria con esso voi non mi adiri, e io come donna libera scriverovvi liberamente e amichevolmente aprirovvi il mio concetto. Desidero sentire che non solo dalla bocca vostra, ma dai vostri scritti ancora, esca quella armonia che sopra ogni altra suol dilettare gli ascoltanti, la qual consiste nel sentirsi lodar da persona lodata come siete voi ...[119]

> In your letter of ıxı [sic] December, you inform me how deeply you wish to honour me and make me famous before the world through your writing, but that you don't dare to do so unless you first ask my permission, fearing that I, being no friend of earthly glory, might be angry with you; and I, as a free woman, freely write you and lovingly explain myself to you. I wish to hear, not only from your mouth, but from your works, that harmony which delights its listeners more than any other, which consists in hearing oneself praised by such as yourself ...

Not only does Ruscelli's recognition please her, she craves it and sees it as a valorization of her own merit:

> ... è gran tempo che io ardo d'un maraviglioso desiderio ... assai lodevole, che vi piaccia d'illustrar l'oscuro mio nome con la luce dei vostri gloriosi scritti, perché *cosí spero che non solamente s'abbia da perpetuare il nome mio nella fama, ma che debba etiandio godermi cosí viva tutta quella autorità che mi pò nascere dal testimonio vostro* ...[120]

> ... for a long time, I have burned with a marvelous desire ... very praiseworthy, that you should wish to honour my obscure name with the light of your glorious works, *for in this way I hope not only to perpetuate the fame of my name but also to benefit, while alive, from all the authority that may come from your support* ...

Far from shunning public recognition, Gonzaga welcomes it, and in this letter makes no secret of her wish to live on through literature. At Ruscelli's hands, she will be granted fame and authority in the realm of letters. At the same time, the letter suggests that writers consulted the objects of their praise before memorializing them in print. Thus, as suggested earlier, even if Gonzaga's *Lettere* were initially Lando's project, she would have been very much involved in it.

As the *Lettere* demonstrate, however, Gonzaga does not rely on others to cement her literary reputation, and several published letters refer to the publication of the very *epistolario* we are reading. In a letter to Giovanni Roncalli, for example, Gonzaga refers to the imminent publication of her own letters. Deftly mixing self-deprecation with self-promotion, Gonzaga insists on the mediocrity of her letters while at the same time repeating for the external reader Roncalli's praise of them:

> Nelle vostre ultime lettere vi rallegrate con esso meco d'aver inteso che abbia fatto un'opra degna di esser letta dalli più elevati ingegni di Europa;

e io vi dico e vi essorto a non lasciarvi ingannare dalla affezione che mi portate, percioché sono certa che, a paragone di quelle che tanti altri divini scrittori hanno mandato fuori, quasi spento carbone al chiaro lume di tante lampadi appena si potrà vedere; quelle, come stelle nella perpetua eternità riluceranno e questa mia nel medesimo giorno forse si spegnerà ch'ella sarà per opra della stampa nel mondo accesa ...[121]

In your latest letters you rejoice with me that I have composed a work worthy of being read by Europe's most exalted minds; and I tell you and implore you not to be deceived by your affection for me, because I am certain that, in comparison to that which many other divine writers have already produced, it will barely shine like spent coal compared to the light of so many lamps; they, like stars, will shine forever, and my own light will burn out in the very day in which its light is shed on the world through print.

Declaring that she expects no acclaim for this endeavour, which will pale like 'spent coal' next to the brilliant works of more established writers, Gonzaga merely hopes not to be condemned for her effort: 'ben sodisfatta me ne terrò se gravemente non ne sarò biasimata' ('as long as I am not gravely condemned, I will consider myself well satisfied'). In order to avoid such an outcome, Gonzaga asks Roncalli's pardon for her temerity, as well as his help in making sure her letters are ready for publication:

... per schifar quel biasimo nel quale son certa che io caderei di esser tenuta temeraria mandandola fuori, come per aventura sono stata tenuta prosuntuosa in comporla, farò che prima ella venga a chiedervi perdono del mio fallo, e sottoporsi alla correzione del vostro intiero e saldo giudizio ...[122]

... to avoid the condemnation I am certain to attract of being audacious in sending it to print, just as I was judged presumptuous for having composed it, I will first send it to you to beg pardon for my fault, and to submit itself to the correction of your whole and sound judgment ...

Of course, such expressions of modesty about one's letters were de rigueur for most writers in this genre. Moreover, as noted earlier, it was not unusual for writers to request one another's aid in revisions. Yet it is interesting to see that Gonzaga includes such a reference to Roncalli, whereas Lando's editorial participation, if it existed, is never mentioned. Perhaps she wished to conceal it. Or perhaps she felt that

Roncalli's stature might better function as a kind of added authorization for the volume. Rather than reflect poorly on her own literary abilities, Gonzaga's request for Roncalli's input adds to the validity of her letters by indicating his willingness to become involved with this project. Similarly, the invocation of Roncalli's editorial aid has the added merit of diminishing Gonzaga's own responsibility for any eventual errors in the letters.

Just as her letters about Manfrone presented a variety of perspectives, however, so do Gonzaga's references to her *Lettere* take more than one form. Lest Gonzaga seem too audacious in her epistolary aspirations, as her letter to Roncalli might suggest, she takes a different tack in another reference to the imminent publication of the volume. In a letter to the printer Niccolò Bevilacqua,[123] Gonzaga professes indignation that 'someone' is gathering her letters for publication: 'Ho presentito che un certo sciagurato, assai men dotto che l'ignoranza, va di qua e di là raccogliendo con inganno e arte alcune mie lettere, scritte ne' miei bisogni, sperando forse di trarne alcun profitto ...' ('I sensed that a certain ruffian, less educated than ignorance itself, is running here and there gathering, through deceit and pretense, some of my letters written in my time of need, perhaps hoping to make a profit'), she writes, and begs Bevilacqua to return her letters to her should they come his way. 'Io son donna che ho imparato a misurare me stessa' ('I am a woman who has learned to take the measure of [her]self'), Gonzaga explains firmly, 'e che conosco che dalla vena del mio rozzo ingegno non possono uscire componimenti degni di questa dotta età' ('and I know that from the vein of my rough imagination no compositions worthy of this learned age can come'). Yet before we can take this disclaimer at face value, Gonzaga quickly adds that, even if she did want to publish her letters, she would want to revise them first: 'quando pure ... che io desiderassi lasciar uscire in publico i scritti miei, io vorrei pure almeno tanto mattorirli, che io potessi togliere la censura di bocca ai calunniatori ...' ('even if ... I wished to allow my writings to appear in public, I would at least want to at fix them up, so that I could pluck the censure from the mouths of [my] detractors').[124]

It is possible that, as Gonzaga claims, someone sought to collect and publish her letters without her consent. We might, for example, envisage Lando in such a role. In that case, the reference to the 'sciagurato' seeking to make a quick profit would be teasing in tone, suggesting a complicity between them while also underscoring Lando's aptitude for exploiting the literary market. However, such an accusation is not uncommon in epistolary collections. In Manuzio's *Lettere volgari*, for example, discussed in chapter 1, several epistolarians claim that their work circulates without their consent, and, fearing the ridicule of their contemporaries, beg to be granted at least the opportunity to revise their correspondence for publication. Whether such protestations are genuine or rather literary devices meant to distance the writer from the act of publication is difficult to know. Publishing one's own letters, as we have noted, has significant implications for a writer, suggesting that he (or she) is confident enough to feel that their personal correspondence is of value to a public readership. Protestations of non-responsibility can function as a strategic tactic to balance such implications with a pose of humility. For a woman writer, these issues were of great importance. It is likely, therefore, that Gonzaga includes this missive to provide an alternate reading for the publication of her letters. She does not say the letters are not hers, only that she has not authorized their publication. In suggesting that the letters may have been published without her consent, not only does she carefully negotiate that gendered border between public and private, between domestic and literary worlds, but she implies that not having had a chance to revise the letters, she should not be condemned for any errors or shortcomings.

Moral and Spiritual Letters

Although there is no firm structure to the *Lettere*, there is some degree of thematic coherence in the grouping of the autobiographical letters most densely at the beginning of the volume, the letters on literary themes in the central pages, and those on moral or spiritual issues in the final third.[125] This general (although not exclusive) structure provides readers with accessible 'blocks' of letters on distinct themes, and might be seen as setting up a structure of progression in which we move from consideration of temporal matters to meditation on larger, spiritual concerns. Thus, Gonzaga's moral and spiritual letters, although concentrated in the last section of the collection, are central both to an overall project of epistolary self-construction and to the structure of the book.

Gonzaga's 'moral' letters are compositions concerning virtue or vice in which the writer positions herself as a kind of humanistic counsellor. Gonzaga is primarily interested in correcting vice, for, just as her letters about Manfrone allow her to appear stronger in comparison, so by reprimanding a correspondent for a moral shortcoming, she distances herself from that failing. In a letter chastising an unnamed correspondent for his excessive pride, Gonzaga casts herself in the superior role of a teacher who corrects a wayward student. 'Ho più volte fra me stessa pensato con quai ragioni e con quai essempi potessi umiliare e abassare la tua superbia' ('Many times I have wondered to myself what explanations and what examples I might use to humble and diminish your pride'), Gonzaga writes, finally reminding her friend that we are all created from dust, and are born only to die.[126] A letter to her brother Carlo rebukes him for losing his temper, while another takes Gonzaga's friend Bonardo to task for playing cards.[127] Avarice and ambition are also targets of Gonzaga's righteous dismay, as is carnal love.[128] Often, the distinction between letters attempting to correct vice and spiritual letters delineating the elements of a faithful life is blurred, as the condemnation of vice segues naturally into a reminder to turn to God. In one case, for example, Gonzaga sets up a direct opposition between carnal and divine love, urging an unnamed correspondent to abandon the corrosive pleasures of the first for the eternal joys of the second:

> … lascia ormai, misera e infelice, le vanità de tuoi amori, il cui puzzo ha di già ammorbato e corrotto quanto di buono apprendeste sotto la disciplina di tua madre […] fa a mio modo; incomincia un poco a gustare l'amor divino, il quale sarà un fermo riposo, una sicura quiete, e una dolce tranquillità. Contempla il suo figliuolo in sulla croce …[129]

> … leave behind, miserable and unhappy woman, the vanities of your loves, the stink of which has weakened and corrupted everything good you learned from your mother […] do as I do; start to taste divine love a little, which will be a reliable refuge, a secure serenity, and a sweet tranquility. Contemplate His son on the cross …

Gonzaga's condemnation of vice is closely linked to her own spirituality. It serves to emphasize and highlight the writer's own virtue by setting her up as a moral guide and allows her to embark on a discussion of her religious views and beliefs.

As we noted earlier, Gonzaga had ample opportunity to come into contact with the religious debates and discussions that swept through Italy before and during the Council of Trent. The strong evangelist bent of many of Gonzaga's spiritual letters, including her emphasis on scripture and on the individual's internal, personal relationship with God, demonstrates that at least some of her religious convictions strayed from orthodoxy – perhaps an early trace of the path that would lead to her Inquisition trial in 1567. Published when the Council of Trent was in its seventh year, Gonzaga's *Lettere* fall well within the period delineated by Delio Cantimori as the 'crisis of evangelism' (beginning with the death of Juan de Valdés in 1541 and continuing through the 1550s), but before the most repressive effects of the Counter-Reformation had begun to be felt.[130] Thus, just as Lando was able to publish his *Dialogo* on scripture (in which Gonzaga plays the role of the student) in the same year without repercussions,[131] Gonzaga, too, was able to include reformist or evangelist ideas in her letters without attracting comment. Indeed, as Anne Jacobson Schutte has shown, vernacular letters were a common vehicle for the circulation of evangelist ideas in this period and did not appear to run into any obstacles to publication even in the early 1550s.[132]

In her study of evangelist content in vernacular letter anthologies, Schutte offers a useful 'checklist' detailing some of the elements common to such collections. It includes advocacy of justification by faith alone; emphasis on scripture and particularly on Paul's epistles; the 'evaluation of other religious books ... in terms of their presentation of the pure Gospel message ...'; stress on personal religious development and the conviction that the writer and/or recipient is part of an 'elect' group of souls; and concern with Church reform.[133] A number of Gonzaga's spiritual letters closely conform to this 'evangelist criteria,' suggesting we might locate her within the heterogeneous spiritual movement referred to by religious historians as 'Italian evangelism.'[134] Diffuse rather than focused (although occasional reference is made to such specific points as justification by faith alone), Gonzaga's beliefs incorporate aspects of Erasmus, Luther, and Valdés, and ultimately consist of an overwhelming faith in the centrality of scripture and a conviction that the purity and intensity of the individual's inner spirituality are of greater import than the external rituals sanctioned by the Church. Such beliefs also closely echo those debated by the characters of Lucrezia and Filalete/Lando in Lando's *Dialogo*.

A letter by Gonzaga to Sor Domitilla emphasizes the importance of the individual's personal relationship with God, declaring that God's truth speaks within us: 'Beata è veramente quella anima che ode Iddio parlar a sé ... la verità favella internamente e senza verun strepito di parole ci favella' ('Truly blessed is that soul who hears God speak within him ... truth speaks inside us and speaks to us without the din of words ...').[135] In a letter to Sor Nicolosa, Gonzaga refuses the nun's request for reading material with the admonishment that she should devote herself rather to the reading of scripture:

> Non vi mando i libri che voi mi avete ne dí passati richiesti, parendomi sieno poco a profitto vostro e avendovi tante volte essortato a leggere le sacre lettere, le quali di gran lunga eccedono la sapienza de tutti i savi del mondo. Le lettere sante sono piene di spirto, e di vita ...[136]

> I am not sending you the books you lately asked me for, as it seems to me they can be of of little profit to you and having urged you many times to read scripture, which greatly exceeds the knowledge of all worldy sages. Scripture is full of spirit and life ...

Like Giovanna Cavalleria in the *Valorose donne* and Filalete in Lando's *Dialogo*, Gonzaga argues that scripture outstrips all other sources of knowledge (although, as we saw earlier, Gonzaga herself read widely in secular literature).[137] Similarly, in a letter to Luciana Garimberti, Gonzaga makes the more unorthodox point that faith, not pilgrimage (i.e., works or ritual) brings us closer to God:

> ... se volete esser cristiana, non far bisogno che per vostro principale oggetto abbiate il voler tutto dí peregrinando visitare i luoghi santi. Non dico già che io ve lo biasimi, ma ben vi affermo per la bocca del vero che la fede si è l'unica porta per andar a Cristo, e di più convenire, che, di lui e delle scritture date e inspirate dallo spirito suo, ottimamente e sinceramente se ne giudichi.[138]

> ... if you wish to be a Christian, you needn't have constant pilgrimage to all the holy places as your primary goal. Not that I condemn such a goal, but I tell you truly that faith is the only door to Christ, and it is better to study his scripture that was inspired by his spirit.

Many of Gonzaga's letters on scripture implicitly or explicitly locate the writer within a community of 'elect' spirits – those who have embarked on the true road to Christ – further situating the *Lettere* within the criteria of 'evangelist' letter collections. This spiritual positioning is evident in a letter to Francesco Carrettona describing the joys of true faith. 'Volete voi gustare una vera voluttà? Gustate l'allegrezza della pura coscientia,' Gonzaga advises. 'Volete assaggiare le più dilicate vivande che gustar si possono? Assagiatele nello studio delle sante scritture? Volete isperimentare la più festevole e la più gioconda compagnia che isperimentar si possa? Isperimentate la comunanza dei fedeli e la raunanza dei buoni' ('Do you wish to taste true joy? Taste the happiness of a pure conscience ... Do you wish to sample the most exquisite victuals there are? Sample them in the study of holy scripture. Do you wish to experience the warmest and most welcoming company there is? Experience the community of the faithful and the gathering of the righteous').[139] Clearly, the 'community of the faithful' and the 'gathering of the righteous' constitute a group of God's elect of which Gonzaga clearly feels she is a part and for whom she is authorized to speak. Similarly, Gonzaga reprimands an anonymous correspondent for not respecting God or His elect ('sprezzando sempre Iddio, beffando i suoi eletti'), thus excluding him from that group while including herself. A letter to Thomaso Ferufino refers to the small but select group of Christ's true followers: 'seguendo Cristo a pochi piacerete, ma quei pochi saranno reputati i migliori' ('following Christ may appeal to few, but those few will be esteemed the best').[140]

Gonzaga takes pains to justify herself as a woman possessed of the moral authority to speak on religious matters. In one of several letters offering guidance or criticism to religious figures, she prefaces her remarks with the declaration that she is as qualified to judge the value of sermons as she is to wield an embroidery needle. Confidently, Gonzaga assures her correspondent that when he hears a certain 'fra Cherubino' preach, '... direte Lucrezia Gonzaga non solo s'intende alquanto di adoperar l'aco, ma anche pò far giudizio dei predicatori' ('... you will say that Lucrezia Gonzaga not only knows how to use a [sewing] needle, but she is also a good judge of preachers').[141] Elsewhere, she acts as an adviser to frate Giovanfrancesco Libertà Trevigiano, encouraging him to continue composing his 'dotti' and 'devoti' sermons, devoted to 'la dottrina vangelica.'[142] Another letter responds to her sister Camilla's doubts about how best to pray to God, thus assuming a position of authority over a cloistered nun.[143] Gonzaga advises Camilla to be heartfelt in her prayers but not overly lengthy, citing the words of Paul (a touchstone for Italian evangelism): 'Paulo loda più tosto cinque parole che diecimila profferite solo con le labbra e non punto intese' ('Paul praises five words, more than ten thousand that are offered only with the lips and not understood').[144]

Finally, a letter explaining how to draw closer to Christ, in addition to reiterating the religious views expressed in the previous letters, may provide a key to interpreting the moral letters we have discussed here. To be 'with Christ,' Gonzaga declares, we must leave behind all vice:

'per esser con Cristo, che faremo noi? Lasciaremo l'ambizione, la superbia, l'ozio, le delizie, i piaceri, la libidine, i sfrenati desideri et i disonesti appetiti ...' ('We must abandon ambition, pride, sloth, delight, pleasure, lust, unbridled desires and dishonest appetites ...').[145] Thus the letters on vice in the volume, which deal with precisely these issues – ambition, pride, lust – as well as the story of Manfrone, which functions as a kind of morality tale, not only set up Gonzaga as a moral figure attempting to guide her readers by turning them away from such vices, but also fit into her larger spiritual consciousness. To be part of the 'elect' means to transcend these vices. The moral and spiritual letters are intertwined, mutually ancillary aspects of Gonzaga's *epistolario*.

The religious aspect of Gonzaga's letters is central to our understanding of the volume as a whole, for together with the narrative and literary elements, it constitutes the third of three principal 'threads' (autobiographical, literary, and spiritual) which together form (and inform) Gonzaga's epistolary persona. These compositions not only help us to better understand where Gonzaga stood within the complex, shifting territory of religious debate in the early 1550s, but also shed further light on her objectives for the published volume. Not only did Gonzaga's letterbook aim to create an enduring public representation of the woman, but it also sought to disseminate her religious convictions through the popular new vehicle of the vernacular letterbook. Finally, the religious content of Gonzaga's letters constitute another link to Lando and to their literary partnership. The ideas she expresses privileging scripture, justification by faith, and the community of the elect, are all present in Lando's *Dialogo* on scripture, which preceded the publication of the *Lettere* by a matter of months. There, she plays the role of a student, bright and well educated, but obediently led by her teacher. Here, she has become the teacher, assuming the active role played by many women (such as Vittoria Colonna) within the evangelist movement in Italy. Lando's clear fascination with Gonzaga, as demonstrated by his representation of her in the *Valorose donne*, the *Dialogo*, and the *Panegirico* suggests that her *Lettere* might indeed constitute the apex of a broader Landian project to promote Gonzaga and, through her, his own religious views. At the same time, however, it is difficult to separate Lando's views from those of Gonzaga, for they shared a common interest in evangelism as well as in literature (the former attested to by Gonzaga's later Inquistion trial, the latter by the praise of her contemporaries). Given the textual and thematic similarities between the *Lettere* and Lando's works, along with his indisputable fascination for Gonzaga as a protagonist, we must accept his role as an editor and promoter of her letters. We can do so, however, without discounting the authorial contribution of Gonzaga herself.

As the first *epistolario* to be published under a female name following the *Valorose donne* (and indeed the first such collection to follow Aretino's ground-breaking example), Gonzaga's *Lettere* cannot help but draw comparison to their Landian predecessor. It is in such comparison, however, that the innovation of her *Lettere* stands out. Where the *Valorose donne* are choral in nature, the *Lettere* promote a single, identifiable woman. If the *Valorose donne* are often parodic, the *Lettere* take the epistolary genre and women's contribution to it seriously. Most significantly, where the *Valorose donne* purport to represent authentic women's discourse through discussions of such intimate aspects of the female experience as childbirth and nursing and through recipes for health, beauty, and fertility, the content of Gonzaga's *Lettere* is strikingly different. With the exception of marriage, an unavoidable subject given the narrative centrality appointed to Manfrone's story, the *Lettere* are largely devoid of the 'female' content so important to the *Valorose donne*. Instead, they focus almost exclusively on constructing Gonzaga as an exemplary, authoritative female figure who is capable of dispensing moral and religious counsel as well as of participating in literary discourse.

As we see in the next chapters, the tendency of the vernacular letter genre over the course of the sixteenth century is to move from thematic specificity to generality, avoiding the problems that may arise when letters are too closely identifiable with the writer. Gonzaga's *epistolario*, therefore, is a unique hybrid. Inhabiting a transitional space within the epistolary genre, the *Lettere* move between the specificity of experience that characterized such collections as that of Aretino, and the abstract, generalized framework of later letterbooks, in which the epistolary persona is not necessarily identifiable with the writer, and the letters themselves function as literary and moral models rather than aspire to the appearance of actual correspondence. If, in the tension between the dual tenets of *utilità* and *diletto*, the first quality gradually overshadows the second in sixteenth-century epistolarity on the whole, Gonzaga manages to balance the two, artfully combining a personal narrative with an emphasis on general moral and spiritual guidance. By doing so, she is able to present herself as a valid participant in literary culture, while simultaneously attenuating any criticism that her foray into such public self-construction might have provoked. As we go on to examine the letter collections of Veronica Franco, Isabella Andreini, and Arcangela Tarabotti in part three of this study, we will find similar strategies at work as these writers attempt to promote themselves as writers while also publicizing a still more marginalized female experience.

PART THREE

Epistolary Space and Female Experience

4 The Courtesan's Voice: Veronica Franco's *Lettere familiari*

I. The 'Honest Courtesan'

As the sixteenth century progressed, early modern writers continued to capitalize on the converging trends of epistolary literature and widespread interest in describing the female experience, turning increasingly to manuals and repertories for guidance. On the one hand, popular epistolary narratives such as the *Lettere amorose* of Madonna Celia and those of Girolamo Parabosco began to codify representations of the woman writer as an epistolary character motivated by passion and lovesickness. Models for such fictionalized and generalized female narrators, who fell from grace as they abandoned the feminine ideals of chastity and silence to follow their hearts, abounded.[1] On the other hand, women letter writers themselves did not always subscribe to this characterization. Some replaced it with a different kind of epistolary self-representation, privileging portraits of reason and restraint over unchecked passion, literature over love. Nowhere is the integration – or, perhaps, collision – of the linked arenas of epistolary writing and women's experience more evident than in the *epistolario* of the famous Venetian courtesan, Veronica Franco (1546–91), who published her *Lettere familiari* in 1580.[2]

Franco's text, which combines literary self-promotion with a glimpse of the life of a high-status courtesan, is a distinct departure from the lovelorn female letter writer depicted by Madonna Celia and Parabosco and introduces a new arena of female experience to the realm of epistolary representation. Although love relationships play an important role in Franco's text (as in her life), her letters strive to establish her as a voice of reason, not passion – a Cicero, rather than a Celia – while never discounting her identity as a courtesan. By integrating her own voice into the structure and themes of humanist letter writers, Franco rethinks conventional characterizations of both the courtesan and the female letter writer. Franco's volume further reflects the influence of Aretino, who understood and exploited the power of letters to establish literary position, reward patrons and admirers, and dismiss detractors. The letter collection constituted an opportunity for Franco to increase her own fame, as well as a way to respond to the negative characterizations of the courtesan that circulated in early modern literary culture, despite her 'celebrity' status.[3]

The *cortigiana onesta*, or 'honest courtesan,' negotiated a difficult position as the object of both desire and anxiety.[4] As a new wave of scholarship has increasingly shown, the courtesan trafficked not only in sexual services but also in literary and cultural capital.[5] In addition to her beauty, it was her ability to carry on learned conversation, and indeed to produce her own literary works, that secured her status as a sought after, socially mobile, economically independent figure. A prominent performer in the *ridotto* (salon) culture that was off-limits to respectable women, the courtesan participated in and also inspired cultural production.[6] Yet even a *cortigiana onesta* was defined first and foremost by her sexual function. No matter how intellectually gifted, how sophisticated a conversationalist, she was a sexualized commodity in an economic transaction. Ambiguously situated as both object of and partner in this transaction, her position was further complicated by the peculiar obligation incurred by the courtesan as a result of the patronage of her clients, at once her admirers and the source of her wealth and status.[7]

Because courtesans depended on their reputation for learning as well as their more corporeal gifts to secure their economic stability and advance their status in society, many saw writing as a way to enhance this reputation. Writing had a practical as well as a creative function. As Fiora Bassanese points out, 'literary talent provided a competitive edge in the day-to-day business of marketing the honest courtesan.'[8] Literary recognition of any kind added to a courtesan's cachet, and courtesans, supported by wealthy and powerful patrons, wrote and circulated their compositions in both manuscript and print. Fiammetta Malaspina, Camilla Pisana, and Franceschina Baffo all composed poetry; the renowned *cortigiana onesta* Tullia D'Aragona, backed by a series of influential patrons, published a Neoplatonic dialogue on love as well as a volume of *Rime*. Franco herself, supported by Domenico Venier, published a volume of *Rime* in addition to her *Lettere*, edited a poetry collection, and composed an epic poem (although this went unpublished).⁹ In a sense, the honest courtesan existed as the very embodiment of the cultural pairing of female speech and sexuality we examined in the introduction. By expecting the *cortigiana onesta* to be both learned and sexually accessible, a provider of sexual services as well as literary products, the society that produced and shaped her reinforced a gender ideology that associated women's learning and speech with sexual availability. Her learnedness and her public exercise of voice in the production of literature could be explained and contained within this schema, for the courtesan was already a public figure, a woman who no longer possessed the 'honour' (that is, chastity) that noblewomen were expected to guard so carefully. As a result, she could, at least in theory, express herself more freely in print.

Recent work by Ann Rosalind Jones and Diana Robin has emphasized how the interests of courtesans and printers both coincided and collided in a literary market that was particularly receptive to texts with an erotic charge. If courtesans sought increased status, fame, and authority through print, then printers capitalized on the frisson created by the authors' 'other' profession in order to sell books.[10] Paula Findlen's work on the emergence of pornography in early modern Italy further emphasizes the important connections between the advent of print and the commodification of an erotic culture that had previously been available only to the cultural elite.[11] Texts by courtesans piqued the interest of the same audience that fuelled the success of Aretino's most scandalous works, while also circulating as part of salon culture. In turn, the courtesan's literary works were as integral to her public persona as her sexual practice, and variously underscored her intellect, virtue, or sexual desirability and expertise. They allowed her to create and manipulate her public persona as she wished. Tullia d'Aragona, for example, emphasized her intellectual brilliance over her identity as a courtesan (even obtaining the right to forego, as a poet, the courtesan's yellow veil), while Franco reiterated her sexual authority even as she established herself as a literary figure, combining both aspects of her persona in unique ways.

Although courtesans published poetry and, to a lesser extent, prose works like Tullia D'Aragona's *Dell'infinità d'amore*, Franco was virtually alone among her contemporaries in publishing a book of letters (although many wrote letters privately).[12] Indeed, she was one of only a few authors, male or female, to produce a true volume of 'familiar' letters in the later sixteenth century, when publishers were primarily issuing reprints of already-existing volumes or promoting generic volumes of love letters and didactic writing manuals.[13] Perhaps Franco's counterparts, despite their participation in the 'alternative' feminine economy of prostitution, were hesitant to cross this last threshold between public and private persona. The first-person narrative of the letterbook, as Aretino had so brilliantly shown, held great possibility as a vehicle for self-promotion and literary advancement, but required in return that the writer negotiate the pitfalls of epistolary authorship by establishing authority, demonstrating the utility of his enterprise, and avoiding the suggestion of literary narcissism. It was a delicate balance for any writer and one particularly complicated for women, given the cultural idealization of female restraint. While the courtesan's primary profession located her outside the private, chaste world idealized for gentlewomen, it did not automatically clear the way for her literary aspirations: women's writing inevitably met with resentment from some. What, then, persuaded Franco to undertake such an endeavour, even financing the publication of her letters herself in 1580 (her last such literary effort before the decline of her fortunes and her death in 1591)?[14] Franco's *Lettere familiari* can be read as a work of both literary and professional self-promotion, a final effort to rehabilitate her reputation and revive her clientele in the wake of diminishing tolerance for courtesans in Venice, as well as in light of her damaging Inquisition trial of 1580. The city that had once paraded and celebrated its courtesans as reflections of its glory held them culpable for its misfortune following the plague years of 1575–7, while the accusations of sorcery brought against Franco by her children's tutor had a distinct undertone of hostility to the power and influence she had accrued throughout the city. By highlighting her epistolary relationships with an array of lovers and literary patrons, Franco sought to strengthen her position and status by advertising and reinforcing her social, sexual, and literary connections, expertise, and erudition. More restrained in erotic imagery than her earlier book of *Terze rime*, Franco's letters responded to a changing cultural climate as well as an increasing body of anti-courtesan literature by fashioning a new public image for the courtesan, one that sought association with the authority of classical tradition through the Ciceronian vehicle of the familiar letter.[15] Although still a figure of female sexual power, Franco is also – principally – a dispenser of the kind of wisdom and counsel traditionally reserved for men in the classical tradition and in its humanist evolutions, as Maria Luisa Doglio first noted in her important study of Franco.[16] Seeking literary authority and acceptance, Franco draws not only on classical epistolary tradition but on the growing body of didactic epistolary literature that informed earlier works like Ortensio Lando's *Lettere di molte valorose donne* and the *Lettere della ... donna Lucrezia Gonzaga*, especially epistolary manuals that dictated the proper form for letters according to topic and audience. At the same time, Franco appropriates in her letters the very discourse of commerce that governs her life as a courtesan, adopting an extensive vocabulary of mercantile imagery to describe and define her position as both counsellor and lover. Thus, she creates in her *Lettere* an epistolary persona that combines and conflates traditional aspects of male and female literary and sexual identity and culture. Her epistolary performance of gender prefigures in many ways the more extensive performances enacted in the texts of certain seventeenth-century women writers (for example, Isabella Andreini, discussed in chapter 5).

II. Prostitution, Power, and Patronage

According to some estimates, there were close to 12,000 courtesans in Venice in the sixteenth century, most of them clustered near the Rialto.[17] One traveller to the city, Thomas Coryat, marvelled over these creatures at length, describing the richness of their dress and possessions and the dangerous power of their alluring speech. At once attracted and repelled by the courtesans, Coryat advised other visitors to Venice to turn their eyes away and fortify their ears 'against the attractive inchauntments of their plausible speeches.'[18] His warning evokes at once the strong linkage drawn between female sexuality and speech, and the curious power of the courtesan's voice as an instrument of desire, authority, and anxiety.[19] If the inherent structure of the sexual transaction between courtesan and client was conditioned by the patriarchal society in which it transpired, sex, as Guido Ruggiero remarks, notoriously escapes any rigid schemas of order. The sexual transaction was constructed as an orderly one in which the client retained control by purchasing the courtesan's body, but sexual passion was an unruly emotion that threatened to destabilize that transaction.[20] Moreover, the function of the *cortigiana onesta* as a kind of mirror for her patrons in elite Renaissance society – who saw their intellectual aspirations reflected in her erudition, their social ambitions in their ability to purchase her as a kind of luxury good – created anxiety in the relationship.[21] The courtesan trafficked in illusion as well as sex. As Ruggiero explains, she sold her patrons precisely what they wished to procure:

'the illusion of men being elite, refined lovers; the illusion of men being discriminating in their choice of mistresses; the illusion of men being mannered and intellectual.'[22] Lynn Lawner adds that in constructing the courtesan as his own 'idealized' other, the patrician male expected to retain control over this 'other' self. When the courtesan proved she couldn't be wholly controlled (or rather, when the client found himself ruled by his own disorderly passions), this illusion shattered.[23] The results of such disillusionment could be brutal. Consider, for example, the punishment purportedly inflicted upon the famous courtesan Angela del Moro for rebuffing her lover: according to Lorenzo Venier's infamous account of the incident in his 1531 poem *Il trentuno della Zaffetta*, Angela's assertion of autonomy resulted in her sexual assault by eighty men.[24] The courtesan's power over the passions of her clients may help to explain such antagonism towards courtesans, even on the part of the men who frequented them.

Over the course of her career as a courtesan, Franco negotiated this complicated position and navigated the resulting alliances and enmities that it engendered. She knew periods of success and wealth as well as times of personal trial and economic hardship. The years in which she was involved with the influential literary circle of Domenico Venier, the leader of one of Venice's most well-known literary salons and a supporter of several women writers including Tullia D'Aragona and Moderata Fonte, were her most productive and were fundamental in establishing her literary persona.[25] During this period, Franco engaged with Venice's literary elite, circulating her poetry and with it her sexualized image as a courtesan-writer. She published a collection of dialogic poems in which, using the structure of the *capitolo*, she brilliantly established herself as a literary figure capable of jousting with the best of Venier's literary set, and created an erotic poetic voice that still resounds with readers today.[26] Franco was also the editor of at least one poetic anthology, reflecting her immersion in a salon culture that encouraged and promoted what has been termed the 'poetics of group identity' by producing and publishing collective volumes of verse and letters, essentially auto-promoting its members as both creators and arbiters of culture.[27]

By the time her *Lettere familiari* were printed in 1580, Franco had been married and separated, raised several children, and achieved considerable recognition both as a courtesan and as a writer.[28] At the peak of her career, Franco was visited by Henri III of Valois on his way from Poland to be crowned King of France – a great honour, though one that went unpublicized until Franco herself pointedly described the encounter in her *Lettere*. The great essayist Montaigne even mentioned Franco's *epistolario* in his *Journal de voyage en Italie,* making a note that: 'Le lundy a souper, 6 de novembre, la signora Veronica Franco, gentifemme venitienne, envoia vers lui pour lui presenter un petit livre de lettres qu'elle a composé' ('Monday 6 November, at dinnertime, the Venetian lady signora Veronica Franco presented him with a little book of letters composed by her').[29] Franco herself had sent him the volume, a sure clue that the letters were part of a plan for marketing herself as a literary figure and courtesan of the highest stature.

Despite her efforts at self-promotion, however, the publication of Franco's letters coincided with the beginning of her fall from grace as an elite, successful *cortigiana onesta*. As noted above, a city scarred by recent plague increasingly targeted marginal figures like the courtesan as scapegoats for its tribulations, while the presence of the Inquisition in Venice exerted a sobering force on the population. It seemed the citizens of La Serenissima had become more willing to heed Coryat's warning that 'such uncleanesse should be an occasion to draw down upon them God's curses and vengeance from heaven …'[30] Franco had been harshly ridiculed in verse by her enemies beginning much earlier, most notably as the target of a series of dialect poems by Maffio Venier, against which she defended herself in both the *Rime* and the *Lettere*.[31] In 1580 – the year in which her letters were published – such attacks took a more ominous turn when Ridolfo Vannitelli, the tutor of one of Franco's sons, accused her of performing heretical incantations in an effort to retrieve lost objects. Transcripts of the Inquisition's preliminary examination suggest that Vannitelli was motivated by deep personal resentment. Not only did he denounce Franco as a 'fattucchiera puttana pubblica' ('witch and a public whore') who never attended mass, but, threatened by the position Franco had achieved through her carefully chosen friendships, he complained '… ha ella troppo grande aiuto in questa città, et è favorita da molti, dai quali vorrebbe esser odiata' ('… she has too much support in this city, and is favoured by many who ought to despise her').[32] Serving as her own defence, Franco proved as capable in the courtroom as she was with the pen, and after two separate hearings her trial was suspended and she was released without being made to abjure. Despite her escape from the Inquisition, however, the event marked a turning point in her life. Her luck would soon change for the worse, likely, at least in part, as a result of the damage to her reputation caused by the trial. After a ten year period characterized by economic comfort, literary production, and a certain social prestige, Franco would find herself struggling to survive on a meagre annual income and living in much reduced circumstances in a neighbourhood that housed some of Venice's poorest prostitutes. When she died on 22 July 1591 after a month of illness, Franco was forty-five years old. She had published no works since her volume of *Lettere familiari*.

III. The Courtesan as Epistolary Category

Hostility towards the courtesan like that faced by Franco was not a new phenomenon. Indeed, it played a prominent role in literary works by Aretino, Erasmus, Speroni, and others.[33] Such works targeted the courtesan as a symbol of Venice's social and moral decay, singling out her presumed avarice and promiscuity. Many also reflected a deep anxiety about the writers' own relationship to patronage, which they deflected onto the courtesan.[34] Such a parallelism lies at the heart, for example, of Aretino's satirical representation of the Roman court in his *La Cortigiana*. In his *Sei giornate*, too, the figure of the prostitute serves as a vehicle for a broad critique of the social, moral, and religious corruption of Venetian society, as reflected in Antonia's and Nanna's conclusion that prostitution is the least hypocritical option for women. Unlike the nun or the wife, Antonia explains, the prostitute betrays no insitution or vows but rather 'fa come un soldato che è pagato per far male' ('does as a soldier who is paid to do ill').[35] While the prostitute served as a convenient tool for such social commentary, however, the honest courtesan's participation in culture and her desire for literary recognition sparked antagonism among these same writers. Hence the change in tone when Aretino's Nanna contrasts courtesans with prostitutes in the *Sei giornate*, disdainfully remarking that Venetians prefer 'la lingua melata' ('honeyed tongue') of the common prostitute to '[la lingua] addottorata' ('learned tongue') of the *cortigiana onesta*, the latter a false and less desirable version of the former.[36] Were she a man, Nanna adds, she would far rather hold in her arms 'una robba sfoggiata' ('a rotten mess') than 'messer Dante' himself.[37] The courtesan's transgressive combination of erudition and sexuality is disorienting to such narrators, male or female.

In a number of mid-sixteenth century *epistolari* the courtesan emerges as a kind of epistolary category unto herself, a generic type satirized by letter writers for her social and cultural pretensions, her avarice, and her venality. Letter collections such as those of Andrea Calmo, Nicolò Franco, and Aretino himself include missives to courtesans real and imagined that range from exaggerated flattery to sexual double entendre and denunciation; while in the early seventeenth century, women writers themselves, such as Isabella Andreini and Margherita Costa, would also target courtesans in their epistolary collections. Aretino's celebrated first volume of *Lettere* contains a letter to Angela del Moro, la 'Zaffetta' who, as we saw above, was the subject of Lorenzo Venier's obscene poem. Framed as a flattering letter intended to differentiate Angela from other courtesans, Aretino's composition actually serves to promote typical negative characterizations of courtesans. So adept is Angela at her profession, so straightforward in her greed, that her clients are barely aware of all they spend on her: 'Voi non essercitate l'astuzia, anima de l'arte cortigiana, col mezzo dei tradimenti, ma con sí fatta destrezza che chi spende giura d'avanzare' ('You don't exercise cunning, the heart of the courtesan's art, through betrayal, but with such dexterity that he who loses would swear he had gained').[38] Angela takes care not to make her lovers jealous, takes their money without leaving them penniless, and is largely free of the vices of envy, gossip, and lying; in all these virtues, Aretino notes, she differs from the typical courtesan.[39]

Thus, Aretino's 'praise' of Angela in distinguishing her as unique serves as a vehicle for condemning courtesans in general as mercenary, duplicitous, and untrustworthy. Even Angela, finally, is deemed praiseworthy for her ability to simulate honesty despite her profession, not for her honesty itself, emphasizing the performative nature of the courtesan's profession. 'Io vi do la palma,' Aretino writes, '... poiché voi più ch'altra avete saputo porre al volto de la lascivia la mascara de l'onestade' ('I praise you ... because, more than anyone else, you know how to make lust masquerade as respectability').[40] A letter to the lovely 'Franceschina' in Aretino's Book IV reiterates the courtesan's duplicitous nature, comparing her to a refreshing drink that seems sweet but soon proves bitter and poisonous, while a letter to a certain 'Veneranda' derides her for withholding her sexual favours.[41] A missive addressed to Zufolina, finally, a Pistoian courtesan at the French court, plays on fears about the courtesan's transgressive sexuality, describing her as a hermaphrodite who changes her sex according to the situation: 'Certo che la natura vi ha in modo composta in l'utriousque sesso, che in uno istante vi dimostrate maschio e in un subito femina' ('Clearly nature has made you both sexes, for in one instant you are male and then you are suddenly female').[42] Here the hermaphrodite creates anxiety, but courtesans themselves capitalized on the erotic charge of their liminal gender status, for example by dressing in men's clothes, as evidenced in costume books like Cesare Vecellio's *Degli habiti antichi et moderni* (1590). Frequently, moreover, they found themselves the targets of sumptuary laws that sought to prevent them from passing for respectable women.[43] The courtesan's ability to simulate the appearance and characteristics of different genders and classes was among her most alluring and most threatening qualities. Zufolina challenges the physical boundaries of gender, dressing sometimes as a man and sometimes as a woman, but it is, according to Aretino, her combination of female speech with male comportment that makes her a 'wolf that devours both hens and roosters'; that is, a danger to both sexes in equal measure. Aretino's description of the hermaphroditic courtesan who combines female speech with male behaviour could be aptly applied to the Franco of the *Lettere familiari*, who constructs herself as a voice of female authority in a male context, appropriating and manipulating the conventions of male literary tradition through a female lens.

Perhaps the most extensive epistolary invocation of the courtesan comes in Andrea Calmo's four books of letters written in Venetian dialect and published in the period from 1547 to 1566. Calmo was a semiprofessional actor known for his portrayals of the *commedia dell'arte* character Pantalone, the old man who chases young women, and his stage persona is reflected in the fictional compositions included in his opus. Book IV of Calmo's letters is composed entirely of letters to women, most of whom were probably courtesans, that play on the Pantalone/young woman trope.[44] While playful in tone, many of these letters target the greed, duplicity, and social pretensions of the courtesan attacked in other literary genres (while also satirizing the 'old man' writer himself). A letter to a certain 'Brunela,' for example, castigates her as 'piena de lazzi, de ingani, e de trapole' ('full of deceits, tricks, and traps'), prone to stealing her clients' money as they sleep.[45] Their relationship, Calmo complains, has left him so poor that he is reduced to pleading with his former lover to hire him as her servant. Another letter mocks 'Balzana' for thinking she can improve her station through her alliances with important men, while still another woos 'Lucida' with an exaggerated account of the author's possessions – again appealing to the courtesan's 'natural' avarice.[46] Even flattering letters extolling the beauty or culture of particular courtesans, such as an elegy of Madonna Vitruvia detailing every aspect of her physical perfection, assume a parodic tone in the exaggerated rhetoric of their praise.[47] Whether condemnatory or adulatory, the letters addressed by

Calmo to courtesans reflect the diffusion of the epistolary category of 'the courtesan' in sixteenth-century letters. Even Parabosco's *Lettere amorose*, which were comprised primarily of pseudo-epistolary compositions devoid of the recipients' names, included one letter to a specific *destinataria*, the courtesan Franchescina Baffo.[48]

In addition to missives addressed to courtesans, some letter collections included the 'responses' of the courtesans themselves, composed by the male author of the *epistolario*, recalling the Landian ventriloquism of the *Lettere di molte valorose donne* described in chapter 2. Nicolò Franco's *Pistole Volgari* (1542), for example, include a lengthy, fictitious letter addressed to 'le puttane'; that is, to prostitutes in general. In it, he emphasizes the power enjoyed by these 'potentissime ... Madone' and effects to laud them for having fled patriarchal authority to seek autonomy.[49] Of course, Venetian perceptions of courtesans tended rather to cast them in the opposite light: like courtiers, courtesans, too, were considered slaves to the will of their *padroni* and competitors for their favours.[50] In spite of his ostensible admiration, Nicolò takes a mocking approach to his *destinatarie*, 'praising' them by opposing them to a standard model of female virtue, the Roman Lucrezia, whose steadfast chastity, Nicolò writes, made her a 'mostro de la natura.'[51] His letter to 'le puttane' is followed by a response issued by this collective, generic *destinataria* that acknowledges receipt of his letter and expresses the desire to demonstrate that there are educated women among their number. It is a rare choral representation of the prostitute; yet, it is Nicolò's voice that informs the letter, and the prostitutes' 'self'-presentation as serious epistolary interlocutors is undermined by the subtext of mockery and negative stereotypes that pervades even their 'own' response. Their preoccupation with money, for example, is echoed in their qualification that they welcome Nicolò's epistolary advances only if his letter is a 'messaggiera del soldo,' a portent of economic gain. The conclusion to their missive, moreover, invokes the potential power they wield over their clients' bodies and reflects a (male) anxiety about this power as they threaten, 'Come a chi ne dona pochi denari, noi doniamo del mal francioso assai' ('As for him who rewards us too meagerly, we will return the favour with plenty of *mal francioso* [syphilis]').[52] Vague fears of the courtesan's hold over the male body are thus given form as the courtesans specify the ill they can inflict upon those who do not reimburse them properly for their services. Throughout Nicolò's own letter and the prostitutes' imagined reply, it is the male writer who controls the epistolary exchange, and the women who are subject to the negative characterization imposed upon them.

Veronica Franco responds to these epistolary representations in her *Lettere familiari*, draining the familiar epistolary satires of power by presenting the courtesan in a new key. The courtesan to whom Aretino and Calmo addressed their letters, and in whose voice Nicolò Franco wrote, was a male construction of a female 'type,' and the epistolary exchange that was initiated in such letter collections was, like the sexual transaction, inherently conditioned by the goals and biases of the male partner. By publishing her own letters, Franco replaced this male-constructed version of the courtesan's epistolary voice with one very much at odds with male depictions of the courtesan in any genre, and of which she could retain full control.[53] Offering advice to male correspondents struggling with despair, jealousy, or ill fortune, Franco locates herself in the authoritative position of moral counsellor. She frequently explains that her intention is to repay her correspondent for some kindness or favour done her, thus cancelling any debt she feels lies between them and emphasizing her innate honesty. Like the *epistolari* of other women writers, most notably Arcangela Tarabotti (discussed in chapter 6), several of Franco's letters address literary projects, reinforcing the image she wishes to project of herself as a literary figure, or defend her against the calumny of her enemies. In one instance, finally, she turns her focus to the concerns of women in particular. Throughout the letters, Franco does not conceal her identity as a courtesan, but she is careful to show that she is never driven by merely economic concerns. Rather, she is drawn to virtue rather than wealth, literary works rather than words, and offended by idle flattery and the assumption that she can be had by the highest bidder. Franco seeks to neutralize any suggestion that she is in some way indebted to her patrons by 'repaying' them – and her public – with a display of literary and moral virtue in her letters. At the same time, she reaps the benefit of her public association with them, as, for example, in her commemoration of her encounter with Henri III, the dedication of her book to Cardinal Luigi II D'Este, or her evocation of Tintoretto's portrait of her.[54]

IV. Franco's *Lettere familiari*

If Franco's *Lettere familiari* are a performance of literary virtue and sexual authority, a dual exercise in self-promotion and self-defence, their first concern is to present the public with an alternative to the negative imagery of the courtesan offered by texts like Aretino's *La cortigiana*, Lorenzo Venier's *Il Trentuno della Zaffetta*, and contemporary epistolary collections, while showcasing the author's exceptional talents. Accordingly, Franco takes pains throughout her letters both to refute general charges of greed and moral corruption, and to publicize her own literary activity, emphasizing her participation in the sphere of letters as an integral part of her activity as a courtesan. Letters XXXII and XL, for example, address the anthology she was assembling in honour of Estor Martinengo, a Venetian military hero. Letters XLI, XLVIII, and XLIX, probably meant for Domenico Venier, request aid with revisions, the collaboration with so influential a figure validating rather than diminishing her work. Franco also highlights her own desirability as a sexual and romantic partner, but focuses primarily on her own honourable conduct as an equal partner in this arena. Her reasoned and practical treatment of the love relationship – a topic that enjoyed considerable popularity in epistolary form well into the seventeenth century – has little in common with that of the love-struck Madonna Celia, for example, nor with Parabosco's female letter writers. Accurately assessing the direction increasingly taken by epistolary texts towards generic model letters and, increasingly, love letters, Franco situates her unconventional epistolary voice within a conventional epistolary framework that draws not only on the classical sources that scholars have rightly emphasized, but also on a growing body of contemporary letter-writing manuals. Influenced by didactic texts like Miniatore's *Formulario*, Sansovino's *Secretario*, and Toscanella's handbooks for the study of classical and humanist letters, Franco combines her unique form of self-fashioning with a willingness and capacity to demonstrate her skills within mainstream literary forms.[55] In her *Rime*, Franco vowed to engage her opponent with whatever literary weapon he chose, whether Tuscan or Venetian dialect, high or comic verse.[56] In the epistolary realm, too, she is determined to compete with men in their own territory and with their own literary instruments.

The influence of didactic epistolary texts is apparent throughout Franco's *Lettere*. The subjects she chooses to address are, with some exceptions, common to letterbooks of the period, from letters of thanks and congratulations to consolatory letters, love letters, and 'lettere di complimento.' Repertory texts like Garimberto's *Concetti* (utilized in the *Lettere* of Lucrezia Gonzaga) offered extensive examples of phrases of gratitude or condolence, while Sansovino's *Secretario* and similar texts emphasized the social implications of epistolary exchange and the proper rules to follow in composing a letter. Franco's opening compositions, two sonnets addressed to Henri III of Valois, for example, follow many of the conventions laid out in such manuals. These were important compositions for Franco. Documenting the king's visit to her in 1574, they functioned as the book's 'official' opening following the dedication to Luigi II D'Este, and validated Franco's own social position and prestige as a courtesan singled out by a king. Of the collection's fifty-two components, the letter to Henri is one of only three in which the recipient is explicitly named (the others are Cardinal D'Este and Tintoretto), and with it Franco communicates two things to her readers. First, she makes it clear that she will neither hide nor apologize for her profession, but, rather, exploit it for creative inspiration as well as personal and literary recognition. Second, she places herself in illustrious company by highlighting her relationship with royalty, aware that the king's glory will not only redound to her in the eyes of her public, it will also lend authority to her writings. Her letter to Henri closely follows standard protocol for addressing royalty, as described in many epistolary manuals. Sansovino's *Secretario* offered detailed instructions for the opening and closing salutations of such missives, advising that a letter to the King of France be addressed 'all' Invittissimo & Cristianissimo … Re di Francia' and signed 'di Vostra Altezza divotissimo et umilissimo servo …' (other monarchs were to be addressed with slightly different titles, for example the 'Re Cattolico di Spagna …').[57] Collections like Girolamo Ruscelli's *Lettere di principi* and Stefano Guazzo's *epistolario* included model letters to Henri III in specific; addressed, respectively, to the 'invitissimo et cristianissimo Sire' and the 'Cristianissimo Re di Francia,' suggesting that Franco was not alone in considering a letter to the king of France a suitable mode of displaying lofty connections.[58] Franco follows Sansovino's prescription in her own letter, addressing herself to the 'invittissimo e cristianissimo re Enrico III di Francia e I di Polonia' – heeding his further advice to list all relevant titles of one's correspondent – and signs herself, as he suggests, 'umilissima et divotissima serva della Maestà Vostra.' Similarly, she follows the advice of various epistolary manuals for other forms of subscription in other letters, signing herself, for example, 'vostra amorevol quanto sorella' or 'vostra affezionattisma servitrice' – in keeping with appropriate formulas listed in Giovanni Antonio Taglienti's *Componimento di parlamento* – and wishing her correspondents good health and long life, as advised by Sansovino.[59]

If the structure of Franco's letter to Henri III follows the protocol advised by male letter writers, the body of it embraces new territory in the connection it traces between literary and sexual exchange, between courtesan and king. Franco's reference to Henri's visit serves as both commemoration of the great honour that his recognition has conferred upon her, and a reminder of the unequal nature of the sexual transaction, rendered particularly complex by the network of gratitude and obligation created by this specific visit. Although Franco has provided a service to the king in the form of her body and her company, his greater social status has left her in the position of one who must repay a debt, and this she undertakes to do through her literary production. Again following the prescriptions of didactic manuals, Franco insists she is unable to reciprocate the great honour done her by the King's royal visit. That he should have taken her portrait with him when he left, moreover, is an exchange described by Franco as 'cambio per me troppo aventuroso e felice' ('an exchange for me too fortunate').[60] Sansovino's *Secretario*, along with other similar texts, offered detailed instructions on composing letters of thanks for gifts or favours. These included acknowledging the enormity of the favour and the recipient's unworthiness in comparison, along with his (or her) desire to repay the favour in kind.[61] Accordingly, Franco laments that she is unable to properly respond: 'qual cosa può nascer da me che sia degna della suprema altezza dell'animo suo celeste?' ('what could I possibly produce that would be worthy of the greatness of your celestial self?').[62] Yet despite her requisite declarations of unworthiness (common to epistolary writers of either gender), Franco devotes the remainder of her letter and the two sonnets that accompany it to reestablishing an equilibrium with Henri through her writing: her compositions are offered as the 'disegno ... della mia gratitudine' ('the representation ... of my gratitude'), the material representation of Franco's thanks and the repayment of the honour he has done her.[63] Franco's sonnets to Henri celebrating their encounter thus fulfil an obligation. Although each sonnet acknowledges the honour of the king's visit, it is Franco who figures most prominently, evoked through the poetic reconstruction of the moment in which she gives Henri the gift of her portrait. The first sonnet closes by evoking the moment in which Henri took possession of her image: 'l'imagin mia di smalt' e di colore / prese al partir con grat'animo aperto'; ('my image crafted in colored enamel / he gratefully took away with him') while the second opens by describing the verisimilitude of the portrait, the 'scolpito e colorato aspetto, / in cui 'l mio vivo e natural s'intende' ('sculpted and vivid likeness, / that represents my real and true self').[64] Each sonnet emphasizes the dichotomy between self and image, and subsumes any commercial aspect of the encounter under the guise of the 'gift' Franco makes of her company. Although Franco liberally engages Henri in flattery, calling the transaction that has occurred between them 'an exchange for me too fortunate,' she makes herself the king's co-protagonist in these three compositions. With the gift of her portrait, and of her poetry, Franco weaves together the commerce of sex, art, and literature, and allows the principle of exchange to cancel her debt.

Not only does Franco reference epistolary manuals in her *Lettere familiari*, she also incorporates into her letters the themes of a growing prescriptive literature that increasingly sought to define and regulate the roles of both men and women in the Renaissance household. Treatises like Lodovico Dolce's *De la institution delle donne*, Juan Luis Vives' *De Institutione Feminae Christianae*, and Leon Battista Alberti's *Libri della famiglia* approached such problems quite seriously, while epistolary texts like Lando's *Lettere di molte valorose donne* and Aretino's own *Lettere* took more flexible, sometimes satirical, approaches to the subject. Lando's letters played a kind of pseudo-didactic role in this regard, as we saw in chapter 2, for example, instructing women how to be good wives and household managers, dispensing medical advice for common ailments, and addressing letters to servants (even as they advanced a social and cultural critique). Aretino's own satirical response to prescriptive literature is evident in his *Ragionamento,* in which Nanna describes the 'three states' of women (wife, prostitute, nun) – ultimately preferring prostitution – and in his own letters addressed to servants, such as that written to the maladroit Lucietta, who flees his household after having broken an exaggerated series of objects.[65]

Franco, too, evokes these and other themes throughout her own *Lettere*. The advice she offers ranges from governing servants to navigating the trials of ill fortune, curing melancholy, or gaining her love through admirable deeds. In some cases, her advice is aimed at women in particular, as when she congratulates a friend who has recently given birth. Her evocation here of the 'molestie della gravidanza' (pregnancy problems) and the 'fatiche e le doglie' ('difficulty and pain') of giving birth rewrite typical congratulatory missives found in epistolary manuals that tend rather to be addressed to the new father who has gained an heir,[66] and has new resonance in its direct address to the mother from one who has been in her position. A famous letter discouraging a friend from setting her daughter on the path of prostitution, discussed in detail further on, introduces an entirely new type of counsel to the epistolary genre – the first-person account of the problems faced by the sex worker – and stands in stark contrast to the satirical speeches of Aretino's Nanna. Franco's evocation of prescriptive literature, with its growing focus on domestic economy, can best be seen, however, in letter xv, in which she evokes in sober tones the semi-serious letters of Aretino and Lando to their hired help, advising a male correspondent on how to govern servants. Here, she assumes the role played by male writers like Alberti, for example, who addressed the management of the home at length in his *Libri della famiglia*. Even as she acknowledges that her friend is already 'experienced in the economy of the household,' Franco advises him with the authority of experience, as one head of household to another – a clear indication of her different status and role from that of a married woman, who governed her servants but reported to her husband.[67] Franco's advice to adopt a balance between severity and indulgence when dealing with servants is offered in the moderate register that is typical of all her letters, whether addressing the home, fortune, or matters of love (and indeed, characteristic of Venetian humanism, as Margaret King has shown).[68] Similarly, a letter regarding a mutual friend suffering from 'l'angoscioso pensiero' ('anguished thoughts') urges calmness and moderation over passion and turbulence.

Recasting the kind of medical counsel that abounded in popular manuals and was given epistolary form in Lando's *Valorose donne*, Franco advises setting aside all 'beveraggi medicinali' ('medicinal potions') that only contribute to the 'violentissime perturbazioni dell'animo' ('the violent disturbances of the soul') and dispensing with the apothecary altogether.[69] The trials of the soul must run their natural course until, exhausted, the soul can return to its customary tranquility. The letter melds together practical advice with philosophical counsel, Franco performing both functions. In closing, Franco excuses herself for appearing to challenge her friend's authority in such matters, but insists that it is she, not he, who understands the true nature of the patient's indisposition. Not just a courtesan, then, Franco is both a household manager and a student of the soul.

Franco continues to position herself throughout the letters as a figure of authority, addressing friends suffering from the loss of a loved one or a change in fortunes, favoured topics for sixteenth-century letter collections. Consolatory letters were a favourite instrument of humanist writers, who used them to demonstrate their capacity for moral and spiritual counsel as well as their mastery of an important literary form. Bembo approached the genre by recalling the excellent qualities of the deceased, while Guazzo employed conventional tropes regarding the inevitability of death.⁷⁰ Chiara Matraini, who published a book of letters not long after Franco, probably also with the intent of rehabilitating her reputation, penned consolatory letters urging bereaved mothers and wives to be moderate in their grief and trust in God's will.⁷¹ Sansovino's *Secretario* lists a number of 'capi della consolazione' ('types of consolatory letters') a writer might address, including consolation for death, illness, loss of property or friends, prison, exile, and poverty; while the *Concetti* offer a wide selection of ready phrases for such occasions.⁷² Battista Ceci's *Compendio* describes exactly how to console someone in these events. For a lost thing, one should remind the person that they will find another object of equal or greater value, for a lost loved one, they ought to meditate on the necessity of death and the trials of life.⁷³ In letters like these, Franco again assumes the humanist role of counsellor, and continues to be guided by epistolary manuals. Her efforts in this arena, however, were more complex, requiring not only that she transcend her sex to adopt this role but also that she accomplish this without negating her profession. Significantly, Franco employs the very language of that profession in order to do so, applying the imagery of the economic transaction to the trope of the consolatory letter (and indeed to most of her letters). The same concern for maintaining a balance between debt and obligation displayed in her letter to Henri III, for example, together with the commercial imagery that emerges in her letters on melancholy or on household governance (where she speaks of profit and loss), are present here, too.⁷⁴

In a letter written to a friend facing economic disaster, Franco uses the language of debt as she attempts to establish herself as a steady, stern adviser to her *destinatario*. Skillfully overturning the schema of patriarchal authority, Franco offers advice to a male friend who has once done the same for her:

> E perché, in occasione che anco io, secondo l'uso del mondo, sono stata assai travagliata, v'ho trovato prontissimo a consolarmi con le vostre efficaci ragioni... non debbo mancar di far con voi questo medesimo officio di consolarvi nelle vostre sciagure ...⁷⁵

> And since I, too, as is the way of the world, have had my share of troubles, and found you more than ready to console me with your reasonable advice ... I must not fail to perform this same service for you by comforting you in your adversity ...

Repaying her friend for his past advice to her, while at the same time drawing a parallel between his current state and her own past troubles, Franco erases her debt to him and establishes a parity between them. If the moral and literary support Franco proposes is based on the reciprocal exchange of counsel (which Franco terms 'virtú'), however, the exchange is described in overtly economic terms:

> ... fate conto che, nel pagarvi il mio debito io venga a restituirvi quella propria moneta a punto che voi m'avete dato: tal è ricambio della virtú, che s'attegna non pur in similitudine, ma in forma d'un medesimo modo.[76]

> ... understand that, in paying back my debt to you, I am making restitution with the very same coin which you gave to me; such is the repayment of virtue to which I aspire not just through simile, but in the very same mode.

Not only is the moral support of a friend a display of virtue that requires restitution, but also that restitution is envisioned in an explicitly monetary framework. This imagery is echoed elsewhere in the collection, in a letter regarding the kindness of another friend, again characterized as a debt Franco would like to repay. Her words are similarly placed in a commercial framework as she expresses a 'pronto desiderio di pagare quanto più conosco il creditore apparecchiato non pur a farmi ogni commodità di esborsamento, ma a rimettermi tutto 'l credito ancora' ('a ready wish to [re]pay, strengthened by the knowledge that the lender is prepared not only to lend me any sum, but even to extend me full credit').[77]

In the case of Letter IV, it is significant that Franco's intention to repay her friend with his own coin means repaying him with his own words. Franco writes, 'vi parlerò con le vostre parole e vi discorrerò col vostro stesso discorso' ('I'll speak to you with your words and reason with you using your own reasoning'), echoing her readiness in the *Rime* to respond to her critic in the language of his choosing.[78] Although Franco suggests that the knowledge she possesses derives from her correspondent, her discourse is necessarily different as a result of the fact that she, a woman, is proposing it. Jones' discussion of the concept of poetic negotiation, discussed in chapter 2, is useful here. As Jones explains in her study of the Renaissance love lyric, even when writing within the parameters of hegemonic literary discourse, women exerted a destabilizing force with regard to gender conventions.[79] Thus, even as Franco acknowledges a debt she feels she has incurred towards her correspondent, she demonstrates that she has absorbed and reformulated his advice to her, and can advise him from a position of equal moral footing.

The destabilization inherent in Franco's appropriation of a male discourse of consolation is evident in the way she reworks rhetorical structures from a female standpoint in the same letter. To convince her friend of his own good fortune in life, Franco creates a scale of fortune, establishing a series of positive/negative oppositions that increase in force. The hierarchy she sketches recalls, in several aspects, one proposed in a handbook for the study of Cicero's familiar letters by Toscanella. There, Toscanella uses a kind of graph to demonstrate how to broach the subject of failing or improving health: one begins by describing the ailment, then its qualities, followed by the sex, age, and social status of the victim, his degree of learnedness, and the role of fortune in the vicissitudes of life.[80] Similarly, Franco's consolatory letter first identifies her friend's problem (a reversal of fortune), then describes his social status (high), sex (male) and degree of wealth (sufficient), and finally reminds him of mankind's common subjection to the ups and downs of Fortune.[81] Franco's take on the ladder of Fortune, however, has a distinctly gendered element, her identification of her correspondent as a man a pointed bite. At the bottom of the scale, Franco explains, he is lucky to have been born a man and not a beast, but this good fortune is closely followed by his having been born a man and not a woman:

> ... ringraziate la bontà divina ... che, potendovi far nascer della più immonda e delle più vil specie di tutte le bestie, v'abbia fatto nascer nella perfettissima umana, e di questa v'abbia attribuito il sesso del maschio e non, sí come a me, quel della femina ...[82]

> ... thank God ... that, although He might have generated you from the lowest species of all beasts, He allowed you to be born into the most perfect human species, and within this species he made you a man and not, as in my case, a woman.

If Franco is, as she asserts, only returning the counsel offered her by her friend, one wonders how he might have originally constructed this scale to console her. By inserting her own status as a woman into this rhetorical scale as a contrast to her male friend's biological good fortune, Franco calls attention to the gendered inequalities of the social structure.

On Franco's ladder of fortune, however, gender is followed by an element Franco considers of still more importance – and in which she can participate – that is, citizenship. Franco reminds her interlocutor how fortunate he is to belong to a city like Venice, which she describes in distinctly feminine terms:

> ... una città non barbara, non serva, ma gentile, e non pur libera ma signora del mare e della più bella parte dell'Europa. Città veramente donzella immacolata e inviolata, senza macchia d'ingiustizia, e non mai offesa in se stessa da forza nemica per incendio di guerra né per combustion di mondo ...[83]

> ... not a barbarian or subservient city, but a noble one, and not only free, but mistress of the sea and of the most beautiful part of Europe. A city that is truly an immaculate maiden, unstained by injustice, and never offended by enemy force through the fire of war or the trials of the world ...

While Franco's evocation of Venice as an immaculate maiden, innately just and physically unsullied by the assaults on her by foreign powers, is undoubtedly linked to her own identity as a *cortigiana onesta*, this kind of imagery was widespread in the civic mythology of Venice and adopted by both male and female writers.[84] Moderata Fonte, for example, seems to echo Franco in her *Merito delle donne* when she emphasizes Venice's unique position as an inviolable fortress protected by the boundaries of the sea. For Fonte, the sea repels Venice's enemies but also creates a bond among its citizens, all of whom must navigate its waterways. Like Franco's, Fonte's exaltation of Venice as a uniquely just city is complicated by her concurrent evocation of the real limitations placed on women, but the desire to claim the rights of citizenship in such a city is central to the self-fashioning of both women.[85] Just as significant as Fonte's elegy of Venice as a free and just city, however, is her admiration for its powerful position as a centre of commerce. She is quick to note, for example, that '[q]ui corre il denaro più che in altro luogo' ('[t]here is more money here than anywhere else').[86] If the exaltation of the city functions as a way for the writer to talk about herself and assert her independence in a socially acceptable metaphoric system, Venice's economic power, described by Fonte, has added weight for Franco. The parallels Franco sketches acquire significance not only in terms of moral worth (she, like Venice, remains pure in the face of challenges to her honour), but also with regard to commerce. Venice is glorious and powerful both as a result of, and in spite of, its reliance on commerce; so, too, the courtesan has a paradoxical relationship to her own commercial function.

Significantly, given the stereotypes that circulated about avaricious courtesans, it is money that wields the most power in the strata of good fortune Franco elaborates in Letter IV. Money has a central, practical importance for Franco, for whom economic security was a very real preoccupation, but she protects herself from the stigma of greed by characterizing that importance as a necessary product of living in a money-corrupted society. She admonishes her friend:

> Vi mancano forse le ricchezze? Guardate di quanto poco sia contenta la natura a conoscere quanto vi sopravanza ... E se non vi par d'aver tanto che basti all'usanza del mondo corrotto dal soverchio uso, considerate quanto meno potreste avere e quanto potreste star peggio ...[87]

> Perhaps you don't have enough money? Look at how little nature needs and recognize how much you have ... And if you don't think you have enough for a world corrupted by excess, consider how much less you might have and how much worse off you might be ...

The resignation to one's destiny urged by Franco in these lines is a topos that resonates with new meaning in the explicitly monetary context in which it is placed. In rejecting the pursuit of ever-greater wealth, moreover, Franco was, of course, countering the label of avarice pinned on the courtesan by literary tradition and by epistolary works like the letters of Calmo and Aretino in particular. Her advice to her friend, in fact, culminates in the observation that true wealth is measured not in money but in virtue:

> ... la vera ricchezza consiste nella tranquillità della mente e nel contentarsi; ed il contentarsi dell'anima nostra non è altro che il possesso della virtú, la quale grandemente si conosce nelle sue operazioni, che hanno forza, contro ogni nemico sforzo di contraria fortuna, a render l'uomo felice.[88]

> ... true wealth consists in tranquility of mind and contentment, and our soul's contentment is nothing but the possession of virtue, which is known through its actions, which stand against all aggression of ill fortune to make man happy.

In contrast to depictions of the courtesan like those offered by Aretino, Calmo, Lorenzo and Maffio Venier, and others, Franco demonstrates her integrity here by valuing virtue over money. It is she, the courtesan, who understands that true happiness transcends material wealth. While Franco rejects money as something that can lead to imbalance and excess, the recurrence of the economic metaphor in her work attests to the particular importance of money as a concern for her. This dual rapport is a challenging course for Franco to negotiate in her letters.

As she is mindful in letter IV to avoid appearing fond of money for its own sake, so in several other letters Franco pays close attention to the way she approaches the issue of money, particularly where matters of love are concerned. The eighteenth letter of the collection, for example, seems designed to illustrate the writer's strong sense of (monetary) fairness and (moral) equality by underscoring her determination to accept only that payment which is rightfully due her – again offering an alternative portrait of the courtesan to that presented by many male writers. Rather than accept the gifts of a hopeful lover, Franco immediately establishes that she is emotionally and physically unavailable, but comforts her suitor by stressing the sincerity of her rejection. She could have easily handled the situation in a much less honourable manner, had she chosen to do so:

> Poich'io non posso ricambiarvi con l'egual corrispondenza di quell'amore che voi fate professione di portarmi, avendo già collocato il mio pensiero altrove ... vi sarò almeno grata e cortese nel cercar di giovarvi col discoprimento di quella verità, la quale, mentre io, tacendola con mio beneficio, potrei celarla ...[89]

> Since I can't return the love you profess for me in equal measure, having already focused my attention on another ... I will be at least gracious and courteous in trying to help you by telling you the truth, even though I could conceal it for my own benefit ...

Rigorously honest, Franco refuses to profit from her suitor's affections when she knows her own are already spoken for, and in this she openly challenges the stereotype of the mercenary courtesan: 'Avrei potuto, usando l'artificio dell'adulazione ... imprimervi nell'opinione del falso, per valermi ... di voi, che pur sète gentiluomo di gran qualità, dal quale potrei aspettare in molti modi aiuto e favore' ('I could have let you believe falsely, using the artifice of adulation, in order to have power ...

over you, since you are a grand gentleman from whom I could expect help and favours in a variety of forms').[90] Instead, Franco is careful to clear away any debt to her suitor's attentions, and where she refers to her honesty and the lover's affections as equal sums of silver and gold, it is certainly the influence of the economic transaction that structures her discourse: 'pretendo di pagarvi con la mia lealtà il debito dell'affezzione in quel modo a punto che s'io vi restituissi alcuna somma d'oro da voi prestatami con altretanto argento o con altretanta altra moneta equivalente' ('I propose to repay with my loyalty the debt of affection, exactly as if I were repaying a loan of gold with an equal amount of silver or some other equivalent sum').[91] Offended by the message implicit in the attentions of her admirer, who by attempting to buy her love attributes to her the vice of avarice and mistakes her for a common prostitute, Franco admonishes:

> E con queste righe torno ad accertarvi della medesima disposizione dell'animo mio, al quale voi fate espresso torto con l'imputarmi d'avarizia, mentre credete con premi poter comprar l'amor mio, il quale, benché sia amor di donna che non concorre di ricchezze né di certe altre circostanze con un par vostro, non è però di vil femina che per convenuto prezzo obligasse alcuna parte del suo corpo, nonché tutto l'animo ...[92]

> And with these lines I remind you again of my character, which you impugn by implying that I am avaricious, whereas you think with gifts to buy my love, which, although it is a woman's love and can't compete in richness or anything else with one of your position, it is not that of a low woman who for an agreed-upon sum forces any part of her body, let alone her soul ...

Again resorting to the imagery of the market, Franco accuses her correspondent of increasing his offer 'con accrescimento di prezzo, quasi facendo mercato' ('by raising the sum, as if making a deal'), as if haggling over a strictly economic transaction.[93] The honest courtesan, this letter declares, is one who enters into relationships for love, respect, or esteem, but never for material gains alone.

This theme is again reinforced in a letter in which Franco reminds a suitor that the way to earn her affection is through virtue and intellectual prowess:

> Voi sapete benissimo che tra tutti coloro che pretendono di poter insinuarsi nel mio amore a me sono estremamente cari quei che s'affatican

nell'essercizio delle discipline e dell'arti ingenue, delle quali (se ben donna di poco sapere ...) io sono tanto vaga, e con tanto mio diletto converso con coloro che sanno, per aver occasione ancora di imparare ...[94]

You well know that, of all those who try to insinuate themselves into my affections, dearest to me are they who exert themselves in the exercise of the liberal arts and disciplines, whom (although I am a woman of little learning ...) I hold most dear, and it is my pleasure to converse with those who know, in order to have the opportunity to learn ...

Although she modestly dismisses her own intellectual abilities (even as she easily inserts a reference to Dante [*Inf*. IV, 131] into her words with the phrase 'coloro che sanno'), Franco goes on to exclaim that she herself would happily spend all her time conversing with other *letterati*, if she could: '... se la mia fortuna il comportasse, io farei tutta la mia vita e spenderei tutto 'l mio tempo dolcemente nell'academie degli uomini virtuosi' ('... If my fortune allowed it, with pleasure I would spend all my time among the academies of virtuous men').[95] By way of encouragement, Franco assures her suitor that he has the advantage of being well educated ('avendo industria ... di bella letteratura') and that he should devote himself to study if he wants to earn her love. The fruits of that intellectual labour, rather than any material gift, are what she prizes: '... col farmi veder spesso il profitto che fate nell'essercizio dell'oneste dottrine, mi potrete indur più che con tutte le cose del mondo ad amarvi e tenervi caro' ('... by showing me the profit you reap in the exercise of honest studies, you will be more able to persuade me to love and esteem you than with anything else in the world').[96] Thus Franco, again dismantling stereotypical characterizations of the avaricious and corrupt courtesan, constructs herself as one who seeks and prizes the attribute of virtue rather than material wealth, in others as well as in herself, and who maintains a measured control over love and its turbulent passions, in contrast to other depictions of women lovers in epistolary literature.

Franco also addresses lovers she has accepted. Here, too, the love relationship revolves primarily around an exchange of virtue: the attentions of an esteemed suitor are an honor Franco feels duty-bound to repay.[97] In letter XXXVIII, Franco is anxious to respond to her lover's missives despite her lament that the letter is a poor substitute for the physical exchange of words and breath. It is interesting to note that she calls deliberate attention here to her careful adherence to the form of the familiar letter in particular, which counts sincerity, rather than length, as the more important quality ('... non rispondo con più lunghezza, dovendosi attender nelle lettere familiari al vero affetto con che si scrive piu che alle molte parole ...' ['I don't answer at greater length, since true feeling is more important than length in the familiar letter']).[98] In letter XIX, Franco chooses to repay her lover with a literary offering: not only in the form of the letter itself, but with a 'certa raccolta di sonetti da me fatta' ('a certain collection of sonnets I made') that she sends along with it.[99] This exchange once again emphasizes the primary importance Franco attaches to intellectual virtue: love is both inspired and repaid by intellectual and literary endeavours.

Like the sonnets offered to her suitor in letter XIX, the literary artifact, symbol of Franco's intellectual equality, and a common element in humanist epistolary exchanges, makes numerous appearances in the *Lettere familiari*. In Franco's letters, writing itself becomes an instrument with which to cancel and repay her debts, thus assuring the writer's continuing independence. In letter V, for example, Franco offers her work in exchange for the religious consolation given her by a friend in the Church, conscious of having 'acquistato ricchissimo capitale' ('acquired great capital') through her relationship with him. Letter VI, perhaps to Marco or Domenico Venier, offers 'due sonetti fatti per l'istesse rime dei quattro vostri' ('two sonnets written according to the same rhyme scheme as your four') as a token of thanks ('in segno della mia gratitudine'), as well as demonstration of her ability to compete on male literary terms. Franco's *epistolario* itself is dedicated to Cardinal D'Este with the expectation of his continued support. Indeed, it is in this dedicatory letter that Franco's use of her literary works as an instrument of exchange is perhaps most evident, functioning as a catalyst for creative production and the promotion of emotional as well as material bonds.[100]

Implicitly correcting perceptions of the courtesan as rich and extravagant by placing herself in opposition to the wealthy and powerful who will no doubt make the cardinal gifts of 'maggior prezzo' ('greater worth'), Franco offers him a gift of a value that transcends the commercial: her letter(s).[101] Using the typically humble language of the dedicatory letter, Franco goes on to describe the 'inadequacy' of her epistolary endeavour, but even standard expressions of deference acquire in Franco's hand a particular resonance. Her apology for the 'poorness' of her offering ('minimo segno di devozione'), which turns on the idea of the relative worth of gifts as determined by intent and cost to the giver (amply articulated in Sansovino's *Secretario*), anticipates Franco's attempts in the body of her *epistolario* to establish herself on equal ground with her correspondents and to rewrite the trope of the venal courtesan.[102] True wealth, Franco explains, lies not in its material expression, but rather in the devotion of the giver: 'poiché Iddio Signor dell'universo ha rispetto più alla prontezza dell'animo, accompagnata con la forza di chi dona, che alle qualità del dono' ('since God, the master of the universe, cares more for the eagerness of the soul, along with the intentions of the one who makes a gift, than to the quality of the gift').[103] As Franco continues to address the cardinal, she explicitly calls attention to her own participation in the male realm of literary production, declaring that her confidence in the cardinal's reception of her work gives her the courage to take part in the 'concorso di molt'uomini famosi di dottrina che del continuo indrizzano a Lei opere maravigliose di scienza e di elegantissimi studi e anco delle proprie lodi vostre ...' ('contest of many famous and learned men who constantly address to you marvellous works of science and elegant studies and even praise of you'). Striking a balance between 'feminine' modesty and assertiveness, Franco simultaneously valorizes and de-valorizes herself, calling herself a 'donna inesperta delle discipline e povera d'invenzione e di lingua' ('a woman unschooled in study and lacking in imagination and eloquence') even as she explicitly puts herself in competition with these 'famous, learned men' who also seek the cardinal's attention. That she fully intends to establish herself on equal ground is evident, however, by the fact that she already has future literary projects in mind, more ambitious than this 'poco libro.' She muses about her literary capacities, which will increase with time and practice, while at the same time acknowledging her need for the cardinal's patronage: 'Forse che a tempo di maggior occasione e di più prospera fortuna e di più essercitato stile, ardirò con l'aiuto della vostra divina umanità tentar impresa di maggior espressione dell'animo e dell'obbligo mio ...' ('Perhaps at a better and more propitious time and with a more practiced hand I will dare, with your divine aid, to attempt a greater expression of my heart and my obligation').[104]

This subtle bid for the cardinal's future support of her writing is important. In addition to functioning as a token of the writer's admiration for her dedicatee, Franco's gift of her *Lettere familiari* to the cardinal is offered with the expectation of some return. In a study of the exchange of books as gifts in sixteenth-century France, Natalie Zemon Davis considers the delicate and complex implications of gift-giving in general. She notes that the gift, which carries with it something of its giver, raises an expectation of reciprocity. It sets in motion a cycle of mutual obligation and exchange, a 'potentiality for benefits,' in the words of Marshall Sahlins, '... which it would be immoral for the recipient to profit from at the others' expense.'[105] Recent work by Mark Osteen and Nicoletta Pireddu, among others, poses similar questions regarding the circulation and consumption of the aesthetic object.[106] For Franco, it is this mutually beneficial exchange, this state of equilibrium, she seeks in presenting the cardinal and others with the gift of her literary work. In doing so, she could have expected not only to promote her literary product and elicit continued support from the cardinal, but also to minimize her debt to him for his patronage while assuring his loyalty.

If Franco uses her *Lettere familiari* to publicize herself as a courtesan-writer of the highest culture, she also employs her letters to respond directly to her detractors. Letters VIII, XXX, XXXI, and XLVII, for example, chronicle her misunderstanding with Marco Venier over the poems targeted at her by Maffio Venier satirizing her literary and social pretensions.[107] In the first of these letters, Franco sternly rebukes Marco for his presumed attack on her, which she finds unworthy of him.[108] Rather than linger over her anger, however, Franco casts herself as a picture of restraint and moral concern who is duty-bound to help her attacker see his error:

> Né vi scrivo ... per darvi speranza che, procedendo con contraria maniera, possiate avanzar meco in alcuna, benché minima sodisfazzione ... ma quest'ufficio io 'l faccio per discarico della mia coscienza, nella qual sono per civiltà tenuta di mostrarvi la via dritta, mentre vi veggio piegar al precipizio dell'errore.[109]

> Nor do I write you ... to give you hope that, acting in an opposite manner, you might gain some, even minimal satisfaction from me ... but I do this to appease my conscience, which requires me to show you the proper path, when I see you at the precipice of error.

Similarly, in letter XXX Franco continues her efforts to convince Marco of his fault, reminding him of their former closeness: '... ricordatevi di quel ch'avete fatto in casa mia' ('... remember all you have done in my home').[110] In Letter XXXI, Franco is relieved to learn she is mistaken in her identification of Marco as the author of the poems, and in letter LXVII she confronts Maffio, the real author. As she does in her *Rime*, here too Franco derides Maffio's poems and proclaims her own literary superiority, challenging her adversary to a duel of words in whatever language he chooses: '... in quella lingua che le sarà di più destro uso' ('... in whatever language is easiest for you').[111] Such letters serve to ground Franco's more general project of rewriting the courtesan as an epistolary 'type' within the narrative specificity of her own individual experience.

One of Franco's most well-known letters, finally, written to a female friend who is considering initiating her daughter into the sex trade, evokes the complexity of her position as a courtesan – a profession from which she profits in certain ways, but one in which questions of autonomy and integrity are always at stake. In letter XXII, Franco turns for the first and only time to an explicit critique of the sexual transaction and the female partner's lack of control over it. Again positioning herself as adviser and counsellor, Franco now addresses in unembellished terms the life of the prostitute. Taking her correspondent to task for having asked her advice only to ignore it (even attributing Franco's discouraging words to professional jealousy), Franco warns that the mother will be gravely at fault if she should push her daughter into this profession:

> ... la rovina di lei non può esser separata dalla vostra ... s'ella diventasse femina del mondo, voi diventereste sua messaggiera col mondo e sareste da punir acerbamente, dove forse il fallo di lei sarebbe non del tutto incapace di scusa, fondata sopra le vostre colpe.[112]

> ... her ruin cannot be separated from yours ... if she were to become a public woman, you would become her go-between to the world and you would merit harsh punishment, whereas her fault would perhaps not be completely inexcusable, being the result of your actions.

The tone and thrust of Franco's dissuasive discourse would seem to locate this letter within the realm of what Garimberto's *Concetti* describes as *riprendere* (reproof), a form of *biasimare* (condemnation) that derives from love rather than hate.[113] Here, Franco seeks to save the woman, her friend, from falling off a 'precipizio nascosto' ('hidden precipice'), as much as to help her daughter. Recent analyses of this letter have argued that Franco's focus here is on the prostitute of lower status, rather than her own position as a cultured and learned courtesan.[114] Franco herself states that the girl in question has neither the beauty nor the quick wit necessary for a successful courtesan: 'è così poco bella ... ed ha così poca grazia, e poco spirito nel converser ...' ('she is so unattractive ... and has very little grace and wit ...'). By calling attention to this girl's lack of suitability for the profession, Franco seems to highlight her own superior beauty, poise, and learning. Nonetheless, her words are tinged with the lessons of her own experience. Nowhere else in the collection do we encounter the forceful directness of the sharp analysis of the female lot that follows – a description that could be applied, it has been noted, to most women in early modern Venice, not just prostitutes or courtesans.[115] In Franco's stark evocation of the loss of autonomy over one's body and destiny we can read not only the plight of the prostitute but that of all women who are pawns in patriarchal society:

> Darsi in preda di tanti ... mangiar con l'altrui bocca, dormir con gli occhi altrui, muoversi secondo l'altrui desiderio, correndo in manifesto naufragio sempre della facoltà e della vita ... Credete a me: tra tutte le sciagure mondane questa è l'estrema ...[116]

> To give oneself over to many ... to eat with the mouth of another, sleep with the eyes of another, move according to the wishes of another, always risking the shipwreck of one's faculties and life ... Believe me: of all wordly tribulations, this is the worst ...

In addition to painting a cautionary picture of the prostitute's experience, and perhaps that of all women, Franco is again responding to and reworking depictions of the courtesan by male writers. As Jones and Rosenthal point out, her words here have a specific resonance to this effect, for they echo a conversation between the elderly prostitute Nanna and her daughter Pippa in Aretino's *Dialoghi*, in which Nanna complains of having to sleep with someone else's eyes and eat with someone else's mouth. Whereas Aretino means to speak metaphorically of the subservience of courtier to prince, however, Franco speaks literally for 'women who have experienced the actual enslavement of their bodies and their daily activities to their clients' desires ...'[117] At the same time, Franco's description also recalls instructions intended specifically for wives, for example Speroni's admonition in his 'Della cura famigliare,' that 'cosi è ragione, ch'il tuo marito sia il cor tuo, gli occhi tuoi, et la lingua tua, in maniera che quello appunto dica et pensi il tuo animo, ch'il tuo marito ti detterà' ('it is right that your husband should be your heart, your eyes, and your tongue, so that your soul should think and speak just as he instructs you to do').[118]

The sharp realism with which Franco treats her subject, in addition to the letter's unusual length and the central position it occupies in the collection, cause this composition to stand out from the others. Moreover, the imagery Franco uses throughout this letter is relentlessly mercantile; the mother, for example, displays her daughter like merchandise: '... l'avete messa sulle vanità del biondeggiarsi e del lisciarsi, e d'improvviso l'avete fatta comparer ... con tutte quell'altre apparenze e con tutti quegli altri abbellimenti che s'usano di fare perché la mercanzia trovi concorrenza nello spedirsi' ('... you've shown her the vanity of bleaching her hair and wearing make-up, and suddenly you've displayed her ... with the appearance and all the embellishments used to help merchandise find an profitable market').[119] Franco's focus here is less the idea of balance and debt than the dynamics of the sexual/commercial transaction. It is a transaction in which, she concludes, it is not the female partner who wields the power. As Franco eloquently reiterates, despite any potential for economic independence, a sex worker's economic autonomy (and here her words certainly are valid, even prophetically so, for a courtesan as well as for a 'common' prostitute) is perpetually unstable, for she constantly risks the sudden loss of all she has: 'ch'un solo un dí ti toglie quanto con molti in molto tempo hai acquistato' ('that a single man in a single day takes from you all that you have acquired over so much time').[120]

Franco's criticism, finally, directed primarily at the mother's actions rather than those of the daughter, targets not the behaviour of the prostitute, but rather her lack of control over her destiny and most particularly the fact that she generally enters the profession at the instigation of someone else (often her mother). As Franco warns her friend not to sacrifice her daughter, using a forceful image ('non sostenete che non pur le carni della misera vostra figliuola si squarcino e si vendano, ma d'esserne voi stessa il macellaio' ['do not allow that the flesh of your own miserable daughter should be butchered and sold, nor that you yourself should be the butcher']), it is not difficult to imagine her thoughts turning to her own mother, Paola Fracassa, who first set Franco on the path of courtesanry.[121] What Franco objects to most strongly is the action of the mother on behalf of the daughter. Even were she to achieve success, the young woman's initial powerlessness can only continue, for although the courtesan may exploit her ambiguous social role to reap greater economic, cultural, and artistic freedom, she cannot escape her subjugation as an object of exchange, the 'flesh' sold by the 'butcher.' In an attempt to break this cycle, Franco offers to help the daughter enter the Casa delle Zitelle, a charitable institution for young women, and to find a husband, promising 'ogni sorte di aiuto' ('every kind of aid').[122] In offering such assistance, Franco is offering one possible alternative: replacing the uncertain revenue of the prostitute with the dowry of a respectable young woman, which will purchase a financially stable future (just as she does in the provision to her second will).[123] Even so, the young woman in question, whether prostitute or wife, will remain subject to a male-constructed system of exchange.

This letter describing the life of the prostitute serves as an important focal point for Franco's *epistolario*. Renowned among *cortigiane oneste*, Franco had a choice to make in crafting her epistolary self-representation. She could suppress her identity as a courtesan in favour of that as a literary figure. Or she could gamble that a frank acknowledgment of her dual role as sexual and literary expert would garner the interest of a curious public. Letter XXII serves both to acknowledge Franco's profession – its pitfalls as well as her own success – and to lend a specificity to her epistolary self-portraiture that was at odds with the increasingly generic letter collections being produced in sixteenth-century Italy. If Franco sought throughout her letters to establish a masculine persona as counsellor and adviser, here she makes it clear that she brings her experience as a woman to her epistolary endeavour. Letter XXII allows Franco to speak compassionately of the prostitute's lot, and in condemning its trials, to appeal perhaps to an increasingly sober cultural climate. At the same time, the letter fulfils a dual function by setting Franco apart from the 'common' prostitute, emphasizing the physical and intellectual qualities she is unique in possessing.

Given the view espoused in many sixteenth-century letter collections that an *epistolario* should instruct the reader or reflect some kind of exemplary experience, Franco's undertaking was an audacious effort. That she should be learned and circulate her literary compositions may have been a requirement of her profession, but to adopt and rework the humanistic vehicle of the familiar letter was a transgressive undertaking. Just as Franco turned to epistolary repertories and manuals to craft her letters, taking them as her guide, so she might have hoped in turn that her own letters would function as exemplary models for others. If, as Julie Campbell notes in a study of women writers and literary circles, '[p]erformances, be they sexual or intellectual, were part of the honest courtesan's stock in trade,' in her *Lettere* Franco performs the role of the *cortigiana onesta* not only as lover and poet, but as counsellor and moral guide.[124] In addition, by acknowledging and even critiquing the courtesan's profession, she allows a new aspect of female experience to come to the forefront of epistolary representation without relinquishing the genre's conventional structure, thus maintaining a discursive framework in which male literary prescription coexists with specifically female concerns. The strength and individuality of Franco's *Lettere familiari*, finally, are the more striking when compared with the increasingly generic letter collections that met with success well into the seventeenth century. As we will see in the next chapter, women writers such as Isabella Andreini accomplished impressive feats of epistolary self-construction even within such fictionalized collections, assuming a variety of identities and emphasizing the performative nature of epistolary writing and, indeed, of gender itself.

5 Between Stage and Page: The Letters of Isabella Andreini

I. *La Pazzia d'Isabella*

L'Isabella ... come pazza se n'andava scorrendo per la Cittade ... parlando hora in Spaguolo, hora in Greco, hora in Italiano, & molti altri linguaggi, ma tutti fuor di proposito ... Si mise poi ad imitare li linguaggi di tutti li suoi Comici, come del Pantalone, del Gratiano, del Zanni, del Pedrolino, del Francatrippa, del Buratino, del Capitan Cardone, & della Franceschina tanto naturalmente, & con tanti dispropositi, che non è possibile il poter con lingua narrare il valore, & la virtú di questa Donna. Finalmente per fintione d'arte Magica ... ritornò nel suo primo essere, & quivi con elegante, & dotto stile esplicando le passioni d'amore, & i travagli ... si fece fine alla Comedia, mostrando nel recitar questa Pazzia il suo sano, e dotto intelletto; lasciando l'Isabella tal marmorio, & meraviglia ne gli ascoltatori, che mentre durerà il mondo, sempre sarà lodata la sua bella eloquenza, & valore.[1]

Isabella ... like a madwoman, went running through the city ... speaking now in Spanish, now in Greek, now in Italian, and many other languages, but all without reason ... She then set to imitating the languages of all her comedians, like that of Pantalone, of Gratiano, of Zanni, of Pedrolino, of Francatrippa, of Burattino, of Capitan Cardone and of Franceschina, so naturally and with such absurdities that it is not possible to put into words the worth and virtue of this woman. Finally, through the deceptions of the art of Magic ... she returned to her former self and then, with elegant and learned style, explaining the passions and travails of love ... she brought the comedy to an end, demonstrating in this madness her sane and learned intellect, Isabella leaving such whispering and wonder in the audience, that as long as the world goes on, her beautiful eloquence and worth will be praised.

This chapter takes us from the realm of the courtesan poet to that of the professional actress/author, and over the threshold into seventeenth-century Venice and the literary baroque. The performer described so admiringly in the passage above was Isabella Andreini, the celebrated comedian whose talent for the stage was mirrored by her equally well-received literary activity, which included a pastoral play, a book of poetry, and a letter collection.[2] When Andreini performed her famous mad scene for the wedding of Ferdinand de' Medici and Christine of Lorraine in Florence in 1589, her audience marvelled not only at the actress' remarkable linguistic facility – she spoke in Spanish, Greek, Italian, and French – but also at the ease with which she assumed the personae of other stock *commedia dell'arte* characters, both male and female: Pantalone, Zanni, Pedrolino, Franceschina.[3] Andreini had earned her fame playing the *prima donna innamorata*, a role which required eloquence and Tuscan diction as well as beauty and stage presence, but her mad scene demonstrated the breadth of her dramatic abilities and the ease with which she could perform characters across boundaries of gender and class, from the *innamorata* to male and female servants like Franceschina and Zanni. This episode underscores how Andreini's activities in the theatrical and literary spheres were intrinsically linked, not only in her referencing of humanist culture via her leaned discourse on love (a theme that reappears throughout her *Lettere*) but in her ability to move easily between different dramatic and literary personae, male and female (also characteristic of her published letters). Andreini may not have performed male roles on stage except as part of a temporary plot twist, but on the printed page she was free to assume whatever guise she chose, and in fact she opted, time and again, to speak in both male and female voices.[4] From the *Mirtilla*, her first work, to her *Rime, Lettere,* and the *Fragmenti* of her *commedia dell'arte* sketches collected and published by her husband Francesco, Andreini experimented with the performativity of gender, creating a literary persona that pulled together cultural constructions of both masculinity and femininity.[5] In her *Rime*, Andreini describes herself as father, mother, and *nutrice* (nurse) to her works, emphasizing this hermaphroditic persona, and in her *Lettere*, a collection of highly stylized discourses on love and its attendant problems, such as passion, jealousy, and separation, she alternates between male and female epistolary voices in a manner unique to epistolary narrative prior to her contribution.[6]

If Andreini's experience as a *commedia dell'arte* performer clearly informed her work as a writer, so too her literary activity influenced her work as an actress, and it is in the kind of gender performance on display in her *Lettere* that this bidirectional influence is most evident. On both stage and page, Andreini manipulated the conventions and connotations of gender as part of her public self-construction, seeking not to erase these categories but rather to draw attention to her skill in impersonating them, thereby impressing and delighting her audience. In Andreini's time, debate raged both in England (where the transvestite stage reigned until the Restoration) as well as Italy (where women where permitted to perform in many, but not all regions) over the problem of cross-dressed actors.[7] If some critics felt these female impersonations were unbelievable, detracting from the spectator's experience of the performance, others, such as Goethe (who described his travels in Italy in *Italian Journey*), maintained that the audience's enjoyment was increased by its awareness of an actor's transvestism, and that the actor's success in sustaining this knowing illusion demonstrated the triumph of art over nature (in playing a woman more convincingly than a biological woman might).[8]

A similar dynamic is at work in Andreini's *Lettere*, which marks a striking departure from the kinds of letterbooks we have examined in the preceding chapters. Devoid of proper names and dates, they are not intended to impart information specific to the writer or to a particular addressee, but rather to engage with and demonstrate mastery of a specific cultural discourse and rhetoric.[9] Rather than present a coherent and recognizable epistolary image, as in the letter collections of Pietro Aretino, Lucrezia Gonzaga, or Veronica Franco, Andreini's letters hinge on the thrill of the knowing illusion described by Goethe, on the performance of gender as a demonstration of rhetorical skill. As Andreini herself cautions in a well-known sonnet, the characters she assumes both on stage and on the page are inherently theatrical. The reader ought not be deceived by the naturalism she exhibits but rather enjoy the performance while keeping in mind its artificiality.

> S'Alcun fia mai, che i versi miei negletti
> Legga, non creda à questi finti ardori,
> Che ne le Scene imaginati amori
> Usa à trattar con non leali affetti:

Con bugiardi non men con finti detti
De le Muse spiegai gli alti furori
Talhor piangendo i falsi miei dolori
Talhor cantando i falsi miei diletti
E come ne' Teatri hor Donna, ed hora
Huom fei rappresentando in vario stile,
Quanto volse insegnar Natura, ed Arte.
Così la stella mia seguendo ancora
Di fuggitiva età nel verde Aprile
Vergai con vario stil ben mille carte.[10]

If ever there is anyone who reads
These my neglected poems, don't believe
In their feigned ardours; loves imagined in
Their scenes I've handled with emotions false.
The Muses' inspirations high I have
Set forth with lies – no less with weasel words –
When my false sorrows sometimes I bewail,
Or sometimes sing my spurious delights;
And, as in theatres, in varied style,
I now have played a woman, now a man,
As Nature would instruct and Art as well,
So in green April, following once more
My star of fleeting years, with varied style,
I ruled lines for at least a thousand leaves.

The love scenarios Andreini depicts in her verse – like those found in her *Lettere* – are fictive: 'falsi dolori' and 'falsi diletti' performed for the enjoyment of the reader. The link between her poetic voice and her experience as an actress is overt, for just as she portrays both men and women 'ne' Teatri' (the reference could be to her own performances, or perhaps to the composition of the pastoral play *La Mirtilla* for the stage), combining natural ease and artistic skill, so too she reenacts the voices of men and women with her pen. Andreini's literary transvestism calls attention to the skill with which it is accomplished, and the reader's awareness of her play on gender adds to the effect rather than detracting from it, resulting in an increased appreciation for her skill.[11]

If the hermaphroditic register of Andreini's letter collection, with its male-female exchanges on love typical of *innamorati* discourse, reflects the influence of her experience on the stage, the impact of her involvement in the *commedia dell'arte* makes itself felt in other ways as well. Indeed, the highly generic quality of the *Lettere* – where no specific reader is addressed – mirrors the structural dynamics of *commedia* performance in general, which was constructed upon an integration of familiarity and spontaneity. Professional troupes like the *Gelosi* to which Andreini and her husband Francesco belonged travelled throughout Italy and Europe armed with a portable selection of costumes, minimal generic scenery, and a repertory of adaptable *scenari* they performed again and again.[12] The audience's appreciation of their performances derived both from the familiarity of the sketches and the characters as well as from the novelty and life injected into them by the actors, who improvised within the broadly drawn lines of the plot. In his important repertory of *commedia scenari*, Flaminio Scala documented not complete scripts, but general sketches, so that other 'bellissimi ingegni' ('inventive minds') might create their own performances from these familiar outlines.[13] Similarly, just as in *commedia dell'arte* performance, the most successful letterbooks of the late sixteenth and early seventeenth centuries were those in which the author, while preserving a well established and familiar structure, brought something new and particularly entertaining to the formula, intertwining structure with improvisation. Like the *commedia scenari* that were at once formalized and improvised, letter collections had become increasingly standardized in their form and content, many veering away from the narrative specificity of mid-sixteenth-century texts like that of Lucrezia Gonzaga, with its readily identifiable protagonist, or Veronica Franco's 1580 *epistolario*, which retained some detail regarding people, places, and events.[14] The movement of many late-sixteenth- and early-seventeenth-century letterbooks was, by contrast, towards a universality that ensured the book could be read, enjoyed, and utilized by any number of readers, regardless of geographic location or even sex. Just as many theatre companies in Italy aimed to make their repertories immediately exportable to any geographical destination by excluding city-specific references and scenery, so too the epistolary genre developed certain universal features that did not require a reader to be particularly familiar with the literary, social, or political culture of, say, Venice over Rome, in order to appreciate the book.[15]

This kind of genericness is particularly evident in love letters like Andreini's, a genre that enjoyed increasing popularity in Italy from Bembo's time well into the seventeenth century (with female narrators the objects of particular admiration). If the epistolary genre was itself considered to be a natural medium, and therefore well suited to a woman's talents, then women were imagined to be particularly capable of discussions of love, which involved instinct rather than art (indeed, the first letter in Andreini's *epistolario* states that she writes her letters just 'as Nature teaches me' ['come la Natura m'insegnerà']).[16] By the late sixteenth century, entire epistolary collections and love letter manuals were devoted to narrating the feminine experience of love and passion – a theme with roots in the Ovidian tradition – and many such texts furnished model letters deemed appropriate to both male and female voices, underscoring the notion that writers might learn to imitate Nature and write like men or like women, regardless of their biological sex.[17] Therefore, the performative element of Andreini's writings must be seen not only as a reflection of her experience in the *commedia dell'arte*, but as part of a broader literary trend, one that was intent on providing literary models for readers of either sex to enjoy and imitate, and one that held women's love letters in particular esteem as expressive of 'authentic' sentiment.[18] Although Andreini's stylized *Lettere* are not letters in the usual sense of the word – so far are they from any actually exchanged correspondence – they clearly fit into the trend towards generic letter collections characteristic of the late Renaissance period. The published *epistolario*, moreover, no matter how abstract its narrative, remained de rigueur in the seventeenth century for writers who wished to cement their reputation among their contemporaries and for posterity. Andreini's composition of these texts, as well as her husband's decision to release them under the rubric *Lettere* after her death, must, therefore, also be seen in this context of literary validation. Not only do the *Lettere*, with their scripted male-female exchanges, constitute a form of literary bravura analogous to that displayed by Ortensio Lando, for example, explored in chapter 3, but they function as a capstone and memorial to Andreini's artistic reputation – a reputation actively promoted by Francesco Andreini, as we will see.

II. Partners on Stage and Page: Francesco and Isabella

When the *Lettere d'Isabella Andreini Padovana comica gelosa et academica intenta* were published in 1607, Andreini had been dead for three years. Although she had begun organizing the collection as early as 1601, it was her husband Francesco Andreini who orchestrated its posthumous publication, imbuing it with his own anxieties, regrets, and grief at the loss of his wife.¹⁹ The desire for immortality and fame expressed by 'Isabella' in the dedicatory letter to Charles Emmanuel of Savoy dated 14 March 1607, although long accepted as the product of Andreini's own pen, must be ascribed rather to Francesco, who undoubtedly added this letter, composed in Isabella's voice, when he edited and published the volume in her memory. As his own works reflect, Francesco, who retired from the stage following his wife's death, was preoccupied with preserving in writing the ephemeral memory of the achievements he and others had made upon the stage.²⁰ The prefatory letter to his *Bravure di Capitano Spavento*, a collection of theatrical dialogues Francesco had created and performed, is illuminating in this respect. In addition to recalling Isabella's memory and noting her various publications ('il suo bellissimo *Canzoniero*, la sua bellissima *Mirtilla* ... ed il Compendio delle sue bellissime *Lettere*'), as in the dedicatory letter to the *Lettere*, Francesco explains that it is because of her example that he now publishes his own work, 'per lasciar qualche memoria di me e per seguitare l'onorato grido della moglie mia' ('in order to leave some record of myself and to follow the honourable example of my wife').²¹ In the theatrical dialogue between 'Corinto Pastore' and his 'defunta Fillide' that precedes the *Bravure*, Francesco also memorializes his wife, this time in the pastoral guise she had made so famous on the stage. He instructs his 'boscareccia Sampogna,' the rustic instrument of his creative spirit, to 'far col tuo suono e col canto ... risonare ... il chiaro nome e l'onorato grido della tua cara e virtuosa Fillide' ('with your music and with song, make ... resound ... the glorious name and honourable fame of your dear and virtuous Fillide').²²

Francesco's hand can also be seen in two compositions included in the body of Isabella's *Lettere* in which a male speaker grieves the death of his wife. The first of these letters, which laments the demise of 'colei, ch'era cagione d'ogni mia allegrezza' ('she who was the reason for my entire happiness')²³ and the writer's own unhappy survival, echoes the torment expressed in the dialogue between Corinto and Fillide in Francesco's *Le Bravure*, where Corinto professed his willingness to follow Fillide to the grave, mixing his own ashes with hers. In the *Bravure*, Corinto explains,

> O quanto volontieri ... accompagnato avrei il suo dolore con le mie proprie essequie? O quanto volontieri averei le mie ossa con le sue ossa, la mia cenere con la sua cenere, rinchiuse in un medesmo tempo ed in un medesmo sepolcro?²⁴

O ... how willingly would I have added my own remains to her pain? How willingly would I have mixed my bones with hers, my ashes with hers, enclosed together in a single sepulchre?

In the *Lettere*, the same lament is displaced onto the baroque conceit of a dialogue between the grieving widower and the 'bellissima chioma' of his deceased wife (the locks of hair cut off during her fever in an effort to cure her). Why, the speaker upbraids these 'bei capegli,' did they not follow their owner to her grave ('perché negaste di chiudervi seco nel sepolcro?'), recalling the words of Corinto in the *Bravure*.[25] The letter ends, like the dialogue, with the realization that death, while cruel, cannot triumph over love: '... se la Morte ha potuto dissolver il mortale, non ha per ciò havuta forza di dissolver l'amore' ('... although Death was able to erase life, it had no strength to erase love').[26]

Analogously, the final letter of Isabella's collection is also written in a male voice and devoted to the 'morte della moglie.' It echoes the grief of the first letter, as well as the desire expressed by Corinto in the *Bravure* to follow his wife beyond death, when the male letter writer states, '... 'l Cielo, il qual soleva risponder benigno a' miei voti or nega d'esaudirmi, negandomi il terminar la vita, la quale noiosissima passo in continuo tormento' ('... Heaven, which once answered my prayers, now ... refuses to end my miserable life, whose unhappy days I pass in constant torment').[27] An even closer textual link comes when the writer of the letter asks that his own ashes be mixed with those of his wife: 'Sia col suo cenere unito il mio' ('let my ashes be mixed with hers'), again echoing Corinto.[28] Most evident in this final letter, however, is the self-appointed role of the speaker as the keeper of the memory of his wife/Isabella. Francesco confronts his loss by devoting himself to preserving Isabella's fame. The desire for immortality, so vividly expressed in the dedicatory letter, is perhaps his own, but one he attributes to her: 'Tu benché mortale sempre avesti pensieri immortali. Lo stesso anch'io vorrei' ('Although mortal, you always thought of immortality. I would like to do the same').[29] Francesco, the bereft husband, becomes Isabella's historian and hagiographer, the promotor of her impeccable image, 'colui, che per altro non vive, che per darti nella sua memoria vita' ('he who lives only to give you life through his memory'); while Isabella is the 'vero ornamento della tua per te fortunatissima etate' ('the true ornament of the age so fortunate to have you') (and in the *Bravure* she is the 'Monarchessa delle donne' [sovereign among women]).[30] Francesco did not create the image of Isabella as a miraculous combination of literary genius, dramatic presence, and female virtue – that reputation was already well established and is evident in the praise of Isabella by writers from Tasso to Chiabrera – but he was intent on preserving it, for her benefit and his own, and the letter collection provided an appropriate vehicle for such an endeavour.[31]

If Francesco was involved in the composition and promotion of Isabella's *Lettere*, what was the extent of his intervention? In a passage from the *Bravure*, Captain Spavento, Francesco's comedic alter ego, slyly states that he is not accustomed to sign his letters with his real name: 'Molti sogliono mettere i nomi propri nel fine delle Lettere loro ... ma io diversamente da ognuno non pongo mai il mio nome ... in qella vece sottoscrivendo dico "Io, il Capitano"' ('Many people sign their names at the end of their letters ... I, on the other hand, never put my name ... but rather sign myself, "I, the Captain"').[32] Could the Captain's words be a clue to Francesco's role in Isabella's letters? Published under Isabella's name, were they actually written by her husband? The answer to this question is no – or rather, not entirely. We are closer here to the kind of literary partnership that likely existed between Ortensio Lando and his muse Lucrezia Gonzaga a half-century earlier, for example, than to a case of complete epistolary appropriation.[33] Isabella and her husband were partners on stage for more than twenty years. They played off one another as the *innamorati* and with Francesco in the role of Captain Spavento, and they knew one another's theatrical voices and personae intimately. We see in the *Bravure* that Francesco was comfortable writing in Isabella's voice: it includes an entire speech written in the voice of Fillide/Isabella, in which 'she' comforts her husband from beyond the grave.[34] It is equally likely that Isabella had her actor-husband in mind as a model for the male voices she assumes in the *Rime* and in the *Lettere*, both of which are replete with speeches composed in the Petrarchan and pastoral tones of the *innamorato*.[35]

Isabella, moreover, was an established author. Before Francesco had committed his *Bravure* or *Ragionamenti* to paper, Isabella had published a pastoral play and a volume of poetry, and had been admitted to the Accademia degli Intenti of Pavia.[36] She had literary aspirations – and was succeeding in achieving them at the time of her death at age forty. Indeed, her second-place performance in a poetic competition with Tasso has become part of her legend; medals were struck with her likeness following her death in Lyons in order to commemorate her.[37] An orthodox writer in many respects, Andreini sought to compete directly with the literary world and therefore created works that would find acceptance and acclaim within that world.[38] This explains, at least in part, her publication of a fashionable pastoral play followed by a book of Petrarchan lyric; and we know that by 1601 she had started work on another timely project, her letter collection.[39] Fictionalized love letters like those that constituted many of Andreini's epistolary compositions were by now a well received literary form, one that functioned as both entertainment and instruction. While Francesco was instrumental in the publication and promotion of Isabella's *Lettere*, it was his wife's own experience as an actress and as a writer who sought recognition in the highest literary circles that formed the basis and inspiration for these compositions, as we will see in the following section.

III. The *Lettere* as Literary and Theatrical Text

While Andreini's *Lettere* owe much to her experience in the theatre – more than half the contents can be linked to thematic material common to the *commedia dell'arte* – they are not simply the written record of a *commedia* performance; they are also, in the words of one critic, a 'prodotto letterario, e perfettamente riuscito'[40] – one fully consonant, that is, with the prevailing literary vogue in early seventeenth-century Italy for women's love letters. They are purposefully packaged and presented by Francesco Andreini as letters in order to locate Isabella within a literary culture that admired and encouraged the production of such works. Rather than risk oversimplifying the *Lettere* as solely a reflection of theatrical repertory, therefore, it is more accurate to read them as a kind of hybrid of literary and theatrical text, of letter and dramatic sketch.[41] In the next few pages I will point out some concrete examples of a linkage between these two arenas, but I will also argue that the influence of stage and page was not unidirectional. Many of the letters derive from Isabella's stage practice, but the monologues and exchanges she performed onstage were equally likely to have been shaped by the pages of literary texts, commonplace books, and indeed epistolary literature (especially love letters).

If *commedia dell'arte* performances featured stock characters, actors also made use of *zibaldoni*, or repertories, of 'concetti' (conceits) for each character and situation, consisting of apposite phrases, dialogues, poems, gestures, and so on. As Robert Henke points out in his study of orality and literature in the *commedia dell'arte*, comedians did not spontaneously recreate their characters in each performance; rather, they relied on a combination of improvisation and structure that helped them organize 'extensive mental storehouses' of material based on the principles of *inventio* and decorum (spontaneity and appropriateness).[42] Henke argues convincingly that actors committed their own 'generici,' or stockpiles of material regarding their characters, to paper, as in the case of the actor Stefanello Bottarga, an actor with the troupe of Zan Ganassa in Spain.[43] The *Fragmenti di alcune scritture della signora Isabella Andreini,* collected and published by Francesco in 1620 as part of his commemorative campaign on Isabella's behalf, although more a memorial project than a practical *generico,* similarly provides a good example of the kinds of exchanges the *innamorati* might have performed on stage. Among the 'contrasti' included in the *Fragmenti* are dialogues *sopra la dignità de gli amanti* ('on lovers' dignity'), *sopra le passioni dell'odio e dell'amore* ('on hatred and love'), *se ogni amato convien che ami* ('whether a beloved ought reciprocate love'), *sopra le morti d'Amore* ('on those who died of love'), *sopra la febre amorosa* ('on love's fever'), *modo di disamare* ('how to fall out of love'), *amor coniugale* ('conjugal love'), *forza d'amore* ('love's power'), *giuramenti* ('vows'), *amor honesto* ('honest love'), *rimedii d'amore* ('remedies for love'), *finger d'amar una, e amare un'altra* ('on pretending to love one woman, while loving another'), and so on. These *contrasti* reflect the sorts of emotional states actors portraying the *innamorati* were required to perform, along with the problems they were expected to explore. The centrality of love and its related dramatic and emotional situations is immediately apparent. It is thus significant that Isabella's own *Lettere* should include compositions similarly titled *forza d'amore, lode d'amore, contra amore, incendio, disperazione, preghiere, lontananza, giuramento degli amanti,* and *rammarichi d'amanti:* these were the tropes of *innamorato* performance. If *commedia* audiences expected to be presented with familiar, generic representations of love onstage and required that sketches play equally well no matter where they were performed, so too letter readers did not expect the story of a real love affair. Rather, they wanted to see all the familiar stages of love addressed, from infatuation and passion to jealousy and despair, and, perhaps, to be able to apply those generic tropes to other situations. Texts like Andreini's *Lettere,* therefore, functioned like reference books, structured to help readers more quickly locate letters on particular subjects. Andreini's letters, for example, are not designated by the people who exchange them (who are nameless), but by the generic circumstances of their composition ('segni di perfetto amore,' 'della bellezza,' 'del dispregio degli amanti,' etc.), easily accessible via a subject index.

Still clearer evidence of the link between stage and page can be found in specific textual correspondence between the *Fragmenti* and the *Lettere*, for example in a discussion of the relationship of jealousy to love that appears in both texts. In the *Fragmenti*, the interlocutors Eliodoro and Teossena debate whether or not jealousy is an essential element of love, with Eliodoro maintaining that jealousy is not to be confused with desperation and insisting, 'Io sono amante, et essendo amante non posso far di meno di non esser geloso, poiché chi ama teme, e la gelosia non è altro, che timore. Dunque chi ama naturalmente teme, e naturalmente è geloso' ('I am a lover, and as such I cannot help but be jealous, because he who loves fears, and jealousy is nothing but fear. Thus he who loves naturally fears, and naturally is jealous').[44] This speech reappears virtually verbatim in Isabella's *Lettere*, albeit in epistolary form and thus as a monologue rather than half of a dialogue (although the second interlocutor is always implied via the reader, the implicit interlocutor). Here, the speaker states,

> se voi siete geloso, siete anche amante, perché la gelosia, è timor mesto d'alcuna speranza ... ma la disperation è certezza d'alcun male privo d'ogni speranza. La gelosia dunque è sempre congiunta con amore, e la disperatione è separate ... *essendo amante non posso far di meno e di non esser geloso, perche chi ama teme, e la gelosia non è altro che timore, dunque chi ama naturalmente teme, e naturalmente è geloso ...*[45]

> if you are jealous, you are also a lover, because jealousy is fear mixed with hope ... but despair is the certainty of pain devoid of all hope. Jealousy, then, is always part of love, but despair is separate ... *since the lover cannot help but be jealous, because he who loves fears, and jealousy is nothing but fear; thus he who loves naturally fears, and naturally is jealous ...*

Later in the same passage from the *Fragmenti*, Elidoro compares love and jealousy to sun and light, lightning and rainbows; while Theossena counters with a metaphor of wine and vinegar:

> ELIODORO: ... amore, e gelosia sono tra loro come il raggio, e la luce, il baleno, e 'l folgore, lo spirito, e la vita; eh, Signora, che sempre la gelosia è segno, et inditio d'amore.[46]

> ... love and jealousy are like the sunbeam and the light, like the rainbow and the lightning bolt, like spirit and life; isn't it true, Signora, that jealousy is always a sign and indication of love.

THEOSSENA: Ancor l'aceto è segno del vino, e la febre inditio della vita; ma non mi negherete già, che il vino non possa star senza l'aceto, e la vita senza la febre, così ancora molto meglio può stare, e sta amore senza gelosia, l'aceto guasta il vino, e la gelosia l'amore; la febre entrando nella vita v'entra piu tosto per ridurla a morte, che per altro, e la gelosia entrando in amore, v'entra più tosto per distruggerlo, e ridurlo in rabbia, che per accrescerlo, & aumentarlo.

Vinegar may be an element of wine, and fever an indication of life; you will not deny that wine does not taste better without vinegar, or that life is not better without fever, and love without jealousy; vinegar ruins wine, and jealousy ruins love; fever comes only to take life, not for any other reason, and when jealousy mixes with love, it comes to destroy it, and reduce it to anger, not to help it grow and bloom.

This exchange, too, reappears in the *Lettere*, where a single speaker now assumes responsibility for both sides of the discussion, guiding it through the objections voiced in the *contrasto* by Theossena to arrive at a conclusion:

... *amore, e gelosia sono tra loro come il raggio, e la luce, il baleno, e 'l folgore, lo spirito, e la vita*. Al ché rispondendo dirò, Che è vero, che la gelosia veramente è segno d'amore e com'è l'aceto segno del vino, e la febre della vita; ma che? Non si negherà già, *che 'l vino non possa star senza l'aceto, e la vita senza la febbre così ancora molto meglio può stare, e sta amore senza gelosia. L'aceto guasta il vino, la gelosia guasta l'amore. La febbre entrando nella vita, entra più tosto per ridurla a morte, che per altro, e la gelosia entrando in amore, v'entra solamente per distruggerlo*.[47]

Love and jealousy are like the sunbeam and the light, the rainbow and the lightning bolt, like spirit and life. To which I respond saying that, while jealousy is truly a sign of love, as vinegar of wine and fever of life, but so? You cannot deny that *wine tastes better without vinegar, and life without fever is far more pleasant, and love without jealousy. Vinegar ruins wine, jealousy ruins love. Fever comes to take life, rather than anything else, and when jealousy mixes with love, it destroys it.*

The correspondence between these passages is important not only for the textual link it creates between performance and text – the speech made in the *Lettere* was performed by Isabella onstage and recorded by

Francesco – but also for what it suggests (or doesn't) about the function of Isabella's *Lettere*. If the *Lettere* were solely the reflection of Andreini's onstage monologues and dialogues, we might expect many such precise correspondences between her text and Francesco's record of her performances in the *Fragmenti*. Instead, the direct correspondences are only occasional, whereas the general similarities in broad themes are pervasive. This thematic similarity – again, with specific regard to love – is more suggestive of the *Lettere* themselves constituting a kind of *commedia dell'arte* 'zibaldone,' rather than functioning as a simple record of stage performance. It is not difficult to imagine epistolary compositions that demonstrate the emotional states of *ira, sdegno, disperazione*, and *dissimulare*, for example, as guidelines for, as well as reflections of, the performance of those states by actors. Such topoi were by this point also commonplaces of the love letter genre, as we will see in section IV below.

As Henke points out, actors had access to a range of sources, oral and printed, on which to base their performances. They could draw on their own observations of other actors' portrayals of a character, of oral descriptions of these performances by others, and on appropriate literary sources, as illustrated in a passage from Domenico Bruni's 'Prologhi' describing the reading material requested by the players of a *commedia* troupe, including Boccaccio's *Elegia di Madonna Fiammetta* and the letters of Andrea Calmo.[48] Here, the actors shape their performance by relying on literary representations of their 'types,' which in some instances in turn derive from the author's own theatre experience: Calmo's letters, for example, revisit the Pantalone figure he was known for portraying on the stage.[49] Other texts, like *Fiammetta* or the works of Plato – utilized by the *innamorati* – are important resources for their relationships to other areas of culture, both literary and philosophical, particularly in the realm of love discourse. Andreini's own *Lettere* include a composition titled 'della pallidezza de gli Amanti' ('on the pallor of lovers') that could have served as a guide for a lovesick character. Her detailed description of the lover's physical state echoes Equicola's *Libro de Natura de Amore* as well as popular adaptations of Equicola such as Ortensio Lando's *Quesiti amorosi* (1552).[50]

If the intertextuality of Andreini's epistolary treatment of love draws on literary sources and perhaps in turn influences the portrayal of this state on stage, her collection includes other stock tropes common to both *commedia* performance and literary tradition, as in her letter portraying the figure of the aged lover. Andreini's treatment of this figure in a comic letter reprimanding a male *destinatario* for his inappropriate passion for a maiden 'tanto dall'esser vostro dissimile' ('so dissimilar to you') has a distinctly visual component, painting a picture of the physically mismatched pair that could easily serve as a guide to an actor seeking to perform the scenario:

> Se questo foglio potesse ridere, riderebbe ... Com'è possibile, che nella vostra età cadente, non vi siate vergognato di mettervi all'impresa d'amar Donna dall'esser vostro dissimile? Com'è possible, che non abbiate scorto, che a quella fronte rugosa, a quel ciglio irsute, et a quella faccia pallida, poco, anzi nulla, si convien amore? Et ancorché facciate ogni sforza, per andar sù la vita, pur si conosce pover'uomo che siete, che 'l soverchio peso degli'anni v'incurva le spalle.[51]

> If this page could laugh, it would laugh ... How is it possible that at your decrepit age, you are not ashamed to pursue a Lady dissimilar to you? How can it be that you do not realize that love does not suit that wrinkled forehead, that hairy brow, and that pallid face? And although you make every effort, it is still obvious, poor man, that the heavy weight of the years bows your shoulders.

Andreini's 'vecchio amante' is a stock figure of ridicule, similar to the awkward old man found on stage as well as throughout Calmo's published letters. Derived from theatrical representations of the Pantalone character, while in turn influencing those same representations, such epistolary representations establish a circular relationship between stage and page, similar to that described by Henke with regard to Calmo.[52] The influence of performance and literature here is thus bi-directional and dynamic. Theatrical performance inspires literary records, while convincing literary representations of characters furnish material for actors' performances.

IV. Love Letters and Literary Manuals

As noted earlier, a clear link between Andreini's experience in the *commedia dell'arte* and her *Lettere* can be seen in the fundamental tension between generic structure and individual innovation that is central to both arenas of artistic expression. This tension mirrors in important ways a broader shift in literary culture towards universalized texts, as evidenced in the proliferation throughout the sixteenth century of literary models, repertories, and manuals of the kind discussed in the preceding chapters. Chapter 1, for example, described how epistolary writing in particular became the focus of an increasing number of texts that sought to teach how to write properly, the initial impetus for such didactic intent deriving from efforts to establish a legitimate form of vernacular literary language, but gaining momentum from the effort to define the contours of a common 'civil conversazione,' or courtly language, seen in works by Castiglione and Guazzo. Texts like Sansovino's *Del secretario*, which was concerned with language as well as the social properties of epistolary exchange, were fundamental in this effort, but the didactic instinct was not limited to the world of the professional secretary. Works like Garimberto's *Concetti*, for example, a kind of general *zibaldone* of ready prose, claimed to contain useful phrases for any situation ('un repositario de tutti luoghi comuni, di qualunque soggetto, o materiali, di che si voglia o ben parlare, o regolatamente scrivere' ['a repository of commonplaces on any subject, or material regarding anything about which one wishes to speak well or write properly']) and we saw in chapter 3 how one epistolary text, the *Lettere ... a gloria del sesso feminile* (1552), used the *Concetti* to good effect.[53] Originality and sincerity are not the goals of such texts, but rather appropriate and interesting application of the models.

If writing manuals in general provided models to imitate, nowhere are these generic models more evident than in the growing corpus of love letters that flourished in the sixteenth and early seventeenth centuries.[54] Sansovino himself published a repertory of model love letters collected from various sources that addressed typical stages of the love relationship, including the nature of love, love's power, the trials of separation, and lovers' suspicions – all themes which come to constitute a common body of material for the love letter genre and which are present in Andreini's letters as well.[55] Some such manuals demonstrate an interest in the hermaphroditic aspect of love letter-writing that presages Andreini's more complex undertaking. This interest is linked not to a theatrical dimension of gender performance, but rather to the notion that the capable writer can learn to imitate Nature by writing either like a man or like a woman. Andrea Zenofonte da Ugubio's *Formulario nuovo da dittar lettere amorose* (1544), for example, a repertory of epistolary situations from joy and passion to despair and abandonment, are written in both male and female voices, allowing readers to study and imitate 'masculine' and 'feminine' representations of the love experience. The adherence of the women's letters included in Zenofonte's text to the gendered dichotomy between nature and art so prevalent in early modern culture is evident. They write fuelled by passion rather than art ('con lagrime e sangue, non inchiostro' ['with tears and blood, not ink']).[56] In this sense they reflect typically gendered associations between love and the female letter writer, echoing the suffering of Ovid's *Heroides* or the experience of Boccaccio's Fiammetta.[57] In similar fashion, the *Lettere amorose di Madonna Celia*, a popular example of 'women's' epistolary love narrative with numerous editions, presents a fictionalized love story from beginning to end, one overtly linked to the model of Boccaccio and devoid of allusions to specific people, places, or events, like Andreini's letters after it.[58]

Repertories and epistolary love narratives like these laid the groundwork for Andreini's *Lettere*, which are as much a product of the literary climate that produced *Madonna Celia* and Sansovino's *Secretario* as they are the reflection of Andreini's experience as a *prima donna innamorata*. In spite of the declaration by Isabella/Francesco in the volume's dedicatory composition that the letters are not intended to 'teach the proper way to write' but only to preserve the memory of the writer, the links between Andreini's *epistolario* and the didactic trend is evident not only in the content of the book, but in its structure, including the *tavola* of subjects that precedes the letters, facilitating the use of the book as a reference tool.[59] The letters themselves are conditioned by the tension between universality and uniqueness characteristic of both the love letter genre and *commedia dell'arte*, as well as by the interest, evident in epistolary manuals and repertories as well as in the theatre, in believably assuming and imitating a variety of voices. Whereas the movement between male and female personae in a text like Zenofonte's is linked to an interest in mastering the 'female' genre of the love letter along with a concern to establish appropriate registers of communication across social classes, Andreini's letters on love take a more specific interest in the performative aspect of gendered writing, one that challenges and questions the parameters of such characterizations. Andreini's are not isolated epistolary compositions, but rather ongoing exchanges between two speakers or on continuing themes, proffered in alternating male and female voices. In this way, Andreini could furnish both sides of the epistolary dialogue, restoring to her women characters the voice that had often been silenced, especially on the stage. Although women were permitted to perform onstage in many parts of Italy, they were often marginalized nonetheless by theatrical texts and performances, relegated to secondary status or to the wings.[60] In writing both the male and female parts of poetic and epistolary exchange, as in the *Rime* and the *Lettere,* Andreini implicitly responded to such marginalization, not only as it occurred in the theatre, but in other genres as well (we need only think of the silent beloved of the Petrarchan tradition).

Some such exchanges are self-referential discussions centred on the letters themselves and their capacity to stand in for real contact (as classical epistolary theory held they should); others are abstract discussions of love that are heavily inflected with the language of lyric poetry and neoplatonism. Still others, while remaining within the constellation of love discourse, introduce debate over the love relationship that explicitly spotlights typical gender conventions and social roles. In a letter entitled 'On the Wisdom of Women,' a female writer counsels caution to other women in choosing lovers, warning that men are false and will use any means possible to 'ingannar le misere donne' ('deceive unfortunate women'), particularly when they are young and trying to prove themselves. Women are too credulous, she cautions, and ought be jealous of their reputations, choosing only worthy lovers of their own social status. Her claims reflect the pressures for women to maintain and project an image of honour and virtue, even while engaging in the love relationships that populated poetic texts and works like Castiglione's *Book of the Courtier.* The letter that responds to this one, by contrast, entitled 'On the Cunning of Women' and written in the male voice, targets such feminine caution as mere cruelty, an obstacle to be overcome. Women, it accuses, revel wickedly in their power over men: 'voi altre crudelissime donne d'altro non godete, che delle nostre avversita …' ('you cruel women enjoy nothing better than our trials').[61] The elaborate dance of courtly love is revealed as a rhetorical game of which each party understands the rules and expectations, an amusement rather than true emotion. This second composition, however, which begins as a rhetorical condemnation of female cruelty to men, takes an interesting turn when the male writer accuses women of valuing rhetoric over sentiment: inverting, that is, the traditional association between nature and femininity and between art and masculinity. It is women, the male speaker claims, who wrongly value elaborate speeches over simple and direct communication. If a man speaks in elaborate phrases, he is admired by the female sex; if he speaks simply and naturally, he is ridiculed.[62]

> S'egli con parole ordinate procura di meglio che sa di significarvi l'insopportabil sua doglia subito dite, Oh ecco l'oratore. So, ch'egli non

lascia addietro i colori dell'arte, io vuol, che ... ne' suoi ragionamenti si scuopra l'ordine, l'invenzione, le locuzione, la memoria, e la pronuncia. Manca sol, ch'egli dica, se la causa è in genere demostrativo, deliberativo, o giudiziale ... S'avvien, che un'altro vinto da soverchio amore, incominciando a ragionar delle sue pene si perda, subbito gli vien addosso una ruinosa poiggia d'ingnorante, dicendo, Oh che balordo.⁶³

If he tries to describe his unbearable suffering with his most eloquent words, you immediately say, Oh what an orator. I know that he does not leave out any artistic adornment ... that his explanations demonstrate order, *inventio*, *elocutio*, memory, and diction. All that's left is for him to say whether the cause is demonstrative, deliberative, or judicial in nature ... If another, overcome by love, loses his place upon beginning to express his suffering, immediately a condemning hail of ignorant women descend on him, saying, Oh what a simpleton.

Not only does this letter writer condemn women's susceptibility to artifice over authenticity, but he also adds that in fact they do not understand love at all. True love cannot be easily expressed, and one who speaks of love glibly does not truly love, but is feigning love, which is also something to be condemned. Here, it is men, not women, who understand love's true emotional essence:

S'è vero, che quel dolor, che ben si sente mal si narra, certo costui non sente dolore, poiché sí ben ne parla, e s'egli non sente dolore, parimente non ama poiché amore non è mai senza dolore, e s'egli non ama, e dice d'amare, ben merita d'esser burlato.⁶⁴

If it is true that the deepest suffering is the hardest to express, then he certainly does not feel pain, if he can speak of it so easily, and if he does not feel pain, than similarly he does not love because love is never without pain, and if he does not love, and says he does, he ought to be ridiculed.

More than an accusation against women for toying with men's emotions, these claims – scripted by a woman but voiced by a male speaker – call into question ideas about letter-writing itself as a spontaneous and specifically feminine form, and love letters in particular as a form driven by instinct over art as laid out by texts like *Madonna Celia*. In fact, this letter suggests, the very models meant to demonstrate the spontaneous beauty of (love) letter-writing have become heavy and artificial. It is an implicit critique of the movement towards generic models in which Andreini herself engages, as well as a challenge to the characterization of the love letter as an inherently feminine genre. Although Andreini herself makes it clear that her writing is a form of performance, as for example in the sonnet from the *Rime* cited earlier, letters like this one express an admiration for 'genuine' sentiment over perfectly crafted, but artificial, declarations of love. The tension between structure and innovation that Andreini resolved on the stage is more difficult to reconcile in the arena of the love letter.

V. Humanism and the 'Woman Question'

Although more than half of Andreini's letters, as we have seen, focus on questions of love, the work does not bill itself specifically as a love letter collection, and some compositions address other issues consonant with her *innamorata* character or linked to other literary trends in evidence at the turn of the seventeenth century. Certain letters, like those treating friendship, Fortune, 'humane miserie' ('human troubles') and the superiority of country life to the world of the court are reminiscent of themes common to humanist discourse and to the humanist epistolary tradition in particular. Other women writers, including Veronica Franco and Chiara Matraini, used some of these same themes as the basis for epistolary composition and literary self-fashioning.[65] The entreaty of one of Andreini's male letter writers to another to 'lasciar l'ingordo desiderio delle richezze, de gli onori, e delle speranze di corte' ('forsake the greedy desire for wealth, honour, and the promises of the court') for the quiet repose of the country, for example, turns on the central problem of liberty versus servitude, the problematic relationship between prince and subject, and the intellectual's need for quiet reflection: 'È pur una pazzia de gli omini, che non hanno mai un giorno di quiete per acquistar facoltà, la quale tanto più cresce, tanto più sa crescer in loro l'affanno di non scemarla' ('It is human folly to go without a day of repose in order to gain knowledge, for the more we learn, the more we value learning').[66] (A second letter on the same theme repositions it in a love context by lamenting that the restorative virtues of the country are not enough to counter the torments of love.)[67] The exaltation of the country life is also linked to the pastoral tradition, present in poetic form in Andreini's *Rime* as well as in dramatic form in the *Mirtilla*. Its application in *commedia dell'arte* performance is similarly widespread, as documented, for example, in Francesco Andreini's

Ragionamenti, which include a dialogue that paints the Court as a den of falsity.[68] Also typical of humanist discourse is a pair of letters regarding the fickle cycles of Fortune, which assumes multiple humanistic valences, encompassing not only Fortune's instability but also the themes of consolation and male friendship, as one male speaker consoles another in his adversity:

> ... è possibile (Amico mio carissimo) che non vogliate ricordarvi, che la Fortuna con l'uomo non serba fede, e che tra lei, e lui, non c'è mai pace ferma? Non si può lungamente durare nelle felicità di Fortuna, atteso che nel colmo de' suoi favori, o ella mutandosi lascia noi, o noi morendo lasciamo lei ...[69]

> ... can it be (my dearest friend) that you do not want to remember that Fortune does not keep faith with man, and that between her and him there is never a steady peace? One can't last long in Fortune's good graces, knowing that at the height of her favours, either she will change and desert us, or we will die and leave her ...

Another letter on male friendship, which praises such a bond as 'quella, che unisce gli animi' ('that which unites hearts'), draws on a long humanist tradition of similar exaltation, while a letter of consolation for the loss of a child, calling on the bereaved parent to remember that his son has gone to a better place, also has roots in an extensive humanist tradition.[70] As MacNeil has noted, one of Andreini's strategies of literary self-presentation is to adopt the masculine costume of humanism in her writing.[71] In letters like these, Andreini utilizes the tropes of male humanistic discourse, but does not appropriate them to a specifically female context. Rather, she demonstrates her ability to 'perform' humanism without relocating it to the female voice.

One of the consequences of sixteenth-century humanism and its focus on the nature of man was a renewal of interest in examining the roles of both men and women in society. Sixteenth-century literary culture across Europe saw the steady production of texts that engaged in 'the woman question,' attempting to define and describe the intellectual capacities, status, and duties of women in relation to men. Gender had come to the forefront of literary debate early in the century and remained there in later works by writers such as Lucrezia Marinella and Moderata Fonte, along with a spate of anti-woman treatises. Although Andreini's *Lettere* do not overtly profess to defend women in the manner of Marinella or Fonte, the *questione della donna* is nonetheless an important and omnipresent subtext to the collection. Whether engaging in self-consciously gendered expressions of literary inferiority (as in the dedicatory letter, which insists that Andreini does not mean to compete with her more learned male counterparts), addressing the nature/art dichotomy in literary production (as in the letter discussed above in section three), or describing the role of women in love and marital relationships (as we will see below), Andreini's letters make a contribution to the debate. Her first foray into protofeminist territory had been her *Mirtilla*, a reworking of Tasso's *Aminta* with a pointed twist on the standard, misogynist satyr scene common to pastoral drama.[72] Her *Lettere*, by contrast, are less pointedly pro-woman. Nonetheless, the message is present, in muted form: women are as capable as men of noble sentiment, honourable behaviour, intellectual accomplishment, and literary eloquence.[73] These qualities are closely tied in Andreini's work to conventional images of female virtue. Scattered throughout the collection are positive depictions of women as chaste and virtuous lovers jealous of their honour, reiterations of standard gender ideologies and reflections of Isabella's *innamorata* role. It is significant, for example, that the female writer of the first letter of the collection praises honour and chastity as the highest virtues to which a woman can aspire.[74] The writer reprimands her audacious lover for endangering her reputation, women's most important possession: 'Siate dunque più geloso della mia reputazione, che non siete stato, e ricordatevi, che 'l disonore è peggior della morte' ('Be more careful of my reputation than you have been, and remember that dishonour is worse than death'). If the 'proprio seggio dell'uomo è la terra' ('man's proper place is in the world') that of women is 'l'onestà' (chastity).[75] Dishonour can destroy entire families, and the public appearance of virtue must be maintained. Accompanying the praise of traditional female virtues is a digression on the merits of silence over speech that evokes widespread notions regarding the links between female silence and chastity, and by contrast female speech and promiscuity: '... ho creduto sempre ... che 'l modesto silenzio di donna aquagli la facondia e l'eloquenza de più purgati intelletti' ('... I've always believed ... that a woman's modest silence is equal to the eloquence of the most learned men').[76] By immediately presenting herself as the virtuous female lover who praises silence and reticence, Isabella manages the paradox that arises from her act of epistolary publication and continues the efforts she made on stage and off to establish an unimpeachable feminine persona in both public and private contexts. Similarly, the two letters on marital love and loss discussed earlier, likely penned by Francesco, eulogize Isabella as a paragon of female virtue.[77]

In some cases, the rhetorical device of scripting both sides of the epistolary exchange permits Andreini to manipulate *querelle des femmes* discussions in new ways, as, for example, when she counters anti-woman claims like those raised by a male speaker who lambastes marriage as 'l'oscura prigione de' nostri spiriti' ('the dark prison of our spirit').[78] Interestingly, this exchange, which ultimately serves as a defence of women, transpires entirely among men, as if in an effort to give it special weight by enlisting male authority. In the first letter of this pair, the writer expresses great – and certainly exaggerated – dismay at his friend's decision to take a wife, a mistake he terms a 'sconcia pazzia' ('terrible folly').[79] He describes marriage as an eternal misery. A wealthy wife will be proud and insolent, a poor one a drain on the household; a pretty one will bring suspicion, an ugly one invites ridicule. Overblown in rhetoric and comic in function, this letter permits the eloquent response of the second male interlocutor, who instead praises marriage as a sacred institution and wives as beloved and precious companions. Accusing the first writer of envying his happiness, he marvels,

> non sa Vostra Signoria che 'l matrimonio è principio, e fondamento dell'ordinazione delle famiglie? Non sapete ... che levato il matrimonio si leverrebbe la conservazione legitima dell'umana spezie? ... Nel matrimonio le richezze, i corpi, e le anime sono communi ...[80]

> Are you not aware, Sir, that marriage is the principle and foundation of the family? Do you not know ... that without marriage we would not be able to perpetuate mankind legitimately? ... In marriage wealth, body, and soul are joined together.

The letter goes on to defend marriage in general and to describe the virtues of this writer's bride in particular. A wife comforts and supports her husband, caring for him when he is ill. His own intended is young and virtuous, of appropriate social status and possessed of the necessary dowry. This description of marriage is a typical one drawing on the Catholic Church's promotion of marriage as an institution for procreation as well as on the reformist emphasis on marriage as companionship. Discussions of marriage and the proper roles of men and (especially) women within the marital bond also abounded in the literary forum, as in Alberti's *Libri della famiglia* (especially Book III) or Vives' *De institutione feminae Christianae*. It is significant, of course, that not only is this letter, which offers some of the highest praise of women in the book, voiced by a man, but that it extols woman in terms of her specific function as marriage partner and mother, rather than in an intellectual capacity. It calls to mind the way in which Andreini herself constructed an essential facet of her image by offsetting her activities on the stage and in the literary sphere with an irreproachable private persona, constructing a 'hermaphroditic persona credible in both male and female authoritative spheres.'[81] At the same time, the mock-condemnation of marriage and its rebuttal was part of *commedia dell'arte* repertory as well as literary expression. Francesco Andreini's *Ragionamenti*, for example, include a dialogue between two fathers in which one urges the other to preserve his son from the dangers of marriage,[82] while in the epistolary context, texts like the *Dell'Ammogliarsi, piacevole contesa fra i due moderni Tassi* (1593) also adopted a pro- and contra- approach to the subject that likely informed Andreini's treatment.[83] Unlike these texts, however, in Andreini's *Lettere* the 'set piece' of the pros and cons of marriage gains context and complexity from the larger backdrop of letters advancing positive depictions of women against which it is positioned, as well as from the spectre of Andreini's own iconic public image as an exemplary wife and mother.

One well-known letter that departs from the conventional rhetoric of many of these other compositions regarding female virtue is entitled 'On the Birth of a Woman,' and offers an important and original approach to the so-called 'woman question.' Written in the female voice, this letter to a father who wishes his newborn daughter had been born a boy makes an eloquent case for the dignity and importance of women. It does so, however, by deftly critiquing women's subservient position in society even as it ostensibly upholds conventional gender ideology, thus displaying an awareness of the ways in which gender, or at least gender roles, are constructed. Fathers, Andreini writes, should rejoice in the birth of daughters who will be docile and obedient to their families, submitting to every command: 'le pazienti donne si contentano di viver in quella soggezione, nella qual nascono ... d'aver il breve confine della casa, per dolce prigione godendo della continua servitù ...' ('patient women are content to live under the subjection into which they are born ... to count their home as a sweet prison, enjoying their perpetual servitude ...').[84] She contrasts the useful passivity of daughters to the misfortune that less obedient sons can bring upon their families, citing Oedipus as an example. Unlike sons, who ignore their duty to their families, or worse, daughters submit quietly, whether to the convent or to marriage, without complaint. Again, however, Andreini's language belies her praise. The convent to which daughters go meekly is a lonely life enclosed amid thick walls ('tra solitarie mura'), marriage an unpleasant yoke ('giogo maritale'), often to the most undesirable of men, while women must demonstrate unflagging patience in tolerating their husbands' innumerable defects. Andreini's unthreatening praise of women for their conformity to societal norms is, at the same time, a knowing critique of those norms. Like many texts of the *querelle des femmes* that informs this letter, Andreini closes her missive with a list of women famous for their virtue and knowledge – women who did honour to their families by proving themselves not only equal, but superior to men in these areas. In contrast to the havoc wreaked by Oedipus and Paris, Andreini states, Corinna, Sappho, Aspasia, Diotima, and dozens of others brought only honour and glory to their sex. With this recollection of admirable and learned women in history, Andreini ties her letter to an important tool of pro-woman discourse, that of the catalogue of 'women worthies.' Used to important effect by Boccaccio, the technique filtered into epistolary rhetoric in works such as Lando's *Lettere di molte valorose donne*, which is virtually constructed upon such lists.[85] Thus Andreini, too, situates her *Lettere* not only in the realm of epistolary writing, but as a means to convey a specifically pro-woman discourse.

Despite Croce's admonition that the Seicento was an era 'devoid of the female presence,' works by Isabella Andreini and others – including Arcangela Tarabotti, discussed in the next chapter – demonstrate that not only did women continue to write and publish in the baroque period, identifying and participating in major literary trends, but also that an audience for works written by women continued to grow.[86] Andreini's *Lettere* demonstrate an engagement with the literary currents of seventeenth-century society and an awareness of the multifaceted nature of epistolary exchange and its possibilities as a vehicle for public self-presentation. Francesco Andreini's posthumous publication of his wife's 'letters' only reinforces the degree to which letter publication had come to serve as the apex of literary achievement and even celebrity. The entire Andreini family – many of whom were still actively invested in the theatre – had an interest in preserving and promoting their matriarch's memory and legacy.[87] Andreini herself, who in publishing works of poetry and pastoral had proved an astute assessor of literary trends, was no less interested in her own public image, and the possibilities of the letter for self-presentation and self-promotion had not escaped her. In her *Lettere* as in her life, she managed a careful balance between a public voice and a private image, her literary achivement and theatrical *innamorata* discourse coexisting carefully with her virtuous image as a loyal wife and mother. The hermaphroditic persona created in the *Lettere* serves as a buffer between the figure of the author and the views she expresses, particularly with regard to the problems posed by the *querelle des femmes*. It creates an added layer of complexity and distance that may help to explain the enduring admiration of and surprising lack of hostility towards Andreini, an actress and a writer with a decidedly pro-woman stance. Thus, the reputation of the renowned Isabella Andreini – who had been crowned with poet's laurels along with Tasso, and who received the honour of a state burial upon her death in Lyons – remained unmarred by this further excursion into male literary space and by this deeper experimentation with the boundaries of gender.

It is perhaps worth noting, finally, that Andreini's unusual hermaphroditic voice went neither unnoticed nor unimitated. The love letters of Margherita Costa, a singer and courtesan who was not an actress by profession but who had many links to the theatre, used this device to even more theatrical effect in a series of male-female dialogues on love in epistolary form.[88] In reading Costa's *Lettere amorose*, we can see the distillation of the hermaphroditic epistolary voice of Andreini's *Lettere* into an even sharper and ultimately comic guise, as the genteel *innamorata* origins of this device give way to the influence of the literary baroque. While echoing many aspects of Andreini's letters, Costa's burlesque re-imagining of the love letter includes missives ascribed to unusual kinds of lovers drawn from the court culture she encountered at Florence.[89] Here we find exchanges not between *commedia dell'arte innamorati*, but rather among lovers who are physically deformed or ill, from *gobbi* and *nani* (hunchbacks and dwarves) to *malfranciosati* and *rognosi* (syphilitics and sufferers of skin diseases). The typical themes of love are all in evidence, but placed in a new comic framework, while the baroque predilection for intriguing imperfections is taken to parodic heights: a recurring figure in Costa's poetry as well as her letters, for example, is the *donna senza naso*, the woman without a nose.[90] It is Costa's 'Zerbino' character in particular, however, who calls direct attention to the gendered complexities of the hermaphroditic text pioneered by Andreini. A dandy who dresses in feminine clothing and affects feminine mannerisms, Zerbino provokes the disdain of the women whose company he seeks. He is the target of spite from a certain 'Bella Donna' who deciphers, in typical baroque fashion, the letters of his name from Z to O: E, the second letter, signifies 'ermafrodito.'[91] Womanish lovers blur the lines of gender in a displeasing manner, the writer reprimands, and fail to incite the appropriate response in women ('non mi fanno gettar sospiri, e pianti' ['they do not move me to sighs and tears']). The madrigal that accompanies this letter, also composed in the female voice, admonishes that the Zerbino's affectation of feminine customs such as make-up and fine clothing makes him distasteful to women, a hermaphroditic figure who cannot be properly categorized:

> Stracciar coi denti il guanto, e 'l fazzoletto,
> romper le scarpe sopra i calcagnini,
> imbrattarsi le gote di rossetto,
> e farsi nella chioma i ricciolini
> a me non piaccion ...
> Che non Zerbini in me godo gli Amanti.[92]
>
> Gnawing at gloves and handkerchief with the teeth,
> ruining shoes at the heel,
> staining cheeks with paint,
> and curling one's hair
> are not pleasing to me ...
> I don't like dandies for my lovers.

It is a curious paradox: almost of all Costa's numerous works, like Andreini's *Lettere*, could be termed hermaphroditic for their assumption of male and female voices, and Costa moves freely between these personae, yet here she adopts an attitude of contempt towards men who test the boundaries of gender in their non-literary behaviour. The ability to perform gender in the literary sphere does not translate to a broader conception of the mobility or flexibility of these concepts in practice.

If the letter collections of Andreini and Costa are marked by a playful, theatrical use of gender, the last epistolary text we will examine utterly rejects such embellishments in favour of a return to a strictly Aretinian style of utilizing the letter as a vehicle not only for self-promotion, but for the establishment of specific alliances and patronage. Writing from within the convent of Sant'Anna in Venice, Arcangela Tarabotti, a cloistered nun, approaches the problem of gender from an entirely different angle. Her concern is not to demonstrate the artificiality of gender constructs, but rather to broach the gendered divisions that segregate the convent world from the literary realm beyond it. If all the collections we have examined to this point have had, in some sense, a didactic component reflective of the broader trend towards teaching how to write in specific registers through imitation, Tarabotti's letters seek less to teach than to promote and to defend the author's reputation and works. Where the letters of Andreini and Costa take us to new degrees of genericity, those of Tarabotti return us to the realm of specificity. Replete with names of people, places, and literary works, her letters require the engagement of the reader with the specific context of seventeenth-century Venice and are aimed at reconstructing for public record the nun's own literary history.

6 The Pen for the Sword: Arcangela Tarabotti's *Lettere familiari e di complimento*

I. La Monaca Forzata

If Isabella Andreini's epistolary compositions are centred on highly stylized discourses on love and humanist set pieces, the letters of Arcangela Tarabotti, the Venetian nun and writer who is the subject of this final chapter, mark a departure from such overtly fictionalized epistolary performance. Tarabotti's *Lettere familiari e di complimento* (1650) constitute rather a return to the use of the letter to promote and defend the self, as pioneered by Aretino. For Tarabotti, a cloistered nun who passed her days within the segregated space of the convent, letters had a uniquely urgent and practical significance. Through letters, and indeed through writing in general, she could broach the confines of the convent, interacting with men and women not only outside its borders but even beyond those of Venice: her contacts included prominent lay and religious figures from other parts of Italy and even France. Tarabotti's literary endeavours were not uncontested, however. The nun struggled constantly to publish her works, which met with opposition both for the socially and politically volatile material they addressed, and their author's religious status, a problem she addresses repeatedly in her *epistolario*.[1] An outspoken advocate for women, who refused to resign herself to her fate as a *monaca forzata* (that is, a nun not by vocation but by coercion), Tarabotti had to contend not only with the barriers to literary participation faced by all women writers, but with the still more deeply institutionalized disapproval she faced as a cloistered nun who sought to participate in public, secular discourse.[2]

Although the *Lettere*, of all Tarabotti's writing, elicited the least open controversy, they were a deeply transgressive work. Intricately tied to the nun's own personal and literary interactions, many (although not all) of these missives had practical origins in real correspondence, in contrast to collections we have examined in the previous chapters. The publication of one's personal letters was, for a cloistered nun, a defiant act, a direct challenge to the codes of separation and silence that, if seen in early modern society as ideally applicable to all women, had in seventeenth-century Venice been actually and directly imposed on nuns. Sixteenth- and seventeenth-century decrees by Venetian officials variously curtailed and prohibited letter-writing by nuns, yet Tarabotti not only exchanged letters, but published them, thereby symbolically and practically crossing the threshold of the most private and female of worlds to claim a place in the public realm. The primary focus of the *Lettere* is on Tarabotti's identity as a writer, as she chronicles the composition of her works and her constant efforts to publish them and targets and dismantles the criticisms that have been levelled against her. On a broader plane, the *Lettere* reflect an acute understanding of the letter as a literary form located at the intersection of public and private communication, as Tarabotti uses her correspondence to influence both internal and external readers' perception of her and to recast the controversies that threaten her. The *Lettere* play an important role in situating Tarabotti within the literary arena of which she constantly strove to be a part, establishing a portrait of the nun as writer, polemicist, and critic that overshadows the religious role so unwelcomely assigned to her.[3]

Born in 1604, Elena Cassandra Tarabotti was, like many girls in Venice, destined for the convent at an early age.[4] Many middle- and upper-class Venetian families placed their daughters in convents as an alternative to marriage, whether to avoid the economic burden of overblown dowries, or to avoid 'marrying down' in the face of a diminishing pool of suitable bridegrooms.[5] The economic rationale of the family was mirrored in the political rationale of the Venetian State, which encouraged the practice as a means of controlling and containing the patriciate.[6] Yet, whereas just a century earlier such a destiny did not necessarily impose strict limits on women's contact with the outside world (indeed, nuns often left the convent for brief periods to visit their families), things were quite different by Tarabotti's time. In an effort to impose order and regularity on religious institutions, the *Decretum de regularibus et monialibus* issued in 1563 at the Council of Trent had made *clausura*, or strict enclosure, mandatory in all women's convents.[7] Unlike many of the decree's other provisions, including those concerning the observation of vows, the renunciation of property, and the establishment of a minimum age of sixteen years for the profession of vows, all of which were equally applicable to both male and female religious, *clausura* was intended only for women, and reflects, as Garbriella Zarri notes, the different value placed on the vows of chastity for male and female religious.[8] It is, Zarri writes, an extension of the general ideals of modesty and seclusion to which women in general were expected to conform.[9] If the preservation of chastity was considered essential for all women, it was in the convents that this dictate was most tangible. Indeed, the ideal structure for convents was considered to be a protected space (although not an isolated one, which might cause its own problems), with high walls, few windows, and *parlatori* – the space in which nuns could receive approved and supervised visits – protected by grates, ensuring the separation of the nun from the outside world even in what limited contact was permitted her.[10] The convent, in effect, was reconceptualized and materially restructured to create a kind of 'additional hymen,' an external barrier to safeguard the virginity of the women inside.[11]

Tarabotti, perhaps because she was lame and had poorer marriage prospects than did her five sisters, entered the convent of Sant'Anna in her neighbourhood of Castello as an *educanda*, or student-boarder, in 1617.[12] Some years later, Tarabotti – now Sister Arcangela – would recall with fury the hypocrisy and deception with which innocent young girls were led into convent life, or, as Tarabotti less generously termed it, 'convent hell,' a never-ending condition of unbearable physical and emotional stasis. Powerless to alter her condition, Tarabotti went on to profess vows in 1623, becoming part of a small community of Benedictine nuns among whom she would live and write until her death in 1652. Although she forged a few close friendships in Sant'Anna, it was, as we will see in our analysis of her letters, the literary life she carried on beyond the convent walls that truly sustained her. Largely self-taught, Tarabotti used her pen as a means to participate in literary and political exchange and debate.[13] The prolific nun published four works in her lifetime and composed at least two others, both of which had some circulation in manuscript form. In all of these texts, Tarabotti's anger and frustration at the systematic subjugation of women – through coerced monachizations, bad marriages, and lack of access to education – are palpable. A true protofeminist, Tarabotti rails not only against her own condition, but against that of all women. Not content with merely describing their lot, she seeks the underlying political and social causes for it.[14] Tarabotti's earliest work, originally called *La tirannia paterna* (the title was changed to *La semplicità ingannata* when the work was published posthumously under the pseudonym Galerana Baratotti), asserts that women are equal to men, God having granted free will to both Adam and Eve, and takes aim, with remarkable political acuity, at the state-sponsored practice of *monacazione forzata*, or coerced monachization.[15] A dual attack on the fathers of Venice, who betray their daughters' trust by consigning them to the convent, and on the State itself, which supports the practice because it poses a limit to the growth of the aristocracy, the work was never published in Tarabotti's lifetime; nor was another early manuscript dealing with the same theme, the *Inferno monacale*. Tarabotti's first published work was rather her *Paradiso monacale*, a celebration of convent life for women with a true religious calling.[16] Long considered a 'revocation' of Tarabotti's thought in the *Tirannia paterna* and the *Inferno monacale*, or evidence of a religious conversion, scholars have more recently agreed that the *Paradiso*, while perhaps constituting an effort by the nun to come to peace with her situation, is not a revocation at all. Tarabotti never takes issue in her works with convent life for those who enter it willingly; but only with the abusive practice of consigning girls to convents to serve economic and political ends.[17] The publisher's preface to the *Paradiso*, which announces several forthcoming works by Tarabotti 'piú piccanti' ('more provocative') than the *Paradiso*, also suggests that Tarabotti had not abandoned her fervent views on this subject. One of these future works is identified as the *Tirannia paterna*; the other was likely the *Inferno monacale*.[18] The *Tirannia* and the *Inferno* are, of course, two of Tarabotti's angriest and most politically engaged works; her intentions to publish them on the heels of the *Paradiso* hardly seem in keeping with any kind of drastic reconsideration of her views on coerced monachization. It is far more likely Tarabotti chose to publish the *Paradiso* first because it was, of her three manuscripts thus far, simply the least controversial in content, and thus the most publishable.[19]

This declaration regarding future Tarabotti volumes, however, never came to pass. Her next work, published not by Oddoni but Valvasense, was rather her *Antisatira*, a response to a 'semi-serious' satire of women's fashion and behaviour by the Sienese academician Francesco Buoninsegni.[20] Using Buoninsegni's own rhetorical tools of exaggeration, paradox, and exempla, the *Antisatira* – published under the initials 'D.A.T.' (D[onna] A[rcangela] T[arabotti]) – turned Buoninsegni's arguments about female vanity back upon the male sex and went on to maintain that if men wished women to give up their worldly preoccupations, they ought not exclude them from learning: women, Tarabotti argued, were naturally superior to men, but were held back by their lack of access to education.²¹ While, unlike the *Tirannia paterna* and the *Inferno monacale*, the *Antisatira* did not make *monacazione forzata* its primary target, its focus on male vanity and hypocrisy was even less palatable to some Venetian readers. Its publication in 1644 was met with great hostility even by Tarabotti's former allies, who easily saw through the text's flimsy anonymity. Perhaps the most vicious reaction came from the friar and writer Angelico Aprosio in the form of his *Maschera scoperta*, a personal attack on the nun that exposed what limited anonymity the *Antisatira's* publication with her initials had granted her. Probably through the influential connections she had managed to establish to the publishing world, Tarabotti was able to keep the *Maschera scoperta* from being printed.²² Even much later, however, after Tarabotti's death, the *Antisatira* was still making waves: a *Censura dell'Antisatira* by Lodovico Sesti appeared in 1656.

Tarabotti published two more books in her lifetime.²³ In 1651, just a year before her death, *Che le donne siano della specie degli uomini* appeared. Like the *Antisatira*, it was a response to a misogynist text. In this case, the claims Tarabotti rebutted were rather more serious: an anonymous treatise, *Disputatio nova contra mulieres, qua probatur eas homines non esse* (generally attributed to the German humanist Valens Acidalius) of 1595 had asserted that women were not human beings. Although a rebuttal had already been issued by the Lutheran Simon Gedik with his *Defensio sexus mulieribus*, a 1647 Italian translation of the *Disputatio* by 'Horatio Plata' (possibly a member of the *Accademia degli Incogniti*) brought renewed attention to Acidalius' controversial arguments.²⁴ The translation did not include Gedik's response, leaving Tarabotti to come to the defence of her sex. In *Che le donne siano*, Tarabotti launches a defence of women by carefully and methodically responding to and dismantling each of Acidalius/Plata's arguments with Biblical examples of her own, an exceptional demonstration of authority by a woman.²⁵

One year prior to *Che le donne siano*, however, Tarabotti had published the text which concerns us here. The nun's *Lettere familiari e di complimento*, printed by the Guerigli of Venice, appeared in 1650 and focused on the defence not of women in general but rather of the writer in particular. Best read as a kind of literary journal, the *Lettere* are overwhelmingly characterized by their attention to and concern with establishing, preserving, and defending Tarabotti's literary identity and reputation: indeed, nearly every letter makes reference in some way to Tarabotti's own works or those of others, and Tarabotti's most frequent correspondents are writers and figures active in the editorial world. Giovan Francesco Loredano, founder of Venice's *Accademia degli Incogniti* and an influential presence in Venetian publishing, appears in the *Lettere* as the recipient of thirteen letters and it is to Loredano that the collection is dedicated.[26] Giacomo Pighetti (Tarabotti's brother-in-law), Francesco Pona, Giovanni Dandolo, Pietro Paolo Bissari, and even Aprosio (all, like Loredano, members of the *Incogniti*), appear frequently in the *Lettere*.[27] Tarabotti's literary network extended even beyond Italy: her collection includes a letter to Gabriel Naudé, librarian to the powerful Cardinal Mazarin of France, as well as a letter to the cardinal himself.[28]

While many of these men admired Tarabotti, the outspoken, protofeminist writer elicited extraordinary hostility from many of Venice's *letterati*. Her detractors attacked her on a number of fronts and even accused her of not having authored the works she published. Her letters serve to counter such allegations by giving readers a history of her writing and laying bare the background and motivation of these literary skirmishes from the privileged vantage point of the epistolary communication, a first-person platform that creates a powerful fiction of authenticity in its claim to transcribe faithfully the experience of the authorial subject. Tarabotti's letters further, in Aretinian fashion, allow the nun to take note publicly of her friends and enemies, rewarding the former with praise and admiration and lambasting the latter with public scorn; as becomes clear upon reading the full collection of 256 letters, however, the distinction between friend and foe is not always clear, nor constant, for in more than one instance Tarabotti's admirers turned against her.

II. The *Lettere familiari e di complimento*

Nuns and Epistolary Exchange

Just as the physical containment of nuns within convents was intended to 'protect' their honour by vastly limiting their contact with the outside, so too were efforts made to prevent or limit less direct forms of interaction with that world, such as letter-writing. Like visits to the *parlatori*, it was feared that epistolary exchange with the outside world might expose nuns to influences from which they ought to be protected. Letter-writing was to be strictly regulated and limited to immediate family and others with express permission, as proclaimed in a decree issued to Venice's female convents in 1636.[29] Ignoring such restrictions could result in confinement to one's cell, suspension of *parlatorio* privileges, the revocation of a voice in convent affairs, and the suspension of eligibility for any kind of office within the convent.[30] Similarly, a 1644 order (issued in the same period in which Tarabotti was engaged in some of the very correspondence later published in her *Lettere*) exhorted nuns not to write letters at all, even to their most immediate family.[31] Even earlier, less severe regulations governing letter-writing insisted that any letters written or received by the nuns were subject to review by the abbess to ensure that both content and correspondent were acceptable.[32] If letter-writing, even to kin, was seen as a threat to the boundaries between the convent and the external world that had been so forcefully constructed in the post-Tridentine climate, then Tarabotti made a remarkably subversive gesture in not only writing, but publishing, a book composed entirely of personal correspondence. Although there were a few precedents for epistolary publication by women religious, including Catherine of Siena, the Dominican tertiary Osanna da Mantova, and the Genovese nun Battistina Vernazza, such texts were – in addition to being published posthumously (and not originally intended for print) – distinctly spiritual in nature, distinguishing them from Tarabotti's manifestly secular letters.[33] As historian Mario Rosa points out, Tarabotti's secular writings made her an 'anomaly' at a time when nuns who chose to write usually produced spiritual works or devotional poetry.[34] Her array of correspondents, moreover, is equally unusual: of 256 letters, only nine are addressed to family – two to Tarabotti's sisters, and the remaining seven to her brother-in-law Pighetti, who played an active role in the nun's literary career. The other 247 missives are directed to writers, diplomats, leaders, and a very few religious figures, mostly male and of no relation at all to Tarabotti; it is, moreover, unlikely that Tarabotti asked for and received permission to correspond with all of these persons as required by the order cited above.[35]

How, then, was it possible for Tarabotti to publish such a work? If her earlier works had resulted in controversy, she must have expected a similar reception for her *Lettere*, a thoroughly secular work of which she, a nun, was the principal protagonist, a defence of her literary oeuvre in which she would take aim at her enemies (and at men in general) while praising her friends, some of them controversial in their own right. Not only was there no shortage of men (and even women) who might resent the way they were depicted in the *Lettere*, but objections were sure to be raised on the basis of the writer's religious status. Moreover, in addition to their single-minded attention to Tarabotti's literary persona, the letters reveal an unmistakable subtext of resistance to the fate of the *monaca forzata* through frequent references to the convent as a prison (*carcere*) and to herself as a 'martyr' of religion. Nor does she miss the opportunity to target, as in her more overtly political works, the *padri di famiglia* guilty of populating the convents with their daughters, predicting that they will be excluded from Paradise. Despite the secular quality of the *Lettere* and their provocative language, however, Tarabotti was able to obtain the *licenza* necessary to publish the work.[36]

One explanation for Tarabotti's success in publishing the *Lettere* lies in the nun's keen understanding of the gendered connotations of epistolary writing as a literary form driven by emotion and passion, as described in the introduction. In seeking permission to publish, Tarabotti downplayed the public, literary aspect of her letters and focused instead on her desire to memorialize her friend and *consorella* Regina Donà, whose death she repeatedly laments throughout the collection and whom she eulogizes in a consolatory work entitled *Le lagrime* ('*Tears*') that she appends to the *Lettere*.[37] Like Lucrezia Gonzaga (discussed in chapter 3), Tarabotti frames her efforts at epistolary composition and publication as a form of consolation: it is her sorrow that leads her to write. Within the *Lettere*, Regina's death functions as one of the few truly conventional thematic threads in the collection, offsetting the volume's primary preoccupation with the author's literary career. Capitalizing on notions of letter-writing as inherently feminine and driven by emotion and spontaneity, Tarabotti makes frequent reference to her sorrow at Regina's death, particularly when addressing female correspondents such as Betta Polani, Guid'Ascania Orsi, and Regina's sister, Andriana Malipieri. On more than one occasion, she explains how this loss inspired her to write the *Lagrime*, as in a letter to Orsi, a Bolognese nun and poet with whom Tarabotti exchanged literary advice:[38]

> Sappia dunque ... che la notte istessa che la mia già dilettissima amica volò nel seno del suo sposo e lasciò me a travagliare, priva della maggior parte di me stessa – quella notte, dico, per soddisfar all'affetto, vergai alcuni fogli in sua lode, ma privi d'ogni buon ordine di retorica, sconcertati ne' periodi, poveri d'eruditioni, ricchi d'errori, e essausti d'ogni buona qualità.[39]

> Know, therefore ... that the very night my once beloved friend flew to the bosom of her spouse and left me here to grieve, bereft of the greatest part of myself – that night, I say, to appease my affection, I drafted a few pages

in praise of her, but devoid of any good rhetorical order, disorganized in their clauses, and lacking in erudition; rich in errors, and without any good qualities at all.

Declaring that the work is the imperfect product of a personal loss, Tarabotti feigns despair that it is about to see the light of day.[40] This is not an uncommon strategy for Tarabotti, who, with a formulaic note of self-deprecation, often professes dismay that her works are published. Nevertheless, it is here that the crux of Tarabotti's literary acuity lies, for by characterizing the *Lagrime* as a personal, 'spontaneous' work, the nun taps into conventional, gendered characterizations of nature and art in literature, presenting the work as the product of the (feminine) former rather than the (masculine) latter (while temporarily obscuring, as we will see, the transgressive force of the less-easily dismissed *Lettere*). Tarabotti makes frequent, strategic use of ideas about the 'natural' and untutored quality of female expression in her *Lettere*, often describing herself as an unlettered woman guided by 'semplice naturalezza' ('simple naturalness').[41] Yet other letters clearly demonstrate that the composition of the *Lagrime* was quite reasoned, and that Tarabotti subsequently took an active role in promoting the work, using it as an acceptable premise capable of passing quickly through the intricacies of publishing procedure, with the more provocative *Lettere familiari* following along with it. Tarabotti's publishing strategy is made evident, for example, in a request to an unidentified correspondent influential in the publishing world.[42] In contrast to her letter to Orsi in which she affects to resist the publication of the *Lagrime*, Tarabotti now presents herself as a strong literary negotiator who has every intention of publishing both the *Lagrime* and the *Lettere*, making it clear that she actively seeks permission to publish both works:

> I miei oscurissimi inchiostri sen vengono agli splendori di Vostra Eccellenza per impetrare lumi da poter anche loro legitamamente comparir nel Teatro del Mondo. Addimandano le licenze dal signor Secretario Quirini, e dal reverendissimo Padre Inquisitore, né credo che Vostra Eccellenza neghi incontro felice a tal richiesta, mentre vedrà nel fine dell'opera delineate le glorie della mia dilettissima amica.[43]

My obscure writings come before your splendor to beg for illumination, that they too might appear legitimately on the World's stage. They request permission from *signor* Secretary Quirini, and from the most reverend

Father Inquisitor; nor do I believe that you would deny a happy outcome to such a request, when you will see the glory of my dearest friend described at the end of the work.

Significantly, Tarabotti downplays her letters, which comprise the major focus of the volume (referring to them as the very 'dark' or 'obscure' products of her pen), in favour of the *Lagrime* (no longer the 'scartafazzi' described in her letter to Orsi, but rather 'glorie' that praise Regina's memory). The phrasing of her request assumes that the presence of the one will prove reason enough to publish the other. Significantly, Tarabotti asks that her application for a *licenza* be kept secret, suggesting that the nun, aware of the objections her letters might arouse, sought to stave off such opposition until the book had already been printed: 'Supplico perciò, genuflessa, Vostra Eccellenza favorire quell'anima santa ed ottenermi con celerità le licenze, *ma che non si sappia ch'io le ricerca*' ('Therefore I beg, on bended knee, that you favour that saintly soul by quickly obtaining a license for me, but that *no one should know that I seek it*').[44] Even here, Regina's irreproachable image adds weight to Tarabotti's words, as the nun ties her request for a speedy conclusion of the matter to a gesture of respect towards Regina (linking the first clause, *'favorire quell'anima santa,'* to the second, *'ed ottenermi con celerità le licenze'*).

That Tarabotti manifests here the desire to publish the *Lagrime* – in obvious contradiction with her letter to Guid'Ascania Orsi – while also making clear her intention to publish the *Lettere* raises some questions for the reader who is provided with two versions of the episode. Why does she allow such contradiction? Tarabotti does, it is true, offer a potential explanation when, in one instance, she distances herself from the actual selection and publication of her letters, claiming: '[Signor N.] ... fece una scelta delle migliori, anzi senza il concorso della mia volontà ha concertato di ponerle alla luce' ('[Signor N.] ... made a selection of the best ones; indeed without my participation he plotted to publish them');[45] such a lack of participation in the assemblage of the collection might account for these discrepancies, were Tarabotti's claim not unconvincing for several reasons. First, as we have seen in earlier chapters, it was common to assert modesty or passivity with regard to the publication of one's work – and perhaps particularly necessary in the case of letters, which rendered an author particularly vulnerable to accusations of self-aggrandizement. More importantly, however, such an assertion of non-involvement is belied by Tarabotti's efforts, chronicled by the writer herself, to publish her letters: indeed, in the same letter to *Signor N.* in which she disavows agency in the affair, Tarabotti asks for the return of her letters to him and notes that they may be published.[46] As Zanette puts it, 'la scelta [delle lettere] ci fu senza dubbio, ma con la sua diretta collaborazione.'[47]

Tarabotti's claims to non-involvement are further belied by evidence suggesting that she altered some of her correspondence before publication. A group of autograph letters from Tarabotti to Angelico Aprosio, for example, demonstrates that the nun subjected her letters to a process of selection before publication, choosing to exclude some of it from the printed collection, and publishing at least one letter in revised form.[48] In one letter, which is not included in the collection, for example, the nun explicitly asks Aprosio (in the friendlier days of their later difficult relationship) to help edit her *Paradiso monacale*.[49] Since, as I argue here, Tarabotti uses her published letters in part to defend herself against accusations of not having authored her own works, she may have 'censored' this letter out of the collection.[50] Another autograph letter, which does not appear in print, offers a particularly severe – perhaps impolitic – criticism of the male species as a whole.[51] The one letter we possess in both autograph and printed form undergoes some slight changes in wording and spelling before being printed;[52] more significantly, an entire passage in which the cloistered nun bleakly refers to herself as 'morta e sepolta già tanti anni sono' ('dead and buried for many years') is deleted from the published letter.[53] A final example from the autograph letters shows that even when Tarabotti excludes a letter from her *epistolario*, parts of it may appear in the published collection, as is the case with the first autograph letter, in which she states (with regard to the *Tirannia paterna*) 'So la materia esser scabrosa, ma contraria al politico vivere, non al cattolico' ('I know the material is delicate, but it goes against political, not Catholic, life'). This phrase reappears in print in a letter to Paolo Donado: 'Conosco la materia scabrosa per esser contraria, se non al catolico, al politico vivere' ('I know the material is delicate because it goes against political, if not Catholic, life').[54] Similar changes are evident in the transition of Tarabotti's letters to Vittoria della Rovere from manuscript to print form: a group of five manuscript letters in Florence show that significant stylistic revisions were made before publication.[55]

Given Tarabotti's attention to the transition between private and public communication, between manuscript and print epistolary forms, the presence of conflicting versions of the publication history of the

Lagrime and the *Lettere* cannot be deemed an oversight. Its purpose might be as simple as the realistic reflection of the shifts and changes over time reflected in epistolary communication: Tarabotti may, in fact, have been truthful when she first insisted that she did not intend to publish the *Lagrime*, yet when she needed leverage to publish her letters, she saw the utility of turning to this earlier composition in order to do so. On the other hand, given her attention to choosing and revising her letters for publication, these different versions suggest a strategy of selective concealment and disclosure similar to that described by some critics in discussions of other genres such as autobiography.[56] Such a strategy, in which a writer reveals some aspects of her experience while concealing others, or, alternatively, reveals certain aspects only to conceal them later, is particularly suited to the complex and often conflicting demands of women's authorship and publication. As Graziella Parati points out, 'To talk, but at the same time, not to say too much, is much more than a woman's desire; it expresses the need to create a document that is only indirectly controversial, a work that invades the literary space crowded by metaphors of male selves, but at the same time negates such an action.'[57] Similarly, Tarabotti's 'conflicting' presentations of the path to publication reflects the inherent conflict in women's epistolary publication, the clash between the desire to 'go public,' on the one hand, and cultural conventions governing women's expression on the other. By presenting herself as both a reticent writer, driven to literary composition by her grief at the death of a dear friend, and a determined author who astutely plays on conventional ideas about epistolary writing in order to publish her quite unconventional *Lettere*, Tarabotti both reveals and conceals, risks and protects herself.

Creating an Epistolary Network

If Regina's memorial rendered the *Lettere* more palatable to the *revisori*, Tarabotti still needed to convince her readers that she, a cloistered nun with little formal education, was a literary figure in her own right whose correspondence was worthy of their attention. By publishing a volume of familiar correspondence, Tarabotti took her place among a host of authors before her who had crowned their literary careers with such a book. The gesture, as we have noted, was a bold one for any writer. In addition to authorizing the writer's experience, an *epistolario* was also a public display of the range of literary, social, or political ties. The publication of the *Lettere* was therefore an essential step in the formation of

Tarabotti's literary persona, and it was important that she secure backing for her enterprise and illustrate the full range of her connections. To this end, she enlisted a number of personages, from the Doge of Venice to Vittoria della Rovere and Cardinal Mazarin of France, seeking the reflected light of their authority and status. It was Loredano, however, with his all-important connections to the world of Venetian publishing, who was of particular importance to Tarabotti in terms of literary validation as well as practical help in getting her works published.

Tarabotti and Loredano had an almost symbiotic association. Tarabotti was dependent upon Loredano's support of her literary career, while Loredano seems to have regarded Tarabotti with some condescension, prizing her as an oddity, charming for her outspokenness and her literary ability, but not to be taken too seriously, nor consistently championed. The nun's epistolary interaction with Loredano is therefore largely shaped by their often unstable literary relationship, and indeed his own letters to her reflect a similar changeability.[58] In the case of the *Lettere,* Loredano encouraged Tarabotti, but – to her consternation – lost interest in the project at least once before helping her to bring it to press. The ups and downs of this interaction are reflected in several letters published in her volume.

That Loredano ultimately supported the publication of the *Lettere* is made clear in the very first pages of the collection, in which she offers the book to him as a gesture of esteem (or repayment). Her baroque *dedicatoria* situates the *Lettere* within a literary, public framework: not only does Tarabotti evoke the protection of one of the most powerful men in Venetian publishing, she also links herself to the literary circle of the *Accademia degli Incogniti* by dedicating her work to its founder. Her letter to Loredano observes the conventions of the literary dedication – extravagant praise for the dedicatee, expression of the author's own humility, request for protection – and Tarabotti explicitly places herself in a literary tradition, saying that in publishing her letters to the honour of Loredano, she is imitating the classical authors: 'risolvo di raccoglier tutte le lettere in un solo volume, e con esso riverir la di lei persona, imitando in questo gli antichi, che ad ogni Nume dedicavano un giorno, e tutto l'anno intiero lo consacravano al sommo Giove' ('I am resolved to collect my letters in a single volume, and with it honour your person, thereby imitating the ancients, who dedicated a day to each god, and consecrated the year entire to Jove on high.')[59]

Into her lavish praise of her patron, Tarabotti weaves a subtle defence of the *Lettere* that works simultaneously to lend authority to the volume while deflecting potential criticism of its unconventional authorship. Tarabotti's humble missives, she tells us directly, have had illustrious recipients outside the religious community, 'cavallieri e personaggi del secolo, grandi per virtú, per nascita, e per condizione' ('gentlemen and personages of the world, great in virtue, birth, and status'). By drawing attention to her correspondence with prominent lay men and women, Tarabotti shows that she is part of a network much larger than the convent world to which she has been confined, with the clear implication that her letters compete in the same field as those of secular writers. Tarabotti then explains that, having honoured such personages with her letters, it is only right that she should honour her patron in similar fashion; thus, she resolves to gather and publish her letters in his honour. Though here Tarabotti assumes responsibility for the decision to publish her letters, her expression of literary agency is offset by her praise of Loredano and the introduction of a note of modesty about her missives, which she describes as 'deboli e imperfetti scritti' ('weak and imperfect scribblings'). In a typical combinination of self-deprecation and self-promotion, however, she quickly adds that she expects them to be successful nonetheless: it is 'proprio dei fogli più leggeri il volar più in alto' ('characteristic of the least substantial pages to fly the highest'). Drawing out this seeming paradox, Tarabotti concludes with the argument that the offerings of the humblest of women are proportionally more valuable than those of the rich or the powerful, underscoring her point with a biblical reference: 'Dio nell'Evangelio, trattandosi d'una povera donna, acolse la sua picciola offerta con più affetto di quello che in alcun tempo abbia giamai ricevuto i ricchi tesori de' grandi' ('In the Gospel, God, when dealing with a poor woman, accepted her small offering with more affection than ever he demonstrated for the rich treasures received from wealthy men').[60]

In the official dedication to the *Lettere*, then, Tarabotti claims that she publishes her letters to honour Loredano, setting up a traditional motivation based on literary imitation and patronage. It is soon apparent, however, that matters were more complex. In spite of the references scattered through the early pages of the volume to Loredano's support of Tarabotti's other works, particularly the *Paradiso*, we find before long that his role as literary champion to the struggling woman writer was not quite so transparent. In contrast to early characterizations of an 'Angelico Loredano' as the nun's protector,[61] Tarabotti soon shows us a different side of Loredano – painting him this time as a man of false promises. In a curt letter to Loredano, Tarabotti – showing herself to be rather more invested in the publication of her *Lettere* than her dedication would imply – complains that her valiant supporter has fallen short of his pledges to help her publish the very volume she later dedicates to his honour:

> Se Vostra Eccellenza m'esortò di far imprimere le mie lettere, e che con gentilissime esibizioni s'offerse d'esser quel nume favorevole che le facesse comparire alla luce, ora parmi che svaniscono i consigli e le promesse, anzi da quell'oracolo ch'ebbi propizie le risposte senza chiederle, veggo troppo differito il sospirato effetto.⁶²

> If you urged me to have my letters printed, and with the kindest of gestures offered himself as that favourable deity who would see that they were brought to light, now it seems to me that all counsel and promises have disappeared; indeed, of that oracle whence I had positive responses without even asking, now I see the longed-for outcome too long deferred.

Tarabotti is expert at the backhanded compliment, and couches her sharp criticism of Loredano's unreliability as a literary mentor within a satirical play on his position as a powerful member of Venetian literary and political society, acknowledging that 'deities' are not bound by their word like mere mortals:

> Non sono però tenute alla parola le deità, e perché incomprensibili sono i lor giudizi non se ne devono doler i mortali. Ben è di dovere chiedere a loro perdono delle proprie colpe, per poter ricevere le grazie. Ond'io, conoscendo questo debito, inchinata inanzi Vostra Eccellenza accuso le mie colpe s'avessi peccato d'ignoranza ...⁶³

> However, gods are not held to their word, and because their judgments are beyond understanding, mortals must not despair. Rather they ought ask forgiveness for their faults, in order to receive favours. Whence I, understanding this debt, kneeling before you, condemn my own failings if I have sinned out of ignorance ...

Read in contrast with the flattering dedication to Loredano, this letter reinforces the multifaceted nature of Tarabotti's collection. As with her references to the *Lagrime*, Tarabotti does not seek to make her representations of Loredano coincide. Again, she presents her experience and interactions from a number of standpoints, alternately revealing and concealing information to suit her purpose – and in this case, perhaps to remind the reader of the fundamental unreliability of even the best-intentioned men.

If Tarabotti dedicates the *Lettere* to Loredano not only to recognize his ultimate support of her, but to benefit from the authority it confers upon her work, so too Giovanni Dandolo, another *Incognito*, is enlisted in the cause of the *Lettere*. In a presentation letter to the editors, Dandolo assures the Guerigli that he has read Tarabotti's *Lettere* in their entirety and can vouch that they are 'degne per le stampe.'[64] In an interesting echo of ideas about femininity and epistolarity, Dandolo states that Tarabotti's letters are a perfect blend of nature and art, of 'heroic' and 'familiar' styles, filled with 'concetti di gran rilievo' ('conceits of great interest') but never 'stirati dall'arte' ('flattened by art'). In essence, Dandolo points out that the letters possess both 'feminine' and 'literary' qualities (they are both natural and artistic). He also testifies that they fulfil the dual requirements of the epistolary genre in their inherent stylistic and thematic worthiness. Dandolo's enthusiastic praise of Tarabotti's 'divino ingegno' ('divine genius') culminates, naturally, in the highest praise of all for a woman: so modest is she, he writes, that in spite of her great talent she has published very little, shrinking from the public spotlight of authorship: in addition to the *Paradiso, Inferno, Purgatorio,* and the *Antisatira*, he writes, 'Molt'altre operette ha composte ... ma poche ne ha date alle stampe, perché i raggi della sua modestia le nascondono ed opprimono ...' ('She has composed many other little works ... but has published few of them, because the rays of her modest nature hide and suppress [her works]'). Dandolo concludes by calling attention to Tarabotti's other fine qualities, feminine and spiritual, including 'la santità dei costumi, l'innocenza della vita, la prudenza, la carità ...' ('the sanctity of her comportment, the innocence of her life, her prudence, her charity ...'), in the hopes that the editors will pay special attention to her *Lettere*. In attaching this letter to her *epistolario*, Tarabotti cleverly invokes the testimony of a well-positioned Venetian nobleman as to her worthiness both as a writer and as a nun. Not only does Dandolo's passing reference to her previous works gloss over the controversy they engendered, but his letter as a whole assures readers not only of the quality of the *Lettere*, but of Tarabotti's good reputation, in an effort to forestall with this portrayal of the writer as a retiring, innocent, modest, and generous woman the objections some might have to the publication of the work. Such a portrayal, naturally, works best when offered not by its subject but by an admiring – and admired – third party.

Having invoked in the pre-text the presence and support of two of Venice's important literary figures, Tarabotti calls upon an important political presence in the first letter of the collection proper: Doge Francesco Erizzo of Venice. Like the *dedicatoria* to Loredano, this letter also interlaces accolades for the recipient with a subtle defence of her own writing. Into her copious praise of Erizzo (whom Tarabotti casts as an ally of women, a son of the Virgin City of Venice, a 'female' city possessed of *giustizia* and all other virtues 'che si chiamano con nome feminile'), Tarabotti weaves many references to her own work, especially the *Paradiso*, which she offers to him as a gift. In offering the *Paradiso* to Erizzo, Tarabotti does not downplay the controversial aspect of her writing, but rather warns Erizzo not to take offence at her frequent critiques of the male sex: 'la prego che non si lasci recar dispiacere da quei sentimenti che vedrà sparsi nell'opere mie contro degli uomini ...' ('I pray you, do not be displeased by those sentiments you will find scattered throughout my works against men'); curiously, she offers no assurances (as she sometimes does) that she does not count him among that group she condemns.[65] Doge from 1631 to 1646, Erizzo was an excellent candidate to be portrayed in such public support of Tarabotti: the nun calls upon him in the period of his greatest glory to lend authority to her *Lettere*, but at their publication, four years had passed since Erizzo's death and he could hardly object to appearing so prominently as an admirer of this outspoken Benedictine nun.[66]

Just as Loredano, Dandolo, and Erizzo are enlisted to lend authority to Tarabotti's *Lettere* and perhaps to forestall objections to the publication of so secular and personal a work by a cloistered nun, so, too, various other public figures are evoked throughout the volume. Some are characters known primarily within the context of Venice, such as various members of the Valier family; others had a wider influence and probably a slightly greater symbolic clout, including the Duke of Parma and Vittoria della Rovere of Tuscany – both of whom Tarabotti engages in her literary struggles.[67] Finally, Tarabotti's *Lettere* illustrate the extended web of her relationships within the French diplomatic community in Venice, including her close friendship with Ambassador Nicolas Bretel de Grémonville and his family. Whether or not such contacts increased Tarabotti's status in Venice, which was hostile to the French during this period, they allowed her to expand her epistolary reach beyond Venice and approach such important personages as Cardinal Mazarin of France and his librarian, Gabriel Naudé, through her letters. Not only did her interaction with these figures, limited though it was, add international and cultural cachet to her epistolary persona, but it also constituted a practical connection for her attempts to circulate her work more widely. Naudé, for example, requested some of her works for the newly-founded Mazarine Library in France, and letters to other French acquaintances tell us that Tarabotti hoped to have her *Tirannia paterna* printed in Paris, a city she considered friendlier to women than her native Venice.[68] Together, Tarabotti's selection of correspondents includes, in addition to closer confidantes such as Betta Polani, Guid'Ascania Orsi, and her brother-in-law Pighetti, a range of contacts both literary and political, all of which lend an aura of authority not only to her *epistolario* but to her literary persona as a whole, and thus even to her prior works that had garnered so much negative controversy.

III. Controversial Texts: Claiming the *Paradiso* and the *Antisatira*

Beginning with Tarabotti's very first published work, the *Paradiso monacale*, accusations flew that she lacked the eloquence and learning necessary for authorship, or, conversely, that the erudition of her works was such that someone had surely helped her to compose them. In the case of the *Paradiso monacale*, Tarabotti's opponents went so far as to accuse her of not having authored the work at all. Such allegations – rendered the more painful for having originated with men she once considered allies, such as Aprosio and Brusoni – infuriated Tarabotti, who felt she understood their origins. Men, she would write in the *Antisatira*, not content to exclude women from education, were so threatened by women's intellectual potential that they could not accept that women could write without male assistance. This, she continues, is precisely what happened with regard to the *Paradiso monacale*.[69] Tarabotti's consciousness of her vulnerability to such allegations is reflected throughout her *Lettere*. Doubly marginalized not only by sex but also by her physical confinement within Sant'Anna, Tarabotti had only her pen with which to defend her reputation. Her discomfort with this position is evident. In a letter written to Girolamo Brusoni, for example, the writer with whom Tarabotti's relationship soured upon seeing the manuscript for his *Amori tragici*, Tarabotti reacts angrily to his discussion in that work of *monache forzate*, cloistered nuns consigned, like Tarabotti, to the convent without vocation.[70] Tarabotti was convinced that Brusoni had trespassed on her own literary territory, marked out with the composition and manuscript circulation of the *Tirannia paterna*, which she had given him to read some time before. At a disadvantage because she had not succeeded in having that work published, Tarabotti feared, not unreasonably, that if Brusoni's work appeared first, hers would seem a mere imitation – a fear made the more galling by her conviction that men inevitably assumed the worst about women's writing. Attempting to head off such an outcome, Tarabotti preemptively wrote to Brusoni accusing him of imitating her; fortunately, she added, enough real gentlemen had seen her *Tirannia paterna* to vouch for its originality:

> Stupisco bene che Vostra Signoria si dichiari d'aver parlato nell'opere sue sopra la materia delle monache forzate, mentre avendo egli veduto l'opera mia, era obligato non parlare di cosa tanto diffusamente da me trattata. Se la *Tirannia paterna* non fosse stata trascorsa da cavalieri degni prima che capitasse sotto gli occhi di lei, confesso che di tali metamorfosi ne sentirei gran dolore.[71]

> I am astounded to hear you say that you speak in your works about coerced nuns, when, having seen my work, you were obliged not to discuss a subject so amply treated by me. Had the *Tirannia paterna* not already been read by worthy gentlemen before coming before you, I confess I would be very aggrieved by such a metamorphosis.

Tarabotti was, necessarily, protective of her literary reputation. If, in the *Antisatira*, Tarabotti had taken the opportunity to respond to the controversy over her *Paradiso*, I suggest that the *Lettere* were conceived with the primary aim of dismantling any negative claims about any of her works, from the unpublished *Tirannia paterna* to the *Paradiso* and the *Antisatira*. As is evident from her letter to Brusoni, Tarabotti understood that she could manipulate the public space of her *Lettere* to turn the tables on her literary foes, recasting key episodes from her point of view and shaping her readers' interpretation of events. By making public her epistolary rebuke of Brusoni, Tarabotti publicized and solidified her own position without ever publishing the work in question. Analogously, by providing in the *Lettere* glimpses into the conception, composition, circulation, and reception of her other works, Tarabotti attempts to set the final parameters for any debate over these texts. The 'eyewitness' testimony of letters is invoked to persuade readers of the authority and authenticity of her version of events.

The Paradiso monacale

That Tarabotti's object was to use her *Lettere* to preserve her literary integrity is made particularly clear in a letter directed to Nicolas Bretel de Grémonville, the French ambassador to Venice.[72] During his stormy tenure in La Serenissima, Bretel established a warm friendship with Tarabotti, visiting her in Sant'Anna and exchanging frequent letters with her, even having his two daughters educated at the convent.[73] Tarabotti, for her part, claimed she could confide 'tutte le cose mie' ('all my affairs') in her friend Bretel.[74] In this letter to the Ambassador, Tarabotti makes it clear that her primary motive in publishing her *Lettere familiari* is to defend herself against the hostile response to her works and to preserve her literary reputation. In answer to her friend's inquiry regarding the insinuations and injurious treatment she has received at the hands of men like Aprosio and Brusoni, Tarabotti details the various responses to her *Antisatira*, calling Brusoni's unpublished *Antisatira satirizzata*, with irony, 'la migliore' ('the best') and making angry reference to Aprosio's *Maschera scoperta*.[75] She goes on to rebut some of the faults which her critics have found in her work, but is incensed, most of all, by accusations which call into question the authorship of her work, particularly the *Paradiso monacale*: 'Mi tacciano che lo stile del *Paradiso* e dell'*Antisatira* siano diversi' ('They accuse me that the style of the *Paradiso* and the *Antisatira* are different'), she writes – an accusation to which she refers in several other letters as well, as we will see further on.[76] Her published letters, she tells Bretel distinctly, are intended to combat those malicious voices. First, they will demonstrate that she is a capable and accomplished writer who counts many illustrious figures among her correspondents. Second, by following her familiar correspondence as it develops, her readers will be able to trace Tarabotti's literary history: they will, that is, see for themselves how she has struggled over the composition and publication of her works, and they will be convinced of their legitimacy. Finally, her correspondents will attest to the authenticity of the letters themselves, verifying that they appear in the same form in which they were originally dispatched. Tarabotti explains to Bretel:

> Tuttavolta, dicano ciò che vogliono, lasciamoli ciarlare, già che il mondo in un volume delle mie lettere, che fra poco si lascerà veder alla luce, potrà comprendere s'è vera quella ciancia che i miei scritti abbiano bisogno della lor lima per illustrarsi. Vostra Eccellenza e altri soggetti di vaglia potranno

sempre attestare se le mie lettere siano capitate nelle loro gloriose mani in quella forma, per apunto, che saranno impresse dallo stampatore.[77]

Nonetheless, let them say what they want, we'll let them chatter, since in a volume of my letters that will soon be published, the world will find out if that charge that my writings have need of their help is true. You and other important personages can always attest as to whether my letters reached their glorious hands in that same form in which they are printed by the printer.

These themes reappear persistently in the *Lettere:* Tarabotti constantly reminds both internal and external reader that by studying her literary history, her authorship of all her works can be vindicated. By making public what was once private, by exposing her familiar correspondence – and with it, the background of her literary evolution – to the eyes of the general reader, Tarabotti proposes to protect her literary reputation.

Within this framework, Tarabotti begins to unravel for readers of the *Lettere* the complicated background to the rumours about her *Antisatira* and *Paradiso monacale*, introducing these controversies early in the collection and referring to them throughout. Again seeking the reflected authority of some of the more important members of the Venetian literary milieu, Tarabotti quickly establishes her alliances with prominent figures such as Loredano, Giovanni Polani, her own brother-in-law Pighetti, and others. In the early pages of the collection, for example, Tarabotti thanks Polani for his support of her work and asks him to deliver a copy of her *Paradiso monacale* to Loredano, who contributed a presentation letter to it. In calling attention to Loredano's connection to the *Paradiso*, which had become the object of much negative speculation after the publication of the *Antisatira*, Tarabotti manages both to compliment Loredano's contribution to the book and to remind her readers of the authority it confers upon the *Paradiso*. A subsequent letter to Loredano himself leaves no doubt that Tarabotti sees her patron's letter for the *Paradiso* as a gesture of invaluable support: here, Tarabotti casts Loredano as a champion who protects her literary *Paradiso* against its foes, just as the cherubim protect earthly Paradise and St Peter the Empyrean: 'Il mio *Paradiso* si vanterà più glorioso di un tal diffensore che 'l Terrestre del Cherubino, e l'Empireo del Pescatore,' Tarabotti writes, adding: 'Cedano dunque l'uno e l'altro all'angelico Loredano, che più di loro valoroso, col lucidissimo scudo della sua lettera non lascia entrar nel mio *Paradiso* le malignità degli Aretini' ('My *Paradiso* will boast of a more glorious defender than the Earthly Paradise with the cherubim, or the Empyrean with St Peter. Let the one and the other cede, then, to Loredano, who, more courageous than they, with the shining shield of his letter does not permit the wickedness of the Aretines to enter my *Paradiso*').[78] Loredano is thus presented as an ally with the power and influence to protect Tarabotti and her reputation, and in whose authority the *Paradiso* takes refuge. Tarabotti reiterates this sentiment in another letter in which, again praising Loredano's letter for the *Paradiso*, she remarks that a single word from her patron would suffice to lend lasting authority and validity to even the most unworthy text.[79] Again, Tarabotti casts Loredano as her shield against the rumours about the *Paradiso*, confessing that she alone cannot fend off her attackers. Loredano, at least for now, is Tarabotti's well-connected chivalric knight: by repeatedly making reference to his role in the *Paradiso* Tarabotti draws her readers' attention to this important ally.

If Tarabotti saw Loredano as the *Paradiso's* protector against the 'malignità degli Aretini,' she is also careful to explain – in order to deride – the nature of the 'malice' that threatens the work. In a letter to a certain 'Padre N.' (in this case Aprosio), Tarabotti responds to the doubts Aprosio has expressed in a recent letter concerning the authorship of her works. Perhaps because another correspondent had insinuated that it was the nuns of Sant'Anna who had started the rumours about their *consorella*'s books, Tarabotti is careful here to show that she has the support of her Benedictine sisters.[80] In fact, she writes, a certain 'monaca di chiesa' told her that Aprosio had expressed to her 'concetti tanto lontani dalla verità quanto sono l'Indie maggiori da questo nostro clima' regarding Tarabotti's writing ('ideas as far from the truth as the greater Indies are from this climate of ours').[81] Tarabotti goes on to express her utter amazement upon hearing Aprosio's accusation, adding that her surprise resulted not from naivete, but rather from the disgust experienced by an immaculate conscience upon hearing such slander. She insists that not out of vanity, but only to defend her integrity does she respond in her own defence, exclaiming, '… i miei parti non ebbero giamai altro padre ch'è il mio rozzo ingegno, né altra madre che la mia stessa ignoranza, e chi altramente suppone se n'inganna' ('my offspring never had any father other than my own untutored imagination, nor any mother but my own ignorance, and he who supposes otherwise is fooling himself').[82] She brings her letter to a close by challenging Aprosio to visit her to discuss the matter in person.

In another letter to Aprosio, the 'concetti tanto lontani dalla verità' referred to more obliquely in the letter above are spelled out: 'M'è arrivato all'orrecchio che Vostra Paternità abbia qualche dubbio che 'l *Paradiso Monacale* uscito alla luce delle stampe non sia opera dell'ingegno mio; forsi ch'ella non creda ch'una femina, in emenda della prima delle donne che distrusse un paradiso, possa formarne un nuovo' ('I have heard that *Vostra Paternità* has some doubt that the *Paradiso Monacale* that has been printed is not the work of my own mind; perhaps you don't think a woman, making amends for the first woman who destroyed a paradise, is capable of forming a new one').[83] Tarabotti turns Aprosio's insinuations on end, however, by noting that they are actually a form of praise, implying that her critics find her work so good that they can only assume it has been written by a more experienced or gifted writer than she. Once again, Tarabotti insists that she does not protest out of vanity – indeed, she would prefer to say nothing at all, were not her accuser a man of the Church. Again making a play on the title of the disputed work, Tarabotti insists, 'non posso soffrire in pace che un religioso neghi la fede al *Paradiso*' ('I cannot suffer in silence that a man of the cloth should deny faith in the *Paradiso*').[84]

Some of the criticism directed at the *Paradiso*, however, concerned actual errors in the text. Tarabotti responds to these criticisms, too, in the *Lettere*, arguing that the errors were introduced by the printer.[85] In a letter to an unnamed correspondent, for example, Tarabotti complains: 'Gli errori sono infiniti, e di maniera conspicui, che non paiono della stampa ma di chi ha scritto' ('The errors are innumerable, and conspicuous in nature, so that they seem not to derive from the printer but from the author').[86] The distinction is significant: the errors are especially vexing because they are not common printers' errors, and might appear to be those of Tarabotti herself. Ever conscious of her vulnerability as a woman author and as a nun, Tarabotti knows that her public will be quick to turn on her. 'Mi sento morire di passione,' she writes, 'perché a questo modo non posso se non tirarmi dietro le risa d'ognuno, tanto più che come donna, parerà al volgo ch'abbia voluto a guisa di scimia immitar i litterati senza saper quello che mi dica' ('I feel myself die of shame, because in this manner I cannot help but draw the laughter of everyone; the more so because, as a woman, it will seem to the public that, like a monkey, I wanted to imitate the educated men without knowing what I was saying').[87] In another letter, she refers to the errors in the *Paradiso*'s Latin citations, insisting that they are not hers and offering the testimony of her friend Giovanni Polani as corroboration of her claim: 'Che nel *Paradiso* vi siano molti errori nelle sentenze latine lo so anch'io, ma sono più della stampa che miei, come l'illustrissimo signor Gio[vanni] Polani e altri ne ponno far fede' ('I, too, am aware that there are many mistakes in the Latin citations, but the printer is more to blame than I, as the illustrious signor Giovanni Polani and others can attest'); once again, Tarabotti seeks the authorization of an ally in the world beyond Sant'Anna.[88] She goes on, however, to argue disingenuously (as with the *Lagrime*) that she never intended to publish the *Paradiso*, but was pushed into it by her brother-in-law. This pronouncement is consistent with Tarabotti's strategy throughout the *Lettere*, for she frequently attempts to distance herself from agency in the publication of her works and deliberately falls back on stereotypical ideas about 'untrained' women writers to deflect any criticism of her writing. At the same time, she just as often reverses that approach, acknowledging her active role in publication and defending her literary capabilities.

The *Antisatira*

If there was controversy over the *Paradiso*, it was largely the publication of the still more controversial *Antisatira* that fanned the flames. After the publication of the *Antisatira*, even those who had praised the *Paradiso* shifted sides, as Tarabotti herself remarks in one letter: '... questi gran scrittori che già con mille adulazioni avendomi loro esortata ad esponer alla publica luce il mio *Paradiso monacale*, ora con perfidia ... lo biasimano, e dubitano se possa esser frutto de' miei sudori ...' ('... these great writers who, having once urged me with a thousand flatteries to publish my *Paradiso monacale*, now with perfidy ... condemn it, and doubt whether it can be the fruit of my travails ...').[89] The witty, cutting, and decidedly secular *Antisatira* offended many in Venetian society, both for its content and its perceived attack on Buoninsegni, and led Tarabotti's critics to argue that it was so different in style from the *Paradiso* as to cast doubt on the authorship of that earlier work. Tarabotti responds disdainfully to this argument in a number of letters, remarking, for example, to Pighetti that it betrays a remarkable lack of understanding of the craft of writing.[90] Similarly, in a letter to Enrico Cornaro, Tarabotti explains that she is sending him two of her works 'tanto differenti di materia, di stile, e di concetti, ch'a pena paiono fratelli' ('so different in content and style and concepts that they hardly seem related') – that is, the *Paradiso monacale* and the *Antisatira* – but pointedly adds that this is merely the opinion of 'gente ch'ha poca cognizione come si scrive' ('people with little understanding of how to write'); whereas her worthy correspondent need not be reminded of the 'necessità di diversificar lo stile in conformità della materia che si tratta' ('need to adapt style to content').[91] In both letters, Tarabotti seizes upon her detractors' own criticisms to portray them as dilettantes who, unable to grasp the essential relationship between style and content, can hardly call themselves writers.

By inserting numerous letters related to the furor over the *Antisatira* into the collection, Tarabotti is able to respond to and disparage the accusations of her critics while guiding the reactions of both internal and external readers to that episode, which was the catalyst for her falling out with her former allies Aprosio, Pighetti, and even Loredano.[92] Tarabotti reveals how Pighetti angered and disappointed her by siding with Aprosio against the *Antisatira* and refusing to acknowledge his early support of the text, and how Aprosio infuriated her with his ungentlemanly bid to expose her as the 'D.A.T.' whose name appeared on the frontispiece of the work. Tarabotti, who upon seeing a copy of Aprosio's *Maschera scoperta*, set out to have its publication suppressed, rejected Pighetti's protestations of innocence regarding his involvement in the affair, and was the more disappointed in seeing this betrayal originate with her own kin.[93] If eventually Tarabotti softened towards her brother-in-law, no such rapprochement was forthcoming with Aprosio, who continued to insist that he never meant to reveal her as the author of the *Antisatira*. Tarabotti makes short work of this denial, informing her adversary that she has seen the manuscript of the *Maschera scoperta* and there can be no mistake: the frontispiece clearly reveals her name.[94] In another letter, she insists that she did not mean to prevent the *Maschera* being published, but only to force Aprosio to refrain from naming her, and adds that her petition was heard because her request was legitimate: 'Se quel senatore m'ha onorata di vietarle che non la stampi col mio nome, questo è stato in riguardo alla convenienza che non vuole che si veda distinto il mio nome, dove io l'ho posto in epilogo, né questo soggetto pretende piú oltre da lei' ('If that senator honoured me by forbidding you to publish it using my name, it was because of the convention that my name should not be displayed, since I placed it at the end, nor does he expect anything more of you').[95] Tarabotti establishes herself in a position of moral and literary superiority, now using to her advantage the deep-seated ideas about (religious) women and public exposure she was accustomed to fight against (and indeed flouted entirely with her *Lettere*). Clearly furious with Aprosio, Tarabotti cuts off contact with him, commanding him to refrain from writing to her: 'Può desistere dallo scrivermi, poiché per l'avvenire le sue lettere non saranno lette da me, e le darò quel ricapito, che meritano ...' ('You may cease writing to me, since in the future your letters will go unread by me, and I will give them the reception they deserve').[96]

The scandal over the *Antisatira* is the backdrop to letters addressed to other figures as well. In a lengthy letter to the Duke of Parma, for example, Tarabotti describes reaction to the *Antisatira*, focusing particularly on the mean-spirited response prepared by Aprosio. Again using her status as a cloistered nun to her advantage, Tarabotti casts herself as a vulnerable innocent set upon by a pack of wolves: 'E chi potrà negar che siano lupi, se vedendo una innocente pecorella se le aventano contro per levarle la vita coll'ingoiarle quel poco d'applauso che le viene dall'ingenuità altrui?' ('And who can deny that they are wolves, if upon seeing an innocent little lamb they launch themselves at her to take her life by swallowing up that little applause she receives from others?').[97] Pointedly, she remarks that not only do her foes come at her in numbers – something by which she pretends to be flattered – but some attack in disguise, 'incogniti sott'abiti ingannevoli' ('disguised in deceitful clothing').[98] Her words here are a clever reference to Aprosio – a member of the *Accademia degli Incogniti* – and his *Maschera*, written under a pseudonym even as it proposed to expose Tarabotti as the author of the *Antisatira*. Tarabotti then goes on to defend her *Antisatira*, arguing that it does not target all men, only those guilty of the vices she condemns. By attacking the *Antisatira* so virulently, writes Tarabotti, her foes show themselves to be threatened by its content, and thus part of the group she targets. Tarabotti insists that she never wrote to offend Buoninsegni: 'non giamai per offenderlo, ma solo per ischerzo' ('never to offend him, but only in jest') did she have *Antisatira* printed.[99]

If Tarabotti tells the Duke of Parma she published the *Antisatira* in a spirit of play, elsewhere she attempts to distance herself from both its conception and publication. To Vittoria della Rovere, to whom she dedicated the work, Tarabotti explains that she composed the *Antisatira* not to defend women's vanity, attacked in Buoninsegni's original text, but rather to obey the wishes of certain noblewomen to whom she was obligated.[100] She repeats this claim in several other letters, and insists that not only did she write it as a favour but also that she never expected to publish it, again recalling her claims regarding the *Lagrime*.[101] In a letter to Pighetti, evidently penned prior to their falling out over this very issue, Tarabotti expresses a similar reluctance regarding the publication of the *Antisatira*; here it appears that it is Pighetti, rather than the noblewomen previously mentioned, who urges his sister-in-law to 'go public' – very much in contrast with his later stance in opposition to the work. Tarabotti modestly resists, insisting that her lack of learning and her religious position prohibit her from such an action: 'La mia soprafina ignoranza non permette che dicerie tali uscite da una mente racchiusa senza lume veruno di lettere compariscano sotto gli occhi del mondo per sottoporsi alla maligna censura degli uomini ... Il mio stato religioso detesta una scrittura tanto profana ...' ('My extreme ignorance does not allow that such scribbles, emanating from an enclosed mind devoid of the light of letters, should appear before the eyes of the world to expose themselves to the wicked censure of men ... My religious state detests such profane writing').[102] Her modest performance of feminine reticence acquires an edge, however, when she adds that women are vulnerable enough to the criticism of men without deliberately subjecting themselves to it by publishing: '... vengono biasimate le donne in generale dagli scrittori, senza ch'io mi metta a periglio d'esser bersaglio delle loro malediche lingue' ('... women in general are condemned by writers, without me placing myself in danger of becoming the target for their condemning tongues').[103] Tarabotti makes a similar argument to Pighetti with regard to the *Paradiso*. While maintaining that it was not her idea to publish that text either, she works in a sharp jab at her former (male) allies, who having once praised her work now profess to doubt its authorship. Men, writes Tarabotti, are fickle and incapable of accepting that women have literary talent, and it is her distrust of their inconstancy – rather than 'feminine' modesty – that makes her reluctant to publish:

> Non è stata ambizione che mi abbia persuasa al metter alle stampe questa mia operetta, poiché pazzo sarebbe chi si fondasse nelle lodi degli uomini che, s'ora essaltano, di là a momenti biasmano e mal trattano; onde poco mi curo che non credino ch'il *Paradiso* o altra sia opera mia, conoscendo molto bene che la virtú è sprezzata e abborrita nelle donne.[104]

> It was not ambition that persuaded me to publish this little work of mine, for he is mad who depends on the praise of men who now praise, and a moment later condemn and mistreat; whence I care little whether they believe that the *Paradiso* or anything else is my own work, knowing full well that virtue in women is belittled and despised.

Elsewhere, Tarabotti wonders if Pighetti's encouragement stems merely from her having exceeded his low expectations of women; but nevertheless reiterates that her works are not worthy of print.[105] Tarabotti's self-deprecation thinly masks a deep distrust of male reactions to women's writing that forms the basis for these ostensible refusals to publish. By stressing Pighetti's repeated encouragement, moreover, Tarabotti uses her letters to create a damning picture of her brother-in-law's inconstancy.

In spite of such protestations to the contrary, however, Tarabotti had far more faith in her work than her retiring words suggest and, in fact, she had shown her work in both manuscript and print form to a number of people, including Vittoria della Rovere, the Duke of Parma, Nicolas Bretel de Grémonville, and, of course, Aprosio. Moreover, she is quite clear at points that her duty is to defend her sex with the only weapon at her disposal; in one letter regarding the *Antisatira* Tarabotti proclaims to wield the pen 'già che non posso la spada per diffender il mio sesso' ('since I cannot use a sword to defend my sex').[106] A letter to Guid'Ascania Orsi shows her determination to publish that work in the face of all objections. '[M]etter alla stampa ci vuole una gran testa,' Tarabotti tells her friend, 'essendo che tutti vogliono dir la sua particolarmente contro di noi, perché ostinatamente gli uomini non vogliono che le donne sappiano comporre senza di loro' ('It takes stubbornness to publish, since everyone wants to say their piece against us, because men obstinately insist that women are incapable of writing without their help').[107] More significantly, a letter to Andrea Valier demonstrates that not only did Tarabotti intend to publish the *Antisatira* but also that she had solicited contributions to embellish the work, such as Valier's sonnet in praise of the volume's dedicatee, Vittoria della Rovere.[108] In a letter to her friend Bissari, Tarabotti, amidst typically overblown declarations of her work's unworthiness – she calls the *Antisatira* a 'caos di errori' ('chaos of errors') – regrets that changing the dedication from Prince Leopold to Vittoria della Rovere has deprived her of the sonnet that Bissari had initially composed for the work. Again, her remarks display not just foreknowledge of the *Antisatira*'s publication, but an active hand in structuring the paratext of the work.[109] A letter to Aprosio, finally, reveals a firm determination to publish the *Antisatira* in spite of the friar's objections, arguing that it is the writer's duty to expose the evils of the world (and of men) to the public eye:

> Il signor Buoninsegni può più che mai attendere l'*Antisatira*, perché quelle cose che sono scritte in detestazione del male e a pro della verità

non si tralasciano da chi vuol arrivar alla perfezione, anzi, che con fervore si devono esporre alla luce del mondo, per trarne frutto per l'anime, essendo molto meglio (com'Ella sa) il predicar rettamente ch'il tacer negligentemente.[110]

Signor Buoninsegni can await the *Antisatira* now more than ever, because those things written against wickedness and in favour of truth are not ignored by one who wishes to achieve perfection; rather, they must be exposed to the light of day with fervor, in order to extract their fruit for the soul, as it is much better (as you know) to preach righteously than to remain negligently silent.

Tarabotti uses her *Lettere* as a public stage on which to defend the story and history of her works, from conception and composition to publication, presenting that history from a variety of angles. As we have seen here and in the previous chapters, the fragmented, one-sided nature of letter collections allows writers to engage in a strategic process of concealment and disclosure as they lead readers through their stories, showcasing different aspects of their persona and of particular events. Indeed, conflicting versions of the same events or varying approaches to epistolary self-representation may be present in a letter collection, tailored to various internal readers. The external reader, by contrast, is left to piece together a fuller, if more ambiguous, interpretation of the writer's persona or of the events she describes. Tarabotti exploits the fragmentary and biased nature of the epistolary form to enlist the reader's complicity in her own version of her story, a version lent weight by the testimonial authority of epistolary narrative. By making public key pieces of her private – and thus apparently authentic – correspondence, Tarabotti shapes her story and 'proves' it to her readers. Her statements to Nicolas Bretel de Grémonville discussed above can be taken, in fact, as a key to interpreting her *epistolario* as a whole. Her letters are intended to be tangible evidence of her literary credibility, proof that she has authored her works.[111] This objective is echoed in a letter to Giovanni Dandolo, in which Tarabotti defends the legitimacy of her entire body of work, declaring forcefully, 'Né vi sia più chi creda i miei parti essere adulterini, già ch'io a guisa dell'acquilotto li faccio conoscere ad ogn'uno per legittimi ...' ('Nor let there be anyone who continues to believe my offspring illegitimate, since, like the eagle, I recognize each of them as legitimate ...').[112] The *Lettere familiari e di complimento* constitute Tarabotti's determined effort to achieve this goal, to abolish any doubt regarding her works and replace it with an enduring epistolary representation in which it is she who shapes the interpretation of her literary history. Through a strategy of concealment and disclosure, a meditated revelation of key pieces of her story through the testimonial force of 'private' correspondence, Tarabotti is able to shape and represent that story with the authority that epistolary exchange evokes. So, too, Tarabotti reconstructs her literary history through a selection of letters, offered to the reader who must piece together her story, and who in this very process of interpretation becomes complicit in its reconstruction on Tarabotti's own terms.

In addition to functioning as defence of her oeuvre, the *Lettere*, finally, allow Tarabotti to showcase the breadth of her contacts in the secular and literary worlds in a defiant challenge to the physical and social confines of her life as a cloistered nun. Just as humanist letter writers used the epistolary collection as a kind of scholarly *dossier*, a reflection of a network of intellectual and cultural relationships, so, too, Tarabotti positions herself in relation to a carefully selected group of correspondents. At the same time, epistolary writing had a unique urgency for the cloistered nun, its function as a tool for both self-promotion and self-defence a new importance. If Aretino famously wielded his pen to bestow 'honour and blame in abundance,' Tarabotti did not shrink from doing likewise: her praise for her supporters is lavish, her condemnation for her detractors harsh.[113] Given the cultural constraints on women's self-expression in general and on that of nuns in particular, Tarabotti's *Lettere* are a remarkable work by a woman who was first and foremost a writer, a protofeminist, and even a political theorist.[114] The originality and transgressive force of the *Lettere*, with their intense focus on the literary career of a cloistered nun and their sharp critique of the oppressive forces of patriarchy, are a forceful challenge to the parameters of epistolary space.

Epilogue: Writing Letters, Performing Gender

As our examination of the letterbooks discussed in the previous pages reveals, the epistolary medium functioned as a unique literary space in which women writers in early modern Italy could position themselves as the protagonists of their narratives. Drawing upon the first-person authority of epistolary discourse, women used letters to record their histories in vivid detail, to engage in social and religious commentary, and to position themselves firmly as literary figures. The widespread interest in women's letters during the sixteenth and early seventeenth centuries suggests a deep curiosity among readers about female experience as well as an openness to women's epistolary publication that belies the cautionary restraint so often advocated in the prescriptive literature aimed at women during the Renaissance period. Ortensio Lando's *Lettere di molte valorose donne* capitalized on this interest by impersonating the epistolary voices of real and imagined women, 'performing' women's experience and epistolary exchange through the pen of a male writer. While some of Lando's letter writers champion women's intelligence and erudition, many of them focus on matters of specifically 'female' import: choosing husbands, raising children, running the household. This focus on the female sphere serves to bring women's domestic experience into the public realm – an important result of Lando's anthology. Yet this deep curiosity about a wholly female world also reflects an element of literary voyeurism, an outsider's reimagining rather than a genuine investigation of female epistolarity.

The letters of Lucrezia Gonzaga, by contrast, focus on the exemplary experience of one woman in particular, positioning it as a model that is meant to reflect positively on the female sex as a whole. Multiple layers of meaning coexist in this collection alongside the description of

Gonzaga's wifely fidelity: no less central to Gonzaga's epistolary self-portrait are her interactions with literary society, her immersion in the heterodox religious thought that flourished in sixteenth-century Italy, and her literary collaboration with Lando. Gonzaga's collection manipulates cultural conventions of the virtuous woman – loyal, modest, and chaste – in order to cement her public image as a literary figure, thus performing the role of the ideal wife while using her husband's predicament to her own literary advantage.

In the collections of both Lando and Gonzaga, the performance of the female epistolary voice, whether male- or female-authored, is further complicated and underscored by the issue of intertextuality. Repertory texts like Textor's *Officina* and Garimberto's *Concetti* furnish much of these letters' content, and Lando and Gonzaga are themselves frequent interlocutors in one another's texts, requiring that the two works be read in dialogue with one another. As Elizabeth D. Harvey has suggested, intertextuality is itself a form of ventriloquism that mirrors the fundamentally imitative and unstable nature of gender. Like gender, intertextuality is the product of multiple sources and experiences, and thus, '[j]ust as intertextuality suggests a transvestitism of voice in which there is no original, so too does this transvestitism of voice imply that gender is a kind of imitation for which there is no original.'[1] The female epistolary voice thus constitutes both the reflection and performance of gender as an artificial category. Analogously, epistolary writing itself is a form of ventriloquism, meant to imitate and substitute convincingly for real conversation. It, too, is a kind of performance, in which ideas about gender are performed by both men and women.

Both the *Valorose donne* and Gonzaga's *Lettere*, finally, are products of the ongoing *questione della donna*, or 'woman question,' as each text investigates and questions common notions regarding gender ideologies and women's roles. The debate over women's capabilities, function, and duties – that is, over the social and cultural construction of gender – lay at the heart of the sixteenth-century *querelle des femmes* and informed in crucial ways all of the women's letter collections examined in this study. The growing didactic literature targeted at women that resulted from this ongoing debate (encompassing comportment texts, medical manuals, beauty books, and *libri di segreti*) similarly influences these collections. If the *Valorose donne* are structured like a domestic handbook for women, replete with recipes for cosmetics and home remedies, the letters of Lucrezia Gonzaga, Veronica Franco, Isabella Andreini, and Arcangela Tarabotti have a different didactic function: to position their protagonists as models to be admired or imitated by readers. Their pursuit of this goal through letters offers a different response to questions about the dignity of the vernacular letter genre than that provided by the *Valorose donne*. Here, the letter is deemed a suitable vehicle for serious tasks, including the defence of women and teaching through example.

It is a striking characteristic of these women's *epistolari* that they avoid the intimate portrayals of female experience offered by Lando's *Valorose donne*. Instead, they concentrate on creating epistolary self-representations that focus ever more exclusively on the letter writer as a literary figure. To do so, Franco and Tarabotti, like Gonzaga before them, take pains to link the literary persona created within their letters to the historical persona who existed outside the literary work. Andreini, by contrast, focuses on literary self-construction to the exclusion of such specific detail. At the same time, however, her collection of highly stylized epistolary compositions reflects in a very real way her own experience as a writer and as an actress on the *commedia dell'arte* stage. Despite their different approaches to the genre, each of these writers is successful in bringing new aspects of female experience to the forefront of epistolary writing.

In publishing an *epistolario*, the letter writer simultaneously plays the part of author, narrator, and protagonist, choosing which aspects of her experience to present to readers and in what light to do so. In this regard, epistolary writing shares certain characteristics with autobiography. Certainly, any narrative representation that seeks to place the 'I' at its centre engages in a process of selection and revision like that which occurs in autobiography. The letter writer, like the autobiographer, shapes the self that emerges from her work. A strategy of concealment and disclosure is at work in autobiographical works, a careful process of selective retelling aimed at forging a particular image of the writer or presenting a sequence of events from a privileged persepective.[2] A similar process of selection is an integral element of any epistolary collection. What the letter writer chooses to describe, as well as what she chooses to leave out, is central to the construction of her epistolary persona. Whether revising letters or composing new missives for publication, choosing to publish some and not others, or simply permitting their letters to be published by someone else, epistolarians shaped the selves and experience that they presented for public scrutiny.[3] This selection process assumes added importance as a result of the fragmentary quality of epistolary communication itself, which by its very nature represents a single first-person view with intrinsic authority. Analogously, the reader who seeks to uncover what is 'real' or 'true' in an *epistolario*, as in an autobiographical account, can only construct it from the elements provided by the writer.[4]

Each of the woman-authored *epistolari* examined in this study engages in a process of persuasion and self-defence, seeking to convince readers of the writer's moral integrity, her literary stature, or the veracity of her version of events. Each author re-presents particular aspects of her experience in order to enlist the readers' support for a specific agenda, whether it be to gain authority as a literary or moral voice, to express religious beliefs, or to defend against literary or personal criticisms. The complicity of the reader in this reenactment or retelling of pivotal events is central to the success of the epistolarian's project. Gonzaga elicits this complicity by focusing on a subject a woman could be admired for writing about in early modern Italy, rather than condemned: her husband, whose arrest and imprisonment she chronicles along with her own efforts to have him released. At the same time, however, the loose narrative lines of Manfrone's story are, in the end, a pretext for more radical concerns. Franco, too, attempts to win over her readers, daring them to recast their negative perceptions of courtesans and attempting to restore lustre to her professional image. Like Gonzaga, Franco aims to establish literary as well as moral authority. To this end, she includes not only letters that emphasize her morality and generosity (in addition to her sexual desirability), but also a number of letters that publicize her links to the Venetian literary circle connected with Domenico Venier. The epistolary space of Franco's *Lettere familiari*, finally, serves as a vehicle for a biting response to Maffio Venier, the adversary who had made Franco the target of his poetic satire. While Andreini's letters do not offer so overt an agenda of self-defence as Franco's, their self-promotional function is similar. Although fictionalized and abstract, composed in the voices of male and female *innamorati* characters, Andreini's letters present an epistolary image of a competent writer as one well versed in the discourses of humanism and neoplatonism as her male counterparts. The letters are a demonstration of rhetorical and dramatic skill meant to elevate Andreini's literary status and memorialize her through the publication of a book of letters. It is in the letters of Tarabotti, ultimately, that the epistolary dynamic of defence and persuasion is enacted most clearly – perhaps because Tarabotti faced the most opposition from her critics. The nun's efforts to win her readers to her side is apparent as she recalls her detractors' accusation that she did not author her *Paradiso monacale*. By presenting readers with the epistolary exchanges she has had with her accusers over time, she draws on the authority of epistolary narration to show how her critics had first praised and encouraged her *Paradiso* before turning on her. Casting herself in the sympathetic position of a vulnerable woman – a nun – set upon by the great literary men of Venice and Italy in an unequal battle, Tarabotti uses gendered tropes to engage her readers' support on her own behalf.

If the aims of the women's *epistolari* examined in this study were individual – that is, each writer sought to represent herself as a singular, recognizable figure in order to gain literary recognition and to defend her integrity – these texts, when considered together, perform an important cultural function. Although each writer focuses on her own experience – as a writer, but also as a wife, courtesan, actress, or cloistered nun – the collective effect of these representations is to bring the myriad aspects of female experience into the public sphere. In writing their experience, these writers supplemented 'official,' or male, culture with their own. Gonzaga's retelling of her husband's story with herself as a main character constitutes an alternative history to the public version found in the court records and annals devoted to these events. Similarly, her location of herself within the literary community of the *Pastori frattegiani* expands our understanding of the composition of that community, while the religious views she expresses in her letters shed light on the vague references to her beliefs found in official correspondence between Rome and the Inquisitor in Mantua in the 1570s. The letters of Franco, too, deepen our knowledge of women's experience in early modern Italy. Franco's contribution to the plethora of representations of courtesans that exist in literature and in legal documents provides a very different vision of the courtesan as a figure possessed of both cultural capital and moral integrity. Like Gonzaga, Franco locates herself within a literary community, enriching our understanding of the dynamics and composition of Venice's salon culture. Likewise, the letters of Andreini reveal much about the efforts of women writers to participate in 'orthodox' literary culture, and also demonstrate clearly the important links between epistolary writing and performance. Tarabotti, lastly, speaking from behind convent walls, offers an alternative to that 'official' history which tells us how many nuns were in convents and the conditions in which they lived, but reveals little of their actual experience. With great socio-political acuity, Tarabotti gives voice through her own experience to this marginalized female community.

The blurring of distinctions between public and private space that occurs in the letters, between internal and external reader, serves to draw the reader into a relationship of complicity through identification with the epistolary 'I.'

Epistolary production in early modern Italy, finally, was truly vast. This study has focused primarily on women's familiar letters; however, the subgenres of epistolary writing are numerous and varied and women's contributions to them remain to be fully investigated. Religious and spiritual letters, comic letters, and love letters might each constitute the subject of a study in its own right; and each of these areas would no doubt raise new and intriguing issues regarding the epistolary construction of gender. More comparative work analysing the epistolary production of Italian women writers with respect to their counterparts elsewhere in Europe remains to be done. As the present study has shown, the impact of women on the epistolary genre was significant, and had repercussions that transcended the realm of epistolary writing. Letter collections like those studied here incorporated ideas about epistolary discourse with ideas about gender, social commentary with religious heterodoxy. These works challenged and expanded the parameters of conventional epistolary discourse by validating and publicizing new areas of female experience, while interrogating the qualities of that experience. These texts, finally, presented women as authoritative protagonists, capable of sustaining their own narratives (and prefiguring in some ways the later emergence of the epistolary novel). In an implicit response to an early modern prescriptive literature that held women's greatest virtues to be silence and a retiring modesty, these letter writers 'went public' with their experience, declaring it worthy of inspection and even imitation by a readership of both men and women.

Why, then, did the vogue for women's epistolary writing diminish and then disappear in the seventeenth century? Tarabotti's *Lettere* of 1650, as we have seen, were the last major collection of familiar letters to be published by a woman in Italy. Never again would letterbooks employ quite the same variety of functions or enjoy such great popularity as in the period between 1538 and 1650; women's epistolary writing in particular did not come back on the scene until the nineteenth century, within the narrative framework of the epistolary novel. The shift may be ascribed, at least in part, to the effects of the changing cultural climate of post-Tridentine Italy on women's writing in general, noted in several recent studies.[5] Tarabotti's own highly politicized and secularized letters are an anomaly in a period marked by the gradual retreat of women's writing (with some exceptions) into safer and more traditional territory, such as religious writing.[6] Moreover, as we have seen, with the passage of the decades, letter collections became increasingly abstract in nature: shifting from the targeted specificity of the Aretinian model, so influential for the writers examined here, to a more generic structure, in keeping with their emerging function as manuals of style and comportment (in this sense, prefiguring the kinds of women's comportment manuals that would resurface by the nineteenth century). The formalized and universal nature of such epistolary collections, in which the imprint of the author as letter writer is greatly de-emphasized, may also been seen within the context of the more restrained and cautious cultural landscape of the post-Tridentine period.

Whatever the causes, letter-writing's moment in the sun – and particularly that of women's letters – had come and gone by the mid-seventeenth century. Even as eighteenth-century anthologists were rediscovering and republishing the work of important female poets of the Renaissance in collections such as Luisa Bergalli's *Componimenti poetici delle più illustri rimatrici di ogni secolo* (1726), no such attention was paid to women's vernacular letters.[7] Although women, and women's writing, would again return to the literary stage in increasing numbers, Italy never saw a resurgence in epistolary writing such as that which accompanied the salon culture of seventeenth-century France. Epistolarity eventually came back into fashion (even as its popularity was declining elsewhere in Europe) in the form of the epistolary novel, embraced by women writers such as Matilde Serao and Marchesa Colombi, but the kinds of letter collections that circulated in the early modern period were never to reemerge. The dexterous blending of historical and literary persona and the brilliant displays of social networks and gender performance that characterize the works of early modern women such as Gonzaga, Franco, Andreini, and Tarabotti, made a fundamental and unique contribution to the literary landscape of early modern Italy. These 'ritratti di lettere' – or 'raccolte di miracoli' (as an admiring contemporary of Tarabotti described her collection)[8] – furnish crucial new facets from which to view women's active engagement with early modern literary culture.

Notes

Introduction

1 Lucrezia Gonzaga da Gazuolo, *Lettere della molto illustre signora … donna Lucrezia Gonzaga da Gazuolo … a gloria del sesso feminile… poste in luce* (Venice: Gualtero Scotto, 1552), 31–2. All translations throughout this study are my own unless otherwise noted. I have modernized accents, punctuation, and, in certain cases, spelling (where necessary for clarity) in the original texts.

2 There is much debate (today as in the sixteenth and seventeenth centuries) over the precise definition of the 'familiar' letter – by nature a fluid form. The term recalls Cicero's *Ad familiares,* a model for humanist letters, as well as Petrarch's *Familiares,* and serves primarily to distinguish letters written 'privately' to friends or family from official correspondence or from other specific epistolary 'types' (*spirituali, amorose, facete, di consolazione, di complimento,* etc). For Erasmus, the familiar letter was one that did not seek to persuade but to narrate. See Judith Rice Henderson, 'On Reading the Rhetoric of the Renaissance Letter,' in *Renaissance Rhetoric*, ed. Heinrich F. Plett (Berlin: Walter de Gruyter, 1993), 150–1. One early modern theoretician held that *all* letters were 'familiar' in that they were letters and not orations, while another claimed the term applied only to those letters which were 'familiar' 'nella materia e nella maniera' ('in content and style'). Cf. Janine Basso, 'La lettera "familiare" nella retorica epistolare del XVI e del XVII secolo in Italia,' *Quaderni di retorica e di poetica* 1 (1985), 61. Cicero himself distinguished the 'familiar' letter from the more elevated style of 'severum et grave,' *Fam.* 2.4; see G. Folena, 'Premessa,' *Quaderni di retorica e poetica* 1 (1985), 7. In 'La lettera 'familiare,"' Basso offers this definition of familiar letters: 'Pare che siano essenzialmente, anche se non

esclusivamente, scritte a nome proprio, personali cioè di interesse privato, indirizzate ad amici più che a parenti ...' but notes that they are never completely without literary artifice (59). Luigi Matt differs slightly from Basso and devotes a chapter of his study of early modern epistolary practice to the problem of definition in his *Teoria e prassi dell'epistolografia italiana tra Cinquecento e primo Seicento* (Rome: Bonacci, 2005), 99–138; see also Henderson, 'Rhetoric,' 149. For my purposes here, I use the term 'familiar' to denote letters in which the author appears as a protagonist and which were not written in an official capacity.

3 For an analysis of *sprezzatura* in Castiglione's *Il libro del cortigiano*, see Harry Berger Jr., *The Absence of Grace: Sprezzatura and Suspicion in Two Renaissance Courtesy Books* (Stanford, CA: Stanford University Press, 2000) and Virginia Cox, *The Renaissance Dialogue: Literary Dialogue in Its Social and Political Contexts, Castiglione to Galileo* (Cambridge: Cambridge University Press, 1992), especially 42–6. Among the numerous efforts to theorize the familiar letter was Juan Luis Vives' epistolary manual, *De conscribendi epistolis* (1536), the first to fully break with the formal heritage of the medieval *ars dictaminis* and embrace the classical tradition. See Judith Rice Henderson, 'Defining the Genre of the Letter in Juan Luis Vives' *De conscribendi epistolis*,' *Renaissance and Reformation* 7 (1983), 89. Erasmus was more reluctant to abandon the rhetorical heritage of the letter. See Judith Rice Henderson, 'The Enigma of Erasmus' *Conficiendarum epistolarum formula*,' *Renaissance and Reformation* 13 (1989), 320. The epistolarian Bernardo Tasso compares his own letters to a 'semplice verginella' ('a simple little maiden') in *Li due libri delle Lettere* (Venice: Vincenzo Valgrisi, 1557), 12; Battista Guarini's handbook *Il secretario* (Venice: Roberto Megretti, 1594) singles out 'purity' as the 'true e infallible' basis of letter-writing (93), as does Battista Ceci's *Compendio d'avertimenti di ben parlare volgare* (Venice: Stamperia Salicata, 1618), 82–3. Later discussions of the topic like that by Stefano Guazzo's *Lettere* (Venice: Barezzo Barezzi, 1606) nuance this view slightly, allowing that letters should be neither overly ornate nor 'pan ruvido' ('rough bread'), but rather seek a 'nobile rustichezza' ('a noble simplicity') (A5v).

4 See, for example, Massimo Prada, *La lingua dell'epistolario volgare di Pietro Bembo* (Genoa: Name, 2000); see also John Najemy, *Between Friends: The Machiavelli-Vettori Correspondence* (Princeton, NJ: Princeton University Press, 1993), and Diana Robin, *Filelfo in Milan: Writings 1451–1477* (Princeton, NJ: Princeton University Press, 1991).

5 Among the first to follow Aretino's example were Nicolò Franco's *Le pistole vulgari* (Venice: Gardane, 1539) and AntonFrancesco Doni's *Libro primo di*

Notes to pages 4–5 223

lettere (Venice: Scoto, 1544). According to Nicola Longo, Franco and Doni were motivated primarily by personal competition with Aretino; see *Del 'buon inchiostro': il sistema letterario nelle* Lettere familiari *di Gerolamo Parabosco* (Urbino: Quattro Venti, 1984), 16. Antonio de Guevara's popular *Epístolas familiares* were published in 1539 (following his previous, also very successful 'romanzo epistolare,' *Marco Aurelio*). Other examples that followed on the heels of Aretino (after the publication of his second and third volumes in 1542 and 1546, respectively) include the letters of Claudio Tolomei (1547), Pietro Bembo (1548), and Bernardo Tasso (1549), as well as a number of anthologies. According to Amedeo Quondam, between 1538 (Aretino's first volume) and 1627 (the letters of Marino), more than 130 letterbooks and twenty-seven anthologies had been published in Italy, some three-quarters of these in Venice. See Quondam's important quantitative study of the genre, *Le carte messaggiere* (Rome: Bulzoni, 1981), esp. 30–49.

6 I draw here on Stephen Greenblatt's conceptualization of self-fashioning in the English tradition, as described in *Renaissance Self-Fashioning: From More to Shakespeare* (Chicago: University of Chicago Press, 1980). For the notion of epistolary performance in a different context (that of seventeenth- and eighteenth-century French love letters and epistolary novels), see Katherine Ann Jensen, *Writing Love: Letters, Women, and the Novel in France, 1605–1776* (Carbondale: Southern Illinois University Press, 1995). Jensen argues that 'Epistolary Woman' is always a 'male creation, the product of specific social and historical forces' (2). In my analysis of early modern Italian letter collections, I show that this performance in many cases became something even more complex.

7 See Maria Luisa Doglio, 'Letter Writing, 1350–1650,' in Letizia Panizza and Sharon Wood, ed., *A History of Women's Writing in Italy*, trans. Jennifer Lorch (Cambridge: Cambridge University Press, 2001), 15. Doglio discusses some of these texts and the issues relating to them here and in her earlier study, *Lettera e donna: Scrittura epistolare al femminile tra Quattro e Cinquecento* (Rome: Bulzoni, 1993). In *Teoria e prassi*, Matt disagrees with Doglio's assessment of Catherine's influence as a letter writer, however, noting that her letters are more like 'spiritual treatises' and are not cited by early modern theoreticians of the genre (12n9).

8 The letterbooks of Nogarola, Fedele, and Cereta have been edited and translated for the University of Chicago Press series The Other Voice in Early Modern Europe, accompanied by analysis and commentary: see Isotta Nogarola, *Complete Writings: Letterbook, Dialogue on Adam and Eve, Orations*, ed. and trans. Margaret L. King and Diana Robin (2004); Cassandra Fedele,

Letters and Orations, ed. and trans. Diana Robin (2000); and Laura Cereta, *Collected Letters of a Renaissance Feminist,* ed. and trans. Diana Robin (1997).
9 See Virginia Cox, *Women's Writing in Italy 1400–1650* (Baltimore: Johns Hopkins University Press, 2008), 14–15. Minutolo's letters are published in *Lettere,* ed. Raffaelle Morabito (Naples: Edizioni Scientifiche Italiane, 1999).
10 Vittoria Colonna, *Rime e lettere di Vittoria Colonna* (Florence: G. Barbèra Editore, 1860); Veronica Gambara, *Rime e lettere di Veronica Gambara* (Brescia: Rizzardi, 1759). Although Gambara corresponded with Aretino, the reigning king of the published letter, it does not appear that she intended to publish her own letters. See Elisabetta Selmi, 'Per l'epistolario di Veronica Gambara,' in *Veronica Gambara e la poesia del suo tempo nell'Italia settentrionale. Atti del convegno (Brescia-Correggio 17–19 ottobre 1985,* ed. Cesare Bozzetti, Pietro Gibellini, and Ennio Sandal (Florence: Leo S. Olschki, 1989), 143–81.
11 See M. Savorgnan and P. Bembo, *Carteggio d'Amore 1500–1501,* ed. Carlo Dionisotti (Florence: Le Monnier, 1950). On Strozzi, see Doglio, 'Letter-writing,' 16–17; and Ann Crabb, 'How to Influence Your Children: Persuasion and Form in Alessandra Macinghi Strozzi's Letters to Her Sons,' in *Women's Letters across Europe, 1400–1700: Form and Persuasion,* ed. Jane Couchman and Ann Crabb (Aldershot, UK: Ashgate, 2005), 21–42; see also Ann Crabb, *The Strozzi of Florence: Widowhood and Family Solidarity in the Renaissance* (Ann Arbor: University of Michigan Press, 2000).
12 See Dava Sobel, *Galileo's Daughter, Letters to Father: A Historical Memoir of Science, Faith and Love* (New York: Walker and Company, 1999); and Dava Sobel, *Letters to Father: Sister Maria Celeste to Galileo, 1623–1630* (New York: Walker and Company, 2001).
13 For the early-modern English context, for example, several new studies look in great detail at women's unpublished correspondence and what it can tell us about issues from literacy to women's social roles and relationships. See, for example, Gary Schneider, *The Culture of Epistolarity: Vernacular Letters and Letter Writing in Early Modern England, 1500–1700* (Newark: University of Delaware Press, 2005); James Daybell, ed., *Early Modern Women's Letter Writing, 1450–1700* (New York: Palgrave, 2001); and James Daybell, 'Women's Letters and Letter-Writing in England, 1540–1603: An Introduction to Issues of Authorship and Construction,' in *Shakespeare Studies* 27 (September 1999), 161–86. On the broader European context, see the edited volume by Couchman and Crabb, *Women's Letters across Europe, 1400–1700,* and, for later examples, Rebecca Earle, ed., *Epistolary Selves: Letters and Letter-Writers 1600–1945* (Aldershot, UK: Ashgate, 1999). For a discussion of unpublished letters by early modern Italian women, see

Maria Grazia Nico Ottaviani, *'Me son missa a scriver questa lettera ...': Lettere e altre scritture femminili tra Umbria, Toscana e Marche nei secoli X–XVI* (Naples: Liguori, 2006); see also the essays in Chemello and Zarri cited in note 14 below.

14 These have been less thoroughly examined, especially in the Italian context. Recent studies include some of the essays included in Adriana Chemello, ed., *Alla lettera: Teorie e pratiche epistolari dai Greci al Novecento* (Milan: Angelo Guerini, 1998); and Gabriella Zarri, ed., *Per lettera: La scrittura epistolare femminile tra archivio e tipografia, secoli xv–xvii* (Rome: Viella, 1999). Doglio's *Lettera e Donna* combines an inquiry into the letters of Franco and Colonna with a reading of Strozzi's unpublished letters but doesn't delve deeply into the theoretical implications of published letters. Quondam's *Le carte messaggiere* remains an indispensable tool but devotes little attention to the specific and complex issues regarding women's epistolary production; similarly, Matt's valuable study, *Teoria e prassi*, offers extensive analysis of letters and letter-writing manuals but excludes women entirely. The introduction to Francesco Erspamer's edition of Aretino's letters, *Lettere: Libro primo*, ed. Francesco Erspamer (Parma: Ugo Guanda, 1995), makes an important contribution to the study of published letters with its location of Aretino as an 'intuitor' of modernity whose fragmentary self-portrait reflects in some respects the social, religious, and political crises of the second half of the Cinquecento in Italy, yet here, too, there are few keys to formulate a gendered reading of women's role within this phenomenon. Studies of the epistolary genre in England and France provide useful foundations for reading women's published epistolary collections in Italy, although many such studies focus on the epistolary novel, which does not constitute part of my own study. See Susan M. Fitzmaurice, *The Familiar Letter in Early Modern English: A Pragmatic Approach* (Amsterdam: John Benjamin's Publishing Company, 2002) and Thomas O. Beebee, *Epistolary Fiction in Europe 1500–1850* (Cambridge: Cambridge University Press, 1999). Janet Altman's *Epistolarity: Approaches to a Form* (Columbus: Ohio State University Press, 1982) sketches a useful structural and theoretical framework for the epistolary medium itself. Linda Kauffman and Elizabeth Goldsmith take specifically feminist approaches to the genre: Linda Kauffman, *Discourses of Desire: Gender, Genre and Epistolary Fictions* (Ithaca, NY: Cornell University Press, 1990); Elizabeth C. Goldsmith, ed., *Writing the Female Voice: Essays on Women's Epistolary Literature* (Boston: Northeastern University Press, 1989).

15 Demetrius' (or pseudo-Demetrius') *De elocutione*, the earliest handbook on letter-writing, was a response to Artemon's lost preface to Aristotle's

letters, which described the letter as a halved dialogue (*On Style*, trans. W. Rhys Roberts [London: The Loeb Classical Library, 1931]). Cicero referred to the letter as 'amicorum colloquia absentium' (*Phillipics* II, 7; reiterated in *Fam.* 2.4.1).

16 This characterization was reiterated in other Renaissance works on letter-writing, such as Francesco Negro's *Opusculum scribendi epistolas* (1488) and Aurelio Brandolini's *De ratione scribendi* (1573). See Erika Rummel, 'Erasmus' Manual of Letter-Writing: Tradition and Innovation,' *Renaissance and Reformation*, new series, 13, no. 3 (1989), 299–312. On Erasmus and letters, see also Lisa Jardine, *Erasmus, Man of Letters* (Princeton: Princeton University Press, 1993), 147–74 and Henderson, 'The Enigma of Erasmus' *Conficiendarum epistolarum formula.*'

17 Francesco Sansovino, *Del secretario* (Venice: N.p., 1573), II, 406.

18 Schneider, *The Culture of Epistolarity*, 22.

19 See Altman, *Epistolarity: Approaches to a Form*, 88. The genre of epistolary fiction shares at least some of the structural attributes of the early modern letter collection (and of other genres, as argued by Beebee, *Epistolary Fiction*).

20 As Andrea Battistini notes, 'una missiva deve sempre e comunque tener conto del destinatario, per cui chi scrive è condizionato da chi legge,' in 'Gli epistolari,' *Manuale di letteratura italiana: Storia per generi e problemi*, ed. F. Brioschi and C. DiGirolamo, vol. 2, *L'io e la memoria* (Turin: Bollati Boringhieri, 1994), 442.

21 According to Adriano Pennacini, 'Situazione e struttura dell'epistola familiare nella teoria classica,' in *Quaderni di retorica e poetica* 1 (1985), 14, the letter is 'la metà di una conversazione orale e improvvisata con un interlocutore lontano collocata nel futuro in sincronia con il momento in cui il destinatario con la lettura della lettera realizzerà e completerà la struttura dialogica.' On the letterbook as a mosaic of diverse representations, see also Diana Robin's essay, 'Cassandra Fedele's *Epistolae* (1488–1521): Biography as Ef-facement,' in *The Rhetorics of Life-Writing in Early Modern Europe*, ed. Thomas F. Mayer and D.R. Woolf (Ann Arbor: University of Michigan Press, 1995), esp. 191.

22 See Anne Jacobson Schutte, 'The *lettera volgare* and the Crisis of Evangelism,' in *Renaissance Quarterly* 28 (1975), 639–88.

23 Fitzmaurice, *The Familiar Letter in Early Modern English*, 1.

24 Battistini, 'Gli epistolari,' 439.

25 My use of the term 'public sphere' draws on early modern conceptualizations of gendered divisions between 'male' and 'female' spaces, which derived from works such as Xenophon's *Oeconomicus* (translated into

Italian in 1540 by Alessandro Piccolomini) and its reinterpretation by pseudo-Aristotle (translated into Italian by Leonardo Bruni in 1419–20), and which were reiterated in Renaissance texts like Leon Battista Alberti's *Libri della famiglia* (1433–4, 1440) and Stefano Guazzo's *La civil conversazione* (1574). The term necessarily calls to mind Jürgen Habermas' conception of the public sphere and its emergence in modern bourgeois society, described in *The Structural Transformation of the Public Sphere: An Inquiry Into a Category of Bourgeois Society*, trans. Thomas Burger with Frederick Lawrence (Cambridge: MIT Press, 1994). Habermas' conceptualization has been usefully applied to women's epistolary writing in such essays as Altman's 'Women's Letters in the Public Sphere,' in *Going Public: Women and Publishing in Early Modern France*, ed. Elizabeth C. Goldsmith and Dena Goodman (Ithaca, NY: Cornell University Press, 1995), 99–115; Mary Jacobus, 'Intimate Connections: Scandalous Memoirs and Epistolary Indiscretion,' in *Women, Writing and the Public Sphere, 1700–1830*, ed. Elizabeth Eger et al. (Cambridge: Cambridge University Press, 2001), 274–89; and Dena Goodman, *The Republic of Letters: A Cultural History of the French Enlightenment* (Ithaca, NY: Cornell University Press, 1996). It has also been the focus of increased critical debate by feminist scholars. See, for example, Nancy Fraser, 'Re-thinking the Public Sphere: A Contribution to the Critique of Actually Existing Democracy,' in *Postmodernism and the Re-reading of Modernity*, ed. Francis Barker, Peter Halme, and Margaret Imerson (Manchester: Manchester University Press, 1992); Joan Landes, ed., *Feminism, the Public and the Private* (Oxford: Oxford University Press, 1998); and Judith C. Brown, 'Gender,' in *Palgrave Advances in Renaissance Historiography*, ed. Jonathan Woolfson (New York: Palgrave, Palgrave Macmillan, 2005), 177–92.

26 Cf. Amedeo Quondam, ed., *Stefano Guazzo e la civil conversazione*, Book 2 (Ferrara: Istituto di studi rinascimentali, 1993),169, and Baldassare Castiglione, *Il libro del cortegiano*, Book 2, ed. A. Quondam (Milan: Garzanti, 1981), where it is observed at numerous points that women must be cautious in their speech in order to preserve their reputations. Such warnings seem to circulate the more furiously as women begin to enter the world of print in greater numbers. Indeed, historians of gender are increasingly recognizing the importance of separating prescription from reality (or reaction) when considering the vast body of literature regarding women's roles. See, for example, Anne Jacobson Schutte, Thomas Kuehn, and Silvana Seidel Menchi, eds., *Time, Space and Women's Lives in Early Modern Europe* (Kirksville, MO: Truman State University Press, 2001), vii–xvii, and Paula Findlen, 'Masculine Prerogatives: Gender, Space, and

Knowledge in the Early Modern Museum,' in *The Architecture of Science*, ed. Peter Galison and Emily Thompson (Cambridge, MA: MIT Press, 1999), 29–57.

27 Peter Stallybrass notes that the connection extended to legal discourse as well as to conduct books; see 'Patriarchal Territories: The Body Enclosed,' in *Rewriting the Renaissance: Discourses of Difference in Early Modern Europe*, ed. Margaret Ferguson, Maureen Quilligan, and Nancy Vickers (Chicago: University of Chicago Press, 1986), 124.

28 Nogarola, *Complete Writings*, 52. Works like Leon Battista Alberti's *Libri della famiglia* fretted that, while women ought to aspire to this most fundamental of female qualities, they were not always capable of it, maintaining that 'ogni cosa possono le femmine eccetto che tacere' ('women are capable of all things, with the exception of silence') and that they could not be trusted with the family's important business, for fear their unchecked speech might endanger its fortunes. Alberti's character Giannozzo links anxiety about women's speech to fears about granting her access to the written word when he forbids his wife to enter the male sanctum of his study where he keeps his written records. Leon Battista Alberti, *I libri della famiglia*, Book 3, ed. Ruggiero Romano and Alberto Tenenti (Turin: Einaudi, 1969) 267–8. On the 'secrecy of mercantile writing' in Alberti and others, see Stephanie Jed, *Chaste Thinking: The Rape of Lucretia and the Birth of Humanism* (Bloomington: Indiana University Press, 1989), 78–89.

29 Francesco Barbaro, *Re uxoria* (1416); cf. Paul Grendler, *Schooling in Renaissance Italy: Literacy and Learning 1300–1600* (Baltimore: Johns Hopkins University Press, 1989), 89. Paolo da Certaldo urged that daughters not be taught to read at all because '... non istà troppo bene a una femina sapere leggere se già no la volessi fare monaca' ('... it is not suitable for a female to know how to read unless she is going to become a nun,' quoted in Maria Ludovica Lenzi, *Donne e madonne: l'educazione femminile nel primo Rinascimento italiano* (Turin: Loescher, 1982), 117–18; Leonardo Bruni excluded women from oratory and disputation, arguing that women had no place in the public realm that required such skills (*De studiis et litteris liber*, 1422–9[?]). Nevertheless, Bruni is more liberal than many on this subject. Francesco da Barbarino's *Reggimento e costumi di donna* (1315[?]) suggests that reading and writing are at best an 'ornament' to women and perhaps a dangerous one at that, necessary only for women who find themselves governing in the event of the death or absence of their husbands (see Lenzi, *Donne e madonne*, 192).

30 On women's education in Renaissance Italy, in addition to Lenzi, *Donne e madonne*, see Giulia Bochi, *L'educazione femminile dall'umanesimo alla*

Controriforma (Bologna: Edizioni Giuseppe Malipiero, 1961) and Barbara Whitehead, ed., *Women's Education in Early Modern Europe* (New York: Garland, 1999). Ann Rosalind Jones discusses some of the texts mentioned here in *The Currency of Eros: Women's Love Lyric in Europe 1540–1620* (Bloomington: Indiana University Press, 1990), 11–35. General overviews of education in the early modern period include Brian Richardson, *Printing, Writers, and Readers in Renaissance Italy* (Cambridge: Cambridge University Press, 1999) and Grendler, *Schooling in Renaissance Italy*.

31 See Agrippa, *Declamation on the Nobility and Preeminence of the Female Sex*, ed. and trans. Albert Rabil Jr. (Chicago: University of Chicago Press, 1996), 55, and Vives, *The Education of a Christian Woman*, ed. and trans. Charles Fantazzi (Chicago: University of Chicago Press, 2000), 47. Vives advocated education for women but distinguished between studying literature and studying 'eloquence,' maintaining that the latter was not appropriate for women. He considered education a means to occupy women's otherwise 'unsettled' minds and keep them from spending their time in 'talking and thinking.' But he drew the line at women passing on what they had learned: 'since a woman is a weak creature and of uncertain judgment ... she should not teach,' ibid., 72.

32 Castiglione, *Il libro del cortigiano*, 266, 246. Despite Castiglione's positive remarks about women, mostly offered through male interlocutors such as the Magnifico Giuliano, it has been argued that his women serve more to facilitate the unfolding of the dialogue among the male courtiers than take an active role in it themselves. See Pamela Bensen's analysis in *The Invention of the Renaissance Woman: The Challenge of Female Independence in the Literature and Thought of Italy and England* (University Park: Pennsylvania State University Press, 1992), 65–90.

33 Some of the highest praise regarding Isabella Andreini, for example, centred on her exceptionality as a woman who exceeded the confines and characteristics of her sex; see Isaac du Ryer's praise in *Le temps perdu* (1610): 'Je ne crois pas qu'Isabelle soit une femme mortale.' Isotta Nogarola was notoriously accused of incest. On learned women as 'intellectual transvestites,' see Patricia Labalme, ed., *Beyond Their Sex: Learned Women of the European Past* (New York: New York University Press, 1980), 5; in the same collection, see also Margaret King, 'Book-lined Cells: Women and Humanism in the Early Renaissance,' 66–90. As King points out, the very idea that learned women were somehow 'beyond their sex' implies that they violated their nature as women (ibid., 75).

34 Laura Cereta, *Collected Letters of a Renaissance Feminist*, ed. and trans. Diana Robin (Chicago: University of Chicago Pres, 1997), 82.

35 See, for example, Virginia Cox's comprehensive investigation of women writers in the early modern period, *Women's Writing in Italy 1400–1650*, and Diana Robin's informative study of women's engagement with academic culture and religious reform movements in sixteenth-century Italy, *Publishing Women: Salons, the Presses and the Counter-Reformation in Sixteenth-Century Italy* (Chicago: University of Chicago Press, 2007). Evidence of women's participation in the literary world can also be found in the more than 100 works published or pending in The Other Voice in Early Modern Europe series edited by Margaret L. King and Albert Rabil Jr. (University of Chicago Press/Centre for Renaissance and Reformation Studies, Toronto).

36 On this connection, see King and Rabil, who note that the writer Barbaro linked woman's silence (which constituted part of her 'education') to 'her perfect unanimity with her husband's will and her unblemished virtue (her chastity).' See the 'Editors' Introduction to the Series' in Moderata Fonte, *The Worth of Women*, trans. Virginia Cox (Chicago: University of Chicago Press, 1997), xxiv. See also Stallybrass, 'Patriarchal Territories,' 127.

37 Claudio Guillén, 'Notes toward the Study of the Renaissance Letter,' in *Renaissance Genres: Essays on Theory, History, and Interpretation*, ed. Barbara Kiefer Lewalski (Cambridge, MA: Harvard University Press, 1989), 80:

38 On the identification made by readers between author and epistolary persona, see Giacomo Moro, 'Selezione, autocensura e progetto letterario: sulla formazione e la pubblicazione dei libri di lettere familiari nel periodo 1542–1552,' *Quaderni di retorica e poetica* I (1985), 67. In *Sent as a Gift: Eight Correspondences from the Eighteenth Century* (Athens: University of Georgia Press, 1993), Allan MacKenzie takes issue with the 'postmodern' critic who attempts to deconstruct the letter, arguing with some sarcasm that letter writers probably thought they were recording actualities, and trusted language to convey their experience (13). Nevertheless, any first-person narrative that claims to reflect the self is necessarily mediated by the artistic process, the act of 'translating' that self from experience to words on paper.

39 Elizabeth Goldsmith notes that '[t]o publish a woman's letters, even if the purpose of publication was to praise female epistolary style, was in some way to violate her personal integrity,' in *Writing the Female Voice: Essays on Epistolary Literature*, ed. E. Goldsmith (Boston: Northeastern University Press, 1989), vii. The conflict between women's literary production and female honour is elegantly explained in Jones' *The Currency of Eros*, in which she theorizes a tension between public accessibility and private chastity, tracing the link drawn between 'women's volubility and their virtue' (see p. 20, and in general pp. 11–35).

40 See the essays in Goldsmith, ed., *Writing the Female Voice*, including Katherine Ann Jensen, 'Male Models of Feminine Epistolarity, or, How to Write Like a Woman in Seventeenth-Century France' (25–45); see also Kauffman, *Discourses of Desire*. According to the editors of *Dear Sister: Medieval Women and the Epistolary Genre* (Philadelphia: University of Pennsylvania Press, 1993), this bias existed in the medieval period as well.

41 Cf. Goldsmith, 'Authority, Authenticity, and the Publication of Letters by Women,' in *Writing the Female Voice*, 47: 'Letters, like conversation, were increasingly valued for their "natural," "authentic," and purportedly inimitable qualities, and good letter writers were said to be those who could make their letters "seem to speak," in a plain and unpedantic style.'

42 Goldsmith, ed., *Writing the Female Voice*, vii.

43 Jensen, 'Male Models …,' 22–45.

44 Cf. ibid., 41: 'To extol women's natural gift for epistolarity amounts to confining women's writing to letter writing and, moreover, limits their letter writing to its social practice.' Jensen's argument is supported by the popularity of the female love letter in particular in sixteenth-century Italy, which strengthened the association of women's letters with emotion rather than reason. See also Jensen, *Writing Love*, esp. 9–35.

45 Daybell shows, for example, that women adopted gendered strategies in early modern letters of petition, emphasizing vulnerability and using maternal imagery. He calls this model the 'scripted' female voice and notes that it could be appropriated by men as well as women. James Daybell, 'Scripting a Female Voice: Women's Epistolary Rhetoric in Sixteenth-Century Letters of Petition,' *Women's Writing* 13, no. 1 (March 2006), 3–22.

46 Cf. Parabosco, 'Alcune lettere scritte per donne,' in *Lettere amorose*, Book 1 (Venice: Giolito, 1545), 60r–66v, where, as a reading of the letters immediately reveals, 'per' has the meaning of agency ('da'). There were four volumes of the *Lettere amorose* in all; Book 1 alone was reprinted thirty-two times by 1617, see Janine Basso, *La genre épistolaire en langue italienne (1538–1662)* (Rome: Bulzoni, 1990), 709. The popularity of these letters would seem to indicate they did not suffer from the condemnation of love letters by the Index of Parma in 1580, and of anonymous love letters in particular by the Index of Sixtus V in 1590 (ibid., 210).

47 *Lettere amorose di Madonna Celia gentildonna Romana, scritte al suo amante* (Venice: Antonio degli Antonii, 1562), attributed to Parabosco by H.M. Adams, *Catalogue of Books Printed on the Continent of Europe 1501–1600*, vol. 1 (Cambridge: Cambridge Libraries, 1967). See also Giuseppe Baretti, *The Italian Library* (London: A. Millar, 1757), 279, who states, 'I have reason

to suspect that the writer of these letters was a man, and not at all in love …' Cox leaves open the possibility that Celia may have existed, noting the presence of a sonnet attributed to her in a sixteenth-century verse collection (*Women's Writing in Italy*, 317n5).

48 Miriam Cyr argues for the authenticity of the *Lettres Portuguaises* in *Letters of a Portuguese Nun: Uncovering the Mystery behind a Seventeenth-Century Forbidden Love: A Historical Mystery* (New York: Hyperion, 2006). The literature on the *Lettres Portugaises* is vast: see Nancy Miller, 'I's in Drag: The Sex of Recollection,' *The Eighteenth Century: Theory and Interpretation* 22 (1981), 47–57, and Peggy Kamuf, 'Writing Like a Woman,' *Women and Language in Literature and Society*, ed. Sally McConnell-Ginet et al. (New York: Praeger, 1980), 284–99; for the debate between them, see Mary McAlpin, 'Poststructuralist Feminism and the Imaginary Woman Writer: The *Lettres portugaises*,' *The Romanic Review* 90, no. 1 (1999), 27–44. Beebee argues that, in fact, all epistolary writing (ventriloquized or not) can be considered epistolary fiction and devotes a brief discussion to Ovid's *Heroides* as an early model for epistolary ventriloquism; see *Epistolary Fiction in Europe*, 103–46.

49 Kauffman, *Discourses of Desire*, 20. A collection of imagined 'letters' that was widely published in early-modern Italy as part of the humanist effort to recuperate classical texts, the *Heroides* were translated into Italian in *ottave* by Domenico da Monticello in 1508, in prose by Carlo Figiovanni in 1532, and in *terza rima* by Vincenzo Menni in 1541. See Basso, *La genre épistolaire*, for a complete sixteenth-century publishing history of the *Heroides* (60–5); on the *Heroides* and the medieval tradition, see Suzanne C. Hagedorn, *Abandoned Women: Rewriting the Classics in Dante, Boccaccio, and Chaucer* (Ann Arbor: University of Michigan Press, 2004), 21–46. On Ovid's female ventriloquism, see also Elizabeth D. Harvey, *Ventriloquized Voices: Feminist Theory and English Renaissance Texts* (London: Routledge, 1992). On Boccaccio's *Fiammetta*, see Janet Levarie Smarr, *Boccaccio and Fiammetta: The Narrator As Lover* (Urbana: University of Illinois Press, 1986), 145–6, and Hagedorn, *Abandoned Women*, 102–29; for a critique of Fiammetta's imitation of her Ovidian predecessors, see Michael A. Calabrese, 'Feminism and the Packaging of Boccaccio's *Fiammetta*,' *Italica* 74, no. 1 (Spring 1997), 20–42. More generally, see Vittore Branca, *Boccaccio medievale* (Florence: Sansoni, 1956) and Robert Hollander, *Boccaccio's Two Venuses* (New York: Columbia University Press, 1977). Recent work by Gerry Milligan approaches the literary performance of gender from the other side; see Milligan, 'The Politics of Effeminacy in *Il Cortegiano*,' *Italica* (2006), 345–66.

50 Cf. Judith Butler, *Gender Trouble: Feminism and the Subversion of Identity* (New York: Routledge, 1990).
51 Goldsmith, ed., *Writing the Female Voice*, vii.
52 See for example Quondam, *Le carte messaggiere*, and Richardson, *Printing, Writers and Readers in Renaissance Italy*.
53 For an illuminating discussion of the models of courtly (or 'civil') conversation as reflected in the genre of dialogue – in many ways related to that of letters – see Cox, *The Renaissance Dialogue*, esp. 22–33. On courtly models for Castiglione, see also Peter Burke, *The Fortunes of the Courtier* (University Park: Penn State University Press, 1995), 19–38.

1 Women's Vernacular Letters in Context

1 Bembo, in a well-known letter to Benedetto Varchi (28 November 1535), made reference to the idea of putting together an 'impression delle lettere volgari,' but he did not do so until 1548, well after Aretino's first volume. Pietro Bembo, *Lettere*, vol. 3 (Venice: Sansovino, 1560), 169.
2 Including reprints. See Amedeo Quondam, *Le carte messaggiere. Retorica e modelli di comunicazione epistolare: per un indice dei libri di lettere del Cinquecento* (Rome: Bulzoni, 1981), 30; and, for the reprints and editions of Aretino's letters, see Bembo, *Lettere*, 287.
3 Margaret King and Albert Rabil Jr. identify three generations of women humanists from the fourteenth and fifteenth centuries, placing Nogarola among the first group along with her sister Ginevra, and Fedele and Cereta in the third group alongside Alessandra Scala in *Her Immaculate Hand: Selected Works by and about the Women Humanists of Quattrocento Italy*, 2nd rev. ed. (Binghamton, NY: Medieval and Renaissance Texts and Studies, 1991), 16–25.
4 While the letters of all three women circulated in manuscript form and were widely known in the fifteenth century, those of Fedele and Cereta did not appear in a printed edition until the seventeenth century and those of Nogarola not until 1886 – although Fedele's *Oratio pro Bertucio Lamberto* appeared in print in 1487, 1488, and 1499; cf. Diana Robin, 'Cassandra Fedele's *Epistolae* (1488–1521): Biography as Ef-facement,' in *The Rhetorics of Life-Writing in Early Modern Europe: Forms of Biography From Cassandra Fedele to Louis XIV*, ed. Thomas F. Mayer and D.R. Woolf (Ann Arbor: University of Michigan Press, 1995), 13n3. See also Jacopo Filippo Tomasini, ed., *Clarissimae Feminae Cassandrae Fidelis venetae: Epistolae et orationes* (Padua: Franciscus Bolzetta, 1636); Jacopo Filippo Tomasini, ed., *Laura Ceretae Brixiensis Feminae Clarissimae Epistolae iam primum e MS in*

lucem productae (Padua: Sebastiano Sardi, 1640); and Eugenius Abel, *Isotae Nogarolae Veronensis opera quae supersunt omnia; accedunt Angelae et Zeneverae Nogarolae epistolae et carmina*, 2 vols. (Vienna: apud Gerold et socios; Budapest apud Fridericum Kilian, 1886). The interpretative issues raised by the relationship of individual letters to one another in each collection is more difficult to pin down than in cases in which authors themselves oversaw and imparted meaning to the collection's structure as a whole – on this problem see further on in this chapter; see also Luigi Matt, *Teoria e prassi dell'epistolografia italiana tra Cinquecento e primo Seicento* (Rome: Bonacci, 2005), 81–99. All three letterbooks have been edited and translated in the University of Chicago Press series The Other Voice in Early Modern Europe: see Isotta Nogarola, *Complete Writings: Letterbook, Dialogue on Adam and Eve, Orations*, ed. and trans. Margaret King and Diana Robin (Chicago: University of Chicago Press, 2004); Cassandra Fedele, *Letters and Orations*, ed. and trans. Diana Robin (Chicago: University of Chicago Press, 2000); and Laura Cereta, *Collected Letters of a Renaissance Feminist*, ed. and trans. Diana Robin (Chicago: University of Chicago Press, 1997). My discussion of Nogarola, Fedele, and Cereta is indebted to the analysis offered by the editors of these editions, and all citations are taken from the translations cited here.

5 Western tradition, moreover, attributes the invention of the genre to a woman, Atossa. See Gabriella Zarri, introduction to *Per lettera: La scrittura epistolare femminile tra archivio e tipografia, secoli xv–xvii* (Rome: Viella, 1999), ix.

6 Petrarch unearthed Cicero's *Letters to Atticus, Quintus and Brutus* in 1345; in 1392, Salutati came upon the *Epistolae ad Familiares* (translated into vernacular Italian in 1544 and titled *Lettere familiari*). On the *ars dictaminis*, see Martin Camargo, *Ars Dictaminis, Ars Dictandi* (Turnhout, Belgium: Brepols, 1991); Roger Chartier et al., ed., *Correspondence: Models of Letter Writing From the Middle Ages to the Nineteenth Century* (Princeton: Princeton University Press, 1997); and James Murphy, *Rhetoric in the Middle Ages* (Berkeley: University of California Press, 1974), 194–268.

7 These are but a few examples; as Paul Oskar Kristeller noted, epistolography was 'perhaps the most extensive branch of Humanist literature,' quoted in Giles Constable, *Letters and Letter-collections* (Belgium: Éditions Brepolis, 1976), 39. There is extensive literature on the humanist letterbooks. See Cecil H. Clough's classic essay, 'The Cult of Antiquity: Letters and Letter Collections,' in *Cultural Aspects of the Italian Renaissance: Essays in Honor of Paul Oskar Kristeller*, ed. Cecil H. Clough (Manchester: Manchester University Press, 1976); M. Fumaroli, 'Genèse de l'épistolographie

classique: rhetorique humaniste de la lettre, de Petrarche à Juste Lipse,'
Revue d'histoire littéraire de la France, 78 (1978), 886–905; Lucia Gualdo Rosa,
'La pubblicazione degli epistolari umanistici: bilancio e prospettive,'
Bullettino dell'Istituto Storico Italiano per il Medio Evo e Archivio Muratoriano
89 (1980/81), 369–92; G. Folena, 'L'espressionismo epistolare di Paolo
Giovio,' in *Il linguaggio del caos: Studi sul plurilinguismo rinascimentale*
(Torino: Bollati Berlinghieri, 1991), 200–41; Judith Rice Henderson, 'Defining the Genre of the Letter in Juan Luis Vives' *De conscribendi epistolis,'*
Renaissance and Reformation 7 (1983), 89–105; Helene Harth,
'L'épistolographie humaniste entre professionalisme et souci littéraire:
L'exèmple de Poggio Bracciolini,' in *La correspondance de Erasme et l'épistolographie humaniste: Colloque international tenu en novembre 1983*
(Bruxelles: Editions de l'Université de Bruxelles, 1985), 135–44; and Diana
Robin, *Filelfo in Milan: Writings 1451–1477* (Princeton: Princeton University
Press, 1991).

8 As Andrea Battistini reiterates, the shift towards the Ciceronian model and away from that of the medieval *artes dictandi* did not necessarily give rise to an epistolary product unmediated by artificial constructs: 'Ciò non significa che la dimensione privata degli studi e delle riflessioni morali, degli enunciati di poetica e dei piaceri intellettuali si traduca in spontaneo e immediato abbandono, giacché i classici sono sempre lí a mediare con il loro modello le tentazioni realistiche.' Andrea Battistini, 'Gli epistolari,' in *Manuale di letteratura italiana: Storia per generi e problemi,* ed. F. Brioschi and C. DiGirolamo, vol. 2, *L'io e la memoria* (Turin: Bollati Boringhieri, 1994), 438.

9 Cf. Vito R. Giustiniani, 'Lo scrittore e l'uomo nell'epistolare di Francesco Filelfo,' *Francesco Filelfo nel quinto centenario della morte: Atti del XVII convegno di studi maceratesi* (Tolentino, 27–30 settembre 1981) (Padova: Editrice Antenore, 1986), 250.

10 Cf. Clough, 'The Cult of Antiquity,' 36. As noted in the introduction, the early modern letter was not the private, personal document we tend to imagine it today, and many letters, humanist and otherwise, were read (and expected to be read) by more than one person. Humanist letters, however, had an overtly intellectual and/or pedagogical purpose. On the different expectations of early modern readers from those today, see Judith Rice Henderson, 'On Reading the Rhetoric of the Renaissance Letter,' in *Renaissance Rhetoric,* ed. Heinrich F. Plett (Berlin: Walter de Gruyter, 1993), 146.

11 Pietro Aretino, *Lettere: Libro primo,* ed. Francesco Erspamer (Parma: Ugo Guanda Editore, 1995), xvii.

12 See, for example, Vito R. Giustiniani, 'La communication érudite: Les lettres humanists et l'article moderne de revue,' in *La correspondance de*

Erasme et l'épistolographie humaniste, Colloque international tenu en novembre 1983 (Bruxelles: Editions de l'Université de Bruxelles, 1985), 109–33; Henderson, 'Defining the Genre of the Letter,' 94; Fedele, *Letters and Orations*, 35; and also Robin, 'Cassandra Fedele's *Epistolae*.' Elsewhere, Giustiniani suggests that the humanist letter resembles today's newspaper and magazine articles, keeping readers current on happenings within the circles of the cultural and political elite (see his 'Lo scrittore e l'uomo,' 251).

13 On the links between letters and dialogue, see Janet Levarie Smarr, *Joining the Conversation: Dialogues by Renaissance Women* (Ann Arbor: University of Michigan Press, 2005), 130–53. Nor did this relationship escape the notice of early modern theoreticians: Guarini's *Segretario* (1594), a reflection on the art of letter-writing, is composed as a dialogue with four interlocutors; other manuals devote sections to the relationship between letters and oratory.

14 As Albert Rabil Jr. states with regard to Cereta's letters, these were '… more than letters: they were occasions for formal presentations of an author's view on various subjects … [that] were favorite themes of many humanist writers,' in *Laura Cereta: Quattrocento Humanist* (Binghamton, NY: Center for Medieval and Early Renaissance Studies, 1981), 24–5.

15 Cereta, *Collected Letters* …, 122.

16 Rabil, *Laura Cereta*, 104, and Cereta, *Collected Letters* …, 123.

17 Fedele, *Letters and Orations*, 56–8. On humanist letters of consolation, see George W. McClure, *Sorrow and Consolation in Italian Humanism* (Princeton: Princeton University Press, 1991); Giovanni Maria Filelfo, *Consolatoria*, ed. Anne Schoysman Zambrini, in *Scelta di curiosità inedite o rare dal secolo XIII al XIX* (Bologna: Commissione per i Testi di Lingua, 1991, Dispensa CCLXXXIII). The letter of consolation was considered appropriate for women, who appear with frequency as both the authors and dedicatees of such texts. In the sixteenth century, Ortensio Lando published a book dedicated entirely to the genre, the *Consolatorie* (Venice, 1550).

18 Cf. Cereta, *Collected Letters* …, 129–33. Robin points out that the letter also contains aspects that are unique to Cereta, including her vivid description of a dream she has had of the underworld, but these serve to highlight Cereta's individuality rather than that of the deceased (ibid., 128).

19 Letter 170, for example, refers obliquely to the 'strano caso del povero signor del Grémonville' ('the strange case of the poor signor Grémonville'), without further explanation. See Arcangela Tarabotti, *Lettere familiari e di complimento*, ed. Meredith Ray and Lynn Westwater (Turin: Rosenberg and Sellier, 2005), 225.

20 As Letizia Panizza states in a recent study of women's writing in Italy, for this reason it can be difficult to speak of a continuity between the early humanists and later women writers: 'The very qualities that made [these writers] so exceptional – classical learning and writing in Latin – ensured that later women, able to gain literary recognition by writing solely in Italian, did not read them,' in Letizia Panizza and Sharon Wood, eds., *A History of Women's Writing in Italy* (Cambridge: Cambridge University Press, 2001), 29. In terms of an epistolary genealogy among women, however, I think we must allow that later writers such as Veronica Franco and Arcangela Tarabotti, both champions of women, would have known of their predecessors by reputation if not necessarily by direct reading; Panizza notes that Tarabotti's contemporary, Lucrezia Marinella, for example, may have been familiar with the works of Fedele and Cereta (ibid., 29n1).

21 Cf. *The Epistles of Erasmus*, vol. 1, ed. Francis Morgan Nichols (New York: Russell and Russell, 1962), letter 137: '... regard my Learning as a suppliant depending upon you, and imploring your aid.' Robin and King discuss the epistolary relationship between Nogarola and Guarino Veronese in Nogarola, *Complete Writings*, 40–62. On Bruni's letter to Battista Malatesta, see King and Rabil, *Her Immaculate Hand*, 13–15.

22 Cereta even addresses a letter to her mother, a figure virtually non-existent in the humanist tradition. As Robin points out, the humanist letterbook generally does not include letters to parents, siblings, or immediate family (Fedele, *Letters and Orations*, 35).

23 It is perhaps worth noting that this last is one of very few anthologies in which all the letters are addressed to one single person. According to the modern editors of the volume, Aretino himself was most likely behind its publication. See *Lettere a Aretino*, ed. Gonoria Floris and Luisa Mulas (Rome: Bulzoni, 1997).

24 Such letters demonstrated, for example, how women ought to address their children, husbands, or other relatives (and vice versa: husbands could learn from these models how to write to their wives, sons to their mothers). Models for composing virtually every kind of letter abounded in the sixteenth century. For an extensive catalogue of compendia and formularies published in the early modern period, see Matt, *Teoria e prassi*.

25 On this point, see also Cereta, *Collected Letters ...*, 25n17.

26 On Cereta as a radically different writer, see Fedele, *Letters and Orations*, 8.

27 Cereta, *Collected Letters*, 25.

28 Discussed in the introduction, note 28.

29 Ibid., 49–50.

30 Ibid., 31–2.
31 On the problem of *otium*, see Cereta, *Collected Letters*, 31–2nn7, 9.
32 Ann Rosalind Jones, *The Currency of Eros: Women's Love Lyric in Europe 1540–1620* (Bloomington: Indiana University Press, 1990), 4.
33 Nogarola, *Complete Writings*, 34.
34 Ibid., 53. Women are also the target of vicious gossip by other women. Nogarola complains, '... I am ridiculed throughout the city; the women mock me' (ibid., 54; see also Cereta, *Collected Letters* ..., 81–2). On Nogarola's exchange with Guarino, see King and Robin, *Isotta Nogarola*, 42–3; see also Margaret King, 'Book-Lined Cells: Women and Humanism in the Early Renaissance,' in *Beyond Their Sex: Learned Women of the European Past*, ed. Patricia Labalme (New York: New York University Press, 1980), 6–90. For an analysis of the 'scripted female voice' in the early modern English context (in women's letters that were not written for publication), see James Daybell, 'Scripting a Female Voice: Women's Epistolary Rhetoric in Sixteenth-Century Letters of Petition,' *Women's Writing* 13, no. 1 (March 2006), 3–22.
35 Fedele, *Letters and Orations*, 21, 37; and Cereta, *Collected Letters* ..., 40. Elsewhere, Robin remarks on Fedele's repeated use of the diminutive form to describe herself; see Robin, 'Cassandra Fedele's *Epistolae* (1488–1521),' 193.
36 On the Renaissance *querelle des femmes*, see Virginia Cox's introduction to Moderata Fonte's *The Worth of Women* (Chicago: University of Chicago Press, 1997); Constance Jordan, *Renaissance Feminism: Literary Texts and Political Models* (Ithaca, NY: Cornell University Press, 1990); Joan Kelly, 'Early Feminist Theory and the Querelle des femmes,' in *Women, History, and Theory* (Chicago: University of Chicago Press, 1986), 65–109; and Patricia Labalme, 'Venetian Women on Women: Three Early Modern Feminists,' *Archivio veneto* 5, no. 117 (1981), 81–108. On the illustrious women tradition, see Beatrice Collina, 'L'esemplarità delle donne illustri fra Umanesimo e Controriforma,' in *Donna, disciplina, creanza cristiana dal XV al XVII secolo*, ed. Gabriella Zarri (Rome: Edizioni di Storia e Letteratura, 1996), 103–19, and Constance Jordan, 'Boccaccio's In-famous Women: Gender and Civic Virtue in the *De claris mulieribus*,' in *Ambiguous Realities: Women in the Middle Ages and Renaissance*, ed. Carole Levin and Jeannie Watson (Detroit: Wayne State University Press, 1987), 25–47.
37 Nogarola, *Complete Writings*, 98–100. On this construct, see my discussion in the introduction.
38 Cereta, *Collected Letters*, 74–80.
39 Ibid., 76.

40 Ibid., 81.
41 Ibid., 79.
42 Ibid. On the lack of a supportive network among the woman humanists, see King, 'Book-Lined Cells,' 71–5.
43 Aretino's were not the first letters to be written in the vernacular – that distinction goes to Guittone d'Arezzo in the thirteenth century – but his letters touched off a new epistolary vogue.
44 Carlo Dionisotti, *Geografia e storia della letteratura italiana* (Turin: Einaudi, 1967), 183–204.
45 On the impact of the advent of printing on readers, writers, and publishers, see Brian Richardson, *Printing, Writers, and Readers in Renaissance Italy* (Cambridge: Cambridge University Press, 1999), and Elizabeth L. Eisenstein, *The Printing Press as an Agent of Change: Communications and Cultural Transformations in Early-Modern Europe* (Cambridge: Cambridge University Press, 1997).
46 The linkage between the rise of the vernacular and the expansion of the printing industry and the impact on authorship is touched on by Richardson in *Printing, Writers, and Readers*: '... the presses ... offered alternative opportunities which enabled writers who came from a variety of social and geographical backgrounds, and who lacked the humanist training that until about 1530 was an essential passport to success in literary society, to establish a reputation outside the milieu of the court. During the sixteenth century, print acted more and more as an incentive to write ...' Specifically, Richardson points out that the proportion of women writers between 1450 and 1550 rose from about 4 per cent to 9 per cent (ibid., 99–100).
47 As John Brewer writes, the 'growing realm of print and of the published word had important effects on the way in which private communication was conducted and the self presented. See 'This, That, and the Other: Public, Social, and Private in the Seventeenth and Eighteenth Centuries,' in *Shifting the Boundaries: Transformation of the Languages of Public and Private in the Eighteenth Century,* ed. Dario Castiglione and Lesley Sharpe (Exeter: University of Exeter Press, 1995), 15.
48 Cf. Andrea Battistini, 'Gli epistolari,' in *L'io e la memoria*, vol. 2, *Manuale di letteratura italiana: Storia per generi e problemi,* ed. F. Brioschi and C. DiGirolamo (Turin: Bolleti Boringhieri, 1994), 439. K.T. Butler describes the following categories of oratory often found in vernacular letters: deliberative (persuasive or dissuasive), demonstrative (narrative or descriptive), and judicial (judgmental: praise, rebuke, etc.). See *The 'Gentlest Art' in Renaissance Italy* (Cambridge: Cambridge University Press, 1954), 17. These

distinctions are present even in many letters that were not written for publication, such as those of Alessandra Macinghi Strozzi. See Maria Luisa Doglio, 'Letter-Writing, 1350–1650,' in *A History of Women's Writing in Italy*, ed. Panizza and Wood, trans. Lorch, 13–24.

49 On the increased element of 'dialogo sociale e cortigiano' in many late Renaissance letters, see Guglielmo Barucci, 'Silenzio epistolare e dovere amicale. I percorsi di un topos dalla teoria greca al Cinquecento,' *Critica letteraria* 126, no. 2 (2005), 213. On 'civil conversation' as a central element of Renaissance literary production, see Virginia Cox, *The Renaissance Dialogue: Literary Dialogue in its Social and Political Contexts, Castiglione to Galileo* (Cambridge: Cambridge University Press, 1992), 23–33, and Peter Burke, *The Fortunes of the Courtier* (University Park: Pennsylvania State University Press, 1995), esp. 8–18.

50 For example, explaining how to choose appropriate super- or subscriptions, as in Miniatore's *Formulario* that allows the reader to choose from Latin salutations collected in an index; or matching content and style to the correspondent's status, as in Ceci's *Compendio*, which urges the reader to remember 'di che qualità sia la persona a chi egli scrive' ('the status of the person to whom he writes'), 83.

51 On this problem, see note 2 in my introduction.

52 Gian Maria Anselmi and Elisabetta Menetti, for example, make note of the 'maniera contraddittoria' in which Aretino managed to intertwine different styles and subjects, combining 'l'ironia e il gusto del grottesco, la serietà di certe riflessioni politiche, letterarie e artistiche, il sarcasmo della polemica, l'ira e lo sdegno, le minacce e le adulazioni, l'amore per le figlie e per le cortigiane.' See Pietro Aretino, *Lettere*, ed. Gian Maria Anselmi, Elisabetta Menetti and Francesca Tomasi (Rome: Carocci, 2000), 15. Aretino's own later volumes of letters, however, displayed increased attention to style and rhetoric compared to the first – cf. Adriana De Nichilo, 'La lettera e il comico,' in *Le carte messaggiere*, 213–17.

53 See Erspamer's introduction to Aretino's *Lettere: Libro primo*, xxxv; see also Paolo Procaccioli, ed., *Pietro Aretino: Lettere*, vol. 1 (Rome: Salerno, 1991–2002), 7.

54 Because of this attention to the self and to quotidian detail, Erspamer sees in Aretino's first volume of letters 'l'affermazione della vita ordinaria e l'individuo nella sua irripetibile differenza, elementi essenziali della trasformazione epistemologica del tardo Rinascimento' (ibid., xxxiv).

55 Cf. Aretino, *Lettere*, ed. Erspamer, 213; I, 216; I, 165.

56 Aretino, *Lettere*, ed. Procaccioli, 6 vols. (Rome: Salerno, 1997–2002), I, 156.

57 Ibid., II, 82.
58 This 'narrative' quality is also present in humanist letters, although it is generally secondary to the other humanistic concerns we have discussed here. The letters of Filelfo, for example, pay particular attention to their own narrative structure. As Robin points out, the collection is 'ordered so as to form an autobiographical novel ... structured for suspense' (although this 'novel' exists amidst formal epistolary essays; see Robin, *Filelfo in Milan*, 6). Nor do all vernacular letter books of the early modern period exhibit this narrative quality, although this type of collection is of particular interest to me. As noted earlier, there was an increased tendency towards abstraction by the end of the sixteenth century, resulting in many letter books that lacked dates, names of addressees, or other identifying information. For an analysis of one such text see chapter 5 here on Isabella Andreini's *Lettere*.
59 Erspamer, for example, notes of Aretino's letters that the 'totale sintonia [del *Primo Libro*] con i suoi tempi lo ha reso, da allora in poi, inattuale' (*Lettere: Libro primo*, x).
60 Ariosto's famous description of Aretino as the 'flagello dei principi' is in *Orlando furioso*, XLVI, 14. In his monograph *Pietro Aretino* (Rome: Salerno, 1997), Paul Larivaille – with some admiration – calls Aretino's letters 'una delle imprese di accattonaggio e addirittura di ricatto più sfacciate e feconde di ogni tempo: opera non tanto di un "flagello dei principi," come ama proclamarsi, quanto ... di un tagliaborse dei principi' (242).
61 In this way Aretino earned enemies as well as friends. See Procaccioli's discussion of Anton Francesco Doni's anti-Aretinian production in Paolo Procaccioli, ed., *Anton Francesco Doni contra Aretinum* (Rome: Vecchiarelli, 1998).
62 Aretino, *Lettere*, ed. Procaccioli, II, letter 5.
63 Ibid., I, letter 100.
64 On this point, see Adriana Chemello, who cites a letter from Aretino to Ludovico Dolce that describes letters as precious jewels to prized and shown off ('... che si possin mostrare di tempo in tempo, come gemme de la gloria ...'). See 'Il codice epistolare femminile,' in *Per lettera: La scrittura epistolare femminile tra archivio e tipografia, secoli XV–XVII*, ed. Gabriella Zarri (Rome: Viella, 1999), 31.
65 Aretino, *Lettere*, ed. Procaccioli, II, letter 131.
66 Brian Richardson observes, 'The kind of transaction which was previously carried out behind the scenes was now spotlighted for the public gaze,' in *Printing, Writers and Readers*, 93.
67 Aretino, *Lettere*, ed. Procaccioli, II, letter 3.

68 The postscript reads: 'Perché il chiedere de le grazie testimonia la grandezza di coloro a cui si chieggono, supplico Vostra Eccellenza a concedermene una. La quale consiste nel degnarvi di far tanto di animo al Duca di Camerino, che si mova a mandarmi il dono che mi promesse è già uno anno' ('Since asking favours is a testament to the greatness of those who are asked, I beg your Excellency to grant me one, which consists in deigning to encourage the Duke of Camerino to send me the gift he promised me more than a year ago'). Ibid.
69 Ibid, IV, letter 573.
70 Aretino, *Lettere*, ed. Procaccioli, IV, letter 434.
71 Ibid.
72 Ibid.
73 For a discussion of Aretino's divergence in this regard from humanist letters, see Aretino, *Lettere*, ed. Erspamer, x.
74 Matt, *Teoria e prassi*, 13.
75 Paolo Manuzio, *Lettere volgari di diversi nobilissimi huomini, et eccellentissimi ingegni, scritte in diverse materie* (Venice: Paolo Manuzio, 1542).
76 In his dedication, Manuzio reminds his *destinatari* that they have always advocated the use of the vernacular: '... la qual cosa voi due, come di volontà, cosí di giudicio congiunti sempre stimaste degna in che l'uomo civile ponesse studio e cura' (Manuzio, *Lettere volgari*, 2r).
77 Ibid.
78 Ibid., 2v.
79 Taglienti, *Formulario nuovo* (Venice: Da Sabbio, 1539), A1v.
80 See Quondam, *Le carte messaggiere*, 41, 44–5. The author of one unpublished letter collection remarked on these qualities and their role in creating *varietas*, saying: 'The words of utility and pleasure in these letters constitute a harmony of writings in which both the indolent can be studious and the bored can be refreshed' (quoted in Constable, *Letters and Letter-collections*, 60).
81 B. Tasso, *Lettere* (Venice: Vincenzo Valgrisi e Baldassar Costantini, 1557), 12. Guazzo dispenses entirely with the notion of resisting publication, stating, 'Io ... senza infingermi (come sogliono alcuni scrittori) che queste lettere vengano fuori malgrado di me stesso, o' senza mia saputa, conffesso d'haver con premeditato disegno posto in aventura il mio ardire ...' ('... without pretending [as some writers are wont to do] that these letters are published in spite of me, or without my knowledge, I confess to having put forth my daring effort with premeditated design') (*Lettere*, A4v), but this is unusual.
82 Manuzio, *Lettere volgari*, 2r-v; emphasis added.

83 In the manuscript tradition, the term 'libro d'autore' is a technical one that refers to 'the definitive manuscript written out and perhaps later revised by the author, which would in turn become the source of other copies' (Richardson, *Printing, Writers and Readers*, 50). I use the term here and throughout in the sense in which it is used by Quondam (*Le carte messaggiere*), that is to distinguish epistolary collections containing the letters of just one writer, and often compiled by that writer, from epistolary anthologies, containing letters by a variety of people and compiled by an editor.

84 On this point, see also John Brewer, 'This, That, and the Other,' 14; and Robert Iliffe, 'Author-Mongering: The "Editor" between Producer and Consumer,' in *The Consumption of Culture 1600–1800: Image, Object, Text*, ed. Ann Bermingham and John Brewer (London: Routledge, 1995), 166–92.

85 Manuzio, *Lettere volgari*, 4.

86 Ibid., 150–3r–v.

87 Having heard that Manuzio is about to publish 'alcuni libri d'epistole volgari' ('some books of vernacular letters'), Molza writes: 'non ho potuto far ch'io non m'allegri con voi di cosí nobile fatica alla quale vi siete mosso per arrichir in questa parte ancora la nostra età ...' ('I could not help but rejoice with you regarding the noble effort you have undertaken in order to enrich our age in this area'). Ibid., 154. For further discussion of this exchange, see Giacomo Moro, 'Selezione, autocensura e progetto letterario: sulla formazione e la pubblicazione dei libri di lettere familiari nel periodo 1542–1552,' *Quaderni di retorica e poetica* I (1985), 67–90. Moro offers a concise discussion of the construction of letter collections and of aspects of Manuzio's anthology in particular, which has received little critical attention.

88 Manuzio, *Lettere volgari*, I, 29v–30, 'Se del scriver lettere latine questa è la vera via, Messer Paolo, io son a cavallo, e caminerò speditamente ... ma sí diversi sono i pareri degli uomini circa questa considerazione, che è molto difficile accertar il vero. A me piace di seguir il vostro iudicio per l'avenire; onde spererò potermi accrescer laude, benché difficilmente può crescere quel che non è ancor nato' ('If this is the proper way to write Latin letters, messer Paolo, count me in, and I will follow along immediately ... but opinions differ so much on this issue, that it is very hard to discern the truth. For my part, I prefer to follow your judgment in the future; whence I will hope to be able to accrue praise, although it is hard for something that has not yet been born to develop').

89 Ibid., I, 29v–30.

90 Ibid., 150v–51r.

91 Moro, 'Selezione, autocensura e progetto letterario,' 75–7. Brewer points out that in eighteenth-century London, booksellers advertised for private letters with no compunctions about permission or privacy, justifying their actions on the grounds that 'even the most intimate private correspondence of a notable was a matter of public importance' ('This, That, and the Other,' 14).

92 Quoted in Moro, 'Selezione, autocensura e progetto letterario,' 75.

93 Manuzio, *Lettere volgari*, 22v. Tolomei entreats Manuzio, at the very least, to print this letter with the others 'acciò ch'ella faccia fede come le poverette si volevano ammendar de lor peccati; ma non hanno avuto né chi l'ascolti, né tempo né modo di poterlo fare' ('that it might testify to the fact that the poor things wanted to correct their sins; but found no one to listen to them, nor time or opportunity to do so'). This letter is also contained in Tolomei's own collection, *Delle lettere di M. Claudio Tolomei* ... (Venice: Iacomo Cornetti, 1585), 180.

94 Manuzio claims, probably referring to the presence of some of his letters in various anthologies, that this has already occurred. 'Non averei mai pensato di mandare in luce [le lettere],' he writes to Antonio d'Avila, 'se non avessi temuto, che, sí come già alcune senza mia saputa, con poco riguardo dell'onor mio, si sono stampate, cosí della maggior parte dell'altre il medesimo dovesse avenire' ('I never would have thought to publish [these letters] if I hadn't feared that, just as some were printed without my knowledge and without reflecting well on me, the same might happen to most of the others' (*Lettere volgari*, 3).

95 Moro, 'Selezione, autocensura e progetto letterario,' 86.

96 Quondam lists 130 'libri d'autore' and twenty-seven anthologies published between 1538 and 1627 (*Le carte messaggiere*, 30). For a complete list of titles, see Quondam's bibliography in *Le carte messaggiere* (279–316), or Janine Basso, *La genre épistolaire en langue italienne (1538–1662)*, 2 vols. (Rome: Bulzoni, 1990).

97 Franceso Sansovino, *Del secretario* (Venice: N.p., 1573), 23v–24r. On the influence of such manuals on actually exchanged correspondence see Sanna-Kaisa Tanskanen, 'Best Patterns for Your Imitation: Early Modern Letter-Writing and Real Correspondence,' in *Discourse Perspectives in English*, ed. Janne Skaffari (Amsterdam: John Benjamins Publishing Company, 2004), 167–95. Some *secretari* were more theoretical in nature, such as that of Tasso (1587), who was concerned primarily with defining the 'ideal' secretary.

98 For a discussion of the increasing abstraction of letter collections, see for example Butler, *The 'Gentlest Art.'*

2 Female Impersonations

1 Vittoria Colonna's small volume of *Lettere*, published in 1544, belongs specifically to the category of spiritual letters, which is not the focus of this study. It was not uncommon for the occasional woman's letter to be inserted into predominately male anthologies (Manuzio's *Lettere volgari*, for example, contains six letters by women: four by Vittoria Colonna and two by Veronica Gambara), but a collection comprised solely of women's letters was in 1548 both a novelty and an anomaly. Jensen, focusing on French anthologies, hypothesizes that the inclusion of a small number of women's letters in dominantly male-authored anthologies functioned as an attempt to 'contain' women's literary power by controlling their participation in the literary realm rather than excluding them from it entirely. See Katherine Ann Jensen, 'Male Models of Female Epistolarity, or How to Write Like a Woman in Seventeenth-Century France,' in *Writing the Female Voice: Essays on Women's Epistolary Literature*, ed. E. Goldsmith (Boston: Northeastern University Press, 1989), 28.

2 Paul Grendler, for example, dismisses the *Valorose donne* as mere 'hackwork for Giolito ... edited (and probably partly written) by Lando,' in *Critics of the Italian World 1530–1560: Anton Francesco Doni, Nicolò Franco & Ortensio Lando* (Madison: University of Wisconsin Press, 1969), 34. Exceptions to this lack of interest are Novella Bellucci, 'Lettere di molte valorose donne ... e di alcune petegolette, ovvero: Di un libro di lettere di Ortensio Lando,' in *Le carte messaggiere*, ed. Amedeo Quondam (Rome: Bulzoni, 1981), 255–76; Constance Jordan, *Renaissance Feminism: Literary Texts and Political Models* (Ithaca, NY: Cornell University Press, 1990), 138–43; and, most recently, Francine Daenens, whose essay 'Donne valorose, eretiche, finte sante. Note sull'antologia giolitina del 1548,' in *Per lettera: La scrittura epistolare femminile*, ed. Zarri (Rome: Viella, 1999), 181–208, is an important resource both for one possible interpretation of the text as well as for the identification of the women represented in it. See also Serena Pezzini, 'Dissimulazione e Paradosso nelle *Lettere di molte valorose donne [1548] a cura di Ortensio Lando*,' *Italianistica* 31, no. 1 (1991), 67–83.

3 On this problem, see Harvey's study of literary ventriloquism in early modern English texts, which concludes that there is a fundamental difference between representations of the female voice authored by men rather than by women and that this difference derives from the unequal distribution of power. Elizabeth D. Harvey, *Ventriloquized Voices: Feminist Theory and English Renaissance Texts* (London: Routledge, 1992), esp. 16–32.

4 See Judith Butler's fundamental study, *Gender Trouble: Feminism and the Subversion of Identity* (New York: Routledge, 1990).
5 Cf. Doni, *Libraria* (Venice: Giolito, 1550), 27r. Although Lando's name does not appear on the frontispiece, it figures in a postscript by Bartolommeo Pestalozza naming him as the compiler of the anthology: 'En habes studiose lector Epistolas … quas ex varijs Italiae locis, multo sudore, multaque impensa Hortensius Lando collegit …' See *Lettere di molte valorose donne* (Venice: Giolito, 1548) (hereafter referred to as *Valorose donne*), 161v, and again in a sonnet by Francesco Sansovino appended to the text and addressed to the 'Onorato M. Ortensio.' Lando's only other 'appearance' is within certain of the letters themselves, for example, when Lucietta Soranza writes to Lucrezia Masippa that 'M. Ortensio … di voi stranamente si scandalizzò …' ('M. Ortensio … was oddly scandalized by you …'), ibid., 32r. All citations are taken from the 1548 edition of the *Valorose donne*.
6 See, for example, Salvatore Bongi, who writes that Lando's authorship is proven by the 'assoluta eguaglianza di lingua, di stile, e di modi di tutte le *Lettere* fra loro, e dalla somiglianza colle altre opere di lui,' in *Annali di Gabriel Giolito* (Rome: Bibliopola, 1965), vol. I, 213; Bellucci, who, while admitting the letters could be 'genuine,' finds that '… complessivamente le *Valorose donne* sono uniformi nello stile e rispondono ad una logica omogenea e ad un criterio di disposizione ben preciso' ('Lettere di molte valorose donne,' 263); and Silvana Seidel Menchi, who notes more generally that the 'elemento unificante' of all of Lando's texts, both anonymous and signed, '*non è l'identita dell'autore*: è l'omogeneità stilistica, è il timbro inconfondibile di una prosa abborracciata e sbilenca ….' See 'Chi fu Ortensio Lando?' in *Rivista storica italiana* III (1994), 504.
7 On Lando's moral themes, cf. for example the *Ragionamenti familiari*, 15, 24, 39, 42. For consolatory letters, see the *Valorose donne*, 78r–v, in which the Marchesa di Meregnano consoles a widowed friend that sudden death at least spares us becoming 'odiosi a parenti et amici' ('hateful to relatives and friends'). Contessa Tassona Etrata accuses the grieving Isabella Tassona Beltrama of envying her father for preceding her to a happier state: rather than mourn him, she ought rejoice for him (ibid., 97r–v). Similarly, in Lando's *Consolatoria del S. Nicolò delli Alberti, alla S. Agnesa di Besta nella morte d'un suo figliuolo*, the bereaved mother is reminded, 'dovereste … del tutto raggiorire l'animo …' ('rather than mourn, you ought … to be overjoyed'), *Consolatoria* (Venice: al segno del pozzo, 1550), 7. The *Paradossi* include compositions entitled 'Meglio è morire, che longamente campare' and 'Non essere da dolersi che la moglie muoia' ('It is

better to die, than live too long' and 'The death of one's wife ought not be grieved'). Camilla Svarda's unsympathetic response in the *Valorose donne* to a friend left lame after an illness, in which she exhorts her to take comfort from such illustrious 'zoppi' ('crippled men') as 'Cocle e Filippo Re de Macedoni' and quips that she ought to be grateful that she is neither a dancer nor a messenger ('datevi pace, Iddio ringraziando che non vi ha fatto né ballarina, né corriera … dove l'esser zoppa disconviene …' ['be at peace, thanking God that he did not make you a dancer, nor a messenger … where it would be a disadvantage to be lame,']), *Valorose donne*, 105v, is rewritten for male interlocutors in the *Consolatorie*. Cf. Francesco Carettono to Gioaniacomo de Medici, 19.

8 Paradox is a central element, obviously, of Lando's *Paradossi*, as well as the *Ragionamenti*, which contain epistolary treatises for and against a variety of subjects. For more on Lando's use of paradox see the discussion below on Lando's stance with regard to the 'difesa della donna,' or defence of women genre.

9 Pezzini, 'Dissimulazione e paradosso …,' 75.

10 Drawing a flattering parallel between her *destinataria* and famous women of antiquity, Ottavia poses a series of questions, for example: 'L'avervi io conosciuto savia et ingegnosa più assai che non fu mai Nicostrata, Diotima, o Targelia, mi fa confidente e molto ardita a chiedervi la soluzione di alcuni dubi … Vorrei da voi sapere per qual causa vaghi sono li amanti di portar nelle mani e poma e fiori … Vorrei intendere dall'alto vostro sapere qual sia la causa che li amanti divengano pallidi nel cospetto delli amati, e altri ve ne sieno che rossi si fanno. Vorrei sapere perché sieno li amanti sí alle lagrime inchinati e pronti …' ('Knowing you to be even wiser and more inventive than ever Nicostrata, Diotima, or Targelia, gives me the courage to dare inquire the solution to certain questions … I would like to know the reason why lovers are so fond of carrying apples and flowers in their hands … I would like you to tell me why lovers go pale in the presence of their beloved, and why others blush. I would know why lovers are so inclined and quick to tears …'), *Valorose donne*, 49r–v. Lando's *Quesiti amorosi* pose identical questions: 'Donde nasce che alcuni amanti veggendo la donna da loro amata si arrossiscono? … Ma donde avien poi che s'impallidiscono? … Da che procede che gli amanti sono sí vaghi di portar in mano e frutti e fiori? … Da che procede che gli amanti sono sí disposti alle lagrime?' ('How is it that some lovers blush upon seeing the woman they love? … Why then do some go pale? … Why is it that lovers are so fond of carrying fruit and flowers in their hands? … Why are lovers so quick to tears?'), *Quesiti amorosi, con le risposte,* in *Vari componimenti di*

M. *Hortensio Lando*... (Venice: Giolito, 1552), 7–8. Camilla's response to Ottavia in the *Valorose donne*, which merely poses more questions, echoes the same text, cf. *Valorose donne*, 50r–v, and *Quesiti amorosi*, 7.

11 I do not rule out the possibility that in some instances Lando may have begun with an actual letter authored by a woman; indeed, Italian archives attest that several of the women who appear in the *Valorose donne* did, in fact, compose letters. My argument is rather that the extent and uniformity of this kind of perpetual citation attests to Lando's heavy intervention, to such an extent that, even in such a case, the letter becomes his creation regardless of its origins.

12 Heavy reliance on examples, lists, and *detti* is apparent in virtually all of Lando's works, from the early *Paradossi* to the later *Cataloghi*. The *Officina* was probably first published around 1520; see Paolo Cherchi, 'La fonte dei *Cataloghi* di O.L.,' in *Studi e problemi di critica testuale* 18 (1979), 136. For a detailed comparison of key passages from the *Valorose donne* and the *Officina*, see Meredith K. Ray, 'Un'officina di donne: le *Lettere di molte valorose donne* e la fonte della "dottrina femminile,"' *Esperienze letterarie* 26, no. 3 (2001), 69–92. Pezzini, in 'Dissimulazione e paradosso,' shows that Lando's sources also included Betussi's *Raverta* and Equicola's *Libro di natura d'amore*.

13 See Paolo Cherchi, *Polimatia di riuso: Mezzo secolo di plagio (1539–1589)* (Rome: Bulzoni, 1998), and Cherchi, 'La fonte dei *Cataloghi* di O.L.,' *Studi e problem de critica testuale* 18 (1979), 142–8.

14 *Lettere amorose di Madonna Celia* (Venice: Antonio degli Antonii, 1562), A2r.

15 All citations are taken from *Officinae Ioannis Ravisii Testoris epitome* (Lugduni: Seb. Gryphium, 1551). Emphases are added in the comparisons of passages.

16 Lando, *Valorose donne*, 17r.

17 Ibid., 31v–32r:

> Adunque non potrete voi credere che *Polla Argentaria* moglie di Lucano scrivesse della guerra di Cesare e di Pompeio, scrivesse dieci libri di selve, scrivesse Saturnali, scrivesse dell'incendio di Roma, dell'incendio di Troia, e della calamità di Priamo? Adunque crederemo che *Claudia* moglie di Stazio dottissima non fusse? Adunque mosse dalla vostra falsa openione non crederemo che *Corrina* (la Tebana) facesse cinque libri de Epigrammi et cinque fiate superasse Pindaro tenuto il prencipe de poeti lirici? Saranno favole per voi le cose memorabili che si raccontano della dottrina di Pamphila, di *Damophila*, di *Sosipatra*, di *Carixena*, e di *Istrina* Reina de Scithi ...?

Therefore can you not believe that *Polla Argentaria*, wife of Lucan, wrote of the war of Caesar and Pompey, that she wrote ten books of *selve*, that she wrote saturnals, that she wrote of the fire of Rome, the fire of Troy, and the diasaster of Priamus? Are we to believe that *Claudia*, wife of Statius, was not extraordinarily erudite? Spurred by your false opinion, shall we not believe that Theban *Corrina* wrote five books of Epigrams and surpassed Pindarus, considered the prince of lyric poets, five times over? The memorable things recounted with regard to the erudition of ... *Damophila, Sosipatra, Carisena,* and *Istrina*, queen of Syths, must be fables to you?

Cf. *Officina*, I: 'Mulieres doctae':

Polla Argentaria,* Lucani fuit uxor (testimonio Martialis: Haes est illa dies, quae magni conscia partus Lucanum populis, et tibi Polla dedit). Tanta dicitur fuisse doctrina, ut maritum iuverit, in emendandis tribus primis libris Pharsaliae ... Statius Papinius uxorem habuit nomine *Claudiam*, magno ingenio, doctrinaque, non vulgari praeditam ... *Corinnae* tres fuerunt. Prima Thebana, seu Tanagraea, Archelodori et Procratiae filia, et Myrtidis discipula, quae Lyricorum principem Pyndarum quinquies vicisse, et Epigrammatum quinque libros edidisse fertur ... *Damophila*, Graeca, uxor Pamphili ... *Sosipatra*, vates fuit Lyda ... Fuit et multorum carminum autor *Charixena* ... *Istrina* Scytharum regina, Aripithis uxor, Sulem filium Graecam linguam literasque edocuit ...'

*The example of Polla is shifted to facilitate comparison.

18 The *Officina* lends a sense of dignity and historical perspective, for example, to the plight of Lucrezia Gonzaga (discussed in chapter 3), whose husband is in prison, as her sister Isabella comforts her with a litany of illustrious antecedents: '... e quando pur a Dio piacesse ch'egli morisse nella prigione, non li averebbe però cosa che non sia avvenuta a maggior uomo di lui: morì prigione *Iugurta*, morì *Siphace*, morì *Enrico III* Imperadore, morì prigione *Celestino quinto, Gioanni primo*, e *Giovanni quarto* decimo pontefice; morì prigione *Aldegisio* figliuolo di Desiderio Re de' Longobardi e *Aristonico* doppoi che egli fu menato in triumfo da Aquilio console' ('... and even should it please God that he die in prison, this is not something that greater men than he have not undergone: *Iugurta* died in prison, as did *Syphax*, the emperor *Henry III, Celestine V, John I*, and *John IV*, the tenth pope; *Aldegisius*, the son of Desiderius, King of the Lombards, died a prisoner, and *Aristonicus* after being led in the triumph of the

consul Aquilus'), *Valorose donne*, 14v. These examples can all be found in the *Officina*, Book I, under the heading 'In carceribus mortui.' See also the Contessa di Scandiano's letter offered in consolation to the mother of a son who is mute (*Valorose donne*, 34r-v), which takes its inspiration entirely from the *Officina*, Book I, 'Muti.' As is the case with more than one of the letters in the *Valorose donne*, these examples are repeated, nearly word-for-word, elsewhere in Lando's opus; cf. Landos, *Consolatorie*, 46.

19 Cf. *Officina*, Book I, 'Ab animalibus diversis amati.'
20 Cf. *Valorose donne*, 141v–142r; 144v–145r. There are a number of other such examples in the *Valorose donne*: Lavinia Sforza's letter to Isabetta Moscarda regarding her brother's drowning (143v–144r); Tadea Centana's to Livia Caraffa, whose brother has been killed by a bear; to console Livia, Tadea lists even stranger incidents in which people have been killed by deer, goats, and even mice (148v–149r). Sibillia Tolomei writes of a Modenese gentleman put to death by being dragged by horses (150v–151r); Diana de Contrari consoles Veronica delli Armelini, whose husband has died falling down a flight of stairs (152v–153r); Violante da Castello consoles Lionella Rossa, whose brother has been killed by an arrow (153r–v); and Teodora Fispogna Calini writes to a friend whose husband has been poisoned (153v–154r).
21 On the phenomenon of *riscrittura* among early modern writers see Cherchi, *Polimatia di riuso* and Cherchi, 'Plagio e/o riscrittura nel Secondo Cinquecento,' in *Furto e plagio nella letteratura del classicismo*, ed. R. Gigliucci (Rome: Bulzoni, 1998), 283–99; see also Amedeo Quondam, 'Note su imitazione, furto e plagio nel Classicismo,' in Paolo Cherchi, *Sondaggi sulla riscrittura del Cinquecento* (Ravenna: Longo, 1998), 373–400.
22 Lando even offers clues to his literary game. One of his epistolarians, for example, lamenting the sorry state of literature, explains that some writers are too dry, others too affected, while still others are 'indegni di esser chiamati scrittori, ma più tosto ladri, *avendo da vari luoghi ripiene le lor carte de furti ...*' ('unworthy of being called writers, but rather thieves, *having filled their pages with material stolen from various places*'), *Valorose donne*, 160r–v (emphasis added). These sentiments are echoed in Lando's satirical *Sferza de scrittori antichi et moderni* of 1550, where the 'anonymous' author, incensed by the lack of originality among writers, pens a more extensive diatribe against the practice of literary 'furto,' writing: 'non vi accorgete voi ... come alcuni ve ne sieno c'hanno le carte loro tutte piene de furti di maniera che se ciascuno si ritogliesse la parte sua rimarebbeno le carte

bianche ...' ('don't you see ... how there are some who have so filled their pages with purloined material that if everyone were to remove their own part, only blank pages would remain ...'), 20r–v.
23 Janet R. Smarr, *Boccaccio and Fiammetta: The Narrator as Lover* (Chicago: University of Illinois Press, 1986), 143. Harvey argues that intertextuality is itself a form of ventriloquism, for no text is completely stable but rather is created from a variety of sources and experiences; cf. *Ventriloquized Voices*, 10.
24 *Valorose donne*, 2r–v.
25 On Lando's use of paradox in his other works, see Paul Grendler, *Critics of the Italian World* (Madison: University of Wisconsin Press, 1969), 31, '... in both the *Paradossi* and the *Confutazione*, Lando used the poverty-wealth paradox to criticize the rich and highborn ... In both books, although arguing seemingly opposed theses, Lando made critical social and moral comments.' Erasmus, whose work Lando read, admired, and often incorporated into his own, was known for his use of paradox. His *Moria* revived the classical genre of 'paradoxical encomium,' while his manual *In Praise of Marriage* approached its subject from both sides. See Erasmus, *The Praise of Folly*, ed. and trans. Clarence H. Miller, 2nd ed. (New Haven: Yale University Press, 2003), xiv, and Erika Rummel, *Erasmus on Women* (Toronto: University of Toronto Press, 1996), 4–7.
26 Traditionally, the term 'poligrafo' has had negative connotations, implying a lack of moral, political, or artistic engagement on the part of the writer, in contrast to those who write for the sake of art or belief, but not for the market. Grendler was among the first to 'rehabilitate' Lando and other 'poligrafi,' emphasizing the element of social criticism in their works. See, for example, Grendler, *Critics of the Italian World*.
27 Lando, *La sferza de' scrittori*, 25v. Lando continues: 'e non ho sentito quella gratitudine che si suol sentir delle più malavagie opre' ('and I did not receive the gratitude customary for even the most malicious of works'), suggesting that Lando labelled these women 'pettegolette' when they proved unmoved by his memorialization of them in print.
28 Ibid., 23v. This and the previous passage are also pointed out by Ireneo Sanesi, 'Tre epistolari del Cinquecento,' *Giornale storico della letteratura* 24 (1894), 11, and by Bellucci, 'Le Lettere di molte valorose donne,' 262, neither of whom, however, addresses the fact that Lando seems to refer to two different texts in these passages, one of which is certainly the *Valorose donne*; the other, quoted here, could refer to the *Ragionamenti*, which includes a composition by Ippolita Palavicina 'contra l'avarizia di alcune signore' ('against the avarice of certain ladies'), 24r.

29 The attribution is made by Conor Fahy, 'Un trattato di Vincenzo Maggi sulle donne e un'opera sconosciuta di Ortensio Lando,' in *Giornale storico della letteratura italiana* 138 (1961), 254–72.
30 Cf. Lando, *Brieve essortatione*, 37r–v, cited in Fahy, ibid., 268.
31 This is always a question when looking at the texts produced by the *querelle des femmes:* Are they serious reflections of the author's own perspective, or merely acts of rhetorical one-upmanship? Erasmus wrote that any author who labelled his text a 'declamatio,' for example, disclaimed all responsibility for the views it put forth. See Desiderius Erasmus, *Collected Works of Erasmus*, ed. Beatrice Corrigan (Toronto: University of Toronto Press, 1974), 71, 91–2; see Rummel, *Erasmus on Women*. Many modern scholars, however, make the point that, regardless, such texts ultimately contributed to the recognition of an existing social problem on the treatment of women, see Albert Rabil Jr., ed. and trans., *Declamation on the Nobility and Preeminence of the Female Sex* (Chicago: University of Chicago Press, 1996), 3–32.
32 Fahy, 'Un trattato ...,' 271.
33 In fact, the *lettera familiare* was used in many cases as a vehicle for religious dissent during this period. On this problem, see Anne Jacobsen Schutte, 'The *lettera volgare* and the Crisis of Evangelism in Italy,' *Renaissance Quarterly* 28 (1975), 639–88, and Paolo Simoncelli, *Evangelismo italiano del Cinquecento: questione religiosa e nicodemismo politico* (Rome: Ist. Storico Italiano per l'èta moderna e contemporanea, 1979).
34 Nancy Miller, '"I's in Drag": The Sex of Recollection,' *The Eighteenth Century: Theory and Interpretation* 22 (1981), 49.
35 See Silvana Seidel Menchi, 'Chi fu Ortensio Lando?' *Rivista storica italiana* 106, no. 3 (1994), 507n17, and Francine Daenens, 'Isabella Sforza: Beyond the Stereotype,' in *Women in Italian Renaissance Culture and Society*, ed. Letizia Panizza (Oxford: European Humanities Research Centre, 2000), 45, which describes this text as 'one of the most important documents of the female identity of Lando the writer.'
36 Isabella Sforza (Ortensio Lando), *Della vera tranquillità dell'animo* (Venice: Eredi di Aldo Manuzio, 1544), 3v: '... ne vi prenda di ciò meraviglia alcuna ... che sí dottamente possa scrivere una donna ... essendo di ingegno elevatissima, di memoria tenacissima, e grandissima osservatrice de savi detti' ('... nor should you marvel at all ... that a woman should be able to write so well ... for she is of the most elevated intellect, tenacious memory, and a great recorder of wise sayings'). The Index of Forbidden Books listed several of Lando's works under the name 'Hortensius Tranquillus' (see n39 below). For a list of Lando's pseudonyms, see Seidel Menchi, 'Chi fu Ortensio Lando?' 505.

37 Including, once again, many of the women who figure in the *Valorose donne*, such as Alda Torella, Isabella Gonzaga da Puvino, and Sulpitia Biraga.
38 Lando, *Consolatorie*, 16v.
39 The Index of May 1544, for example, banned books by 'Hortensius Tranquillus' and 'Philaletis civis Utopiensis,' two of Lando's pseudonyms; see Grendler, *Critics of the Italian World*, 36–7.
40 Daenens, 'Donne valorose …,' 183.
41 Ibid., 'solo se isolate dal contesto storico possono apparire come arbitraria galleria di donne illustri o paradigma astratto.'
42 *Valorose donne*, 3r.
43 The Nicodemetic position (from Nicodemus, a prominent Jew said to have visited Jesus by night) is that the prudent expression of one's religious views can be more effective than an open proclamation that might result in imprisonment, exile, or even death. On the phenomenon of *nicodemismo* in early modern Italy, see Delio Cantimori, *Eretici italiani del Cinquecento* (Florence: Sansoni, 1939), and Carlo Ginzburg, *Il nicodemismo: Simulazione e dissimulazione religiosa nell'Europa del '500* (Turin: Einaudi, 1970).
44 Emphasizing the loosely organized nature of Italian heterodoxy, Susanna Peyronel Rambaldi explains: 'Dopo gli anni quaranta, tutto il movimento eterodosso italiano è caratterizzato dalla formazione di piccoli gruppi che si incontravano clandestinamente nelle case private e che coltivavano rapporti di amicizia …' ('Mogli, madri, figlie: donne nei gruppi eterodossi italiani del Cinquecento'), in *Le donne delle minoranze*, ed. Claire E. Honess and Verina R. Jones (Turin: Claudiana, 1999), 54. For a general discussion of Italian evangelism and heterodoxy, see Simoncelli, *Evangelismo italiano*; on Lando's position specifically, see Grendler, *Critics of the Italian World*.
45 Grendler notes, 'Throughout his life, Lando emphasized Scripture as the foundation of religion,' *Critics of the Italian World*, 120; Lando's *Dialogo… nel quale si ragiona della consolatione, & utilità, che si gusta leggendo la Sacra scrittura* (1552) is entirely devoted to the discussion of scripture. In spite of its tendency to stray from orthodoxy, Lando himself must not have thought the *Dialogo* a risk, for it is one of the few books published under his own name; cf. Grendler, *Critics of the Italian World*, 125.
46 Grendler, *Critics of the Italian World*, 120.
47 *Valorose donne*, 18v–20v. This sentiment, with its Eucharistic overtones, is repeated in Lando's *Dialogo*, 32v, '… non studiate mai altro che questo divino volume, mangiatelo tutto … convertitelo in suco, ed in sangue, perciocché egli farà come lampada a' piedi vostri …' ('… study nothing but this holy text, devour it … transform it to nectar & blood, so that it will be as a light at your feet …').

48 *Valorose donne*, 146v–147r.
49 Cf. *Valorose donne*, 26v–27r and 35r. Lando attributes a heterodox discourse to Isabella Sforza in *La vera tranquillità' dell'animo*, which he published in her name. See Daenens, 'Isabella Sforza,' Seidel Menchi, 'Chi fu Ortensio Lando?' and Meredith K. Ray, 'Textual Collaboration and Spiritual Partnership in Sixteenth-Century Italy: the Case of Ortensio Lando and Lucrezia Gonzaga,' forthcoming in *Renaissance Quarterly* 62, no. 3 (2009).
50 *Valorose donne*, 37v–38v. Numerous similar examples abound in the *Valorose donne*. See, for example, Margherita Pellegrina's letter (47r–48r), which sums up Lando's distrust in the trappings of Christianity and desire for a pure, stripped-down reliance on the Bible.
51 Daenens, 'Donne valorose ...,' 192.
52 See Grendler's comments on Lando's *Dialogo* on scripture, which are equally applicable to the *Valorose donne*: 'In a corollary to his rejection of Renaissance learning, Lando argued that the Bible was superior to all other models of conduct and learning ... Scripture was better than Cicero, Seneca, Plutarch ... for teaching virtue' (*Critics of the Italian World*, 124).
53 Daenens, 'Donne valorose ...,' 192.
54 *Valorose donne*, 17r.
55 Ibid., 91r–v.
56 Ibid., 31r–32r.
57 Ibid., 122r–v, '... non provarno questo ne lor dotti scritti Bernardo Spina, Galeazzo Capra, Cornelio Agrippa, e Ortensio Lando?' ('... was this not proved by Bernardo Spina, Galeazzo Capra, Cornelio Agrippa, and Ortensio Lando in their learned writings?'). Lando thus inserts himself overtly into the pro-woman side of the debate.
58 Ibid.
59 Grendler, *Critics of the Italian World*, 148.
60 *Valorose donne*, 120v.
61 Cf. ibid., 10v–13v; on 10v, we read, 'Con dispiacer ho inteso c'avete lasciato quella ... quella diligente opra di ricamare e di cucire, la quale vi faceva risplendere sopra tutte le donne della città vostrà, e vi siete data tutti in preda alla vana poesia ...' ('I heard with dismay that ... you have left off your diligent embroidery and sewing work, which made you resplendent above all the women in your city, and that you have completely given yourself to idle poetry ...'). The letter writer goes on to mock poets as 'uomini per la maggior parte maligni, iracondi, sazievoli, bizarri e maninconici' ('men for the most part wicked, irate, tiresome, bizarre, and melancholy') and claims that poetry, more dangerous than heresy, will render Margherita 'di giorno in giorno men cristiana che non siete' ('each day less Christian than you are').

62 Ibid., 160r.
63 Ibid., 160v.
64 Ibid., 125v.
65 Ibid., 136r. The question of women's participation in their own subjection was also raised elsewhere, for example in the letters of Laura Cereta; cf. Laura Cereta, *Collected Letters of a Renaissance Feminist*, ed. and trans. Diana Robin (Chicago: University of Chicago Press, 1997), 79. It was later renewed by writers like Moderata Fonte, who defended women and described the difficulties they faced in her dialogue, *Il merito delle donne*. See the modern edition edited by Adriana Chemello (Venice: Eidos, 1988).
66 *Valorose donne*, 95r.
67 Ibid., 131r.
68 Referring perhaps to Aretino or even to Lando himself, Isabella ridicules a certain 'disgraziataccio, il quale ... minaccia di farvi morire con i suo fecciosi e stomacosi scritti, se piacevole, liberale, et affabile non ve li dimostrate' ('scoundrel, who ... threatens to kill you with his despicable and nauseating scribbles if you do not show yourself to be pleasant, generous, and friendly'), ibid.,132r. It is certainly tempting to read this as a sly comment by Lando on the vast appropriation of the female voice at hand.
69 Ibid., 106r.
70 Ibid., 107r.
71 More's *Utopia* was translated as *La republica nuovamente ritrovata, del governo dell'isola Eutopia* ... (Venice, 1548). On Lando as More's translator, see Riccardo Scrivano, 'Ortensio Lando traduttore di Thomas More,' in AAVV, *Studi sulla cultura lombarda in memoria di Mario Apollionio*, vol. I (Milan: Vita e pensiero, 1972), 99–107.
72 On early modern utopias, see Christian Rivoletti, *Le metamorfosi dell'Utopia: Anton Francesco Doni e l'immaginario utopico di metà Cinquecento* (Lucca: Maria Pacini Fazzi Editore, 2003); and Luigi Firpo, 'Thomas More e la sua fortuna in Italia,' *Occidente: Rivista bimestrale di studi politici* 8, nos. 3–4 (1952), 225–41.
73 Cf. Grendler, *Critics of the Italian World*, 148, 'The critics [Lando, Anton Francesco Doni and Nicolò Franco] were not educational philosophers; they offered only hints of an alternative based on experience and on a preference for a rustic or solitary life ...'
74 Cf. Rummel, *Erasmus on Women*, 4.
75 One of the most influential 'books of secrets,' Alessio Piemontese's *La prima parte de' secreti del reverendo donno Alessio piemontese* (Pesaro: Gli heredi di Barolomeo Cesano, 1562) (hereafter *Secreti*), was first published in 1555. The real author of the *Secreti* is thought to have been Girolamo

Ruscelli, a professional writer in the same circle as Lando. On Ruscelli and the *Secreti*, see William Eamon, *Science and the Secrets of Nature: Books of Secrets in Medieval and Early Modern Culture* (Princeton: Princeton University Press, 1994), 134–51; Eamon and Françoise Peheau, 'The Accademia Segreta of Girolamo Ruscell: A Sixteenth-Century Italian Scientific Society,' *Isis* 75 (1984), 327–42; and John K. Ferguson, 'The Secrets of Alexis,' *Proceedings of the Royal Society of Medicine, Section on the History of Medicine* 24 (1931), 225–46. Lando would have had numerous earlier opportunities to encounter the genre, however, either in its Latin incarnations or in the form of the pamphlets that circulated in Italy from about 1520, hawked in the marketplace by *ciarlatani* and peddlers. For a chronological list of such pamphlets between 1520 and 1643, see Eamon, *Science and the Secrets of Nature*, 361–5; for the editions of *libri di segreti* proper, see Eamon, *Science and the Secrets of Nature*, 136 and 13–91 for the tradition prior to the sixteenth century. Of the many *libri di segreti* printed in the sixteenth and seventeenth centuries, only one appeared under a woman's name, that of Isabella Cortese, *Secreti de la signora Isabella Cortese ne' qvali si contengono cose minerali ...*, 1st ed. (Venice: Giovanni Bariletto, 1561). Rudolph Bell speculates that 'she' might have been a 'he,' the female name a marketing gimic to enhance sales; cf. *How to Do It: Guides to Good Living for Renaissance Italians* (Chicago: University of Chicago Press, 1999), 44–5. Cortese's anti-elitist book was quite successful, perhaps due to the novelty of its female authorship; it went through seven reprints from 1561 to 1677.

76 Subsequent to Martin Luther's marriage in 1525, the debate over celibacy versus marriage swirled through Europe. Erasmus, for example, treated the subject in a number of works, such as the *Institutio christiani matrimonii*, which elaborates on themes from his *Colloquia*, see Desiderius Erasmus, *Collected Works of Erasmus*, vol. 39, ed. and trans. Craig R. Thompson (Toronto: University of Toronto Press, 1997), 279–85, 305. It was also addressed in texts like Juan Luis Vives' *De institutione feminae Christianae*, ed. C. Fantazzi and C. Matheussen, trans. C. Fantazzi (1524; reprint, New York: E.J. Brill, 1996), and Lodovico Dolce's *Dialogo della institution delle donne* (Venice: Giolito, 1545).

77 *Valorose donne*, 114v–115r.

78 Virginia suggests that the young man wash with a cloth soaked in wine boiled with myrtle and that he then drink the potion to cure his bad breath; a powder of litharge will stem sweat, while his scabies require a cream of 'lapatio ... fumoterre ... fungia di porco e botiro' made during the month of May (ibid.). For similar problems and remedies see Alessio Piemontese, *Secreti*, Part I, Book I, 25 (bad breath) and Part II, Book I, 4–7 (scabies). See

also Giovani Marinello, *Gli ornamenti delle donne* (Venice: Francesco de' Franceschi Senese, 1562), 8r–15r (scabies), 22–23r (sweat and odour), 281r–v (feet).
79 *Valorose donne*, 16v.
80 See Grendler, *Critics of the Italian World*, 93 and 147, where Grendler writes that '[in the *Vari componimenti*] Lando criticized nearly every human profession as dishonest or vicious'; while physicians in particular were guilty of 'avarice, ignorance, and lack of concern for the poor.' Lando refers to his youthful studies in medicine in the *Sermoni funebri* (ibid., 22).
81 *Valorose donne*, 8v.
82 Ibid., 39v–40v and 127r–v, '… nova cosa non mi pare che le monache de' nostri tempi facciano anch'esse l'amore … elle non sono più di bronzo, né di macigno che siamo noi altre. Troppo nel vero gran forza avrebbe il velo s'egli potesse rafreddare e spegnere i riscaldimenti della carne …' ('… it is not news to me that nuns today make love too … they are no more made of bronze and stone than we are. Truly the veil would have too much power if it were able to cool and extinguish the heat of the flesh …').
83 Ibid., 67v–68r.
84 There is evidence of Lando's presence in Augustinian monasteries in Padua, Genoa, Siena, and Naples, and later Bologna and Pavia, under the name 'Geremia da Milano'; sometime around 1534 he left the monastery and fled to Lyon, see Silvana Seidel Menchi, 'Sulla fortuna di Erasmo in Italia,' *Rivista storica svizzera* 24 (1974), 537–634, and Seidel Menchi, 'Chi fu Ortensio Lando?' 515–16.
85 *Valorose donne*, 23v.
86 The question of the age at which girls should marry is raised in literary sources from Francesco da Barberino's conduct book *Reggimento e costumi di donna* to Dolce's *Dialogo della institution delle donne*. A seventeenth-century dialogue by Francesco Andreini suggests women are ready to marry at eighteen and men at thirty-seven, see *Ragionamenti fantastici …* (Venice: G.A. Somasco, 1612), Ragionamento V, 'Sopra del pigliar moglie,' 41r. On the ages at which marriage actually occurred, see David Herlihy and Christiane Klapisch-Zuber, *Les Toscans et leurs familles: Une étude du cataste Florentine de 1427* (Paris: Presse de la Fondation nationale des sciences politique, 1978); Anthony Molho, *Marriage Alliance in Late Medieval Florence* (Cambridge: Harvard University Press, 1994); Anthony Molho, 'Deception and Marriage Strategy in Renaissance Florence: The Case of Women's Ages,' *Renaissance Quarterly* 41 (1988), 193–217; and Stanley Chojnacki, 'Measuring Adulthood: Adolescence and Gender in Renaissance Venice,' *Journal of Family History* 17 (1992), 371–95.

87 *Valorose donne*, 44v.
88 Ibid., 57r (misnumbered as 7r).
89 Maria de Benedetti, ibid., 53r; Paula Castigliona, ibid., 83r. Here, as is often the case throughout the *Valorose donne*, Lando's satiric intent is evident in the names he assigns his letter writers: Maria de Benedetti the blessed wife who peacefully submits to her submissive role; Leonora Forteguerra constantly at war with her husband.
90 See, for example, Erasmus' *Institutio cristiani matrimonii*, which describes marriage as a kingdom, but not a tyranny, in Rummel, *Erasmus on Women*, 100.
91 *Valorose donne*, 42r–44v.
92 Paolo Manuzio, *Lettere volgari* (Venice, 1545), *dedicatoria* (2r), discussed in chapter 1.
93 *Valorose donne*, 20r. The list of examples clearly calls to mind the *Officina*. Models for letters of congratulations could be found in many epistolary manuals; one useful handbook, Hieronimo Garimberto's *Concetti ... per scrivere familiarmente* (Rome: Valgrisi, 1551) has a section devoted specifically to 'parto.'
94 Palmieri echoes the common notion that a mother passed her own qualities to her child through her breastmilk ('s'appruova il lattare della propria madre, et tanto più quanto di maggiore industria, più valente et nobile fusse' ('[the child's] own mother's milk is best, the more so when the mother is industrious, valorous, and noble'), *La vita civile*, ed. Gino Belloni (Florence: Sansoni, 1982), 17–20. Dolce also argued that mother's milk was best and contained special virtues, not least that it cemented the bond between mother and child (*Dialogo della institution delle donne*, 6v); Henricus Cornelius Agrippa addressed the positive properties of breastmilk as well as menstrual blood in his *Declamation on the Nobility and Preeminence of the Female Sex*, ed. and trans. Rabil Jr., 57–9.
95 For example, increasing or decreasing the mother's milk supply and dealing with breast infection. See, for example, Eustachio Celebrino, *Opera nova piacevole la quale insegna de far compositioni odorifere per far bella ciaschuna donna* (Venice: Bindoni, 1551), 11v; and Piemontese, *Secreti*, 90–1. Francesco Andreini's *Ragionamenti fanstastici* ... offers a rare example of the attribution of this discussion not just to women but to wet nurses themselves: his dialogue between two wet nurses paints the 'real picture' of the life of a *balia*, Ragionamento 4, 'Sopra le Balie, et allevar i Figlioli,' 28r–34v.
96 *Valorose donne*, 24r–v. I have not come across this almost certainly parodical advice in any of the manuals I was able to examine.

97 Ibid., 57r (misnumbered as 7r) and 112r–v. Nicola's description of the perfect *balia* corresponds to general ideas about the ideal female body (see, for example, Marinello's *Ornamenti delle donne*, Book IV, Part II), as well as about *balie* in particular. In spite of encouragement for nursing, many women did use wet nurses and this reality is reflected even in texts that don't condone the practice. Palmieri, for example, says that mothers who do not nurse their children 'meritono odio,' but goes on to describe what qualities to look for in a good *balia* (*La vita civile*, 20). Like Palmieri, Dolce admits that many women choose to use wet nurses, and tries to define the 'condizioni che si debbon ricercar nella balia' ('qualities one should seek in a wet nurse'), *Dialogo della institution de le donne*, 6v–8v.

98 *Valorose donne*, 111v–112r.

99 Cf. for example Piemontese, *Secreti*, Part II, Book I, 91; Pietro Bairo, *Secreti medicinali* ... (Venice: Giorgio Valentini, 1629), 169r–170r.

100 *Valorose donne*, 111r–v; cf. Bairo, *Secreti medicinali*, 166v.

101 On the role and importance of women and gender in the development of the 'books of secrets' genre, see Katherine Park's informative study, *Secrets of Women: Gender, Generation, and the Origins of Human Dissection* (Cambridge, MA: Zone, 2006). See also Allison Kavey, *Books of Secrets: Natural Philosophy in England, 1550–1600* (Champaign: University of Illinois Press, 2007).

102 On the role of the uterus in illness, see Laurinda S. Dixon's fascinating study, *Perilous Chastity: Women and Illness in Pre-Enlightenment Art and Medicine* (Ithaca, NY: Cornell University Press, 1995).

103 *Valorose donne*, 110r–v. If the uterus has descended, she should wash in a mixture of amber, balsam, and musk (cf. Bairo, *Secreti medicinali*, 179v–180). If it should wander out of the body, she gives an an herbal remedy to mix in wine. That this is offered in Latin is surely a sign that Lando was referencing a medical manual, many of which circulated in Latin as well as Italian. Bairo's *Secreti*, for example, was a vernacularization of his Latin handbook *De medendis humanis corporis malis Enchidirion* (1512); see Eamon, *Science and the Secrets of Nature*, 163.

104 *Valorose donne*, 110v.

105 The issue is again raised where Genevra Malatesta solicits the opinion of a group of Ferrarese physicians regarding her friend's menstrual troubles; Genevra distinguishes between truly learned doctors and those who 'ne sanno meno delle loro mule' ('know less about it than their mules'), *Valorose donne*, 118 r–v. On remedies for excessive menstrual flow see Bairo, *Secreti medicinali*, 177.

106 *Valorose donne*, 93r–v; 66r–v.

107 See chapter 1, section two.
108 *Valorose donne*, 36r–37r.
109 Celebrino's *Opera nuova*, for example, teaches how to remove spots from linens or velvet and how to give them a nice perfume (9r). See also Cortese, *Secreti*, Book II, 76–8.
110 Bell, *How to Do It*, 58. Bell does not discuss the *Valorose donne* in his study; presumably he was unaware of the 'medical' content disguised under the rubric of 'letters.'
111 *Valorose donne*,116r–v. Even nuns are in possession of such questionable knowledge: Suor Lucrezia Borgia, for example, while professing a distaste for recipes and potions, offers a prescription for staying young and healthy to Lucrezia Amanio (116v–117r).
112 See for example Bairo, *Secreti medicinali*, 1r–6r, for a potion that promises to 'conservar la gioventù, et ritardar la vecchiezza, et mantaner la persona sempre sana et vigorosa' ('preserve youth, delay old age, and keep the body perpetually healthy and vigorous') and Cortese, *Secreti*, Book IV, 129, for a similar remedy. Another multifaceted potion is furnished by Argentina Rangona to promote health, get rid of freckles, clear up scabies and leprosy, cure gout, and freshen one's eyes after crying, all subjects commonly treated in manuals (*Valorose donne*, 115r–v).
113 Eamon, *Science and the Secrets of Nature*, 138.
114 Ibid., 145.
115 Cf. *Valorose donne*, 116r, where Isabella chides, 'Più volte avete riso di me, perché faccia tutto 'l giorno distillare acque da mastro Cristofero: io ho parimente riso della simplicità vostra e del vostro consorte che non sappiate quanta virtú spesso ci si trovi …' ('You often mock me because each day I distill master Christopher's waters: for my part, I often laugh at the naiveté of you and your husband because you don't see the value that is often found [in such potions]'). Lando's satire works on many levels: Isabella accuses her friends of the same naiveté Lando sees in her. It seems significant, moreover, that Isabella's teacher is a man.
116 On using egg yolk to keep the skin smooth, see Cortese, *Secreti*, Book IV, 100; Celebrino, *Opera nova*, 3v–4r; on hare's blood to remove spots from the face see Marinello, *Delle ornamenti delle donne*, 159.
117 The literature on alchemy in early modern Europe is extensive. Among recent studies, see William R. Newman and Anthony Grafton, eds., *Secrets of Nature: Astrology and Alchemy in Early Modern Europe* (Cambridge, MA: The MIT Press, 2001); Tara Nummedal, *Alchemy and Authority in the Holy Roman Empire* (Chicago: University of Chicago Press, 2007); Tara Nummedal, 'Alchemical Reproduction and the Career of Anna Maria

Zieglerin,' *Ambix* 48 (2001), 56–68; William Eamon, 'Alchemy in Popular Culture: Leonardo Fioravanti and the Search for the Philosopher's Stone,' in *Early Science and Medicine* 5 (2000), 196–214; Piyo Rattansi and Antonio Clericuzio, ed., *Alchemy and Chemistry in the Sixteenth and Seventeenth Centuries* (Dodrecht: Kluwer, 1994); Gareth Roberts, *The Mirror of Alchemy: Alchemical Ideas and Images in Manuscripts and Books from Antiquity to the Seventeenth Century* (London: The British Library, 1994); Alison Coudert, *Alchemy: The Philosopher's Stone* (Boulder: Shambhala, 1980); and Andrea Aromatico, *Alchemy: The Great Secret* (New York: Harry Abrams, 2000).

118 Erasmus, *Alcumistica (Alchemy)*, in *Collected Works of Erasmus*, vol. 39, 545–6.
119 *Valorose donne*, 54r–v.
120 The process of progressive distillation of the *prima materia* is termed 'multiplication' in alchemical texts, see Aromatico, *Alchemy*, 71; Coudert, *Alchemy*, 43, 47–52. Parcelsus counted sulpher and salt among the three principals of matter (together with mercury), see Coudert, ibid., 23.
121 *Valorose donne*, 115v.
122 Argentina, for example, queries her correspondent: 'Parvi che questo segreto possi star al paragon del vostro? ('Do you think this secret can equal yours?'), ibid.
123 Bellucci, 'Lettere di valorose donne,' 271.
124 *Valorose donne*, 48v, 129r, 87r.
125 Ibid., 96v–97r, 123r–v.
126 See Goldsmith, *Writing the Female Voice*, vii.
127 The Masippa daughters, for example, inspire a female friend to write that it is possible to love a stranger through reputation alone, 'Dolcissime figliuole, ora sí che io conosco esser vero che per fama innamor si possa ...' ('Dearest girls, now I see it is true that one can fall in love through reputation alone'), *Valorose donne*, 89r. Lucrezia Corsa introduces herself to Lauretta and Leonora – whom she knows only by reputation – by letter, explaining: 'Non vi meravigliate, bellissime signore, se non conoscendovi di faccia, ma sol di fama e di nome, io ardisca di scrivervi et di richiedervi umilmente che per amica mi accettiate ...' ('Do not marvel, lovely ladies, if I – making your acquaintance not in person, but only through name and reputation – should dare to write you and humbly ask that you accept me for your friend'), ibid., 51r. Letters such as these reflect the reliance of educated women upon epistolary exchange to establish and maintain friendships, as they often lacked the liberty to do so in person.
128 Ibid., 8r.

129 Ibid., 58r, 15r–v, 45r–v.
130 Ibid., 147v–148r.
131 Ibid., 58r–v.
132 As Grendler explains, in Lando's pessimistic world view, 'contemporary learning was not relevant to the spoiled reality' of modern society, *Critics of the Italian World*, 142.
133 Ibid., 148, and chap. 5 in general.
134 Ibid., chap. 5.
135 Linda S. Kauffman, *Discourses of Desire: Gender, Genre and Epistolary Fictions* (Ithaca, NY: Cornell University 1990), 21.
136 See section one above, under 'Lando and the *Difesa della donna*.'
137 As Bellucci points out, the *Valorose donne* present a '... cultura appartenente sostanzialmente alle donne che ne sono molto spesso le creatrici e sempre le utenti e le conservatrici, di grosso spessore anche se priva di benemerenza ufficiali, che in un certo modo vede riconosciuta in quest'opera del Lando una sua dignità, pure se ad ogni scorrer di riga si ha l'impressione che l'arma dell'ironia sia in agguato ...' ('Le lettere di molte valorose donne,' 270).

3 'A gloria del sesso feminile'

1 Lucrezia Gonzaga, *Lettere della molto illustre ... donna Lucretia Gonzaga da Gazuolo con gran diligentia raccolte & a gloria del sesso feminile nuovamente in luce poste* (Venice: Gualtero Scotto, 1552). A modern edition of Gonzaga's *Lettere*, edited by Renzo Bragantini (Rovigo: Minelliana, 2009), was published as this book was going to press; therefore, I was unable to take it into consideration here. I am planning a translation of Gonzaga's letterbook which will be published by the Other Voice in Early Modern Europe series at the Centre for Reformation and Renaissance Studies at the University of Toronto.
2 Ibid., A2r–v.
3 *Annuali di Ferrara*, 1546 (Biblioteca Esense, mss. Filippo Rodi, 431–4). The episode is also recorded by Brasavolo, the physician who administered the antidote to the poisoned pears sent by Manfrone to his sister, the duke, and their families, in *Examen omnium electuariorum* (Venice: Valgrisi, 1548), 5–39, and by Bonaventura Casalini in his *Cronaca Domestica* of 1561, ed. Alfonso Lazzari (Faenza: Lega, 1941).
4 Bartlommeo Ricci, *Deprecatio pro Io. Pau. Manfronio apud Herc. Atestium Ferrariensium Principem* (Ferrara, Giovan Maria de Nicolini de Sabio, 1552). Rodi's *Annuali* make no mention of Gonzaga's role in the commutation of Manfrone's sentence.
5 Cf. Ricci, *Deprecatio*; Ortensio Lando, *Due panegirici nuovamente composti ...* (Venice: Giolito, 1552); Ireneo Affò, *Memorie di tre celebri principesse della*

Famiglia Gonzaga ... (Parma: Carmignani, 1787). One historian offered the romantic but unfounded opinion that Gonzaga desired to join her husband in prison ('avrebbe voluto esserci rinchiusa con [suo marito], ma non le venne concesso ...'), cf. P. Thouar, *Lucrezia Gonzaga* (Biblioteca Archiginnasio di Bologna, Landoni 232), 9.

6 Cf. Pier Francesco Bertioli da Ostiglia, *Rime col commento di Andrea Alciato*, ed. N. Zingarelli (Bologna: Commissione per i Testi di Lingua, 1969). Bertioli, the author of the canzoniere, was accused of conspiring with Manfrone. Tortured into confessing, he then composed a poetic account of the episode that circulated with a detailed gloss by Andrea Alciato. Aspects of the account are confirmed by a manuscript letter in the Archivio di Stato di Modena regarding Manfrone's arrest (Cancelleria Ducale, Archivio per materie, Condottieri) and by Gonzaga's *Lettere* themselves.

7 Anton Francesco Doni, *Libraria seconda* (Venice: Giolito, 1558).

8 The frequently repeated assertion that Lando served as Gonzaga's secretary first put forth by Affò (*Memorie di tre principesse*, 63) is based on the assumption that he wrote her letters.

9 Ortensio Lando, *Due panegirici nuovamente composti* ..., 41. The *Panegirico* slightly predated the *Lettere*. The expression was used by other writers as well, however. A century later, for example, we find Arcangela Tarabotti praising Vittoria della Rovere as 'la gloria del sesso donnesco,' see *Satira e Antisatira*, ed. Elissa Weaver (Rome: Salerno, 1998), 31.

10 Gonzaga, *Lettere*, A2r, '... ho raccolto molte lettere da varie parti, non senza molta fatica ...' ('... I have gathered many letters from all over, not without great difficulty ...'). Such a scenario is taken more or less for granted by C. Di Filippo Bareggi in *Il mestiere di scrivere. Lavoro intellettuale e mercato librario a Venezia nel Cinquecento* (Rome: Bulzoni, 1988) 62–3, and by Paul Grendler in *Critics of the Italian World* (Madison: University of Wisconsin Press, 1969), 35, both of whom devote only passing consideration to the problem.

11 I have found a total of thirteen letters signed by Lucrezia Gonzaga in the archives of Modena and Mantua and in Modena's Biblioteca Estense, ten of which have never been published. The existence of two of these letters is noted by Primo Griguolo in his *Una villa al confine: Documenti storico-letterari su Fratta nel '500* (Fratta: Polesine, 1988), 42–3, and a third is reproduced by Sergio Pagano in his *Il processo di Endimio Calandra e l'Inquisizione a Mantova nel 1567–1568* (Città del Vaticano: Studi e Testi, 1991), 24n69. Francine Daenens refers to a letter by Lucrezia Gonzaga in the Archivio di Stato di Parma; see her 'Donne valorose, eretiche, finte sante: note sull'antologia giolitina del 1548,' in *Per lettera: La scrittura*

epistolare femminile, ed. Gabriella Zarri (Rome: Viella, 1999), 207n57; I was unable to locate this document in my own research in Parma. Unfortunately, although Gonzaga was well known in her own time, she was not a member of the more illustrious branches of the Gonzaga family (and, of course, she was a woman); thus, her correspondence has been only sporadically preserved.

12 The *Rime ... in lode dell'illustrissima signora ... Lucrezia Gonzaga* (Bologna: Giovanni Rossi, 1565) contains contributions by Bandello, Lodovico Dolce, and Laura Terracina. Many of the compositions praise her beauty, virtue, and chastity as a young widow who chose not to remarry, but several make specific reference to her literary gifts. Gonzaga's friend Giovan Maria Bonardo was probably behind the *Rime,* although the book is also catalogued under the name Cornelio Cattaneo at the Biblioteca Nazionale in Florence. Bandello dedicated the *Canti* XI and one of his *Novelle* XXI to Gonzaga; while Scaligero composed an eglogue and an epigram in her honour (*Carm.* vol. I). Ruscelli dedicated his *Imprese illustri* (Venice: Comin da Trino di Monserrato, 1572) to her, as did Federico Luigini da Udine in his *Il libro della bella donna* (Venice: Plinio Pietrasanta, 1554). Lando mentioned her in a number of works, made her an interlocutor in his *Dialogo ... nel quale si ragiona della consolation, e utilità che si gusta leggendo le Sacre Scritture* (Venice: A. Arrivabene, 1552), and praised her in the *Panegirico.* She is also celebrated in Lodovico Paternò, *La Mirtia* (Naples: Gio. Maria Scotto, 1564); Diomede Borghesi, *Rime* (Padua: L. Pasquati, 1566); and Orazio Toscanella, *Madrigali di G.M. Bonardo* (Venice: N.p., 1563). Recently, historians Stefania Malavasi and Primo Griguolo have turned their attention to Gonzaga's biography and cultural context, if not her literary production. See Stefania Malavasi, 'Lucrezia Gonzaga e la vita culturale a Fratta nella prima metà del Cinquecento,' in *Vespasiano Gonzaga e il ducato di Sabbionetta,* ed. Ugo Bazzotti, Daniela Ferrari, and Cesare Mozzarelli (Mantua: Accademia Nazionale Virgiliana di Scienze, Lettere ed Arti, 1993), 301–14, and Griguolo, *Una villa al confine.*

13 Vincenzo Brusantino, *Angelica innamorata* (Venice: Marcolini, 1553). On this text, see Rosanna Alhaique Pettinelli, 'Un tempio/una città: Venezia in un poema cavalleresco alla metà del Cinquecento,' in *La Rassegna della letteratura italiana* 95 (1991), 60–70.

14 Some historians date Gonzaga's birth to 1522, such as D. Bergamaschi, *Storia di Gazuolo e suo marchesato* (Casalmaggiore: Tipografia e Libreria Contini Carlo, 1883), and Malavasi, 'Lucrezia Gonzaga.' Her own claim in the *Lettere* that she married Manfrone at age fourteen (in 1541), along with Lando's claim that she is twenty-five at the time of the *Dialogo,* by contrast,

would put her birth date at 1527. The *Registro dell'Uffizio della Sanità di Mantova*, however, records her death at age fifty-five in 1576, dating her birth to 1521 (Affò, *Memorie di tre celebri principesse,* n3). Pirro Gonzaga was the eldest son of the Bozzolo line; Camilla was the daughter of Annibale and Lucrezia D'Este. Lucrezia Gonzaga had two brothers (Federico and Carlo) and four sisters (Ippolita, Emilia, Camilla, and Isabella). Camilla took vows at the convent of San Giovanni delle Carrette in Mantua; Isabella married Rudolfo Gonzaga of Luzzara and Poviglio; Ippolita married Brunoro di Thiene, who was in the service of the Duke of Mantua; Federico married Lucrezia d'Incisa; and Carlo, Count of Sanmartino, married Emilia Cavuti.

15 See Gonzaga's *Lettere,* 61–2, where she recalls studying Euripedes with Bandello: 'Sovviemmi ancho che interpretandomi voi Euripide, appresi già non esser da considerare la qualità delle richezze, ma bene la qualità di chi le possiede' ('I also recall that in your explanation of Euripedes, I learned to consider not the qualities of wealth, but rather the qualities of those who possess it'). In the same letter she refers to the 'savi precetti, che nel core sí dolcemente a Castel Giuffrè mi instillavate...' ('the wise counsel you so sweetly instilled in my heart at Castel Giuffrè ...'). Bandello remained with Luigi's household until the death of Fregoso and the departure of his wife Costanza, whom Bandello followed into exile.

16 The son of Giulio Manfrone and Beatrice Roverella, Giampaolo Manfrone (sometimes spelled 'Manfroni') is not to be confused with his grandfather of the same name, also a *condottiere.* The appellation 'Fortebraccio' derives from Manfrone's membership in a division of mercenary soldiers, the 'compagnia braccesca' (from its early member Braccio da Montone; cf. Griguolo, *Una villa al confine,* 13–14). Manfrone's violent nature is recalled almost wherever he is remembered; in Lando's *Panegirico,* for example, he is described as '[i]l più spiacevole ... più ritroso ... più folle ... più bizarro uomo che nascesse giamai' ('the most unpleasant ... difficult ... mad ... eccentric man ever born,' 40). Bergamaschi calls him 'uomo astuto, ipocrita, intollerante e feroce' (*Storia di Gazuolo,* 180).

17 Bertioli's *Rime,* for example, recount that Manfrone, infuriated by his wife's dancing at the house of her Gonzaga relatives, beat her severely, then obliged her to excuse his behaviour to the same relatives (cf. *Rime di Pierfrancesco Bertioli,* 35–6; the explanation is in Alciato's commentary).

18 According to her published letters she encountered problems administering what property she did have; in a letter to Luigi da Novale, for example, she complains: 'Essendomi mancato il mio consorte ... e posta in litigi una parte de' nostri beni, restami a sperare dopo Dio solo nella

prudenza vostra ...' ('My spouse being gone ... and there being a dispute over some of our property, I can only hope in God and in your prudence ...' *Lettere*, 259). Manfrone's will is in the Archivio Notarile in Rovigo (notaio Francesco Campagenella, b. 315, cancello n.7, 116–23) and published in Griguolo, *Una villa al confine* (33–8). Manfrone leaves some money for the dowry of his sister Giulia; to Lucrezia he returns her dowry and allows her to retain custody of their daughters so long as she continues to live 'chastely' rather than remarry. Manfrone also makes provisions for his two illegitimate daughters.

19 Autografoteca Campori, 'Lucrezia Gonzaga.' Two of these letters are addressed to Vespasiano, two to his secretary, and one to his first wife, Diana de Contrade (later allegedly murdered by her husband for adultery).

20 Lucrezia Gonzaga to Vespasiano Gonzaga, 9 October 1555 (Biblioteca Estense, Autografi Campori, 'Lucrezia Gonzaga').

21 Cf. Pagano, *Il processo di Endimio Calandra*, 7. Although I have been unable to locate the documents from Gonzaga's trial, it is referred to in a series of letters sent by Camillo Campeggi, the Inquisitor in Mantua, to Rome, conserved in the Vatican's Archivio del Sant'Uffizio (now the Congregazione per la Dottrina della Fede). Some of this correspondence is reproduced in Pagano's study of the trial of Endimio Calandra and suggests that Gonzaga was questioned regarding her views on Purgatory. Campeggi states, for example, 'La signora Lucretia non mi volse confessar chiaro l'articolo del purgatorio che ha creduto di certo, e disse che solamente ha dubitato: ma lo confessarà ...' ('Signora Lucretia did not wish to confess fully to the article of purgatory she certainly believed, and only said she doubted: but she will confess it ...'); letter to Scipione Rebiba, Mantua, 19 September 1567, reproduced in Pagano, *Il processo* ... 40n14. Gonzaga's name also appears in the trial of Odoardo Thiene in 1571; see Silvana Seidel Menchi, 'Chi fu Ortensio Lando?' in *Rivista storica italiana* 106, no. 3 (1994), 535–7.

22 Lucrezia Gonzaga to Isabella Gonzaga, Archivio di Stato di Mantova (ASM), Archivio Gonzaga, b. 2578, c. 371. Cf. Pagano, *Il processo di Endimio Calandra e l'Inquisizione a Mantova nel 1567–1568* (Vatican City: Studi e Testi, 1991), 24n69.

23 Critics sometimes refer to Gonzaga as a poet as well as a writer of letters, but there is no evidence that she published any works besides the *Lettere*. Quadrio attributed a volume of *Rime* to Gonzaga, claiming: 'Di lei ... si veggono alcune belle opere, e fra le altre un Volumetto di Rime, che fu stampato a Venezia,' in *Della storia, e della ragione d'ogni poesia*, vol. 2 (Milano: N.p.,1741), 240. A letter to Gonzaga from Luigi Groto begs her

to entrust him with 'il carico di riformar le sue rime, come ha promesso di dover fare, e tornarle alla stampa ...' ('the job of revising your *rime*, as you promised, and bringing them to print ...'), *Le lettere famigliari di Luigi Groto, Cieco d'Adria* (Venice: Giovacchino Brugnolo, 1601). If such a volume of poetry exists, I have been unable to locate it; it is possible that it circulated only in manuscript form, although I have found no trace of it.

24 Lando, *Panegirico*, 43.
25 Griguolo, 'Giovanni Maria Bonardo e l'ambiente culturale di Fratta nel '500,' in *Palladio e palladianesimo in Polesine*, ed. Luciano Alberti et al. (Rovigo: Associazione culturale Mirelliana, 1984), 82.
26 Malavasi, 'Lucrezia Gonzaga,' 304ff.
27 Ibid., 304–5; M. Maylender, *Storia delle Accademie d'Italia* (Bologna: Cappelli, 1929), 268; and Gio Maria Bonardo, *Origine della Fratta* (Venice: Rocca, 1571). Malavisi's dating of the Academy's formation to around 1555 should be pushed back to before 1552 if Gonzaga's role in the group is not to be discounted, since, as the autograph letters cited here in section one under 'Biographical Sketch' indicate, Gonzaga was cloistered at a convent in Bozzolo for at least three years after Manfrone's death, probably from 1552–5.
28 Malavasi, 'Lucrezia Gonzaga.'
29 Ibid., 304.
30 See John Martin, *Venice's Hidden Enemies: Italian Heretics in a Renaissance City* (Berkeley: University of California Press, 1993), 132n14.
31 See Salvatore Caponetto, *La riforma protestante nell'Italia del Cinquecento* (Turin: Claudiana, 1992), 49. Venice, the clandestine centre for philo-protestant ideas, was infused with reformists from nearby Padua and Vicenza as well as Rovigo and Mantua, while Modena – not far from Fratta – was the 'maggior centro del dissenso antiromano di tutta l'Emilia' after the 1540s (ibid., 227, 303). Mantua, where Gonzaga spent her later years, was greatly influenced by the ideas of Luther, Erasmus, Valdés, Bucer, and others. The Mantuan Inquisition examined by Pagano in a recent study attempted to curb this influence, which had penetrated at all social levels (see Pagano's *Il processo di Endimio Calandra*).
32 Attributions of Gonzaga's *Lettere* to Lando are in G. Tiraboschi, *Storia della letteratura italiana*, vol. 7 (Modena: Società tipografica, 1791), 76–7; Salvatore Bongi, *Introduzione alle Novelle di M. Ortensio Lando* (Lucca: Baccelli, 1851), lvii; Ireneo Sanesi, 'Tre epistolari del Cinquecento,' *Giornale storico della letteratura italiana* 24 (1894), 1–32; Seidel Menchi, 'La circolazione clandestina di Erasmo in Italia,' *Annali della Scuola Normale Superiore di Pisa* 9, no. 2 (1979), 575n7; and most recently, Dieter Steland, 'Ortensio Landos

Lettere di Lucretia Gonzaga und Girolamo Garimbertos *Concetti:* Plagiat, Imitatio, Parodie?' in *Italienisch* 30 (2006), 3–19. There is no lack of supporters for Gonzaga's authorship, however. See, for example, Affò, *Memorie,* and A. Amadei, *Cronaca universale della città di Mantova,* ed. G. Amadei, E. Marani, and G. Pratico, vol. 2 (Mantua: C.I.T.E.M., 1955). Gaetano Melzi and Pietro Ferri incline towards Gonzaga's authorship, although they refrain from definitive judgment; see G. Melzi, *Dizionario di opere anonime e pseudonime di scrittori italiani,* vol. 1 (Milan: L. di Giacomo Pirola, 1848–59), 468; and P. Ferri, *Biblioteca Femminile italiana* (Padua: Crescini, 1842), 189.

33 Gonzaga figures prominently in the *Dialogo* as the spiritual student of Philalete/Lando, who instructs her on the proper reading and appreciation of scripture. Gonzaga also appears in Lando's *Oracoli di moderni ingegni* (1550) as the author of a set of moral *detti,* in his *Ragionamenti familiari* (1550) and in his *Consolatorie* (1550). Lando's *Cataloghi* (1552) are liberally studded with references to Gonzaga, mentioning her in lists of beautiful, chaste, and learned women and even including her Fratta dwelling as an example of the 'piú belli orti che avesse mai et l'antica et la moderna età' ('the most beautiful gardens of antiquity and the modern age'), Book VI, 488–9.

34 *De le Lettere di M. Pietro Lauro Modenese* (Venice, 1552). Cf. Sanesi, 'Tre epistolari,' 21, '[Lauro's book is a] composizione rettorica, una raccolta di lettere, non inviate né punto né poco ai destinatori segnati in capo ad esse, in una parola, un'imitazione dei *Paradossi* e delle *Lettere delle Donne* del Lando.'

35 Gonzaga, *Lettere,* 30–1, 76–7.

36 Sanesi, 'Tre epistolari,' 26.

37 Or meant to appear so. For reasons of her own, Gonzaga might have initially wished to appear ignorant of the book's author.

38 Cf. Sanesi, 'Tre epistolari,' 22: 'Il Lando viveva nel medesimo tempo che Lucrezia Gonzaga e quindi poteva conoscere alla pari di lei gli avvenimenti storici generali; quelli poi riguardanti lei in particolare non gli dovevano essere ignoti, appunto per la molta familiarità che passava fra loro. Quindi egli, fingendo le lettere, le finse, almeno in parte, secondo la realtà storica.'

39 Of the thirteen mansuscript letters I have found, written over a twenty-four-year period from 1546 (the year of Manfrone's arrest) to 1570 (six years before Gonzaga's death), two are addressed to Manfrone in prison, one to the Duke of Ferrara, whom Gonzaga addresses in the *Lettere* on two occasions, and one to a sister, probably Isabella, a frequent *destinataria* in the *Lettere.* I have published and translated a selection of these letters in my

forthcoming 'Textual Collaboration and Spiritual Partnership in Sixteenth-Century Italy: The Case of Ortensio Lando and Lucrezia Gonzaga,' *Renaissance Quarterly* 62, no. 3 (2009).
40 Lucrezia Gonzaga to Giampaolo Manfrone, Venice, 22 November 1546 (Archivio di Stato di Modena [ASMo], Cancelleria Ducale, Archivio per materie, b. 2), '... la stii de bon animo et gubernassi benne et stia sanna, che il Signor Idio proverderà al tutto ...' ('... be of good spirit and take care of yourself and stay well, for the Lord God will see to everything ...').
41 In one letter she refers to an imminent trip, reminding him that 'questo mese la mia andata sarà molto più utile ...' ('my going this month will be much more useful ...'), Lucrezia Gonzaga to Giampaolo Manfrone, Fratta, 13 April 1548 (ASMo, Cancelleria Ducale, Archivio per materie, b. 2). In the other she mentions a trip to Venice, promising to let her husband know 'quello che si è operato et si spera de operare per util et onore de vostra signoria' ('what has been done and what is hoped to be done for your benefit and honour'). The 'util et onore' to which Gonzaga alludes likely concern her efforts to obtain Manfrone's freedom.
42 Giampaolo Manfrone to Lucrezia Gonzaga (n.d., ASMo, Cancelleria Ducale, Archivio per materie, Condottieri), '... la supplico ... veder se li è verso placcar il core del signor Ducca de Ferrara ...' ('... I beg you ... to see if there is any way to placate the heart of the lord Duke of Ferrara ...').
43 Lucrezia Gonzaga to Ercole II d'Este, Fratta, 1 June 1550 (AsMo, Cancelleria Ducale, Archivio per materie, Letterati, b. 24).
44 ASMo, Cancelleria Ducale, Archivio per materie, Condottieri.
45 Francesco Bausi, for example, points to the editorial assistance provided to Tullia D'Aragona by Benedetto Varchi in 'Le rime di e per Tullia D'Aragona,' *Les femmes écrivains en Italie au moyen âge et à la renaissance* (Aix en Provence: Publications de l'Université de Provence, 1994), 278. On collaboration among male writers, for example in the academies and *ridotti*, or salons, see Domenico Zanré, *Cultural Non-Conformity in Early Modern Florence* (Aldershot, UK: Ashgate, 2004). On the phenomenon of Renaissance 'plagiairism,' see Cherchi, *Polimatia di Riuso: Mezzo secolo di plagio (1539–1589)* (Rome: Bulzoni, 1998).
46 Bongi, *Introduzione alle Novelle di M. Ortensio Lando* (Lucca: Baccelli, 1851), 57; cf. Lando, *Vari componimenti*, 273–4 and Gonzaga, *Lettere*, 54–5. Implicit in this fable is also a Landian scorn for alchemical practice, as discussed in chapter 2.
47 Gonzaga, *Lettere*, 54, '... vi voglio raccontare una favola ... applico la mia favoletta al presente ragionamento ...' ('I want to tell you a fable ... I apply my little tale to the discussion at hand').

48 Steland, 'Ortensio Landos *Lettere di Lucretia Gonzaga*...'
49 Cf. Gonzaga, *Lettere*, 156–7, asking Pietro Paolo to convince her husband '... che sia men male una indegna prigione che una indegna libertà ...' ('... that an unworthy prison is preferable to unearned freedom'); she echoes a *detto* attributed to a Bishop Dandino of Carseta in Lando's *Oracoli*, 10, that reads: 'Esser migliore una oscura prigione che una indegna libertà' ('Better a dark prison than an unearned freedom'). Both references can be traced to Garimberto's *Concetti*, 101 ('Consolare di prigionia'): 'È men male una indegna prigione, che una indegna libertà.'
50 Gonzaga, *Lettere*, 11, 'Se per tanto perseverarete sí amaramente piangerlo, parrà ad ognuno o che dubitiate della universal resurrezione de' corpi, dottrina tanto difforme dalla vita cristiana, che sin'ora avete vivuto, o vero crederassi che abbiate invidia ch'ei sia andato a sí lungo e a sí felice riposo' ('If you perservere in mourning him so bitterly, it will seem to everyone that either you doubt in the universal resurrection of the body, a doctrine that is not in keeping with the Christian life you have lived up until now; or people will think you are envious that he has gone to such a long and happy repose'). Cf. Lando, *Consolatorie*, 7, 'voi certo, per lui piangendo, date sospetto a noi che della resurezione de' corpi per aventura non dubitiate, il ché sarebbe troppo grande fallo ... per la sua morte piangendo, dico che ne date sospetto di non avere una tacita invidia al suo dolce riposo ...' ('by mourning him, you clearly cause us to suspect that you doubt in the resurrection of the body, which would be an enormous error ... by mourning his death, I say that you cause people to suspect you of having a tacit envy of his sweet repose').
51 Cf. Lauro, *Lettere*, 156, 'Voglio confortare Vostra Signoria a rallegrarsi de la morte di vostro degnissimo et illustre consorte e mi rendo certo che sarà questo più vero e più amorevole ufficio in farvi conoscer che la morte de nostri piú cari ci dovrebbe far giubilare ...' ('I wish to comfort Vostra Signoria [and remind you] to rejoice in the death of your most worthy and illustrious spouse, and I am certain that it is a true and loving duty to remind you that the death of our loved ones ought cause us to rejoice ...'). Gonzaga's manuscript letter regarding the death of a princess Margaritta is dated 10 April 1567 and states, 'mi confido che vostra Altezza colla sua prudenza mittigarà la passione conformandosi col divino volere' ('I am certain that your Highness will mitigate your passion with prudence, in conformity to divine will'; ASM, Archivio Gonzaga, 2578, f. 371r–v).
52 Cf. Seidel Menchi, *Erasmo in Italia* (Turin: Bollati Boringhieri, 1987), 381n71: 'Come il confronto dimostra, Ortensio Lando prese qui a prestito brani di Erasmo non già traducendoli dal latino (come fece in altre opere), ma

servendosi dalla traduzione del Migli.' See also Seidel Menchi, 'La circolazione clandestina di Erasmo in Italia,' 575 and 575n7, and 'Sulla fortuna di Erasmo in Italia,' *Rivista storica svizzera* 24 (1974), 540.

53 Seidel Menchi cites several writers who 'rewrite' Erasmus in their own works, such as Antonio Brucioli (*Dialogi*, 1537) and Marsilio Andreasi (*Trattato divoto et utilissimo della divina misericordia*, 1542); cf. Menchi, 'La circolazione clandestina.' She further explains that there is still much to be learned about the circulation of Erasmian texts in Italy in this period, noting that the history and landscape of the 'clandestine diffusion' of the works of Erasmus in Italy 'è quasi tutta da ricostruire' (ibid., 573). The possibility that Gonzaga herself, part of a vibrant literary community that counted among its members many figures known for their reformist views, may have had access to and even partially reproduced sections of Erasmus' works should not, therefore, be discounted.

54 Cited in Caponetto, *La riforma protestante* (Turin: Claudiana, 1992), 49.

55 In his case study of the Inquisition in Mantua, Pagano points out that Gonzaga was closely linked to heterodox circles in her area ('... ebbe rapporti con circoli eterodossi veneti e si legò strettamente a Ortensio Lando ...') in his *Il Processo di Endimio Calandra e l'Inquisizione a Mantova nel 1567–1568* (Vatican City: Studi e Testi, 1991), 279n106. Diana Robin's study, *Publishing Women: Salons, the Presses, and the Counter Reformation in Sixteenth-Century Italy* (Chicago: University of Chicago Press, 2007), demonstrates the close links between women and the promotion of new religious doctrines during this period and makes a strong argument regarding collaborative publishing practices between men and women in this context.

56 See, for example, Gonzaga, *Lettere*, 64, 'Il Raymondo mi ha fatto più che certa, e con lettere, e con la viva voce, esservi stato rifferito che io abbia detto mal di voi, il ché mi ha causato al core un estremo dispiacere ... Non posso però pensare che mi abbiate per donna sí leggiera, che io avessi usato parole così aliene dalla natura mia ...' ('Raymond told me clearly, by letter and in person, that you heard I had spoken ill of you, which caused my heart great distress ... I can't believe, however, that you would think so little of me, that I could have used words so alien to my nature ...').

57 See, for example, Gonzaga, *Lettere*, 92, 'Di giorno in giorno sentomi adunque ingannata dalla grandezza dell'amore che vi porto, e voi dubiterete che non vi ami? E voi penserete che alcuna mala lingua possa impedire il corso della benivogliensa mia?' ('Each day I feel more deceived by the depth of my affection for you, and you doubt that I love you? And can you believe that some gossiping tongue could impede the direction of my

272   Notes to pages 92–4

goodwill?'). Interestingly, one of Gonzaga's manuscript letters to Paolo Quaresima contradicts this high-minded position, playfully and overtly positioning Gonzaga as hungry for gossip as she begs for news of her friend's Ferrarese life and loves (Lucrezia Gonzaga to Paolo Quaresima, Mantua, 29 October 1555, ASM, Cancelleria Ducale, Particolari, Gonzaga).

58 Gonzaga, *Lettere*, 285.
59 Ibid., 92.
60 Ibid., 14.
61 Cf. Garimberto, *Concetti di Hieronimo Garimberto, et di più autori raccolti da lui, per scrivere familiarmente* (Rome: Vincenzo Valgrisi, 1551),156r, ('Offerire/Impresto'), 'Se vi par ch'io abbia cosa alcuna, che sia per risultar in onor, et commodo vostro; come sono danari, o qualche altra cosa, ch'io possa prestarvi, tanto mi sarà' caro che ve ne vagliate quanto si ricerca a gli oblighi ch'io ho che ve ne debbiate valere,' qtd. in Steland, 'Ortensio Lando *Lettere*,' 13.
62 See Ray, 'Textual Collaboration and Spiritual Partnership.' Bartolomeo Gamba was among the first to suggest some form of collaboration, arguing that Gonzaga had written the 'domestic' (autobiographical) letters herself, Lando the other (humanist) ones (*Lettere di donne italiane del secolo decimosesto* [Venice: Alvisopoli, 1832], 127–8). Curiously, as Steland demonstrates, it is actually the most 'personal' letters that tend to derive from Garimberto's *Concetti* ('Ortensio Lando *Lettere*,' 6–7). Gamba's theory is updated by both Grendler and Pagano, who make no such thematic claims but do imagine Lando's intervention at an editorial level. Grendler suggests that Lando 'edited a collection of Lucrezia's letters for the printer Gualtiero Scotto, and ... possibly wrote part of it,' in *Critics of the Italian World*, 35. Pagano's identical contention is based on Grendler's, in his *Il processo di Endimio Calandra*, 279n106.
63 Ferri cautions that the problem of authorship is a 'contesa su cui uomini sommi e distinti varia ne diedero sentenza' and predicts, 'lasceranno sempre il dubbio queste lettere della loro originalità' (*Biblioteca Femminile*, 189).
64 Carlo Dionisotti, 'La letteratura italiana all'epoca del Concilio di Trento,' *Geografia e storia della letteratura italiana* (Turin: Einaudi, 1967), 191.
65 A sonnet by Antonio Beffa, for example, describes Gonzaga as 'l'alma GONZAGA di valor Colonna' (*Rime ... in lode di ... Lucrezia Gonzaga*, 2). Colonna, who was much influenced by her friendship with the preacher Bernardino Ochino, was an important model of both spiritual and literary authority within reformist circles. Beffa, therefore, draws a comparison

between Gonzaga and Colonna on both literary and religious levels. On Colonna's involvement in these circles, see Constance Furey, 'Intellects Inflamed in Christ: Women and Spiritualized Scholarship in Renaissance Christianity,' *Journal of Religion* 84 (2004): 1–22; and idem, *Erasmus, Contarini, and the Religious Republic of Letters* (Cambridge: Cambridge University Press, 2006).

66 Zeno's best evidence, in fact, was a lack of documentation asserting Gonzaga's authorship of the text; see his letter to Parisotti, dated 1740, in the *Lettere di Apostolo Zeno* (Venice: Sansoni, 1785), cited in Sanesi, 'Tre epistolari,' 14. This is disproved by Doni's inclusion of Gonzaga in the *Libraria*.

67 Gonzaga, *Lettere*, 5–6 (misnumbered as 26). Emilia was the wife of Lucrezia's brother Carlo, Count of Sanmartino.

68 It was not the first time Manfrone had been accused of violence. His brutal murder of a servant while lodged in the house of Gonzaga's relatives in Mantua had already resulted in his exile from that city. Cardinal Ercole Gonzaga complained of his disgust with Manfrone after this incident in a letter to Benedetto Agnello (Vatican Library, Fondo Barberini Latini 5790, 'Libro segreto di Cardinale Ercole Gonzaga,' 53v–54v). On Manfrone's various crimes see Zingarelli, *Rime di Pierfrancesco Bertioli*, 17ff.

69 Not in a Turkish prison, as stated by Grendler in *Critics of the Italian World*, 35.

70 Gonzaga, *Lettere*, 56.
71 Ibid., 105.
72 Ibid., 8.
73 Ibid., 20.
74 Ibid., 5, 20.
75 Ibid., 22, 17.
76 Ibid., 197.
77 Ibid., 154.
78 Gonzaga, *Lettere*, 99–100. Gonzaga had two daughters, Eleonora and Isabella, who survived to adulthood. Little is known of her sons, who probably died at an early age. Alessandro Farnese (Paul III) was pope from 1534–49.
79 Ibid., 106–7.
80 Ibid., 27. For good measure, Gonzaga also addresses Julius III, Giovanni Maria de' Ciocchi del Monte, pope from 1550–55 (ibid., 101–2), the College of Cardinals (ibid., 102–3), and lesser entities such as the monks of a monastery in Rovigo (ibid., 106–7) and the *convertite* of Giudecca (ibid., 107).

81 Gonzaga thanks the Duke in her letters for the diminished sentence, but continues to press for Manfrone's release: 'ottima speranza prendo ancora che presso la salute della vita, gli habbiate anco a donare la bramata libertà' ('I take heart that along with the bloom of life, you may also grant him the yearned for freedom,') ibid., 158–9.
82 Ibid., 104.
83 Ibid.
84 This letter, with its rythmic, detailed list of church heirarchies, seems more 'Landian' in its structure than any other. Both the technique of the list and the repetitive and evidently satiric emphasis on Church heirarchy recall the style of many of Lando's own works.
85 Gonzaga, *Lettere*, 257–8.
86 Lodovico Dolce, for example, translated a Latin collection of fictional correspondence between the 'gran Turco' and various European sovereigns in his *Lettere del Gran Mahumeto imperadore de' Turchi scritte a diversi re, prencipi, signori, e repubbliche con le risposte loro* (Venice: G.G. de' Ferrari, 1563). For more on this genre, see Paolo Preto, *Venezia e i turchi* (Florence: Sansoni, 1975).
87 Gonzaga, *Lettere*, 24–5, 'Sento poi ritrarmi da cotale impresa e di strana diffidenza tutta mi sento riempire veggendo tosto avicinarsi il sesto anno che prigione si dimora, veggendo poco avergli giovato l'esser vasallo e condottiere della più possente e formidabile repubblica che mai si vedesse fra cristiani ...' ('Then I feel myself shrink from such an endeavour, and I am filled with a strange resignation, seeing that we are upon the sixth year of his imprisonment, seeing that it has been of little service to him to have been vassal and *condottiere* to the most powerful and formidable Republic that ever existed among Christians').
88 To Pietro Paolo she writes that Manfrone 'sopporta di malissima voglia questa sua prigionia' ('is bearing this imprisonment of his very badly') and adds that she is trying to keep his spirits up (ibid., 156). A letter to Thomaso Coccapane responds to news of Manfrone's progressive mental decline with the retort that he was never quite sane to begin with: 'Per le vostre alli xv scritte, mi date nuova che il signor Gioan Paulo è uscito del senno, e io vi dò all'oncontro [sic] nuova ch'egli non fu mai in buon senno, et che ciò sia vero, mirate dove egli è condotto ...' ('In your letters of the xv, you inform me that signor Gioan Paulo has gone mad, and I respond to you with the news that he was never truly sane, and if you want proof, look where he has ended up ...') ibid., 208. To Manfrone himself, Gonzaga expresses concern for his spiritual well being. She advises him to accept his fate bravely: 'Priegovi caro consorte a vivere in qualsivoglia condizione

che vi ritroviate con l'animo quieto ... scoprite ... in questa prigionia la franchezza del vostro animo coperto dell'armi (se non dell'innocenza) ...' ('I implore you, dear spouse, to bear whatever condition in which you find yourself with a tranquil spirit ... discover ... in this prison the courage of your soul, distinguished in war [if not in innocence] ...'), ibid., 156; and urges him to confess his many sins before it is too late: '... se infermo siete (come credo) e che l'ultima ora vostra sia per aventura vicina, non perciò vi dovete sbigotire, anzi col core e con la faccia al ciel rivolto dite: ho peccato, Signore, e consapevole sono de' molti miei delitti ...' ('... if you are ill [as I believe you are] and your final hour is nigh, do not despair, but with your heart and your countenance turned toward heaven say: I have sinned, Lord, and I am cognizant of my many crimes ...'), ibid., 168–70.
89 To Isabella, she writes, 'Piaceravvi darne avviso agli amici e a' parenti, perché io sono sí fattamente fuori di me che a pena di me stessa mi sovviene ... grato mi sarebbe che vi transferisti sino all Fratta, per certo tenendo che la vostra amabilissima presenza e gli ottimi consigli mi debbano alleggerire il mio cordoglio' ('Please let our friends and relatives know, because I am so upset I hardly know what to do with myself ... I would appreciate it if you came to Fratta, for I know that your loving presence and your excellent advice would ease my pain ...'), ibid., 212–13. Isabella was, in fact, a frequent visitor to Fratta, as attested to by her own manuscript letters in the Archivio di Stato di Parma (cf. Fondo Gonzaga, Archivio San Vitale, Serie III [carteggio], bb. 35–6).
90 Gonzaga, *Lettere*, 212.
91 Ibid., 211.
92 Constance Jordan points to these letters as the one area in which Gonzaga advances social criticism in her text, *Renaissance Feminism: Literary Texts and Political Models* (Ithaca, NY: Cornell University Press, 1990), 139.
93 Gonzaga, *Lettere*, 213.
94 Ruscelli focuses on Gonzaga's chastity and virtue, as in this passage describing her life as a young widow: 'Percioché essendo quella signora restata vedova molto giovene, non solo doppo la morte del marito, ma ancora mentr'egli vivea, per la lunga prigionia che egli ebbe, e vi finì dentro, le è convenuto aver cura della casa, delle robe, de' figliuoli, procurar per la liberazion del marito con tanta caldezza quanto mai altra illustre e onorata consorte, o madre, o sorella, o figliuola abbia fatto per marito, figliuolo, o fratello suo ... ella per conservar non meno l'integrità della fama che la vera castità e onestà sua, avea privilegio e monile o catena di molto maggior virtú che quella de' topazi e diamanti terreni e dell'autorità di Cesare imperatore. Del quale scrivono alcuni che solea ad

alcune cerve, o ancor cervi, attaccar al collo un monile con lettere che dicessero: NOLI ME TANGERE, QUIA CAESARIS SUM …' ('Therefore, having been made a widow very young, not just after her husband's death, but while he was alive, due to his long imprisonment, during which he passed away; it fell to her to care for the house, property, and children, to seek the freedom of her husband more fiercely than any other illustrious or famous spouse, mother, sister or daughter ever did for her husband, son, or brother … to preserve the integrity of her reputation for true chastity and honesty, she had a necklace or chain that was of greater virtue than that of earthly topaz or diamonds, and of Caesar's authority. Regarding whom some wrote that he used to attach to the necks of does, or bucks, a necklace with letters that read: NOLI ME TANGERE, QUIA CAESARIS SUM …'), *Imprese illustri* (Venice: Comin da Trino di Monserrato, 1572), 325.

95 Including the likelihood that, by rejecting a second marriage, she ensured that her dowry and property would remain intact for her daughter Isabella, in the absence of any surviving sons; see Malavasi, 'Lucrezia Gonzaga,' 316.
96 Gonzaga, *Lettere*, 214.
97 Ibid., 170.
98 Ibid., 186–7, '… vi faccio sapere che mio marito è ancora prigione et, s'egli avviene che vi muoia, aspettatemi a trapassare il rimanente di mia vita … con essovoi …' ('… I inform you that my husband is still a prisoner and, if he should die, wait for me to come pass the rest of my life … with you …').
99 Gonzaga, *Lettere*, 186.
100 Similarly, when Gonzaga writes of finding Cornelia Giannotti a prospective husband, she is careful to clarify that it is up to Cornelia to decide if she wants him (Gonzaga, *Lettere*, 220).
101 Gonzaga, *Lettere*, 78.
102 Ibid., 53.
103 Ibid., 209, '… mi potreste forse dire, i scrittori latini mi sbigotiscono per le frequenti mettafore e per le spesse figure ch'essi usano; e io ti dico non esservi cosa alcuna tanto alta e difficile che dall'umano ingegno non rimanghi superata …' ('you might tell me, the Latin writers overwhelm me with their constant metaphors and the complex rhetorical figures they use; and I tell you there is nothing so unattainable and difficult that human ingenuity cannot overcome it …').
104 Cf. sonnet CCXII of Stampa's *Canzoniere*, thanking Lando for his praise of her in G. Stampa, *Rime*, introduction by Maria Bellonci, notes by Rodolfo Ceriello (Milan: Rizzoli, 1954).

105 Gonzaga, *Lettere*, 325.
106 Ibid., 153. Terracina later returned the compliment by contributing two sonnets to Bonardo's *Rime* in praise of Gonzaga.
107 Ibid., 153, 'Ho inteso che sono nuovamente uscite dalle stampe le lettere del Muzio, e perché sovviemmi d'averne gia veduto molte, le quali puramente parlavano e sparse di sale e ben ornate in ogni parte si vedevano, pregovi quanto più tosto vi fie possibile a mandarmele' ('I understand that Muzio's letters have just been printed, and because I recall having seen many of them, which spoke purely and were clearly wise and graceful in every respect, I pray you send them to me as soon as possible'). Elsewhere, she writes directly to Muzio to praise his work and request that he send her more (ibid., 147).
108 Ibid., 147–8.
109 Ibid., 31–2.
110 Dolce, *Trasformazioni* (Venice: Giolito, 1553), referred to in Gonzaga, *Lettere*, 283–4.
111 Gonzaga, *Lettere*, 310–11.
112 Ibid., 70, and for the Lando letter, 13–14 (qtd. in section one under 'Agency and Authority').
113 Ibid., 67–8.
114 A letter from Isabella to her husband Ridolfo dated 18 November 1552 asks him to bring her a biography of Vittoria Colonna and works by Bembo and Firenzuola. She writes that this gift will be more precious to her than jewels and hopes he will bring her other books still: 'questo dono ... mi sarà piu caro che tante gioia ... so che la cortesia et liberalità vostra e tale che non solo questi libri che dimando ma due o tre altri appresso ne averò da Vostra Signoria ...' ('this gift ... will be more precious to me than as many jewels ... I know that your courtesy and generosity is such that I will have from you not only these books I request but two or three others ...'); ASP, Fondo Gonzaga-San Vitale, Serie III (Carteggio), b. 57.
115 Gonzaga, *Lettere*, 30–1.
116 Ibid., 76.
117 Ibid., 77.
118 *Il Libro della Bella Donna, composto da Messer Luigini da Udine* (Venice: Plinio Pietrasanta, 1554). Ruscelli's opening letter to Gonzaga explains, 'mi si conveniva allegar l'essempio di persona conosciuta per fama, e degnamente riverita, e adorata da un mondo tutto' ('I wished to include an example of a person who is known for her reputation, justly revered, and adored by all the world'); that is, Gonzaga.
119 Gonzaga, *Lettere*, 131.

120 Ibid. Emphasis added.
121 Ibid., 139.
122 Ibid., 140.
123 Nicolò Bevilacqua (c.1510/20–c.1573) of Trent was apprenticed to Paolo Manuzio and, by 1549, established as a printer in his own right in Venice (primarily of vernacular texts).
124 Gonzaga, *Lettere*, 316.
125 Although letters to Manfrone, for example, sometimes appear after others describing his death, and so on, disturbing the volume's loosely chronological frame.
126 Gonzaga, *Lettere*, 174–5. Several of these 'moral' letters are extremely overt in the artifice of their structure. Unlike the majority of Gonzaga's letters, which bear the name (and sometimes the geographic location) of their recipients, the 'moral' letters are often more general, perhaps to increase their relevance to a wide group of readers (implicitly including them in the reprimand) rather than limit the vice to a particular *destinatario*. The missive cited above, for example, is addressed only to 'un amico suo che di superbia sopra modo peccava' ('a friend of hers who greatly sinned in pride'). Similarly, a letter to a female friend guilty of the same vice and another deploring a male recipient's greed bear no name ('Alla S. ...,' ibid., 304–5; 'Al S...,' ibid., 306–9).
127 Ibid., 204. For the vice of *ira*, cf. ibid., 171, to Carlo Gonzaga, 'Alli dí passati mi fu riferito come Vostra Signoria, tratto da smoderata ira, aveva ferito nelle mani uno de' suoi soldati. Allora fra me stessa considerando e rivolgendo quanto strabocchevol cosa fusse questa passione, deliberai con mie lettere essortarvi ad astenervi di non incorrerci più ...' ('I was recently informed how Vostra Signoria, overcome with anger, wounded one of your soldiers in the hand. Whereby, thinking this over and realizing how excessive was your passion, I decided to use my letters to exhort you to refrain from such passion ...').
128 On avarice and ambition, cf. ibid., 300 to Andronico Volterra, 'Vorrei da voi saper ... perché tanto vi affatichiate in amassare danari ...' ('I would like to know from you ... why you wear yourself out so amassing wealth ...'); 301 to Antonio Rullo, 'Poiché io vego che sí spesso l'ambizione vi tenta ...' ('Since I see that you are so often tempted by ambition ...'); and 306 to an anonymous correspondent in Bergamo, ('Se l'avarizia ... condusse già vostro zio nel mal punto, guardate non conduchi voi nella malora ...' ('If avarice ... steered your uncle wrong, be careful that it doesn't do the same to you ...'). On pp. 292–300 we find a discrete thematic 'nucleus' devoted to such problems as the sordid nature of

physical love (292–3; 293–7), consorting with prostitutes (297–8), and adultery (299–300).

129 Ibid., 166–8.
130 On the 'crisis of evangelism,' see Delio Cantimori, *Prospettive di storia ereticale italiana del Cinquecento* (Bari: Laterza, 1960), 28 and ff. See also Caponetto, *La riforma protestante*, and Stephen D. Bowd, *Reform Before the Reformation: Vincenzo Querini and the Religious Renaissance in Italy* (Leiden: Brill, 2002). Schutte discusses the problem of periodization in 'The *Lettere Volgari* and the Crisis of Evangelism,' *Renaissance Quarterly* 28 (1975), 639–50, where she argues that traditional periodizations placing the end of Italian evangelism in 1542 are inadequate and must be extended by at least a decade to include the 1550s, as Cantimori suggests. Schutte suggests that Dionisotti's idea of an 'openness' which drew to a close around 1560 is helpful for such a periodization.
131 Grendler, *Critics of the Italian World*, 125.
132 Schutte states, 'there is no indication that anyone involved in the composition or publication of the vernacular letter collections felt the need to be particularly cautious' in her article 'The *Lettere Volgari* and the Crisis of Evangelism,' 673, and suggests that letters marked by evangelist sentiment may have escaped censorship because 'the views expressed in them were widely held, and because the writers exercised caution only to the extent that they did not make specific reference to the Northern Reformers' (ibid., 673–4). The anthologies studied by Schutte cover the period 1549–54.
133 Ibid., 662.
134 The exact nature of Italian evangelism is difficult to pin down. Schutte cites George H. Williams' description of evangelism as 'a widespread outcropping of an undogmatic, ethically serious combination of medieval piety and humanistic culture, quickened by Luther's proclamation of salvation by faith alone (solafideism), but disturbed by his seeming antinomianism and programmatic neglect of the traditional means and patterns of personal sanctification ...' (in *The Radical Reformation*, qtd. in Schutte, 'The *Lettere Volgari* and the Crisis of Evangelism,' 642).
135 Gonzaga, *Lettere*, 202.
136 Ibid., 203.
137 Cf. *Valorose donne*, 18v–20v; *Dialogo*, Book I, and chapter 2, note 45.
138 Gonzaga, *Lettere*, 239.
139 Ibid., 254.
140 Ibid., 246.
141 Ibid., 270.

142 Ibid., 271–2.
143 Although Gonzaga herself points out that Camilla ought rather advise her: '... benché non doverebbe mancare che vi sapesse in ciò consigliare meglio di me, essendo retto questo vostro munistero da padri sí prudenti e madri tanto spirituali [sic] ...' ('although really you should know better than me what counsel to give here, since your convent is run by such prudent fathers and spiritual mothers ...'), ibid., 75.
144 Ibid., 276; cf. Paul's First Epistle to the Corinthians 14:19.
145 Ibid., 241.

4 The Courtesan's Voice

1 *Lettere amorose di M. Girolamo Parabosco* (Venice: Giolito, 1564) and *Lettere amorose di madonna Celia gentildonna romana* (Venice: Antonio de gli Antonii, 1562) (attributed to Parabosco; see note 47 in my introduction). For more on the love letter genre, including love letter repertories, see chapter 5. On 'Epistolary Woman' as a specific type, see Katherine Jensen's study of seventeenth- and eighteenth-century French letters, *Writing Love, Letters, Women, and the Novel in France, 1605–1776* (Carbondale: Southern Illinois University Press, 1995), 1–36.
2 See the modern editions of Franco's letters by Benedetto Croce, *Lettere dell'unica edizione del MDLXXX* (Naples: Ricciardi, 1949) and, more recently, Stefano Bianchi's *Lettere* (Rome: Salerno, 1998). A partial English translation can be found in Veronica Franco, *Veronica Franco: Poems and Selected Letters*, ed. Ann Rosalind Jones and Margaret Rosenthal (Chicago: University of Chicago Press, 1998). For a range of critical approaches to Franco's letters, see Pietro Pancrazi, *Nel giardino del Candido,* ed. V. Branca (Florence: Le Monnier, 1961); Elvira Favretti, 'Rime e Lettere di Veronica Franco,' *Giornale storico della letteratura italiana* 163 (1986), 344–82, now in Elvira Favretti, *Figure e fatti del Cinquecento veneto* (Alessandria: Edizioni dell'Orso, 1992), 71–95; Margaret Rosenthal, *The Honest Courtesan: Veronica Franco, Citizen and Writer in Sixteenth-Century Venice* (Chicago: University of Chicago Press, 1992), especially 116–52; Maria Luisa Doglio, 'Scrittura e "offizio di parole" nelle *Lettere familiari* di Veronica Franco,' in *Lettera e donna. Scrittura epistolare tra Quattro e Cinquecento* (Rome: Bulzoni, 1993), 33–48; and Gabriel Niccoli, 'Autobiography and Fiction in Veronica Franco's Epistolary Narrative,' *Canadian Journal of Italian Studies* 16, no. 47 (1993), 129–42.
3 On courtesans and celebrity see Robin, 'Courtesans, Celebrity and Print Culture in Renaissance Venice: Tullia d'Aragona, Gaspara Stampa, and

Veronica Franco,' in *Italian Women and the City*, ed. J. Smarr and D. Valentini (Madison: Fairleigh Dickinson University Press, 1993), 35–59.
4 There is some critical debate over the translation of this term into English. Rosenthal, for example, uses the term 'honest courtesan' for her 1993 biography of Franco, but prefers, with Jones, 'honored courtesan' in their translation of Franco's poems and letters, *Veronica Franco: Poems and Selected Letters*, 3, thus stressing its implications of prestige and status but perhaps erasing some of its sexual valence.
5 See the essays collected in Martha Feldman and Bonnie Gordon, eds., *The Courtesan's Arts: Cross-Cultural Perspectives* (Oxford: Oxford University Press, 2006). On Venetian courtesans, see Rita Casagrande di Villaviera, *Le cortigiane veneziane nel Cinquecento* (Milan: Longanesi, 1968); Paul Larivaille, *La vita quotidiana delle cortigiane nell'Italia del Rinascimento. Roma e Venezia nei secoli XV e XVI*, trans. M. Pizzorno (Milan: Rizzoli, 1975); and G. Padoan, *Il mondo delle cortigiane nella letteratura rinascimentale*, in AA.VV., *Le cortigiane di Venezia dal Trecento al Settecento*, Catalogo della Mostra (Venezia, Casino Municipale, Ca' Vendramin Calergi, 2 febbr.–16 apr. 1990) (Milan: Berenice, 1990), 21–5 and 63–71. See also Georgina Masson, *The Courtesans of the Italian Renaissance* (London: Secker and Warburg, 1975); Antonio Barzaghi, *Donne o cortigiane? La prostituzione a Venezia: Documenti di costume dal XVI al XVIII secolo* (Verona: Bertani, 1980); and Lynn Lawner, *Lives of the Courtesans: Portraits of the Renaissance* (New York: Rizzoli, 1987).
6 For the relationship between courtesans, the literary academies, and salon culture in one particular context, that of Florence, see Domenico Zanré, *Cultural Non-Conformity in Early Modern Florence* (Aldershot, UK: Ashgate, 2004).
7 Cf. Fiora Bassanese, 'Private Lives and Public Lies: Texts by Courtesans of the Italian Renaissance,' in *Texas Studies in Literature and Language* 30, no. 1 (1988), 295. 'More so than any lady, the courtesan had to please and appease the males who were concurrently her admirers, her subjects, and her source of income, status, and reputation.' For a feminist analysis of the 'sexual contract' between courtesan (or prostitute) and client, see Carol Pateman, *The Sexual Contract* (Stanford: Stanford University Press, 1988), who (following Adrienne Rich) argues that an uncoerced, equal exchange is impossible because the prostitute does not merely sell a service. In selling sex, she (however temporarily) places body and self under the control of her client. On women as objects of exchange, see also Gayle Rubin, 'The Traffic in Women: Notes on the Political Economy of Sex,' in *Toward an Anthropology of Women*, ed. Rayna R. Reiter (New York: Monthly Review Press, 1975), 157–210.

8 Bassanese, 'Private Lives,' 302.
9 A 'poema epico' by Franco is alluded to in another epistolary work, Muzio Manfredi's *Lettere brevissime* (Venice: Meglietti, 1606), 249; cf. Bianchi, *Lettere*, 8, 20n4.
10 See Diana Robin, 'Courtesans, Celebrity and Print Culture in Venice,' and Ann Rosalind Jones, 'Bad Press: Modern Editors versus Early Modern Women Poets (Tullia d'Aragona, Gaspara Stampa, Veronica Franco),' in *Strong Voices, Weak History*, ed. P. Benson and V. Kirkham (Ann Arbor: University of Michigan Press, 2005), 287–313.
11 Paula Findlen, 'Humanism, Politics and Pornography in Renaissance Italy,' in *The Invention of Pornography: Obscenity and the Origins of Modernity, 1500–1800*, ed. Lynn Hunt (New York: Zone Books, 1993), 49–108.
12 For a selection of private correspondence by early modern courtesans, see *Cortigiane del secolo XVI* (Florence: Il 'Giornale di Erudizione,' 1892), and Angelo Romano, *Lettere di cortigiane del Rinascimento* (Rome: Salerno, 1990). See also Thea Picquet, 'Profession: Courtisane,' in *Les femmes écrivains en Italie au Moyen Age et à la Renaissance*, ed. G. Ulysse, Actes du colloque internationale Aix-en-Provence, 12, 13, 14 novembre 1992 (Provence: Publications de l'Université de Provence, 1994), 119–37.
13 Cf. Amedeo Quondam, *Le carte messaggiere, Retorica e modelli di comunicazione epistolare: per un indice dei libri di lettere del Cinquecento* (Rome: Bulzoni, 1981), 49–50.
14 On Franco's private publication of the *Lettere familiari*, see Rosenthal, *The Honest Courtesan*, 117–18.
15 On the cultural shift from love lyric towards literature of a more serious tone, see Robin, 'Courtesans, Celebrity and Print Culture in Renaissance Venice,' 50.
16 Cf. Doglio, 'Scrittura e "Offizio di Parole,"' 41.
17 The Venetian diarist Marin Sanudo estimated the number of Venetian courtesans at 11,654 (cited in Picquet, 'Profession: Courtisane,' 119).
18 Thomas Coryat, *Coryat's Crudities*, ed. James Maclehouse, 2 vols. (Glasgow: University of Glasgow Press, 1905), 406. For other travellers' descriptions of Venice and its courtesans, see Barzaghi, *Donne o cortigiane*.
19 On the erotic connotations of the courtesan's voice, see Bonnie Gordon, 'The Courtesan's Singing Body as Cultural Capital in Seventeenth-Century Italy,' in Feldman and Gordon, eds., *The Courtesan's Arts*, 182–98.
20 Cf. Ruggiero, *Binding Passions: Tales of Magic, Marriage, and Power at the End of the Renaissance* (New York: Oxford University Press, 1993), 32.
21 Ibid, 42. See also Bassanese, 'Private Lives,' 295: 'Entertainer, hostess, siren, substitute lady, and prostitute, [the courtesan] fashioned herself to reflect

the characteristics of the dominant group she served.' More recently, Ruggiero has discussed the tensions that arose from the client/patron's desire to be considered worthy of the courtesan's attentions, see 'Who's Afraid of Giulia Napolitana? Pleasure, Fear, and Imagining the Arts of the Renaissance Courtesan,' in Feldman and Gordon, eds., *The Courtesan's Arts*, 280–92.

22 Cf. Ruggiero, *Binding Passions*, 42.
23 Lawner, *Lives of the Courtesans*, 65.
24 As Courtney Quaintance notes, whether or not this attack actually took place is beside the point – its rhetorical hostility remains striking; see 'Defaming the Courtesan Satire and Invective in Sixteenth Century Italy,' 201, in Feldman and Gordon, eds., *The Courtesan's Arts*. It is the spurned lover himself, Lorenzo, who tells the story of the assault on Angela, a courtesan also known as 'Zaffetta.' On Venier's text and the 'trentuno' attack, see also Rosenthal, *The Honest Courtesan*, 38.
25 On Venier and his literary academy see Martha Feldman, *City Culture and the Madrigal at Venice* (Berkeley: University of California Press, 1995), esp. 83–197, and Martha Feldman, 'The Academy of Domenico Venier, Music's Literary Muse in Mid-Cinquecento Venice,' in *Renaissance Quarterly* 44, no. 3 (1991), 476–512.
26 Franco's *Rime* (Venice, 1575) include poetic interchanges with Marco and Maffio Venier, both nephews of Domenico, as well as with (an unnamed) Domenico himself. The *Rime* are published in a modern edition as Veronica Franco, *Rime*, ed. Stefano Bianchi (Milan: Mursia, 1995); they are translated by Rosenthal and Jones in *Veronica Franco: Poems and Selected Letters*. On the *Rime*, see Sara Maria Adler, 'Veronica Franco's Petrarchan *Terze Rime:* Subverting the Master's Plan,' *Italica* 65, no. 3 (1988), 213–33; Margaret Rosenthal, 'A Courtesan's Voice: Epistolary Self-Portraiture in Veronica Franco's *Terze Rime*,' in *Writing the Female Voice: Essays on Women's Epistolary Literature*, ed. Elizabeth C. Goldsmith (Boston: Northeastern University Press, 1989) 3–24; Margaret Rosenthal, 'Veronica Franco's *Terze rime:* The Venetian Courtesan's Defense,' *Renaissance Quarterly* 42, no. 2 (1989), 227–57; Mary Rogers, 'Fashioning Identities For Venetian Courtesans,' in *Fashioning Identities in Renaissance Art*, ed. Mary Rogers (Aldershot, UK: Ashgate, 2000), esp. 96–100; and Courtney Quaintance, 'Veronica Franco's Poems in Terza Rima,' in *Italian Literature and its Times*, ed. Joyce Moss (Detroit: Thomson Gale, 2005), 351–9.
27 This term is in Ann Rosalind Jones, 'The Poetics of Group Identity: Self-Commemoration through Dialogue in Pernette du Guillet and Tullia d'Aragona,' in Ann Rosalind Jones, *The Currency of Eros: Women's Love Lyric*

in Europe, 1540–1620 (Bloomington: Indiana University Press, 1990), 79–117. In addition to nine of Franco's own sonnets, her *Rime di diversi eccellentissimi auttori nella morte dell'illustre signor Estor Martinengo Conte di Malpaga* (date and place of publication unknown; probably 1575) included seventeen others by members of Domenico Venier's *ridotto*. Franco also contributed sonnets to a manuscript anthology entitled *Canzoniere di Bartolommeo Zacco Gentiluomo Padovano*, which she may have intended to edit and publish (cf. Rosenthal, *The Honest Courtesan*, 99–100).

28 Biographies of Franco include, in addition to Rosenthal's *The Honest Courtesan:* Alvise Zorzi, *Veronica Franco e i suoi poeti* (Milan: Camunia, 1986; now Milan: Rizzoli, 1993) and M. Diberti Leigh, *Veronica Franco. Donna poetessa e cortigiana del Rinascimento* (Ivrea: Priuli and Verucca, 1988). Franco married Paolo Panizza in the early 1560s, but separated from him shortly afterward, as her will of 1564, which requests the return of her dowry, indicates (Rosenthal, *Honest Courtesan*, 288n20). She had six children (none with her husband), three of whom did not survive infancy.

29 Michel de Montaigne, *Journal de voyage en Italie*, ed. Maurice Rat (Paris: Éditions Garnier, 1955), 1183. Of note is Montaigne's description of Franco as a 'lady': courtesans were famous – and reviled – for their efforts to dress and 'pass' as noblewoman (see note 43 below). On Franco's gift to Montaigne, see François Rigolot, 'Montaigne and Veronica Franco,' *Montaigne Studies* 15, nos. 1–2 (2003), 117–30.

30 Coryat, *Coryat's Crudities*, 402. Such a conflation of anxieties is reflected, for example, in Maffio Venier's poems (see Rosenthal, *The Honest Courtesan*, 45–8). On the plague in Venice, see Paolo Preto, *Peste e società a Venezia, 1576* (Vicenza: Neri Pozza, 1978), and on the Inquisition trials, with specific reference to women, see Ruth Martin, *Witchcraft and the Inquisition in Venice 1550–1650* (New York: Basil Blackwell, 1989).

31 Maffio Venier's satirical poems ('An fia, cuomodo? A che muodo zioghemo?,' 'Franca, credeme, che per San Maffio,' and 'Veronica, ver unica puttana') circulated among Venice's *letterati*, much to Franco's consternation. Initially, Franco suspected her friend and lover Marco Venier (Maffio's cousin) to be the author: her confusion and anger over the episode are chronicled in both her poems and letters. On Maffio Venier, see Manlio Dazzi, *Il fiore della lirica veneziana*, vol. 2, *Il libro segreto (chiuso)* (Vicenza: Neri Pozza, 1956).

32 Vannitelli's statement is contained in the Processi del Sant'Uffizi for 1580 (b. 46) at the Archivio di Stato di Venezia. For an overview of the archival documents regarding Veronica Franco, such as birth, tax, and death

records, as well as proceedings from the Inquisition's examination of her, see Alessandra Schiavon, 'Per la biografia di Veronica Franco. Nuovi documenti,' *Atti dell'Istituto Veneto di Scienze, Lettere ed Arti* 137 (1978–9), 243–56. For a reproduction of the trial documents, see also Rosenthal, *The Honest Courtesan*, 197–203. On Franco's trial, see Marisa Milani, 'L'"incanto' di Veronica Franco,' *Giornale Storico della letteratura italiana* 262, no. 518 (1985), 250–63.
33 For example, Aretino's *La Cortigiana* (1525) and his *Sei Giornate* (1534); Erasmus' *Dialogo di un giovane e d una meretrice* (1549); and Sperone Speroni's *Orazione contro le cortigiane* (1575).
34 On this anxiety, see Rosenthal, *The Honest Courtesan*, 18–19.
35 Pietro Aretino, *Ragionamenti/Dialogo*, ed. Nino Borsellino (Milan: Garzanti, 1984), 203. The title *Sei giornate* is generally used to denote all six 'days' of dialogue that comprise the *Ragionamento* and the *Dialogo*, published together as one organic work. Translations from all works cited here, including Franco's, are mine.
36 Ibid., 263. Similarly, in Lodovico Domenichi's play *Le due cortigiane* (Florence: Giorgio Mariscotti, 1563), the 'dolci paroline' ('sweet little words') of beautiful and mercenary twin courtesans serve to snare two young men and their fathers, and the women are described repeatedly as the cause of the young men's financial and moral ruin.
37 Aretino, *Ragionamenti/Dialogo*, 263.
38 Aretino, *Lettere, Libro Primo*, ed. Francesco Erspamer (Parma: Ugo Guanda, 1995), 609.
39 Ibid., 611, 'La bugia, l'invidia, e la maladicenza, quinto elemento de le cortigiane, non vi tengono in continuo moto l'animo e la lingua' ('Lies, envy, and gossip, the quintessence of courtesans, don't constantly fuel your soul and tongue').
40 Ibid., 609.
41 Cf. Aretino, *Lettere*, 6 vols., ed. Paolo Proccaccioli (Rome: Salerno, 1997–2002), vol. 4, letter 512, and vol. 2, letter 275.
42 Ibid., vol. 4, letter 471.
43 Early modern legislation against courtesans' dress, for example, reflects the anxiety of both Venetian men and women that a courtesan might, as a result of her elaborate costume, be taken for a patrician lady (or vice versa). See Margaret Rosenthal, 'Cutting a Good Figure: The Fashions of Venetian Courtesans in the Illustrated Albums of Early Modern Travelers,' in Feldman and Gordon, eds., *The Courtesan's Arts*, 52–74; Casagrande, *Le cortigiane veneziane*, 64ff; Diane Owen Hughes, 'Sumptuary Laws and Social Relations in Renaissance Italy,' in *Disputes and Settlements: Law and*

Human Relations in the West, ed. John Bossy (Cambridge: Cambridge University Press, 1983), 343–55.

44 The designation of Calmo's *destinatarie* as courtesans is proposed in Vittorio Rossi's edition of Calmo's letters, *Le lettere di Messer Andrea Calmo, riprodotte sulle stampe migliori* (Turin: Ermanno Loescher, 1888), which observed that many of the women Calmo addresses are listed in the *Catalogo di tutte le principali et più onorate cortigiane di Venetia*. Piermario Vescovo, however, argues that Calmo's women are likely fictitious in *Da Ruzante a Calmo. Tra 'Signore Comedie' e 'Onorandissime stampe'* (Padua: Editrice Antenore, 1996), 180–1.

45 Calmo, *Lettere*, vol. 4, 284–6.

46 Ibid., 258–60, 260–2.

47 Ibid., 309–10.

48 Parabosco, *Lettere amorose libro primo*, 66v–66r.

49 Nicolò Franco, *Pistole Vulgari* (Venice: Gardane, 1542). See letter CCLVI, 'Pistola di M. N. Franco, nela quale scrive a le puttane' (217v–224).

50 Cf. for example Lawner, *Lives of the Courtesans*, 65.

51 N. Franco, *Pistole*, 224.

52 Ibid., 225v.

53 See also Rosenthal, *The Honest Courtesan*, 117, and 'Epistolary Self-Portraiture in Veronica Franco's *Terze rime*,' 4.

54 See Franco, *Lettere familiari*, letter I, dedicatory letter; and letter XXI.

55 Bartolommeo Miniatore, *Formulario, overo epistolario volgare* (Venice: [F. De Leno], 1568 [i.e. 1569]); Francesco Sansovino, *Del secretario* (Venice: N.p., 1573); Orazio Toscanella, *Concetti et forme di Cicerone, del Boccaccio, del Bembo* (Venice: L. degli Avanzi, 1560), and Orazio Toscanella, *Modo di studiare le Epistole Famigliari di M. Tullio Cicerone* (Venice: Giolito, 1567). On the development of such manuals, see Luigi Matt's useful study, *Teoria e prassi dell'epistolografia italiana tra Cinquecento e primo Seicento* (Rome: Bonacci, 2005).

56 Franco, capitolo 16, vv 112–17, 'La spada, che 'n vostra rade e fora,/ de la lingua venezïana,/ s'a voi piace d'usar, piace a me ancora;/ e se volete entrar ne la toscana, / scegliete voi la seria o la burlesca,/ che l'una e l'altra è a me facile e piana' ('The sword you wield in your hand,/ of the Venetian language,/if that's what you wish to use, then I do, too;/and if you want to use Tuscan,/ you can choose the high or comic style,/for both are equally easy for me').

57 Sansovino, *Del secretario*, 18r, 22v.

58 Girolamo Ruscelli, *Lettere di Principi, le quali si scrivono o da principi, o a principi, o ragionano di principi* (Venice: Giordano Ziletti, 1577), Book III, 218v; Stefano Guazzo, *Lettere*, 373–76.

59 On subscriptions, see Sansovino, *Del secretario*, 12r–13v; Taglienti, *Componimento di parlamenti* (Venice: Gli eredi di Luigi Valvassore, 1584).
60 Franco, *Lettere*, 7. All citations from the *Lettere* are taken from Bianchi's edition.
61 See for example, Sansovino, *Del secretario*, 88r–v.
62 Franco, *Lettere*, 30.
63 Ibid.
64 Ibid., 31–2.
65 Aretino, *Lettere*, vol. 4, letter 434.
66 Perhaps simply reflecting, at least in part, greater rates of literacy among men. There are a few examples of humanist letters to pregnant women and new mothers, for example Bembo's to his daughter Elena in Pietro Bembo, *Lettere*, ed. Ernesto Travi, vol. 4 (Bologna: Commissione per i Testi di Lingua, 1993), 530–1. Most of Garimberto's congratulatory phrases are addressed to fathers (*Concetti*, 10r).
67 Franco, *Lettere*, 54–6.
68 See Margaret King, *Venetian Humanism in an Age of Patrician Dominance* (Princeton: Princeton University Press, 1986), esp. 175–7, on Venetian humanists' privileging of reason and control over passion.
69 Franco, *Lettere*, 34–5. On medical manuals and popular advice, see chapter 2 in this volume.
70 See, for example, Bembo, *Lettere*, III, 40–1; Guazzo, *Lettere*, 614. Ortensio Lando published an entire collection of such missives, titled *Consolatorie de diversi autori* (Venice, al Segno del Pozzo, 1550). For a discussion of the *consolatoria* genre, see Giovanni Maria Filelfo, *Consolatoria*, ed. Anne Schoysman Zambrini, in *Scelta di curiosita inededite o rare dal secolo XIII al XIX* (Bologna: Commissione per i Testi di Lingua, 1991), xi–l.
71 Cf. Chiara Matraini, 'Chiara Matraini: Rime e Lettere,' ed. Giovanna Rabitti, in *Scelta di curiosita inededite o rare dal secolo XIII al XIX* (Bologna: Commissione per i Testi di Lingua, 1991), 177–81 and 185–7. See also Lucrezia Gonzaga, *Lettere*, 11.
72 Sansovino, *Del secretario*, 96v; Garimberto, *Concetti*, 36r–50r.
73 Battista Ceci, *Compendio d'avvertimenti di ben parlare volgare* (Venice: N.p., 1618), 86–7.
74 Cf. Franco, *Lettere*, 34 and 55–6. I first formulated the discussion of Franco's commercial imagery that follows in my article 'Settling the Debt: Veronica Franco's Literary Economics,' *RLA: Romance Languages Annual* 8 (1996), 303–10.
75 Franco, *Lettere*, 35–6.
76 Ibid., 36.

77 Ibid., XLII, 105.
78 Ibid., IV, 36.
79 Jones, *The Currency of Eros*, 4.
80 Among other points. Cf. Toscanella, *Modo di studiare le Epistole Famigliari di M. Tullio Cicerone*, 52.
81 Franco, *Lettere*, IV, 35–41.
82 Ibid., 37.
83 Ibid.
84 On Franco's identification with Venice's civic mythology, see Rosenthal, *The Honest Courtesan*, 58–111, and 'Veronica Franco's *Terze rime*,' 227–57, as well as Jones, *The Currency of Eros*, 30.
85 Cf. Moderata Fonte, *Il merito delle donne*, ed. Adriana Chemello (Venice: Eidos, 1988), 13, 'La nobilissima città di Venezia ... giace mirabilmente situata nell'estrema parte del mare Adriatico, e sí come ha per fondamento esso mare, cosí le mura che la circondano, le fortezze che la guardano, e le porte che la Serrano, non sono altro che il medesimo mare ... Il mare l'è via publica e aperta campagna ...' ('The most noble city of Venice ... lies remarkably situated at the extreme end of the Adriatic sea, and just as the sea is its foundation, so the walls that surround it, the fortresses that protect it, and the gates that enclose it, are the very same sea ... The sea is [Venice's] public road and open countryside'). On Fonte's elegy of Venice, see Paola Malpezzi Price, '*Venetia Figurata* and Women in Sixteenth-Century Venice: Moderata Fonte's Writings,' in *Italian Women and the City*, ed. Janet Levarie Smarr and Daria Valentini (Madison: Fairleigh Dickinson University Press, 1993), 18–34.
86 Fonte, *Il merito delle donne*, 14.
87 Franco, *Lettere*, 38.
88 Ibid., 40.
89 Ibid., XVIII, 62.
90 Ibid.
91 Ibid.
92 Ibid., 63.
93 Ibid., 64.
94 Ibid., XVII, 59–60.
95 Ibid., 60.
96 Ibid.
97 For example, in letter XIX, 65, 'Sì come la vostra cortesia è stata incredibile a far che voi, per avermi a pena solamente veduta, m'abbiate posto ... grandissimo amore e mi abbiate oltre ad ogni mio merito stimata degna d'essere onorata e compiaciuta da un gentiluomo par vostro, così la

relazione fattami dal signor N. della vostra affezzione verso di me ... ha avuto forza di farmi pigliar la penna in mano per ringraziarvi, sì come faccio con queste poche righe, della vostra soverchia umanità e del mio infinito obligo ...' ('Just as your incredible courtesy has led you to love me almost at first sight, and you have deemed me worthy of the attentions of a gentleman such as yourself, so signor N.'s description of your love for me ... inspired me to take pen in hand in order to thank you, as I do with these few lines, for your overwhelming kindness and my own infinite obligation').

98 Ibid., xxxviii, 99.
99 Ibid., xix, 65.
100 Here I am following Nicoletta Pireddu's analysis of aesthetic exchange; cf. Nicoletta Pireddu, 'Gabriele D'Annuzio: The Art of Squandering and the Economy of Sacrifice,' in *The Question of the Gift: Essays across Disciplines*, ed. Mark Osteen (London: Routledge, 2002), 172–90; see also Nicoletta Pireddu, *Antropologie alla corte della bellezza. Decadenza ed economia simbolica nell'Europa fin de siècle* (Verona: Edizioni Fiorni, 2002).
101 Cf. Franco, *Lettere familiari*, 3, 'Sí come può ciascuna persona, quantunque posta in umilissima fortuna, rendere onore e gloria nei sacrifici e nei voti dell'Altissimo Iddio proporzionevolmente in concorrenza degli uomini più ricchi e più abondevoli di tutti i beni ... cosí ... non può fallire che non accetti più volontieri un minimo segno di devozione ch'un opera infinita ...' ('Just as anyone, no matter how lowly their status, can render honour and glory to God through vows and sacrifices in direct proportion to the efforts of richer and more well-off men ... thus ... you cannot fail to accept more readily the poorest sign of devotion rather than an infinite work ...').
102 Cf. for example, Sansovino, *Del Secretario*, 87v–88v.
103 Franco, *Lettere*, 3.
104 Ibid., 4.
105 Cited in Natalie Zemon Davis, 'Beyond the Market: Books as Gifts in Sixteenth-century France,' *Transactions of the Royal Historical Society* 33 (1983), 70. Davis considers the significance of the exchange of books, discussing at some length the function of dedications and prefaces within this context.
106 See the essays collected in Osteen, ed., *The Question of the Gift*.
107 See note 34 above.
108 Franco, *Lettere*, viii, 18.
109 Ibid., 19.
110 Ibid., xxx, 48.

111 Franco, *Lettere*, 66. Cf. idem, *Rime*, capitoli 16, 17, 23, and 47.
112 Ibid., XXII, 36.
113 Cf. Garimberto, *Concetti*, 21r, 'Biasimare ... [c]omprende ... il riprendere, ma propriamente il riprendere nasce d'amore, onde la riprensione è propria dell'amico' ('Condemnation ... includes ... reproof, but reproof born of love; whereas reproof is the duty of a friend').
114 See, for example, Jones and Rosenthal, *Veronica Franco*, 12, who argue that Franco's depiction of the harsh realities of courtesanry is not meant to apply to her own experience, but rather to her specific fears for her friend's daughter, who lacks the beauty and intelligence to succeed as a *cortigiana onesta*: '... [Franco] is distinguishing herself from the lower ranks of sex workers which this daughter is likely to join.'
115 Cf. Gordon, 'The Courtesan's Singing Body,' 92.
116 Franco, *Lettere*, XXII, 38.
117 Jones and Rosenthal, *Veronica Franco*, 13.
118 Cf. Sperone Speroni, 'Della cura famigliare,' in *Dialoghi di Sperone Speroni* (Venice: Fra Lorenzini da Torino, 1550), 54r.
119 Franco, *Lettere*, XXII, 37.
120 Ibid., 38.
121 It was not unusual for a daughter to follow in her courtesan-mother's footsteps as Franco evidently did. Paola is listed as Veronica's procuress in the *Catalogo di tutte le principali et più honorate cortigiane di Venezia*, reprinted in Casagrande di Villaviera, *Le cortigiane veneziane*.
122 Franco, *Lettere*, XXII, 39. On the Casa delle Zitelle, see, for example, Monica Chojnacka, 'Women, Charity and Community in Early Modern Venice: The Casa delle Zitelle,' *Renaissance Quarterly* 51 (1998), 68–91.
123 For Franco's will, see Rosenthal, *The Honest Courtesan*, 111–15.
124 Julie Campbell, *Literary Circles and Gender in Early Modern Europe* (Aldershot, UK: Ashgate, 2006), 22.

5 Between Stage and Page

1 Giuseppe Pavoni, *Diario descritto da Giuseppe Pavoni* ... (Bologna, 1589), cited and translated in Anne MacNeil, 'The Divine Madness of Isabella Andreini,' *Journal of the Royal Music Association* 120 (1995), 198–9. On the *Pazzia d'Isabella*, see also Louise George Clubb, *Italian Drama in Shakespeare's Time* (New Haven, CT: Yale University Press, 1989), 263–4; Luigi Rasi, *I comici italiani* (Florence: Fratelli Bocca, 1897), 91; Ferdinando Taviani, ed., *La Commedia dell'Arte e la società barocca*, vol. 2 (Rome: Bulzoni, 1969), 164; Cesare Molinari, 'L'altra faccia del 1589: Isabella

Andreini e la sua 'pazzia,' in *Firenze e la Toscana dei Medici nell'Europa del Cinquecento*, vol. 2 (Florence: Olschki, 1983), 565–73; and Cesare Molinari, *La Commedia dell'Arte* (Milan: Mondadori, 1985), 119–22.

2 On Isabella Andreini and her works, see, for example, Armand Baschet, *Les comédiens italiens a la cour de France* (Paris: E. Plon and Co., 1882); F.S. Bartoli, *Notizie istoriche de' comici italiani che fiorirono intorno all'anno MDC fino ai giorni presenti*, 2 vols. (Padua, 1782; facsimile edition, Bologna: Arnaldo Forni, 1978), 31–7; Achille Fiocco, 'Isabella Andreini,' *Enciclopedia dello spettacolo* 1 (Rome: Casa Editrice Le Maschere, 1954), 555–8; L. Panella, 'Isabella Canali,' in *Dizionario biografico degli italiani*, vol. 30 (Rome: Istituto della Enciclopedia Italiana , 1960–), 704–5; F. Marotti and G. Romei, eds., *La Commedia dell'Arte e la società barocca. La professione del teatro*, vol. 1b (Rome: Bulzoni, 1991), 163–208; Roberto Tessari, 'Sotto il segno di Giano: La Commedia dell'Arte di Isabella e Francesco Andreini,' in *The Commedia dell'Arte From the Renaissance to Dario Fo*, ed. Christopher Cairns (Lampeter: Edwin Mellen Press, 1989), 1–33; Nancy Dersofi, 'Isabella Andreini (1562–1604),' in *Italian Women Writers: A Bio-Bibliographic Sourcebook*, ed. Rinaldina Russell (Westport, CT: Greenwood Press, 1994), 18–25; Anne MacNeil, 'The Virtue of Gender,' in *La femme lettrée à la Renaissance*, ed. Michel Bastianesen (Louvain, Belgium: Poetas, 1997), 147–64; Anne MacNeil, *Music and Women of the Commedia dell'Arte in the Late Sixteenth Century* (Oxford: Oxford University Press, 2003), 187–263, which contains a detailed chronology of her life.

3 The bibliography on *commedia dell'arte* is extremely rich; I offer here an abbreviated guide to some of the most important contributions. For general sources, see M. Apollonio, *Storia della Commedia dell'Arte* (Rome-Milan, 1930; facsimile edition Florence: Sasoni, 1982); Taviani, ed., *La commedia dell'Arte e la società barocca I. La fascinazione del teatro*; Marotti and Romei, eds., *La commedia dell'Arte e la società barocca II. La professione del teatro*; V. Pandolfi, ed., *La commedia dell'Arte. Storia e testi*, 2 vols. (Florence: Sansoni Antiquariato, 1957–9; facsimile edition Florence: Sansoni, 1988); S. Ferrone, ed., *Commedie dell'arte* (Milan: Mursia, 1985–6); B. Croce, 'Intorno alla 'Commedia dell'Arte,' in *Poesia popolare e poesia d'arte* (Bari: LaTerza, 1933); S. Ferrone, *Attori mercanti corsari. La Commedia dell'Arte in Europa tra Cinque e Seicento* (Turin: Einaudi, 1993); K.M. Lea, *Italian Popular Comedy: A Study in the Commedia dell'Arte, 1520–1620. With special reference to the English stage*, 2 vols. (Oxford: Clarendon Press, 1934); F. Marotti, introduction to F. Scala, *Il Teatro delle Favole Rappresentative*, vol. 1 (Milan: Il Polifilo, 1976), ix–lxiii; Allardyce Nicoll, *Il mondo di Arlecchino* (Milan: Bompiani, 1980); E. Petraccone, *La Commedia dell'Arte. Storia, tecnica, scenari* (Naples:

Ricciardi, 1927); I. Sanesi, 'Note sulla Commedia dell'Arte,' *Giornale storico della letteratura italiana* 111 (1938), 5–76; F. Taviani and M. Schino, *Il segreto della Commedia dell'Arte. La memoria delle compagnie italiane del XVI, XVII e XVIII secolo* (Florence: La Casa Usher, 1982); Ferdinando Taviani, 'Un vivo contrasto: Seminario su attori e attrici della Commedia dell'Arte,' *Teatro e Storia* 2 (1986), 25–75; Roberto Tessari, *La Commedia dell'Arte nel Seicento. 'Industria' e 'arte giocosa' della civilta' barocca* (Florence: Olschki, 1969); Jane Tylus, 'Women at the Windows: Commedia dell'arte and Theatrical Practice in Early Modern Italy,' *Theatre Journal* 49, no. 3 (1997), 323–42. On *commedia dell'arte* activity outside of Italy, see Delia Gambelli, *Arlecchino a Parigi, Dall'Inferno alla corte del Re Sole* (Rome: Bulzoni, 1993); R. Guardenti, *Gli italiani a Parigi. La Comédie Italienne (1660–1697). Storia, pratica scenica, iconografia*, 2 vols. (Rome: Bulzoni, 1990).

4 Andreini may have performed the male lead in Tasso's *Aminta*. See Ferdinando Taviani's important discussion of the links between Andreini and Tasso in 'Bella d'Asia. Torquato Tasso, gli attori e l'immortalita,' *Paragone/Letteratura* 35 (1984), 3–76, esp. 6–9.

5 Andreini's literary voice has been variously described as 'androgynous' and 'hermaphroditic.' See the comments of Anne MacNeil, ed., *Selected Poems of Isabella Andreini*, trans. James Wyatt Cook (Lantham, MA: The Scarecrow Press, 2005), ix, 2–3; and MacNeil, *Music and Women ...*, 89. Although historically these terms have been used interchangeably, they suggest a different emphasis. The androgyne is neither recognizably male nor female; the hermaphrodite, beginning with Plato's formulation in the *Symposium*, is clearly both. In Andreini's case, the second term, 'hermaphroditic,' is the more apt: Andreini does not present herself as being *neither* male nor female but rather as *both* male and female. On literary and cultural hermaphroditism and androgyny, see Linda Woodbridge, *Women and the English Renaissance: Literature and the Nature of Womankind* (Urbana: University of Illinois Press, 1984), 140–1; see also Constance Jordan's discussion of symbolic androgyny in early modern texts in *Renaissance Feminism: Literary Texts and Political Models* (Ithaca, NY: Cornell University Press, 1990), 134–8.

6 See the dedication to Cardinal Giorgio Cinzio Aldobrandini, that accompanies the *Rime* [*parte prima*] (Milan: Bordone, 1601): 'io ... che sola a' questi miei figli son Padre, Madre, e Nutrice ... iscusami appresso di lei la maternal pietà, che 'l bene della sua prole continuamente desidera ...' ('I ... who alone am Father, Mother, and Nurse to these my children ... excuse my maternal piety before you, which perpetually desires the good of its offspring'; all translations are mine throughout, unless otherwise noted).

The praise of the academician Erycius Puteanus, with whom Isabella exchanged a number of letters, is indicative of this hermaphroditic public persona. He repeatedly extols her as a 'an equal partner' in 'male glory,' a woman who has transcended the limitations of her sex (cf. Epistle 19, Erycius Puteanus to Isabella Andreini, 9 November 1601). Puteanus insists that Isabella ought more properly be called a man and, indeed, that she even surpasses 'the virtue of the male' (Epistle 5, 14 December 1601). The correspondence between Andreini and Puteanus is transcribed and translated in MacNeil, *Music and Women* ..., 305–23, based on Charles Reulens, *Eryicius Puteanus et Isabelle Andreini: Lecture faite à l'Académie d'Archéologie le 3 Février 1889* (Antwerp: N.p., 1889). Like Puteanus, many of Isabella's admirers described her as 'manly' in her virtue, or an exception among women, as, for example, in Isaac du Ryer's poem written in her honour: 'Je ne crois point qu'Isabelle soit une femme mortale' (*Le temps perdu*, 1610). On Andreini's mingling of masculine and feminine cultural attributes in the construction of her public reputation, which remained immaculate despite the common perception of actresses as morally unreliable, see MacNeil, *Music and Women* ..., 89–91, and MacNeil, 'The Virtue of Gender'; see also Robert L. Erenstein, 'Isabella Andreini: A Lady of Virtue and High Renown,' in *Essays on Drama and Theatre: Liber amicorum Benjamin Hunnigher* (Amsterdam: Moussalt's Uitgeverij, 1973), 37–49. On the perception that actresses were immoral, see Richard Andrews, 'Isabella Andreini and Others: Women on Stage in the Late Cinquecento,' in *Women in Italian Renaissance Culture and Society*, ed. Letizia Panizza (London: Legenda, 2005), 316–33; Taviani and Schino, *Il segreto della Commedia dell'Arte*, 337; and Stephen Orgel, *Impersonations: The Performance of Gender in Shakespeare's England* (Cambridge: Cambridge University Press, 1996), 1. Many of Isabella's biographers praised her for maintaining an impeccable reputation in both arenas. Crescimbeni, for example, wrote admiringly of Isabella: '... seppe accompagnare ad un'arte riputata universalmente pericolosa per l'onore delle Donne, una somma castità, e un costume inocentissimo,' in *Commentarij ... intorno alla sua istoria della vulgar poesia*, vol. 4, Book III (Rome: Antonio de' Rossi, 1710), 148. Francesco Bartoli effused, '... ella fu eccellente Poetessa, saggia Filosofa, e valorosa Commediante. V'aggiungerò ancora, che fu Moglie fedele, Madre amorosa, ed esemplarissima Cristiana; pregi tutti che la resero un vero modello di virtù, ed uno specchio di saviezza, e d'onestà,' in Bartoli, *Notizie istoriche de' comici italiani*, 32–3. Garzoni's praise of her in *La Piazza universale* as a 'spettacolo superbo non meno di virtù che di bellezza' whose name will live on forever is well known; cited in Marotti and Romei, eds., *La commedia dell'arte e la società barocca*, vol. 2, 12.

7 Although women were forbidden to appear on stage in early modern England until the 1660s and women's parts were played by men or boys, in Italy women appeared on stage from the 1540s, with some exceptions. The practice of male actors portraying female characters remained common, however, especially in *commedia erudita* (cf. Andrews, 'Isabella Andreini and Others,' 316–33). Thomas Coryat marvelled that while in Italy 'I saw a woman acte, a thing that I never saw before ... and they performed it with as good a grace, action, gesture, and whatsoever convenient for a Player, as ever I saw any masculine Actor,' in *Coryat's Crudities*, vol. 1 (Glasgow: James MacLehose and Sons, and New York: Macmillan, 1905), 386. On the emergence of women actors see Clubb, *Italian Drama in Shakespeare's Time*, 257, and Maggie Günsberg, *Gender and the Italian Stage: From the Renaissance to the Present Day* (Cambridge: Cambridge University Press, 1997), 49, 58. On the problem of the transvestite stage and the spectator's experience in early modern England, see the important work by Stephen Greenblatt, 'Fiction and Friction,' in *Reconstructing Individualism: Autonomy, Individualism and the Self in Western Thought*, ed. Thomas C. Heller et al. (Stanford: Stanford University Press, 1986), 30–52; Peter Stallybrass, 'Transvestitism and the "Body Beneath": Speculating on the Boy Actor,' in *Erotic Politics: Desire on the Renaissance Stage*, ed. Susan Zimmerman (New York: Routledge, 1992), 64–83; Stephen Orgel, 'Nobody's Perfect, Or, Why Did the English Stage Take Boys for Girls?' in *Displacing Homophobia: Gay Male Perspectives in Literature and Culture*, ed. Ronald R. Butters, John M. Clum, and Michael Moon (Durham, NC: Duke University Press, 1989), 7–30; and Lisa Jardine, *Still Harping on Daughters: Women and Drama in the Age of Shakespeare* (Sussex: The Harvester Press, 1983), esp. chap 1. On England's all-male theatre, see also Orgel, *Impersonations*. For a brief summary of these critical positions and an overview of cross-dressing in historical perspective, see Vern L. Bullough and Bonnie Bullough, *Cross Dressing, Sex, and Gender* (Philadelphia: University of Pennsylvania Press, 1993). Sue Ellen Case, *Feminism and Theatre* (New York: Methuen, 1988) offers a general discussion of cross-dressing on stage: see esp. chap. 1. On the transition to women on the English stage, see Ann Thompson, '"Woman/Women" and the Stage,' in *Women and Literature in Britain, 1500–1700*, ed. Helen Wilcox (Cambridge: Cambridge University Press, 1996), 110–16, and Elizabeth Howe, *The First English Actresses: Women and Drama 1660–1700* (Cambridge: Cambridge University Press, 1992).
8 The German writers von Archenholtz and Volkmann, for example, along with Goethe, debated whether the use of *castrati* in Roman opera detracted from the illusion; or whether the deep voice of the *istrione* in the "'teatri di

prosa' was realistic. Cf. Alesandro Ademollo, *I teatri di Roma nel secolo decimosettimo* (Bologna: Forni, 1969), xviii–xxv. Goethe commented: '... the enjoyment is doubled by the fact that these are not women, but rather portray women,' from *Italian Journey,* cited in Ademollo, ibid., xxiv, my translation.

9 The only proper name to appear in Andreini's *Lettere* is that of Tasso, to whom an elegiac letter is devoted (107–9v).
10 Citations are taken from the 1611 edition of the *Rime d'Isabella Andreini Padovana* ... (Milan: Girolamo Bordone). This translation is from MacNeil, ed., and Cook, trans., *Selected Poems of Isabella Andreini,* 31.
11 In a discussion of works by Titian and Michelangelo, Frederica Jacobs notes a similar dynamic in which the viewer admires (but is never confused by) the merging of male and female characteristics. 'Aretino and Michelangelo, Dolce and Titian: Femmina, Masculo, Grazia,' *Art Bulletin* 82, no. 1 (March 2000), 51–67.
12 Michael Anderson writes, '... the Gelosi used no essential scenery in their performances: in the public *stanzone* they would play in front of drapes and at court they were quite happy to act in front of perspective scenery designed for a different play,' in 'Making Room: *Commedia* and the Privatisation of the Theatre,' in *The Commedia dell'Arte From the Renaissance to Dario Fo,* ed. Christopher Cairns (Lampeter: Edwin Mellen Press, 1989), 86. This was the case in the performance of the *Pazzia d'Isabella* at the Medici Court; see MacNeil, 'The Divine Madness of Isabella Andreini,' 96.
13 Although not specific about dialogue, Scala gave detailed instructions regarding props and costumes: words might be improvised, but appearance was codified. See Flaminio Scala, *Il Teatro delle Favole Rappresentative,* dedicatory letter by Franceso Andreini, 'E perchè più agevolmente si possano rappresentare l'opere sue, e porre in scena, egli ha a ciascheduna d'esse fatto il suo non disdicevole argomento, ha dichiarati, e distinti i personaggi, et ha per ordine posto tutti gli abiti che in esse si ricercano per non generar confusione nel vestire' ('So that his works can be more easily performed, [the *capocomico*] has provided each one with its own suitable subject, he has identified and distinguished the characters, and he has listed all the clothing needed for each one so as not to create confusion in the costumes'). Scala was part of the *Confidenti* troupe until 1621, but perhaps not, as some have suggested, its director. Cf. Molinari, *La Commedia dell'Arte,* 136. On Scala's *Teatro,* see also Marotti, 'Il *Teatro delle Favole Rappresentative*: un progetto utopico,' *Biblioteca Teatrale,* nos. 15–16 (1976), 191–215, and Marotti and Romei, eds., *La Commedia dell'Arte e la società barocca,* vol. 1b, 55–62.

14 On these works, see chapters 3 and 4 in this volume.
15 In contrast, for example, to a text like Gonzaga's *Lettere,* which is replete with references to people, places, and events that require the reader to be familiar with the writer's particular context. On the generality or universality of *commedia dell'arte* repertory, see the discussion by L. Bianconi and T. Walker in 'Dalla Finta Pazza alla Veremonda,' *Rivista italiana di musicologia* 10 (1975), 379–454, regarding Ottonelli's description of three types of theatre (*principesco, academico,* and *mercenario*). Of the three, mercenary theatre must be geographically mobile and thus more general, requiring 'per poter essere agita ovunque, la rinuncia ad ogni allusione direttamente riferita a una città, a una specifica tradizione locale, e perciò comprensibile a un pubblico solo' (412–13). Michael Anderson notes that Italian companies had established touring circuits by the early seventeenth century ('Making Room,' 82).
16 I cite from the 1607 edition of the *Lettere d'Isabella Andreini padovana, comica gelosa et academica intenta nominata l'accesa* (Venice: Marc'Antonio Zaltieri), 2r.
17 For a discussion of these problems as they relate to the development of the love letter and, eventually, the novel in seventeenth- and eighteenth-century France, see Katherine Ann Jensen, *Writing Love: Letters, Women, and the Novel in France, 1605–1776* (Carbondale, IL: Southern Illinois University Press, 1995).
18 Andreini's pastoral play *La Mirtilla* is, obviously, the most 'theatrical' of her writings because it was written for the stage (and performed); I am interested here in the theatricality of works not written for the stage but nonetheless dramatic in nature, like the *Lettere*. For Isabella's *Mirtilla*, see the modern edition edited by Maria Luisa Doglio (Lucca: M. Pacini Fazzi, 1995) and the translation by Julie Campbell (Tempe, Arizona: Arizona Center for Medieval and Renaissance Studies, 2002). A relationship between Andreini's experience on stage and her literary production has been noted by various critics. See, for example, Taviani, ed., *La Commedia dell'Arte e la società barocca,* for whom Andreini's *Lettere* 'partecipano – forse piu di ogni altro scritto dei comici dell'arte – della frequentazione di due universi culturali' (165–6); see also Clubb, *Italian Drama in Shakespeare's Time,* 257; Tessari, 'Sotto il segno di Giano,' 5; and Tessari, *La Commedia dell'Arte nel Seicento,* 200. For a wide-ranging discussion of the links between *commedia dell'arte* and literary culture, see Robert Henke's informative study, *Performance and Literature in the Commedia dell'Arte* (Cambridge: Cambridge University Press, 2002).
19 Andreini's letters were published posthumously and reprinted numerous times up until 1663. For a list and description of the various edi-

tions, see Janine Basso, *La genre épistolaire en langue italienne (1538–1662),* 2 vols. (Rome: Bulzoni, 1990), 414–20, and Amedeo Quondam, *Le carte messaggiere. Retorica e modelli di comunicazione epistolare: per un indice dei libri di lettere del Cinquecento* (Rome: Bulzoni, 1981), 286. Andreini referred to her letter collection in a letter to Erycius Puteanus, dated 19 November 1601, that states, '... quand'io non fossi per hora data alla fatica delle mie Lettere, le quali come diverse di stile non lasciano ch'io possa invocare a vostra contemplatione le muse,' in Reulens, 'Erycius Puteanus et Isabelle Andreini,' 25–6, transcribed and translated in MacNeil, *Music and Women* ..., 'were I not at the moment working on my Letters which, so different in style, do not permit me to call forth the Muses to your contemplation,' 307–9. Although Isabella had begun work on the letters by 1601, MacNeil's reference to a 1602 edition of this book (in *Music and Women,* 325) is inaccurate. The first edition is the posthumous edition of 1607.

20 Flaminio Scala sought to address this problem in his *Teatro delle Favole Rappresentative,* and Francesco Andreini did the same in a series of publications under his name and that of his wife (see Tessari, 'Sotto il segno di Giano,' 3). On the literary production of comedians and the factors behind it, see Molinari and Guardenti, eds., *La Commedia dell'Arte,* iv–xvii, and Tessari, *La Commedia dell'Arte nel Seicento,* esp. 57–60, where he points out that actors tended to write all kinds of literature except the *scenari* they performed. See also Maria Galli Stampino, 'Publish or Perish: An Early Seventeenth-Century Paradox,' *RLA: Romance Languages Annual* 10 (1998), 373–9. On Francesco's composition of the dedicatory letter, see Taviani, 'Bella d'Asia,' 11–15.

21 Francesco Andreini, *Le Bravure di Capitano Spavento,* cited in Marotti and Romei, eds., *La commedia dell'arte e la società barocca,* vol. 2, 218. First published in 1607 (the *parte seconda* in 1624), *Le Bravure* were also adapted into French by J. de Fontery in 1608 as *Les Bravacheries du capitaine Spavente* ...; cf. Delia Gambelli, *Arlecchino a Parigi: Dall'Inferno alla corte del Re Sole* (Rome: Bulzoni, 1993), 200n8. On Francesco Andreini and his *Bravure,* see Tessari, 'Francesco Andreini e la maschera del Capitano. Una strategia dell sogno a occhi aperti,' introductory essay to his edition of *Le bravure del Capitano Spavento* (Pisa: Giardini, 1987), 8–44, and Marotti and Romei, eds., *La Commedia dell'Arte e la società barocca,* vol. 2, 209–302. In the opening letter to a collection of theatrical dialogues collected and published by Francesco under Isabella's name, he again cites his wife as an inspiration for his own literary activity, saying, 'I morti sono quelli, che fanno parlar' i vivi' ('It is the dead who cause the living to speak'). Francesco Andreini,

Fragmenti di alcune scritture della signora Isabella Andreini ... Raccolti da Francesco Andreini... (Venice: Combi, 1627).
22 F. Andreini, *Le bravure,* 216.
23 I. Andreini, *Lettere,* 136r.
24 Indeed, only the thought of their beloved children ('nostri teneri fanciulli e nostri communi figli') restrains him. F. Andreini, *Le bravure,* 215.
25 I. Andreini, *Lettere,* 137r.
26 Ibid., 137v.
27 Ibid.,154r.
28 Ibid.,155r–v.
29 Ibid., 155r.
30 Ibid.; F. Andreini, *Le bravure,* 234.
31 Laudatory compositions by Tasso and Marini accompany Andreini's *Lettere;* Chiabrera praised Isabella's mad scene from the *Pazzia* (cf. Marotti and Romei, *La professione del teatro,* 55). Andreini's poetry circulated in compendia like the *Gioie poetiche di madrigali del Sig. Hieronimo Casone, e d'altri celebri poeti de' nostri tempi ... raccolte da Gherardo Borgogni* (Pavia, 1593) and Frate Maurizio di Gregorio's *Rosario delle stampe di tutti i poeti e le poetesse* (Naples, 1614).
32 F. Andreini, *Le bravure,* Ragionamento IV, 235.
33 On the literary 'partnership' between Lando and Gonzaga, see chapter 3 in this volume.
34 F. Andreini, *Le bravure,* 216.
35 On the Petrarchan elements of Andreini's work, see Rosalind Kerr, 'Isabella Andreini, Comica Gelosa 1562–1604: Petrarchism for the Theatre Public,' *Quaderni d'Italianistica* 27, no. 2 (2006), 71–92.
36 On the Accademia degli Intenti see Michele Maylender, *Storia delle accademie d'Italia* (Bologna: A. Forni, 1926–30), s.v. 'Intenti' and 'Affidati.' Isabella became a member of the Intenti in 1601.
37 See the description in Bartoli of the 'mensa fattale dall'Eminentissimo Cardinale Cinzio Aldobrandini gran Mecenante de' virtuosi, dove erano per commensali sei Cardinali ... Tasso ... ed altri Poeti chiarissimi, fra quali in bella gara scrivendo, e improvvisando Sonetti l'Andreini spiritosamente dopo il gran Torquato ne riportò il primo vanto' (*Notizie istoriche,* 32). On the commemorative medal, see Tessari, 'Sotto il segno di Giano,' 18–20. See also Taviani, 'Bella d'Asia,' 26–40, on both subjects.
38 Taviani contrasts Isabella's desire to be part of the *mondo accademico* via publications in keeping with its tastes with her husband's more ambivalent approach to authorship (which according to Taviani derived from a desire to preserve his memory as an actor, not as a writer; cf. *La Commedia dell'Arte e la società barocca,* I, 166, 209).

39 Single letters composed by Isabella appeared in other collections, including one that was dedicated to her, the *Secondo libro di lettere dedicatorie di diversi all'Ill. Et compitissima signora la Sig. Isabella Andreini, comica gelosa et acad. Intenta* (Bergamo: Comin Ventura, 1602); cf. Basso, *La genre épistolaire en langue italienne*, 378.
40 Francesca de' Angelis, *La divina Isabella* (Florence: Sansoni, 1991), 104.
41 Such an approach is suggested by Giovanni Malquori Fondi (cf. 'De la "lettre-canevas" à la "pièce de cabinet": les *Lettere d'Isabella Andreini*, tràduites par Francois de Grenaille,' in *Contacts culturels et échanges linguistiques au XVIIe siècle en France: actes du 3e Colloque du Centre international de rencotres sur le XVIIe siècle, Université de Fribourg (Suisse) 1996* (Paris: Papers on French Seventeenth-Century Literature, 1997), 132.
42 Henke, *Performance and Literature*, 43–4. See also Adolfo Bartoli, *Scenari inediti della Commedia dell'Arte* (Padua, 1782; facsimile edition Bologna: Arnaldo Forni, 1978), LXXVII.
43 Bottarga's manuscript (contained at the Biblioteca Teatrale del Bucarda di Roma) includes a variety of compositions including poems, prologues, and dialogues that 'probably represented [his] actual stage repertoire' (cf. Henke, *Performance and Literature*, 44). Henke also points to Domenico Bruni's undated manuscript 'Dialoghi scenici' as an example of a *generico* closely tied to stage performance. It contains material catalogued under various subject headings such as 'amorous war,' 'disdain placated,' and so on, 'which could furnish the actress verbal material for codified scenes appropriate to the aulic and Petrarchan decorum of her character' (ibid., 45; such titles are similar to the headings of Isabella's *Lettere*). In Henke's view, the 'dearth of extant mansuscript *generici*,' which has led some to suggest they were a mental tool not committed to paper, can be ascribed to fact that they circulated among actors rather than being addressed to figures of higher social status, and were not preserved (ibid., 45).
44 I. Andreini, *Fragmenti*, 135.
45 I. Andreini, *Lettere*, 48v. Emphasis added.
46 I. Andreini, *Fragmenti*, 137.
47 I. Andreini, *Lettere*, 49v–50r. Emphasis added.
48 Bruni, *Prologhi*, 'La matina la Signora mi chiama: "Olà, Ricciolina, portami la innamorata *Fiametta* che voglio studiare." Pantalone mi dimanda le *Lettere* del Calmo. Il Capitano le *Bravure* del Capitan Spavento. Il Zanni le *Astuzie* di Bertoldo ... Graziano le *Sentenze* dell'Erborenze ... Franceschina vuole la *Celestina* per imparare di far la ruffiana. Lo innamorato vuol l'opere di Platone ...' ('In the morning the Prima Donna calls me, "Oh Ricciolina, bring me Boccaccio's *Fiammetta*, which I want to study."

Pantalone asks me for Calmo's letters, the Capitano for *Le Bravure di Capitano Spavento,* the Zanni for the *Astuzie di Bertoldo* ... Graziano for the *Sentenze dell'Eborenze* ... Franceschina wants the *Celestina* to help her play the bawd, and the Lover calls for Plato's works'), qtd. in Marotti and Romei, eds., *La Commedia dell'Arte e la società barocca,* Book II, 388–9, translated in Henke, *Performance and Literature,* 46–7.

49 Andrea Calmo, *Lettere,* ed. Vittorio Rossi (Turin: Ermanno Loescher, 1888). See Henke, *Performance and Literature,* 47. As Lea notes, the name 'Pantalone' does not occur in Calmo's letters, but '[t]he type of Pantalone is there all but the name in Calmo's old men, Coccolin, Collophonio, Melindo, and Zurlotto ... We do not want a better Magnifico' (*Italian Popular Comedy,* 240). On the relationship between Calmo's literary and theatrical activity, see Piermarco Vescovo, *Da Ruzante a Calmo. Tra 'signore comedie' e 'onorandissime stampe'* (Padua: Editrice Antenore, 1996). Henke points out the curious circularity of the use of the *Bravure* by the actor portraying the Captain, noting that here 'we have an actor ... recirculating into performance a literary redaction of original stage material' (Henke, *Performance and Literature,* 47).

50 I. Andreini, *Lettere,* 12 r–v; cf. Lando, *Quesiti amorosi* (Venice: Giolito, 1552), 7–8.

51 I. Andreini, *Lettere,* 19r.

52 See note 49 above. A similar but still more comic epistolary representation of this figure can be found in the *Lettere amorose* of Margherita Costa (Venice: N.p., 1639), 210–14, 226–30, published after (and influenced by) those of Andreini. On Costa, see pages 181–2 of this chapter.

53 Hieronimo Garimberto, *Concetti di Hieronimo Garimberto, et di più autori raccolti da lui, per scrivere familiarmente* (Rome: Vincenzo Valgrisi, 1551), dedicatory letter; on Gonzaga's use of this text see chapter 3, section one, 'Agency and Authorship.'

54 Pietro Bembo's forays into the literary explication of love and its effects in the *Asolani* (Venice, 1505) and in the *Lettere giovenili et amorose di M. Pietro Bembo et altri eccelenti autori* (Venice, 1553) as well as in his own *epistolario* (*Lettere,* Venice, 1552), were influential for the development of this epistolary subgenre. Important contributions to it included Anton Francesco Doni, *Pistolotti amorosi* (Venice, 1552); Girolamo Parabosco, *Libro primo delle lettere amorose* (Venice, 1581); the *Lettere amorose di Madonna Celia* (1562); *Lettere amorose del Mag. M. Alvise Pasqualigo libri III, ne' quali sotto maravigliosi concetti si contengono tutti gli accidenti d'amore* (Venice, D. Farni, 1581) and numerous other examples. For a partial analysis of Parabosco's *Lettere amorose* in particular, see Martha Feldman,

City Culture and the Madrigal (Berkeley: University of California Press, 1995), 55–8.

55 *Delle lettere amorose di diversi huomini illustri ... Nelle quali si leggono nobilissimi, et leggiadri concetti, in tutte le materie occorrenti ne' casi d'Amore* (Venice: Appresso gli Eredi del Bonelli, 1574), 'Ai Lettori.' '...Qual'è quell'ingegno accorto,' Sansovino asks in the *Letter to Readers*, 'che non si possa servire delle presenti letter, in cose, et di stato, et di negocij, facendone estratti di concetti, di voci, di periodi, et di mille altri ornamenti ...?' ('Who is that brilliant mind that cannot make use of these letters to express emotion and take action, extracting from them ideas, terms, phrases, and a thousand other ornaments?')

56 Andrea Zenophonte da Ugubio, *Formulario nuovo da dittar lettere amorose messive et responsive* (Venice: Francesco Bindoni and Mapheo Pasini, 1544), C1v. Another letter writer laments, '... io piango, mi lamento, ploro, consumo, struggo, e moro ...' ('... I weep, I despair, I beg, I burn, I struggle, and I die ...'), ibid., C3.

57 The link between the woman writer and the love letter was cemented in the *Heroides* and renewed in Boccaccio's *Fiammetta*. The *Heroides* were first translated into Italian in octave form by Domenico da Monticello in 1508 and reappeared in many other forms throughout the sixteenth and seventeenth centuries; see Basso, *Le genre épistolaire*, 60–5, for a complete publishing history.

58 For the attribution of Celia's letters to Gerolamo Parabosco, see H.M. Adams, *Catalogue of Books printed on the Continent of Europe 1501–1600*, vol. 1 (Cambridge: Cambridge Libraries, 1967).

59 The demurral that the letters are not meant as models is a gendered one. As a woman, the author would not presume to usurp the province of male writers: '... s'alcuno dicesse, che fu sempre intenzione di chi mandò lettere alle stampe d'insegnar il vero modo di scriverle, sappia quell tale, ch'io non ebbi mai cosi temerario pensiero, sapendo, ch'è solamente dato a gli uomini più intendenti l'avere, e 'l conseguir simil fine' ('if anyone were to say that one who publishes letters means to teach the proper way to write them, they should know that my intent was never so audacious, since I am aware that it is the province of men more learned than I to have and execute such a goal'), I. Andreini, *Lettere*, dedicatory letter.

60 Günsberg, for example, notes the common Renaissance phenomenon of theatrical ventriloquism, in which '... a female character who is never seen or heard to be the subject of an action, but is always its object, and who is talked about rather than speaking for herself, is relentlessly marginalized in terms of audience perception' (*Gender and the Italian Stage*, 48).

61 I. Andreini, *Lettere*, 147r–151r.
62 The accusation of the male lover in Andreini's text that women are inordinately susceptible to rhetoric over sentiment, for example, quoted above, is reversed in Margherita Costa's *Lettere amorose della Signora Margherita Costa, Romana* (Venice: N.p., 1639), where it is the female lover who warns, in a more typical formulation, against artificial declarations of passion, 'se poi voglio credere, che lo facciate per scherzo ... abborrisco la vostra simulazione' ('if I must think that you [speak of love] as an exercise ... I detest your simulation') (28).
63 I. Andreini, *Lettere*, 149r–v.
64 Ibid, 149v.
65 Matraini's letters, which I do not focus on in this study, include formal humanist compositions on subjects such as friendship, consolation, and the debate over arms versus letters. See the modern edition by Giovanni Rabitti, *Chiara Matraini Rime e Lettere* (Bologna: Commissione per i Testi di Lingua, 1989). On humanistic elements in Veronica Franco's *Lettere familiari* (1580), see chapter 4 of this volume.
66 I. Andreini, *Lettere*, 138r.
67 Ibid., 140v–141r.
68 Cf. I. Andreini, *Rime*, Egloga I, likening the *vita pastorale* to the Golden Age, far from the court and its problems; and F. Andreini, *Ragionamenti*, ragionamento 14.
69 I. Andreini, *Lettere*, 121 r–v.
70 Ibid., 12v–13v and 89v–90v. Letters of consolation like this one are found in other letterbooks, such as that of Lucrezia Gonzaga, as well as in epistolary manuals like Stefano Guazzo's *Lettere* (Venice: Barezzo Barezzi, 1606) and Battista Ceci's *Compendio d'avertimenti di ben parlare volgare* (Venice: N.p., 1618). Garimberto's *Concetti* contains similar sentiments that can be inserted into letters (36v).
71 MacNeil, *Music and Woman*, 51–2.
72 On the satyr trope and sexual violence in the pastoral, see my 'La Castità Conquistata: The Function of the Satyr in Pastoral Drama,' *Romance Languages Annual*, 9 (1997), 312–21.
73 As the dedicatory letter states, Andreini has set aside the traditional tools of women's work – 'ago, conocchia, e arcolaio' ('needle, wool-winder, and distaff') – to devote herself fully and nobly to the pursuit of learning. I. Andreini, *Lettere*, dedicatory letter.
74 Ibid., 'Di quanto pregio sia l'Onore' ('On the Value of Honour'), 1r–2r.
75 Ibid., 1v.
76 Ibid.

77 Ibid. 135v–137v, 154v–155r.
78 Ibid., 30v–33v.
79 Ibid., 31v.
80 Ibid., 33v–34r.
81 Cf. MacNeil, *Music and Women*, 89.
82 F. Andreini, *Ragionamenti*, Ragionamento 5, 35r–42v.
83 For the editions of this text, reprinted a number of times, see Basso, *Le genre épistolaire*, 288–9.
84 I. Andreini, 'Del Nascimento della Donna,' *Lettere*, 18v–20r.
85 Giovanni Boccaccio, *On Famous Women*, ed. and trans. Virginia Brown (Cambridge, MA: Harvard University Press, 2001). On the 'women worthies' who populate the *Lettere di molte valorose donne* (and their derivation from a Latin humanist repertory), see chapter 2 in this volume.
86 Cf. Benedetto Croce, *Nuovi saggi sulla letteratura italiana del Seicento* (Bari: N.p., 1968), 160, 'La società del Seicento è senza alito di muliebrità.'
87 See Taviani, *La Commedia dell'Arte e la società barocca*, I, 209. Isabella and Francesco's son Giovanni Battista Andreini became an actor and playwright who formed the *Fedeli* troupe; both his first and second wives were actresses. On G.B. Andreini and his works see, Maurizio Rebaudengo, *Giovan Battista Andreini, tra poetica e drammaturgia* (Turin: Rosenberg and Sellier, 1994).
88 Costa, *Lettere amorose*. Most sources concur that Costa was a courtesan, although Paolo Mandosio defended her in his *Bibliotheca Romana* (Rome: Typis ac sumptibus Ignatij de Lazzaris, 1692) 26–8, arguing that she was merely the target of hostile slander. The debate is summarized in C. Arlía, 'Un bandito e una cortigiana letterati,' *Il bibliofilo* Anno II agosto-settembre, nos. 8–9 (1881), 164–6. Little is known about Costa and her family, except that her sister was likely the singer Anna Francesca Costa and her brother may have been in the service of the Barberini family; see S. Ferrone, 'Margherita Costa, *Li buffoni*,' in *Commedie dell'Arte*, vol. 2, 235. Interestingly, Costa can be linked to Andreini through Isabella's son G.B. Andreini, with whom Costa participated in an operatic competition while in France in 1646; see Ferrone, 'Margherita Costa,' 237–8. On Costa's life and works see the important article by D. Bianchi in three installments, 'Una cortegiana rimatrice del Seicento: Margherita Costa,' *Rassegna critica della letteratura italiana* 29 (1924), 1–31 and 187–203, and *Rassegna critica della letteratura italiana* 30 (1925), 158–211. See also M. Capucci, 'Margherita Costa,' in *Dizionario biografico degli italiani*, vol. 30 (Rome: Istituto della enciclopedia italiana, 1960-), 234; F.S. Quadrio, *Della storia e della ragione d'ognia poesia* (Milan: N.p., 1731); and L. Allacci, *Drammaturgia, accresciuta e*

continuata fino all'ano 1754 (Venice: Pasquali, 1755), 62, 150, 339, 363. More recent contributions to the study of Costa are by Teresa Megale, 'La commedia decifrata: Metamorfosi e rispechhiamenti in *Li Buffoni* di Margherita Costa,' *Il Castello di Elsinore* 2 (1988), 64–76, and Teresa Megale, 'Una cantratrice, un buffone, una commedia del Seicento: "Li Buffoni" di Margherita Costa' (PhD diss., University of Florence, 1987–8). Virginia Cox devotes several pages to Costa in *Women's Writing in Italy 1400–1650* (Baltimore: Johns Hopkins University Press, 2008), 212–16.

89 On Costa's use of these figures in her work – and their correspondence to people actually in attendance at the Medici court during her years in Florence – see Megale, 'La commedia decifrata' and Megale, 'Il mestiere di buffone tra Cinque e Seicento,' introduction to Teresa Megale, *Il Tedeschino, overo Difesa dell'arte del cavalier del piacere, Con l'epistolario e altri documenti*, ed. B. Ricci (Florence: Le Lettere, 2003), 7–59.

90 There can be no beauty without imperfection, writes her lover (described as *l'amante monco,* the maimed lover). Cf. Costa, *Lettere amorose,* 252, '[la natura] non si diede mai, che i suoi parti perfezzionati partorisse: ne' v'è bellezza così stimabile, che di qualche bruteza non richieda il biasimo' ('Nature never made her children perfect: there is no beauty so great that it is devoid of some flaw'). The noseless woman is also the figure of syphilis: in Costa's *Lo stipo* (Venice: N.p., 1639), 209, she cautions other women to avoid her fate, which she links to an injudicious faith in the power of the love letter. Other 'imperfect' figures in Costa's letters include lovers marred by freckles, pitted skin, crossed eyes, blindness, and various other afflictions.

91 Costa, *Lo stipo,* 207, 'A dio Zerbini a Dio, a Dio Narcisi / Ganimedi io vi lascio, e von voi cedo / L'opre del Zerbinar tra dolci risi' ('Farewell dandies, farewell Narcissi / I bid you farewell, Ganimedes, and to you I leave / the dandy's work among sweet laughter'). Cf. Costa, *Lettere amorose,* 257.

92 Costa, *Lettere amorose,* 257.

6 The Pen for the Sword

1 Tarabotti was the author of at least six works including the *Lettere,* five of which have been published in modern editions. See *L''Inferno monacale,' di Arcangela Tarabotti*, ed. Francesca Medioli (Turin: Rosenberg and Sellier, 1990); *La semplicità ingannata*, ed. Simona Bortot (Venice: Il Poligrafo, 2007); *Paternal Tyranny*, ed. Letizia Panizza (Chicago: University of Chicago Press, 2004); *Satira e Antisatira*, ed. Elissa Weaver (Rome: Salerno, 1998); *Che le*

donne siano della spezie degli uomini: Difesa della donna (1651), ed. Letizia Panizza (London: Institute of Romance Studies, 1994); also translated in Theresa M. Kenney, *'Women Are Not Human': An Anonymous Treatise and Responses* (New York: Crossroad Publishing Company, 1998); *Lettere familiari e di complimento*, ed. Meredith Ray and Lynn Westwater (Turin: Rosenberg and Sellier, 2005); translation by Ray and Westwater forthcoming in the series The Other Voice in Early Modern Europe (Toronto: Centre for Renaissance and Reformation Studies). An edition of Tarabotti's *Paradiso monacale* is planned by Ray and Westwater. Early studies on Tarabotti's life and work are Giuseppe Portigliotti, *Penombre claustrali* (Milan: Fratelli Treves Editori, 1930), and Emilio Zanette, *Suor Arcangela monaca del Seicento veneziano* (Rome–Venice: Istituto per la Collaborazione Culturale, 1960) – which, although undermined by its paternalism, remains essential for its rich archival findings. In recent years there has been renewed interest in Tarabotti, particularly on the part of scholars who have focused on the protofeminist and political aspects of her work. See Ginevra Conti Odorisio, *Donna e società nel Seicento* (Rome: Bulzoni, 1979); Medioli, *L"Inferno monacale'*; and the essays collected in Elissa Weaver, ed., *Arcangela Tarabotti: A Literary Nun in Baroque Venice* (Ravenna: Longo, 2006).

2 A wave of important recent scholarship has focused increasingly on the ways in which nuns were able to interact with and contribute to the secular community despite their cloistered status, through family networks, brokerage activities, the production of various goods and services, and through music and performance: see, for example, Silvia Evangelisti, *Nuns: A History of Convent Life 1450–1700* (Oxford: Oxford University Press, 2007); Gabriella Zarri and Gianna Pomata, eds., *I monasteri femminili come centri di cultura fra rinascimento e barocco* (Rome: Edizioni di Storia e Letteratura, 2005); Kate Lowe, *Nuns' Chronicles and Convent Culture in Renaissance and Counter-Reformation Italy* (Cambridge: Cambridge University Press, 2003); Elissa Weaver, *Convent Theater in Early Modern Italy: Spiritual Fun and Learning for Women* (Cambridge: Cambridge University Press, 2002); R. Kendrick, *Celestial Sirens: Nuns and Their Music in Early Modern Milan* (Oxford: Clarendon Press, 1996). Sharon Strocchia's forthcoming *Nuns and Nunneries in Renaissance Florence* (Baltimore: Johns Hopkins University Press, 2009), promises to offer much new information in this regard. Tarabotti was likewise active in the life of her city in many ways, for example in her brokerage of the lace produced by the nuns of Sant'Anna; see my 'Letters and Lace: Arcangela Tarabotti and Convent Culture in Seicento Venice,' in *Early Modern Women and Transnational Communities of Letters*, ed. J. Campbell and A. Larsen (Aldershot, UK: Ashgate, 2009, in press). Nonetheless, in her

literary activity Tarabotti is unique in her organized protofeminist argument which originates from within the cloister.
3 Earlier versions of portions of this chapter appear in Meredith Kennedy Ray, 'Letters from the Cloister: Defending the Literary Self in Arcangela Tarabotti's *Lettere familiari e di complimento,*' *Italica* 81, no. 1 (2004), 24–42, and Meredith Kennedy Ray, 'Making the Private Public: Arcangela Tarabotti's *Lettere familiari,*' in *Arcangela Tarabotti,* ed. Weaver, 173–89.
4 By the mid-seventeenth century, there were about 2,500 cloistered nuns in Venice's thirty-some convents, a large proportion considering the size of the patriciate from which many of them came: about 4,000; cf. Francesca Medioli, 'Monache e monacazioni nel Seicento,' in G. Zarri, F. Medioli, and P. Chiappa, 'De monialibus,' *Rivista di storia e letteratura religiosa* 33, no. 3 (1997), 677–8. Historian Jutta Sperling estimates the number of nuns in Venice at 2,905 in 1642, with about 69 per cent of these coming from patrician families; according to Sperling's calculations, in 1642 more than 80 per cent of patrician girls were nuns; from *Convents and the Body Politic in Late Renaissance Venice* (Chicago: University of Chicago Press, 1999), 28, table 2. On coerced monachization, see also Francesca Medioli, 'The Dimensions of the Cloister: Enclosure, Constraint, and Protection in Seventeenth Century Italy,' in *Time, Space, and Women's Lives in Early Modern Italy,* ed. Anne Jacobson Schutte, Thomas Kuehn, and Silvana Seidel Menchi (Kirksville, MO: Truman State University Press, 2001), 165–80, and Francesca Medioli, 'Monacazioni forzate: Donne ribelle al proprio destino,' in *Clio: Trimestral di studi storici* 30 (1994), 431–54; Mary Laven, *Virgins of Venice: Broken Vows and Cloistered Lives in the Renaissance Convent* (New York: Penguin, 2002), and Mary Laven, 'Cast Out and Shut In: The Experience of Nuns in Counter-Reformation Venice,' in *At the Margins: Minority Groups in Premodern Italy,* ed. Stephen J. Milner (Mineapolis: University of Minnesota Press, 2005), 72–93; Giovanna Paolin, *Lo spazio del silenzio: Monacazioni forzate, clausura e proposte di vita religiosa femminile nell'età moderna* (Pordenone: Biblioteca dell'Immagine, 1996), and Giovanna Paolin, 'Monache e donne nel Friuli del Cinquecento,' in *Società e cultura del Cinquecento nel Friuli occidentale. Studi,* ed. Andrea del Col (Pordenone: Edizioni della Provincia di Pordenone, 1984), 201–28; Romano Canosa, *Il velo e il cappuccio: monacazioni forzate e sessualità nei conventi femminili in Italia tra Quattrocento e Settecento* (Rome: Sapere, 2000).
5 See Anthony Molho, *Marriage Alliance in Late Medieval Florence* (Cambridge: Cambridge University Press, 1994), 308; and Stanley Chojnacki, 'Daughters and Oligarchs: Gender and the Early Renaissance State,' in *Gender and Society in Early Renaissance Italy,* ed. Judith Brown and Robert C. Davis

(London: Longman 1998), 70. By this period, the *dote spirituale,* or dowry, now required by convents was about 1,000 ducats for all convents and was fixed by the *Pregadì,* the Venetian senate. This amount was still far less than the average dowry for marriage, which, depending on the bride's social class, ranged from eight to forty times more (cf. Medioli, 'De monialibus,' 688). In *Convents and the Body Politic in Late Renaissance Venice,* Sperling posits a complementary rather than causal relationship between inflated dowries and high rates of 'coerced monachizations,' and argues that the increasing numbers of nuns had less to do with the escalation of dowries than with the patriciate's reluctance to surrender its grip on exclusivity: that is, faced with a diminishing pool of potential grooms, patrician families preferred the convent to a downwardly-mobile marriage for their daughters. Sperling's argument, however, is meant to explain the high levels of monachization for patrician girls. Tarabotti was not of a patrician family and her consignment to the convent may have stemmed from other, perhaps more specifically economic factors.

6 Tarabotti herself astutely makes this connection in several of her works: in the *Inferno monacale,* she pleads with families to recognize the base economic and political factors behind the cloistering of women without religious vocations; see *'L''Inferno monacale,'* 93, and *La semplicità ingannata* (Leida: Sambix [i.e., J. Elzevier], 1654), 138. For a discussion of the 'ideologia cittadina' behind the practice of *monacazione forzata,* or coerced monachization, see Zarri, 'Monasteri femminili e città (secoli xvxviii),' in *Storia d'Italia. Annali 9. La chiesa e il potere politico,* ed. G. Chittolini and G. Miccoli (Turin: Einaudi, 1986), 359–429.

7 See Giuseppe Alberigo, Giuseppe L. Dossetti, Perikle P. Joannou, Claudio Leonardo, and Paolo Prodi, eds., *Conciliorum Oecumenicorum Decreta* (Bologna: Istituto per le scienze religiose di Bologna, 1973).

8 Zarri, 'De monialibus,' 660–1. Historian Mario Rosa echoes this view in his assertion that seventeenth-century convent reform placed more emphasis on chastity than on poverty or obedience, making convents places for the preservation of virtue rather than the fostering of sanctity; see 'La religiosa,' in *L'uomo barocco,* ed. Rosario Villari (Bari: Laterza, 1991), 226.

9 Zarri, ibid., 661, '... il nesso tra pudicizia, come virtú prettamente femminile, e ritiratezza, come mezzo per conservarla, era elemento centrale della cultura del tempo e non si riferiva esclusivamente alla condizione monastica.'

10 On convent architecture, see Anne Jacobson Schutte, 'The Permeable Cloister?' in *Arcangela Tarabotti,* ed. Weaver, 19–33; Helen Hills, *Invisible City: The Architecture of Devotion in Seventeenth Century Neapolitan Convents*

(Oxford: Oxford University Press, 2004); Marilynn Dunn, 'Spaces Shaped for Spiritual Perfection' in *Architecture and the Politics of Gender*, ed. Helen Hills (Aldershot, UK: Ashgate, 2003), 151–76; Gabriella Zarri, *Recinti: Donne, clausura e matrimonio nella prima eta moderna* (Bologna: Il Mulino, 2000), esp. 117–340; and Zarri, 'Monasteri femminili e città,' 411–12; and for the case of late medieval English nunneries, Roberta Gilchrist, *Gender and Material Culture: The Archaeology of Religious Women* (London: Routledge, 1994).

11 Sperling, *Convents and the Body Politic*, 134.

12 Two of Tarabotti's sisters, Lorenzina and Innocenza Elisabetta, married while the other sisters remained unmarried and stayed at home. Tarabotti refers to herself as 'zoppa' (lame) in her *Lettere*, and implies that she inherited the condition from her father (*Lettere*, 110; all references to Tarabotti's *Lettere* are to page numbers in the modern edition by Ray and Westwater). *Educande*, sometimes referred to as 'putte a spese,' were the young girls who boarded at most convents and received a rudimentary education from the nuns. Tarabotti writes that she entered Sant'Anna at age eleven, which would have been in 1615 (cf. *Lettere*, 158). Zanette's research, however, suggests that she entered in 1617 (*Suor Arcangela*, 27); other scholars concur (see, for example, Medioli, L'"*Inferno monacale*,' 113).

13 While all *educande* received basic instruction in reading and writing so that they could read the breviary and other religious materials and help with the daily running of the convent, they did not receive any systematic or sustained education, a problem Tarabotti repeatedly laments in her works, including her *Lettere*, where she refers to herself as 'una donna a cui manca il lume dell'arte e dello studio necessario a chi professa belle lettere' ('a woman who lacks the illumination of the art and the study necessary to one who is lettered'), *Lettere*, 50; see also ibid., 124.

14 As Conti Odorisio notes, 'L'aspetto piú singolare della scrittrice veneziana è quello di riuscire a fare della sua vicenda autobiografica l'emblema della situazione generale femminile e cogliere i nessi che la legano alla politica' (*Donna e società*, 90).

15 *La semplicità ingannata*, published in Leyden in 1654 by 'Sambix' (actually Jean and Daniel Elzevier). The work was placed on the Index of Forbidden Books in 1660. For a description of the censured points in this text, see Natalia Costa-Zalessow, 'Tarabotti's *La Semplicità ingannata* and its Twentieth-Century Interpreters, with Unpublished Documents Regarding Its Condemnation to the *Index*,' *Italica* 78, no. 3 (2001), 314–25, which reproduces, in translation, some of the documents from the deliberations.

16 Venice: Guglielmo Oddoni, 1643. The date on the frontispiece, MDCLXIII, is an error for MDCXLIII.

17 In the *Semplicità ingannata*, for example, Tarabotti clarifies, 'Biasimo la monacata a forza, non quelle che chiamate dalle voci dello Santo Spirito si ritirano volontariamente a servir Dio ne' monasteri' ('I speak against she who is enclosed by force, not against those who, called by the voices of the Holy Spirit, willingly withdraw to serve God in the convents'; 'Al lettore,' *La simplicità ingannata*, ed. Bortot, 175, my translation).

18 Zanette argues convincingly that Tarabotti and her publisher were in collusion here, with Oddoni publicizing these controversial works while Tarabotti claimed in the text of the *Paradiso* that two manuscripts had been stolen from her, thus distancing herself, as authors often did, from the proposed publication of the works (*Suor Arcangela*, 120).

19 Here I am in agreement with Medioli, *L'"Inferno monacale,"* 155–61, and Zanette, *Suor Arcangela*, 241. Conti Odoriso writes that the traditional interpretation of the *Paradiso* as an 'opera mistica' or the product of the writer's conversion fails to take into account the work's content or the dates of its composition and publication early in Tarabotti's literary career (*Donna e società*, 98–9).

20 Buoninsegni read his satire to an academy audience in Siena in 1632; it was later published in Venice in 1638 with the title *Contro 'l lusso donnesco satira menippea* (the modern edition is edited by Weaver; see note 1 above).

21 See Weaver, *Satira e Antisatira*, introduction and 20–2.

22 On this subject, see Emilia Biga, *Una polemica antifemminista del '600. 'La Maschera scoperta' di Angelico Aprosio* (Ventimiglia: Civica Biblioteca Aprosiana, 1989). The writer Girolamo Brusoni, another one-time supporter of Tarabotti, also composed a response to the *Antisatira*; it too went unpublished (see Tarabotti's *Lettere*, 70, no. 2 and no. 80).

23 There are indications that she may have written others, but these have never been located. Tarabotti makes reference in the *Antisatira* to a work entitled *Purgatorio delle malmaritate*, which would have constituted the middle installment of her 'trilogy' that included the *Inferno monacale* and the *Paradiso monacale* (see *Satira e Antisatira*, 59), and in a letter to Betta Polani she mentions several devotional works: *La via lastricata per andare al cielo, La contemplazione dell'anima amante,* and *La luce monacale* (*Lettere*, 47).

24 *Che le donne non siano della spetie degli huomini. Discorso piavevole, tradotto da Horatio Plata Romano* (1647), ed. Letizia Panizza (London: Institute of Romance Studies, 1994). Zanette holds that the translator was Giovan Francesco Loredano, Tarabotti's friend and the founder of Venice's *Accademia degli Incogniti* (Zanette, *Suor Arcangela*, 387–406), while Giorgio Spini, who more cautiously suggests that the translator was a member of the *Accademia degli Incogniti*, does not name Loredano specifically; see

310 Notes to pages 188–9

Ricerca dei libertini. La teoria delle religioni nel Seicento italiano (Florence: La Nuova Italia, 1983), 221–2. The translation caused a huge furor in Venice, leading to the trial and imprisonment of the printer Valvasense, suspected of having published it, and the placing of the work on the Index of Forbidden Books in 1651. For a reading of Acidalius' text, see Manfred P. Fleischer, '"Are Women Human?" The Debate of 1595 between Valens Acidalius and Simon Gediccus,' *Sixteenth Century Journal* 12, no. 2 (Summer 1981), 107–20.

25 See Panizza, *Che le donne siano*, introduction, vii. Not only was Tarabotti the only woman to have entered this particular dispute about women's lack of a human soul, but 'it was exceptional ... for a woman in Counter-Reformation Italy to be interpreting Scripture and pitting her theological and philosophical opinions against men's in the public press.' The texts of the debate, excluding the Italian translation, are published in English by Kenney, *'Women Are Not Human'* (see note 1 above).

26 A prolific writer of both religious and profane works, Loredano (1606–61) held a number of important positions within the Venetian Republic. The *Accademia degli Incogniti* which he co-founded dates to about 1631 (in an earlier incarnation it was known as the *Accademia Loredana*) and was one of the most well known of the numerous Venetian academies in this period. On the *Incogniti*, see Mario Infelise, 'Books and Politics in Arcangela Tarabotti's Venice,' in *Arcangela Tarabotti*, ed. Weaver, 57–72; first published in Italian as 'Libri e politica nella Venezia di Arcangela Tarabotti,' *Annali di storia moderna e contemporanea* 8 (2002), 31–45; in the same volume, see also Daria Perocco, 'Prose Production in Venice in the Early Seicento,' 73–87. See also Spini, *Ricerca dei libertini*.

27 Pighetti, a lawyer and writer from Bergamo and a member of the *Accademia degli Incogniti*, was married to Tarabotti's sister Lorenzina. It was probably through Pighetti that Tarabotti first established ties to this Academy. Pona (1594–1660), a Veronese doctor, was a member of the *Incogniti* and the author of *La lucerna*, which was placed on the Index of Forbidden Books; Dandolo (1613–61) was also an *Incognito*. Bissari (1595–1662), a Vicentine writer, was the founder in 1649 of the *Accademia dei Rifioriti* in Vicenza as well as a member of the *Incogniti*; while Aprosio (1607–81) was a friar of the order of Augustinian Hermits who spent time in Genoa, Siena, Pisa, and Venice. A member of the *Incogniti*, as well as of several other literary academies, Aprosio published a number of works under a variety of pseudonyms; Portigliotti records Belloni's description of Aprosio in *Il Seicento* as a 'bizzaro tipo di grafomane ... davvero ... figlio del suo secolo, perché del suo secolo ebbe tutta la stravaganza, la smania

dell'inusato, il gusto barocco, l'eccessiva fecondità letteraria, il nessun senso di misure ...' (cited in Portigliotti, *Penombre*, 280). For a detailed examination of Aprosio and his work, see Biga, *Una polemica antifemminista*.
28 Jules Mazarin (Giulio Mazarino; 1602–61), a French cardinal of Italian birth, succeeded Richelieu as prime minister in 1642 and served the Queen Regent Anne of Austria after the death of Louis XIII. In 1642, Mazarin founded a library (known today as the Bibliothèque Mazarine), for which his librarian, Gabriel Naudé – author of a treatise on establishing libraries, *Advis pour dresser une bibliothèque* (Paris: Liseux Editeur, 1876) – sought books during a sojourn in Italy.
29 Issued by Cardinal Cornelius Patriarch, the decree warns that in order to protect the honour and sanctity of Venice's convents,

> ... commettiamo in virtú di santa obedienza a tutte le abbadesse, priore, et superiore che sono et che saranno pro tempore delli monasteri di monache a noi soggetti, che né per loro stesse, né per altre monache permettino in modo alcuno qualsivoglia visita o colloquio etiandio per poco spatio di tempo, e sotto qualsisia imaginabil pretesto, ne' parlatori o altro luogo, overo pratica et intelligenza, o per messi, *o per lettere*, o per via di presenti, o in altra maniera con persone straniere, o forestiere, ancorché fossero personaggi grandi cosí ecclesiastici come secolari di qualsisia grado, qualità, e stato, e sotto che colore esser si voglia, *se non saranno parenti in primo o secondo grado di esse monache, o se non vi sarà la nostra licenza speciale in scritto,* sottoscritta da noi medesimi, et sigillata col nostro proprio sigillo, veduta, et approvata dalla superiora ...

> ... in the name of holy obedience we command all current and future abbesses, prioresses, and superiors of the convents under our jurisdiction that they in no way permit any visit or interview, even of brief duration, or for any possible reason, in the parlors or anywhere else, nor any form of discourse or exchange via messengers, *via letters*, or in person, or in any other manner with strangers or outsiders, even high-ranking Church officials or secular personages, *if they are not relatives in the first or second degree of these nuns, or if they do not have our special permission in writing,* undersigned by ourselves, and sealed with our own seal, witnessed and approved by the mother superior ...

(Archivio Patriarcale, Venezia, Sezione Antica, Monalium 7, Order of Cardinal Cornelius Patriarch; my translation and italics; I have modernized punctuation and dissolved abbreviations for clarity.)

30 Ibid., my translation:

> ... sotto pena contravenendo a quest'ordine in qualsivoglia parte alle abbadesse, priore, e superiore sudette di restare immediatemente prive del loro carico, incapaci et inhabili per sempre di poterne havere altri; at alle monache di dover star per sei mesi almeno continuati in una cella senza poter mai uscire, et di piú di esser immediatemente prive per tre anni, oltre li detti sei mesi, di voce attiva e passiva, de' gradi, carichi et preeminenze che havessero o potessero pretendere di qualsivoglia sorte, e di poter accostar<s>i a' parlatori, porte, ruode, et altri luoghi etiandio per occasione de' loro propri congionti, et sotto altre pene maggiori ...

> ... under pain of violating this order in any respect, the aforementioned abbesses, prioresses, and superiors are to be immediately removed from their position, nor permitted to hold any other position in the future; and the nuns are to be confined to their cells for six months without leaving, and what's more they are to lose, for three years, in addition to the six months, their active and passive voice, their status and position of any kind, and the privilege of going to the parlor, the doors, the wheel, or any other place to visit with their relatives, under pain of greater punishment ...

31 Order of Giovan Francesco Morosini, cited in Zanette, *Suor Arcangela*, 365–7.
32 See Bishop Antonio Grimani's *Constitutioni, et decreti approvati nella sinoda diocesana, sopra la retta disciplina monacale sotto L'illustrissimo, & Reverendissimo Monsignor Antonio Grimani Vescovo di Torcello. L'anno della Natività del Nostro Signore. 1592. Il giorno 7.8. & 9. d'aprile*, cap. XLVI 'Delle Lettere, & Polize' (Venice, 1592), and Patriarch Lorenzo Priuli, *Ordini, & avvertimenti, che si devono osservare ne' Monasteri di Monache di Venetia: Sopra le visite, & clausura*, 10r. (Venice, 1591).
33 Generally considered to be the first female-authored book of vernacular letters in Italy, Catherine of Siena's spiritual letters – which she dictated to a scribe – were first printed in 1500 by Manuzio. The letters of Osanna da Mantova were published with an account of her life written by her confessor: *Libretto della vita et transito de la beata Osanna da Mantova nuovamente corretto et con una nova aggiunta* (Bologna, 1524). On Osanna da Mantova, see Zarri, *Sante Vive: Profezie di corte e devozione femminile tra '400 e '500* (Turin: Rosenberg and Sellier, 1990). Battistina Vernazza was the author of various devotional works; her spiritual letters were published posthumously by Scotto in 1602; see Daniela Soffaroli Camillocci, 'La

monaca esemplare: Lettere spirituali di madre Battistina Vernazza,' in *Per Lettera: La scrittura epistolare femminile tra archivio e tipografia secoli XV–XVII*, ed. G. Zarri (Rome: Viella, 1999), 235–61.
34 Rosa, 'La religiosa,' *L'uomo barocco*, 234, 'Anomala ... e isolata nel panorama secentesco, la scrittura della Tarabotti. Alle religiose in generale, che amavano coltivare le lettere, si apriva generalmente in un secolo ... il campo della letteratura di pietà o la pratica della poesia devota.'
35 Many of Tarabotti's correspondents could hardly have been considered appropriate contacts for a nun: Brusoni, for example, was an apostate monk of the Carthusian order and the author of several texts of 'libertine' imprint, while Loredano, Bissari, Pona, and even Pighetti were members of the *Accademia degli incogniti*, noted for its libertine tendencies (on this, see Spini, *Ricerca dei libertini*).
36 The publication permit issued by the *Riformatori dello studio di Padova* and the Inquisitor of Venice attesting to a work's suitability for printing: specifically, that it contained no heretical material.
37 See, for example, Tarabotti's letter to Nicolò Crasso describing Regina's virtues and reporting her death (*Lettere*, 132–3). According to Zanette, Regina and Arcangela were both 'clothed' (*vestite*) as nuns on 8 September 1620; Regina died on 31 March 1645 at age thirty-six (Zanette, *Suor Arcangela*, 20, 30). On Tarabotti, Regina, and the *Lagrime*, see Ray, 'Making the Public Private,' 179–82.
38 On Orsi, see Elisabetta Graziosi, 'Arcipelago sommerso: Le rime delle monache tra obbedienza e trasgressione,' in *I monasteri femminili come centri di cultura fra rinascimento e barocco, atti del convegno internazionale Bologna, 8–10 dicembre 2000*, ed. Zarri and Gianna Pomata (Rome: Edizioni di Storia e Letteratura, 2005), 146–81. Like Tarabotti, Orsi also corresponded with Loredano; see Loredano, *Delle Lettere del Signor Gio. Francesco Loredano ... divise in cinquantadue capitoli* (Venice: F. Prodocimo, 1692), 20, 48, 178.
39 Tarabotti, *Lettere*, 185.
40 Ibid.: 'Conobbi l'imperfezioni loro, e se bene traffitta, e fuor di me dal dolore, li viddi indegni di comparir alla luce, anzi meritevoli di starsene eternamente sepolti' ('I recognized their imperfections, and, although wounded and out of my mind with grief, I knew they were unworthy of appearing in the light of day; rather, they merited eternal burial'). Tarabotti goes on to emphasize her 'passive' role in the publication of the *Lagrime*, making it clear that her 'worthless pages' leave the convent walls only at the urging of their heroine's sister, Andriana Malipieri, and offers a similar explanation to Henrico Cornaro (ibid., 170).

314 Notes to pages 192–4

41 In one letter, for example, Tarabotti uses this characterization to decry the attacks made against her by men better educated than she. Making a virtue of the lack of access to formal education that so galled her, and manipulating stereotypical binaries of woman/nature, man/art, Tarabotti expresses disdain for her attackers, who as educated men should hardly be wasting their time on a mere woman, whose only talent is that with which she was born: 'Consideri ... se averia del buono e del termine cavallaresco che un essercito di penne addottrinate nei maggiori studi si movesse contro quella d'una donna che non ha potuto volare che sopra la superficie delle Scritture, guidata dalla semplice naturalezza' ('Consider ... whether it be courteous behaviour that an army of highly educated pens should advance against a woman who has not been permitted to fly beyond the surface of the Gospel, guided by simple naturalness', ibid., 251).
42 Zanette's suggestion that this letter was intended for Bertucci Valier (*Suor Arcangela*, 377n1) is based in part on a later letter to Valier thanking him for his help in obtaining the proper publishing permit for an unidentified book that could be the *Lettere* (*Lettere*, 206); see also Zanette, ibid., 378–9.
43 *Lettere*, 206.
44 Ibid. Emphasis added.
45 Ibid., 214.
46 Ibid.: 'Manderò asseverantemente le sue [lettere] uno di questi giorni, ed ella deve fare lo stesso delle mie, le quali se siano stampate, o in che stato s'attrovino, io non lo so ...' ('I will most certainly send [your letters] one of these days, and you must do the same with mine, although whether they are to be published, or in what state they find themselves, I do not know'). Zanette identifies the recipient of this letter as Brusoni (*Suor Arcangela*, 376); underlying Tarabotti's efforts to effect the return of her letters is not only the possibility of publication, but also the fact that the two had a falling out, leading to a mutual return of correspondence.
47 Zanette, *Suor Arcangela*, 370.
48 Francesa Medioli and Flavia De Rubeis have published a transcription of seven of Tarabotti's autograph letters in 'La scrittura forzata. Le lettere autografe di Arcangela Tarabotti,' *Rivista di storia e letteratura religiosa* 32, no. 1 (1996), 142–55. The transcriptions follow Medioli's discussion of the autograph letters in the same journal, entitled 'Alcune lettere autografe di Arcangela Tarabotti: Autocensura e immagine di sé,' 133–41. The autograph letters themselves are contained in the Biblioteca Universitaria di Genova (Manoscritti aprosiani, v. E, VI, 22, cc. 122r–134v).
49 See Medioli, 'Alcune lettere,' letter III, 'et mi avisi se debbo mandarLe il *Paradiso*, acciò la gentilezza di V.S. m'honori di farle le margini come La mi

promise' ('and you must advise me as to whether I should send you the *Paradiso*, so that the kindness of *Vostra Eccellenza* might honour me by editing it as you promised me'; my translation).

50 On the other hand, a similar request made to Pighetti finds its way into the published collection: perhaps because it refers only to a letter Tarabotti had composed, as opposed to an entire work (the authorship of which had been specifically called into question), there was no need to censor it out (see *Lettere*, 119).

51 See Medioli, 'Alcune lettere,' letter IV, '... non v'è ne pure un sol grano di formento buono in tutta la massa del sesso maschile, essendo ognuno di loro o spiche piene di vitii o vuote di virtù, o paglia cui il vento della superbia e pretensione disperde, o pietre pesanti di falsità e peccati che ai precipizi non meno dell'anime proprie si conducono, che di quelle semplici che credono loro. Ciò dico in universale, lasciando che i buoni si sottragano con le sante operazioni dal numero degli iniqui ...' ('... nor is there even a single kernel of good corn among the entire male sex, since each of them is an ear filled with vice or empty of virtue, or a blade of straw scattered by the wind of pride and pretension, or stones laden down with falsity and sins that lead not only their own souls to the precipice, but those of the innocents who believe them. I say this universally, leaving the good ones to remove themselves from the wicked through their good works ...'; my translation).

52 De Rubeis calls these changes a *ripulitura*, which could have been made either by Tarabotti or by someone directly involved with the printing of the collection (see Medioli and De Rubeis, 'La scrittura forzata,' 146).

53 See Medioli and De Rubeis, 'Alcune lettere,' letter VII. This is a bleak elaboration on the words pronounced by nuns in the profession ceremony, which Tarabotti incorporates into a published letter to 'Signor N.' that declares, 'La libertà che Vostra Signoria essercita meco mi sarebbe favore singolarissimo quando non fossi astratta da tutti gl'interessi mondani, *anzi morta al mondo, per viver in Dio*' ('The liberty shown me by *Vostra Signoria* would be a great favour, were I not so removed from worldly interests, *indeed dead to the world, that I might live in God*'; *Lettere*, 216). Emphasis added.

54 *Lettere*, 297.

55 Transcribed by Medioli in 'Arcangela Tarabotti's Reliability about Herself: Publication and Self-Representation (Together with a Small Collection of Previously Unpublished Letters),' *The Italianist* 23, no. 1 (2003), 54–101. Medioli found five letters from Tarabotti to Vittoria della Rovere (and three by Vittoria in response), three of which Tarabotti published in her *Lettere*.

56 See, for example, Graziella Parati, *Public History, Private Stories: Italian Women's Autobiography* (Minneapolis: University of Minnesota Press, 1996), and Leigh Gilmore, *Autobiographics: A Feminist Theory of Women's Self-Representation* (Ithaca, NY: Cornell University Press, 1994).
57 Parati, *Public History*, 29.
58 Loredano's *Lettere* include business-like notes regarding the publication of Tarabotti's letters (50), extravagant praise of Tarabotti's literary ability, particularly with regard to her *Paradiso* (96), and a virulent condemnation of the nun following the publication of the *Antisatira* (272–4).
59 Tarabotti, *Lettere*, dedication (43).
60 In the dedication of her *Lettere familiari* to Cardinal Luigi d'Este, Veronica Franco uses the same double-edged metaphor to profess literary inferiority, and simultaneously to claim literary (and moral) power. Franco's *dedicatoria* is discussed in chapter four, 148–9. Tarabotti does not make reference to Franco's work, but the similarity to her letter is striking. We know Tarabotti read other women writers, such as Moderata Fonte and Lucrezia Marinella (both lauded in Tarabotti's *La semplicità ingannata*); perhaps she knew this book as well.
61 Tarabotti explicitly solicits Loredano's literary protection claiming him to be the 'difensore' of her *Paradiso monacale* in particular (see chapter 6, section two, 'The *Paradiso monacale*.')
62 Tarabotti, *Lettere*, 74. Loredano's involvement with the project is reflected in his own *epistolario* as well. In a letter to Tarabotti, Loredano breaks the news to her that the printed *Lettere* are full of printer's errors: 'Tutte le diligenze sono riuscite inutili per rendere la stampa delle *Lettere* di Vostra Signoria senza errori. La copia ben corretta e 'l compositore intendente, il correttore non trascurato e affettuoso, non hanno potuto supplire che non siano corse alcune minuzie, poco considerabili in numero e in qualità. L'emmacolato non è epiteto per le stampe, dove etiandio correggendo si falla. Il cielo può vedersi alle volte senza nubi, ma la stampa giamai senza errori' ('All diligence was useless in printing your *Lettere* without errors. The properly corrected copy, the experienced compositor, and the attentive and affectionate editor were unable to prevent a few minute errors, of little import in number and quality. The term immaculate ought not be applied to printing, where even in the act of correcting, one makes mistakes. The sky might sometimes be cloudless, but printing is never without errors'); Loredano, *Lettere*, 50, my translation.
63 Ibid., 74.
64 Ibid., 44.
65 Ibid., 49.

66 Tarabotti addresses two other missives to Erizzo. In the first of these, she calls attention to the 'adorabili saluti' proffered her by the Doge on more than one occasion (75). In the second she wishes him well in the struggle against the Turks (111–12). In both, her reverent praise becomes the vehicle through which to establish a connection between herself and the secular world, and to claim validation through that connection. Significantly, Tarabotti's *Lettere* also include a letter to Erizzo's successor Francesco Molin (1646–55), offering him a copy of her *Paradiso* (118–19).

67 She complains to Ferdinando (really Odoardo) Farnese of Parma (1612–46) about the hostile reaction to her *Antisatira* (*Lettere*, 70–4) and seeks Vittoria's support in publishing the *Tirannia paterna* (ibid., 151–2).

68 See Tarabotti's letter to Cardinal Mazarin in which she writes that Signor Naudeo '... fu a richiedermi l'opere mie per ricovrarle nella fioritissima biblioteca di Vostra Eminenza' ('... came to ask for my works to bring them to the splendid library of *Vostra Eminenza*'); *Lettere*, 195–7. Tarabotti refers to Paris as the 'paradiso delle donne,' but goes on to say that, for her, Paris has become an 'inferno' due to a complicated affair involving her *Tirannia paterna*, which she had hoped to have published there. In what would turn into an ongoing struggle, Tarabotti gave the mansucript to a certain monsieur Colisson (secretary to Tarabotti's acquaintance, Renata di Claramonte), who had expressed admiration for it and promised to have it published in France. As months passed and Tarabotti heard nothing from Colisson, she became suspicious and upset, and complained both to Renata and to Naudé and Mazarin.

69 Cf. Weaver, *Satira e Antisatira*, 73–4, 'Costoro ... per parere protomaestri di tutto il mondo litterario, se per sorte vedono da una donna invece dell'ago adoprarsi la penna, con mille invenzioni contro quei scritti attestano come Evangelo che non può essere ch'una femina scriva, se non ricorre a pigliar in prestito dal perfettissimo lume de' loro begl'intelletti un picciolo lumicino. Perciò è avvenuto che molti maligni o ignoranti asseriscano che 'l *Paradiso monacale* non possa esser dettame dell'ingegno mio, o volo della mia penna, o pur, che, essendo, sia anche necessità ch'abbia ricevuto ornamento, fregi, e ricchezze di tratti di filosofia e teologia da spiriti elevati e intelligent.' ('These men ... in order to appear masters of the entire literary world, if they should happen to see a woman use a pen rather than an embroidery needle, with a thousand comments against her work they attest, as if it were the Gospel, that there is no such thing as a woman who writes, unless she has borrowed a little flame from the most perfect light of their high intellects. Therefore it has come to pass that many wicked or ignorant men assert that the *Paradiso monacale* could not have been the

product of my own mind, or the flight of my pen, or that, if it were, it must have received ornamentation, flourishes, and riches of philosophy and theology from elevated and intelligent minds'; my translation).

70 Tarabotti's relationship with Brusoni was surely not helped by his composition of a response to her *Antisatira*, the *Anstisatira satirizzata* to which she refers rather bitterly in the letter to Nicolas Bretel de Grémonville, quoted in this chapter 6, section two, 'The *Paradiso monacale*.'
71 Tarabotti, *Lettere*, 292.
72 Ibid., 157–9. Nicolas Bretel de Grémonville was in Venice from 1645–7, a period of intense Venetian distrust of the French. Because Venice's French guests were forbidden to have contact with the Venetian aristocracy, the *parlatorio* at Sant'Anna was one of the few places Grémonville could turn for conversation and company (see Zanette, *Suor Arcangela*, 313).
73 See Tarabotti's letter to the girls' mother, Madame de Grémonville (*Lettere*, 199), and her fond farewell to them upon their return to France (ibid., 218). On Tarabotti's interactions with this family, see also Ray, 'Letters and Lace.' On the practice of boarding and educating girls in the convent, known as *serbanza*, see Strocchia, 'Taken into Custody: Girls and Convent Guardianship in Renaissance Florence,' *Renaissance Studies* 17, no. 2 (2003), 177–200.
74 Tarabotti, *Lettere*, 157.
75 As Biga points out, Brusoni's response to Tarabotti's *Antisatira* may have never actually been completed (*Una polemica antifemminista*, 83–5). Tarabotti proposes that both texts be burned, along with another forthcoming response by Silvio Foccacci, *Le funerali delle pompe femminili* (cf. Zanette, *Suor Arcangela*, 278).
76 Tarabotti's critics rebuke her for calling Alexander the Great 'incontinente,' referring to Dante as 'poeta vano,' and for having confused Saint Anthony with Saint Paul, all complaints which she finds of incredible insignificance: 'questi sono oppositioni di nessuna sussistenza, e hanno più del maligno che del critico appasionato' ('these are objections of no substance, and are more characteristic of the wicked than of the passionate critic'; *Lettere*, 158).
77 *Lettere*, 159.
78 Ibid., 59.
79 Ibid., 52, 'Una sola parola, non ch'una lode cosí spiritosa e gentile, contenuta in una lettera dell'eccellentissimo Loredano in favore di qualsivoglia più imperfetto scritto, basterebbe ad accreditarlo per degno in tutti i secoli' ('One word alone, not to mention such spirited and kind praise, contained in a letter by the most excellent Loredano in favour of any imperfect work at all, would suffice to validate it as worthy for all time').

80 In a letter to Brusoni, Tarabotti takes great offense at the insinuation, writing: 'Se il credere che le mie monache avessero disseminata quella zizania che Vostra Signoria m'accenna fosse punto di fede, morirei certamente eretica e più tosto crederei di veder il diavolo a farsi la croce, che supponere una tal improprietade ...' ('If it were a point of faith to believe that my fellow nuns had disseminated this rumour to which you allude, I would certainly die a heretic, and I would sooner believe I had seen the Devil make the sign of the cross than suppose such an impropriety [as this] ...'); *Lettere*, 277.
81 Ibid., 64.
82 Ibid., 65.
83 Ibid., 107–8.
84 Ibid., 108.
85 As, for the most part, they were (see Zanette, *Suor Arcangela*, 252).
86 Tarabotti, *Lettere*, 140–1.
87 Ibid., 141.
88 Ibid., 145.
89 Ibid., 72.
90 Ibid., 173.
91 Ibid., 254–5.
92 Loredano too was irritated by the *Antisatira*, as reflected in his own published letters (see Loredano, *Lettere*, 234–44).
93 Zanette hypothesizes that Brusoni, who was in prison during this period, may have received a copy of the work and sold it to Tarabotti, who then went to work to keep it from being published (cf. *Suor Arcangela*, 259; see Biga, *Una polemica antifemminista*, for a detailed discussion of these events).
94 Tarabotti, *Lettere*, 246–7, 'A fin che Vostra Signoria Reverenda sappia non aver del verisimile ch'ella non abbia pensiero di stampar la sua *Maschera* con il mio nome distinto e ch'io con giusta causa mi son mossa di farGlielo cancellare, Le mando il frontespicio copiato dall'originale fatto di Sua propria mano' ('So that you might know that it is entirely unbelievable that you had no thought of publishing your *Maschera* with my name clearly indicated, and that I with just cause took steps to make you remove it, I send you the frontispiece copied from the original in your own hand').
95 Ibid., 295–6.
96 Ibid., 94–5.
97 Ibid., 71. Similarly, in a letter to a certain 'Signor N.' Tarabotti marvels at hearing 'ch'io mi ponga in stato d'irritarmi contro le più celebri penne d'Italia,' ('that I am annoying the most celebrated pens of Italy'), adding, 'Gran vigliacheria sarebbe certo a mio parere di questi tali se congiurassero

contro una sola donna ...' ('It would indeed by great cowardice, in my opinion, if these men were to plot against a lone woman ...'), ibid., 250.
98 Ibid., 71. Just as she argues to Aprosio regarding the *Paradiso*, Tarabotti insists here that the negative reaction to her *Antisatira* is flattering: 'Non creda ... ch'io nutrisca mal'animo contro costoro,' she writes to the Duke of Parma, 'anzi mi tengo loro obligata ch'essi mostrano d'aver così gran concetto di me che mi stimino più robusta d'un Ercole, venendomi contra a gran schiere' ('Do not think ... that I harbour ill will against these men; indeed I am obligated to them for demonstrating so great an admiration for me that they esteem me more robust than a Hercules, coming after me in great numbers').
99 Ibid., 73, and reiterated in a letter to Aprosio which states '... non pretesi d'offendere il Signor Buoninsegni o altri nella mia *Antisatira*, né mai ho parlato di quelli che non lo meritano' ('... I did not mean to offend Signor Buoninsegni or others in my *Antisatira*, nor did I ever speak of those who did not deserve it'), ibid., 80. Buoninsegni himself expressed admiration for Tarabotti in a letter to Aprosio, writing: 'Io rendo infinite grazie a quella madre che ha voluto onorarmi, stimando le mie bagatelle, fatte per far ridere un'ora nell'Accademia il nostro serenissimo padrone, degne delle censure dell'ingegno elevato di cotesta madre' ('I extend infinite thanks to that mother who wished to honour me, deeming my little jest [composed to make our most serene patron laugh for an hour at the Academy] worthy of the censure of the high intellect of this mother'); letter dated Siena, 15 September 1644, BUG, E VI 6, Int. I, cited in Portigliotti, 285, and in Weaver, *Satira e Antisatira*, 25.
100 Ibid., 90. Initially Tarabotti had thought to dedicate her *Antisatira* to Prince Leopold de' Medici, but instead decided on Vittoria della Rovere, who was known for taking an interest in the nuns of Florence (Weaver, *Satira e Antisatira*, 19).
101 Tarabotti, *Lettere*, 295.
102 Ibid., 139.
103 Ibid., 140.
104 Ibid., 173.
105 Ibid., 178.
106 Ibid., 78
107 Ibid., 81.
108 Valier (1615–91) was a senator, general, and historian, and member of a prominent Venetian family. In thanking him for his sonnet in this letter, Tarabotti also expresses regret that Valier's name is not attached to it; in fact, it appears anonymously at the beginning of the *Antisatira* and is dedicated to Vittoria della Rovere.

109 Another letter to Bissari reveals a similar knowledge of the publication process – and certainly no surprise to find her *Antisatira* in the midst of it – as Tarabotti apologizes for her delay in sending Bissari a copy of the work, which is still in the hands of the *revisori* (*Lettere*, 298). A letter to Bertucci Valier reporting that the *Antisatira* has received the necessary license for publication also shows her engagement with the process: 'Trasmetto a Vostra Eccellenza la mia *Antisatira*, la quale servirà per testimonio verace che l'inscrizione di A. e T. ha conseguite ancora le licenze ...' ('I send you my *Antisatira*, which will serve as true testimony that the inscription A. and T. has once again received a permit ...'), ibid., 266.
110 Ibid., 181.
111 In addition to a reliance on the 'authenticity' and testimonial force of letters, Tarabotti demonstrates a deep faith in the power of the physical object of the written document itself as tangible evidence, not only in her letter to Bretel, but also in a letter to Francesco Mula regarding the *Tirannia paterna* in which the physical evidence of an early, hand-written draft is offered as the strongest defence of authorship: 'Acciò che Vostra Signoria Illustrissima veda gli attestati miei esser veridichi, le mando la *Tirannia Paterna* in foglio rozza e incolta, nello stato apunto che l'ho partorita' ('So that you may see my statements to be truthful, I send you a rough draft of the *Tirannia Paterna*, exactly as I first gave birth to it'), ibid., 243.
112 Ibid., 96.
113 Cf. Aretino, *Lettere*, ed. Proccaccioli, I, 144, '... la mia penna paga altri d'onore e di biasimi in contanti: Io in una mattina senza altre istorie divulgo le lodi e i vituperi di coloro non ch'io adoro e odio, ma di quegli che meritano d'essere adorati e odiati' ('... my pen repays others with the currency of honour and blame: In a single morning, without hesitation, I divulge praise and condemnation, not of those I adore and despise, but of those who merit adoration and hatred'); my translation.
114 Stephanie Jed terms Tarabotti a 'political theorist' in her article: 'Arcangela Tarabotti and Gabriel Naudé: Libraries, Taxonomies and *Ragion di Stato*,' in *Arcangela Tarabotti*, in *Arcangela Tarabotti*, ed. Weaver, 139.

Epilogue

1 Elizabeth D. Harvey, *Ventriloquized Voices: Feminist Theory and English Renaissance Texts* (London: Routledge, 1992), 10.
2 See Leigh Gilmore, *Autobiographics: A Feminist Theory of Women's Self-Representation* (Ithaca, NY: Cornell University Press, 1994), xi.

3 Printers and editors also played a role in this regard: they influenced, to various degrees, the order and even the selection of the letters they published. On editors' influence over style in the publication of sixteenth- and seventeenth-century texts, see Brian Richardson, *Print Culture in Renaissance Italy* (Cambridge: Cambridge University Press, 1994), and Paolo Trovato, *Con ogni diligenza corretto* (Bologna: Il Mulino, 1991).
4 Cf. Gilmore, *Autobiographics*, 107 and 122 on this issue with regard to autobiography.
5 Cf. Virginia Cox, *Women's Writing in Italy 1400–1650* (Baltimore: Johns Hopkins University Press, 2008), and Diana Robin, *Publishing Women: Salons, the Presses, and the Counter Reformation in Sixteenth-Century Italy* (Chicago: University of Chicago Press, 2007).
6 Cox, *Women's Writing in Italy*, 212–13, characterizes this period as one marked by the 'reconventualization' of women's writing.
7 Luisa Bergalli (1703–79) published a number of poetic anthologies, including *Componimenti poetici delle più illustri rimatrici di ogni secolo* (Venice: N.p., 1726), the first such anthology to be planned and edited by a woman; see Pamela D. Stewart, 'Luisa Bergalli,' in Rinaldina Russell, *Italian Women Writers A Bio-Bibliographic Sourcebook* (Westport, CT: Greenwood Press, 1994), 50–7; Adriana Chemello, 'Literary Critics and Scholars, 1700–1850,' trans. Peter Brand, in *A History of Women's Writing in Italy*, ed. L. Panizza and S. Wood (Cambridge: Cambridge University Press, 2001), 135–9. The first anthologies of women's vernacular letters began to appear in the nineteenth century, for example, with Bartolomeo Gamba's *Lettere di donne italiane del secolo decimosesto* (Venice: Alvisopoli, 1832).
8 Cf. Arcangela Tarabotti, *Lettere familiari e di complimento della sign. Arcangela Tarabotti*, ed. Meredith Ray and Lynn Westwater (Turin: Rosenberg and Sellier, 2005), 45, dedicatory letter by Giovanni Dandolo to the publishers, '… pare a me che invece di ritratto di lettere si possa dire con buona coscienza raccolta di miracoli, perchè ogni lettera è un miracolo dell'arte e della natura' ('… it seems to me that rather than a portrait in letters, one may in good conscience call it a collection of miracles, because each letter is a miracle of art and nature').

Bibliography

I. Manuscript Sources

Archivio di Stato di Mantova: Archivio Gonzaga, Busta 2578, fol. 370–1.
Archivio di Stato di Modena: Cancelleria Ducale, Archivio per Materie, Condottieri, Buste 1–2; Cancelleria Ducale, Archivio per Materie, Letterati, Busta 24; Cancelleria Ducale, Archivio per Materie, Particolari, Gonzaga, Busta 818.
Archivio di Stato di Parma: Fondo Gonzaga-San Vitale, Serie III, Buste 35–7.
Archivio di Stato di Rovigo: Archivio notarile, notaio Francesco Campagella, Busta 315, cancello n.7, fol.116–23.
Archivio Patriarcale di Venezia. Sezione Antica, Monalium, 7.
Biblioteca Estense di Modena: Autografoteca Campori, Gonzaga; mss. Filippo Rodi, *Annuali di Ferrara* (1546).
Vatican Library: Fondo Barberini Latini 5790.

II. Printed Primary Sources

Agrippa, Henricus Cornelius. *Declamation on the Nobility and Preeminence of the Female Sex*. Edited and translated by Albert Rabil Jr. Chicago: University of Chicago Press, 1996.
Alberigo, Giuseppe, Giuseppe L. Dossetti, Perikle P. Joannou, Claudio Leonardo, and Paolo Prodi, eds. *Conciliorum Oecumenicorum Decreta*. Bologna: Istituto per le scienze religiose di Bologna, 1973.
Alberti, Leon Battista. *I libri della famiglia*. Edited by Ruggiero Romano and Alberto Tenenti. Turin: Einaudi, 1980.

Andreini, Francesco. *Ragionamenti fantastici di Francesco Andreini da Pistoia comico Geloso, detto il Capitano Spavento, posti in forma di dialoghi rappresentativi.* Venice: G.A. Somasco, 1612.
- *Fragmenti di alcune scritture della signora Isabella Andreini comica gelosa, & academica intenta. Raccolti da Francesco Andreini comico geloso, detto il Capitan Spavento. E dati in luce da Flaminio Scala Comico.* Venice: Combi, 1627.
- *Le bravure del Capitano Spavento.* Edited by Roberto Tessari. Pisa: Giardini, 1987.

Andreini, Isabella. *Lettere d'Isabella Andreini padovana, comica gelosa.* Venice: Marc'Antonio Zaltieri, 1607.
- *Rime d'Isabella Andreini Padovana ...* Milan: Girolamo Bordone, 1611.
- *Mirtilla.* Edited by Maria Luisa Doglio. Lucca: M. Pacini Fazzi, 1995.
- *La Mirtilla.* Edited and translated by Julie Campbell. Tempe, Arizona: Arizona Center for Medieval and Renaissance Studies, 2002.

Aretino, Pietro. *La cortigiana.* In *Tutte le commedie.* Edited by G.B. DeSanctis. Milan: Mursia, 1968.
- *Ragionamento/Dialogo.* Edited by Nino Borsellino. Milan: Garzanti, 1984.
- *Lettere: Libro Primo.* Edited by Francesco Erspamer. Parma: Ugo Guanda Editore, 1995.
- *Lettere.* 6 vols. Edited by Paolo Procaccioli. Rome: Salerno, 1997–2002.
- *Lettere: Libro Secundo.* Edited by Francesco Erspamer. Parma: Ugo Guanda Editore, 1998.
- *Lettere.* Edited by Gian Maria Anselmi, Elisabetta Menetti, and Francesca Tomasi. Rome: Carocci, 2000.

Aristotle. *Oeconomica.* Edited by E.S. Forster. Oxford: Clarendon Press, 1921.

Atanagi, Dionigi. *De le lettere di tredici huomini illustri.* Venice: Vincenzo Valgrisi, 1554.

Bairo, Pietro. *Secreti medicinali ... nei quali si contengono i rimedij, che si possono usar in tutte l'infermità, che vengono all'huomo, cominciando da capelli fino alla pianta de piedi.* Venice: Giorgio Valentini, 1629.

Bandello, Matteo. *Novelle.* Vienna: Antonio Reboglio, 1545.
- *Canti XI.* Edited by Luigi Russo and Ettore Mazzali. Milan: Rizzoli, 1990.

Bembo, Pietro. *Lettere giovenili et amorose di M. Pietro Bembo et altri eccelenti autori.* Venice: N.p., 1553.
- *Delle lettere di M. Pietro Bembo...Di nuovo riveduto e corretto da Francesco Sansovino, con la giunta della Vita del Bembo, descritta per il medesimo.* Venice: Sansovino, 1560.
- *Asolani.* Edited by Giorgio Dilemmi. Florence: Accademia della Crusca, 1991.

Bergalli, Luisa. *Componimenti poetici delle più illustri rimatrici di ogni secolo.* Venice: Antonio Mora, 1726.

Boccaccio, Giovanni. *De mulieribus claris.* Edited by Vittore Branca. Milan: Mondadori, 1970.
– *Decamerone.* Edited by Vittore Branca. Turin: Einaudi, 1980.
– *Elegia di Madonna Fiammetta: Corbaccio.* Edited by Francesco Erbani. Milan: Garzanti, 1988.
– *On Famous Women.* Edited and translated by Virginia Brown. Cambridge, MA: Harvard University Press, 2001.
Bonardo, Gio Maria. *Madrigali: Dedicati alla illustrissima sig. Lucretia Gonzaga.* Venice: Rocca, 1571.
– *Origine della Fratta.* Venice: Rocca, 1571.
Borghesi, Diomede. *Rime.* Padua: L. Pasquati, 1566.
Borgogni, Gherardo. *Gioie poetiche di madrigali del Sign. Hieronimo Casoni, e d'altri celebri poeti de' nostri tempi ... raccolti da Gherardo Borgogni.* Pavia: Per gli heredi del Bartoli, 1593.
Brusantino, Vincenzo. *Angelica Innamorata.* Venice: Marcolini, 1553.
Brusoni, Girolamo. *La Orestilla.* Venice: Guerigli, 1652.
Calmo, Andrea. *Lettere.* Edited by Vittorio Rossi. Turin: Ermanno Loescher, 1888.
Caro, Annibal. *Lettere familiari.* Edited by Aulo Greco. Florence: Le Monnier, 1957–61.
Casalini, Bonaventura. *Cronaca domestica.* Edited by Alfonso Lazzari. Faenza: Lega, 1941.
Castiglione, Baldassare. *Il libro del cortigiano.* Edited by Amedeo Quondam. Milan: Garzanti, 1981.
Cattaneo, Cornelio. *Rime di diversi nobilissimi et eccellentissimi auttori in lode dell'illustrissima Signora, La Signora Lucretia Gonzaga marchesana.* Bologna: Giovanni Rossi, 1565.
Ceci, Battista. *Compendio d'avertimenti di ben parlare volgare.* Venice: Stamperia Salicata, 1618.
Celebrino, Eustachio. *Opera nova piacevole la quale insegna di far compositioni odorifere per far bella ciaschuna donna.* Venice: Bindoni, 1551.
Cereta, Laura. *Collected Letters of a Renaissance Feminist.* Edited and translated by Diana Robin. Chicago: University of Chicago Press, 1997.
Colonna, Vittoria. *Rime e lettere di Vittoria Colonna.* Florence: G. Barbèra Editore, 1860.
Cortese, Isabella. *Secreti de la signora Isabella Cortese ne' qvali si contengono cose minerali medicinali alchimiche.* 1st ed. Venice: Giovanni Bariletto, 1561; 2nd ed. 1574.
Coryat, Thomas. *Coryat's Crudities.* Vol. 1. Glasgow: James MacLehose and Sons, and New York: Macmillan, 1905.

Costa, Margarita. *Lettere amorose della Signora Margherita Costa, Romana*. Venice: N.p., 1639.
– *Lo stipo*. Venice: N.p., 1639.
– *Li buffoni*. In *Commedie dell'Arte*. Vol. 2. Edited by S. Ferroni, 235–59. Milan: Mursia, 1986.
[Delicado, Francisco?]. *Dialogo dello Zoppino. De la vita e genealogia di tutte le cortigiane di Roma*. Edited by G. Lanfranchi. Milan: L'Editrice del libro raro, 1922.
Demetrius, *On Style*. Translated by W. Rhys Roberts. London: The Loeb Classical Library, 1931.
di Gregorio, Frate Maurizio. *Rosario delle stampe di tutti i poeti e le poetesse*. Naples: N.p., 1614.
Dolce, Lodovico. *Dialogo della institution delle donne*. Venice: Giolito, 1545.
– *Lettere del Gran Mahumeto Imperadore de' Turchi scritte a diversi re, prencipi, signori, e repubbliche con le risposte loro*. Venice: G.G. de' Ferrari, 1563.
Domenichi, Lodovico. *Le due cortigiane*. Florence: Giorgio Mariscotti, 1563.
Doni, Anton Francesco. *Libraria*. Venice: Giolito, 1550.
– *Pistolotti amorosi*. Venice: Gabriel Giolito, 1552.
– *Tre libri di lettere del Doni*. Venice: Marcolino, 1552.
– *Libraria seconda*. Venice: Giolito, 1558.
Erasmus, Desiderius. *The Epistles of Erasmus*. Edited by Francis Morgan Nichols. New York: Russell and Russell, 1962.
– *Collected Works of Erasmus*. Edited by Beatrice Corrigan. Toronto: University of Toronto Press, 1974.
– *Collected Works of Erasmus*. Vol. 39. Edited and translated by Craig R. Thompson. Toronto: University of Toronto Press, 1997.
– *The Praise of Folly*. Edited and translated by Clarence H. Miller. 2nd ed. New Haven: Yale University Press, 2003.
Fedele, Cassandra. *Letters and Orations*. Edited and translated by Diana Robin. Chicago: University of Chicago Press, 2000.
Filelfo, Giovanni Maria. *Consolatoria*. Edited by Anne Schoysman Zambrini. In *Scelta di curiosità inedite o rare dal secolo XIII al XIX*. Bologna: Commissione per i Testi di Lingua, 1991, Dispensa CCLXXXIII.
Firenzuola, Agnolo. *Le bellezze, le lodi, gli amori & i costumi delle donne* ...Venice: Barezzo Barezzi, 1622.
Fonte, Moderata. *Il merito delle donne*. Edited by Adriana Chemello. Venice: Eidos, 1988.
– *The Worth of Women*. Edited and translated by Virginia Cox. Chicago: University of Chicago Press, 1997.
Franco, Nicolò. *Le pistole vulgari*. Venice: Gardane, 1542.

Franco, Veronica. *Terze rime e sonetti*. Edited by G. Beccari. Lanciano: Carabba, 1912.
– *Lettere dall'unica edizione del MDLXXX con proemio e nota iconografica*. Edited by Benedetto Croce. Naples: Ricciardi, 1949.
– *Lettere*. Edited by Stefano Bianchi. Rome: Salerno, 1988.
– *Rime*. Edited by Stefano Bianchi. Milan: Mursia, 1995.
– *Veronica Franco: Poems and Selected Letters*. Edited and translated by Ann Rosalind Jones and Margaret F. Rosenthal. Chicago: University of Chicago Press, 1998.
Gambara, Veronica. *Rime e lettere di Veronica Gambara*. Brescia: Rizzardi, 1759.
Garimberto, Hieronimo. *Concetti di Hieronimo Garimberto, et di più autori raccolti da lui, per scrivere familiarmente*. Rome: Vincenzo Valgrisi, 1551.
Gonzaga, Lucrezia. *Lettere della molta illustre ... donna Lucretia Gonzaga da Gazuolo ...* Venice: Gualtero Scotto, 1552.
Grimani, Antonio. *Constitutioni, et decreti approvati nella sinoda diocesana, sopra la retta disciplina monacale sotto L'Illustrissimo, et Reverendissimo Monsignor Antonio Grimani Vescovo di Torcello*. Venice: N.p., 1592.
Groto, Luigi ['Il Cieco d'Adria']. *Le lettere famigliari di Luigi Groto, Cieco d'Adria*. Venice: Giovacchino Brugnolo, 1601.
Guarini, Battista. *Il segretario*. Venice: Roberto Megretti, 1594.
Guazzo Stefano. *Lettere*. Venice: Barezzo Barezzi, 1606.
– *La civil conversazione*. Edited by A. Quondam. Modena: Panini, 1993.
Lando, Ortensio. *Paradossi ...* Lione: G. Pullon da Trino, 1543.
– *Lettere di molte valorose donne, nelle quali chiaramente appare non esser né di eloquentia né di dottrina alli huomini inferiori*. Venice: Giolito, 1548.
– *Consolatorie de diversi autori*. Venice: Al segno del pozzo, 1550.
– *La sferza de scrittori antichi et moderni ...* Venice: N.p., 1550.
– *Oracoli de moderni ingegni ...* Venice: Giolito, 1550.
– *Ragionamenti familiari di diversi autori ...* Venice: Al segno del pozzo, 1550.
– *Dialogo ... nel quale si ragiona della consolatione, e utilità che si gusta leggendo la Sacra Scrittura*. Venice: A. Arrivabene, 1552.
– *Due panegirici nuovamente composti de quali l'uno è in lode della marchesana della Padula, et l'altro in comendatione della S. Donna Lucretia Gonzaga da Gazuolo*. Venice: Giolito, 1552.
– *Questi amorosi*. Venice: Giolito, 1552.
– *Sette libri di cataloghi a varie cose appartenenti, non solo antiche, ma anche moderne*. Venice: Giolito, 1552.
– *Vari componimenti di M. Hortensio Lando*. Venice: Giolito, 1552.
Lauro, Pietro. *Lettere*. Venice: N.p., 1552.
Lettere a Aretino. Edited by Gonoria Floris and Luisa Mulas. Rome: Bulzoni, 1997.

Lettere del Cinquecento. Edited by Giuseppe Guido Ferrero. Turin: U.T.E.T., 1967.
Lettere di cortigiane del XVI secolo. Edited by Luigi Ferrai. Florence: Libreria Dante, 1884.
Lettere di donne italiane del secolo decimosesto. Edited by Bartolomeo Gamba. Venice: Alvisopoli, 1832.
Lettere facete e piacevoli di diversi grandi uomini e chiari ingegni. Edited by Silvia Longhi. Ferrara: Arnaldo Forni Editore, 1991.
Lettere scritte al signor Pietro Aretino.... Venice: Marcolini, 1551.
Lettere volgari di diversi nobilissimi uomini ... in diverse materie. Venice: Paolo Manuzio, 1545.
Loredano, Giovan Francesco. *Le glorie degli Incogniti*. Venice: Valvasense, 1647.
– *Delle lettere del Signor Gio. Francesco Loredano ... divise in cinquantadue capitoli*. Venice: F. Prodocimo, 1692.
Luigini da Udine, Federico. *Il libro della bella donna*. Venice: Plinio Pietrasanta, 1554.
Mandosio, Paolo. *Bibliotheca Romana*. Rome: Typis ac sumptibus Ignatij de Lazzaris, 1692.
Manfredi, Muzio. *Lettere brevissime*. Venice: Meglietti, 1606.
Marinello, Giovani. *Gli ornamenti delle donne*. Venice: Francesco de' Franceschi Senese, 1562.
– *De le medicine pertinenti alle donne*. Venice: Francesco de' Franceschi, 1563.
Matraini, Chiara Cantarini. 'Chiara Matraini: Rime e Lettere.' Edited by Giovanna Rabitti. In *Scelta di curiosita inedite o rare dal secolo XIII al XIX*. Bologna: Commissione per i Testi di Lingua, 1991. Dispensa CCLXXXIII.
Miniatore, Bartolomeo. *Formulario, overo epistolario volgare...* Venice: [F. de Leno], 1568 [i.e., 1569].
Montaigne, Michel de. *Journal de voyage en Italie*. Edited by Maurice Rat. Paris: Éditions Garnier, 1955.
More, Thomas. *Utopia*. Edited by Clarence H. Miller. New Haven: Yale University Press, 2001.
Nogarola, Isotta. *Complete Writings. Letterbook, Dialogue on Adam and Eve, Orations*. Edited and translated by Margaret King and Diana Robin. Chicago: University of Chicago Press, 2004.
Novo libro di lettere scritte da i più vari autori e professori della lingua volgare italiana. Edited by Giacomo Moro. Ferrara: Arnaldo Forni, 1987.
Ostiglia, Pier Francesco Bertioli da. *Rime col commento di Andrea Alciato*. Edited by N. Zingarelli. Bologna: Commissione per i Testi di Lingua, 1969.
Ovid. *Heroides*. Translated by Harold Isbell. London: Penguin Books, 1990.
Paleario, Aonio. *Dell'Economia o vero del governo della casa*. Edited by Salvatore Caponetto. Florence: Olschki, 1983.

Palmieri, Matteo. *La vita civile*. Edited by Gino Belloni. Florence: Sansoni, 1982.
[Parabosco, Girolamo.?] *Lettere amorose di Madonna Celia gentildonna Romana, scritte al suo amante*. Venice: Antonio de gli Antonii, 1562.
Parabosco, Girolamo. *Il primo libro delle lettere famigliari*. Venice: Giovan. Griffio, 1551.
– *Lettere amorose di M. Girolamo Parabosco*. Venice: Giolito, 1564.
– *Libro primo delle lettere amorose*. Venice: D. Forni, 1581.
Pasqualigo, Alvise. *Lettere amorose del Mag. M. Alvise Pasqualigo libri III, ne' quali sotto maravigliosi concetti si contengono tutti gli accidenti d'amore*. Venice: D. Farni, 1581.
Paternò, Lodovico. *La Mirtia*. Naples: Gio Maria Scotto, 1564.
Pavoni, Giuseppe. *Diario descritto da Giuseppe Pavoni. Delle feste celebrate nelle solenissime nozzi delli serenissimi sposi, il sig. Don Ferdinando Medici, & la sig. Donna Christina di Loreno gran duchi di Toscana. Nel quale con brevità si esplica il torneo, la battaglia navale, la comedia con gli intermedii, & altre feste occorse di giorno in giorno per tutto il di 15 Magio. MDLXXXIX*. Bologna, 1589.
Petrarca, Francesco. *Familiares*. In *Opere di Francesco Petrarca*. Edited by Emilio Bigi. Milan: Mursia, 1963.
Piemontese, Alessio [Girolamo Ruscelli?]. *La prima parte de' secreti del reverendo donno Alessio piemontese*. Pesaro: Gli heredi di Barolomeo Cesano, 1562.
Plato. *The Symposium*. In *Collected Dialogues Including the Letters*. Edited by E. Hamilton and H. Cairns. Princeton: Princeton University Press, 1961.
Priuli, Lorenzo. *Ordini, & avvertimenti, che si devono osservare ne' Monasteri di Monache di Venetia: Sopre le visite, & clausura*. Venice: N.p., 1591.
Ricci, Bartolomeo. *Deprecatio pro Io. Pau. Manfronio apud Herc. Atestium Ferrariensium Principem*. Ferrara: Giovan Maria de Nicolini de Sabio, 1552.
Rime ... in lode dell'illustrissima signora ... Lucrezia Gonzaga. Bologna: Giovanni Rossi, 1965.
Ruscelli, Gerolamo. *Le imprese illustri ...*. Venice: Comin da Trino di Monserrato, 1572.
– *Lettere di Principi*. Venice: Giordano Ziletti, 1577.
Sansovino, Francesco. *Del secretario*. Venice: N.p., 1573.
– *Delle lettere amorose di diversi huomini illustri ... Nelle quali si leggono nobilissimi, et leggiadri concetti, in tutte le materie occorrenti ne' casi d'Amore*. Venice: Gli Eredi del Bonelli, 1574.
– *Del secretario*. Edited by Pietro Calamandrei. Florence: Le Monnier, 1942.
Savorgnan, Maria, and Pietro Bembo. *Carteggio d'Amore 1500–1501*. Edited by Carlo Dionisotti. Florence: Le Monnier, 1950.
Scala, Flaminio. *Il Teatro delle Favole Rappresentative*. Edited by Ferruccio Marotti. Milan: Il Polifilo, 1976.

Sforza, Isabella (Ortensio Lando). *Della vera tranquillità dell'animo*. Venice: Eredi di Aldo Manuzio, 1544.
Speroni, Sperone. *Dialoghi di Sperone Speroni*. Venice: Fra Lorenzini da Torino, 1550.
Stampa, Gaspara. *Rime*. Edited by Maria Bellonci and Rodolfo Ceriello. Milan: Rizzoli, 1954.
Taglienti, G.A. *Formulario nuovo che insegna dittar lettere missive e responsive* ... Venice: Da Sabbio, 1539.
– *Componimento di Parlamenti*. Venice: Gli eredi di Luigi Valvassore, 1584.
Tarabotti, Arcangela. *Il Paradiso monacale*. Venice: Guglielmo Oddoni, 1663 (i.e., 1643).
– *La semplicità ingannata*. Leyden: Sambix (i.e., Jean and Daniel Elzevier), 1654.
– *L'inferno monacale di Arcangela Tarabotti*. [*ante quem* 1643]. Edited by Francesca Medioli. Turin: Rosenberg and Sellier, 1990.
– *Che le donne siano della spetie degli uomini*. Edited by Letizia Panizza. London: Institute of Romance Studies, 1994.
– *Antisatira*. In *Satira e Antisatira*. Edited by Elissa Weaver. Rome: Salerno, 1998.
– *Paternal Tyranny*. Edited by Letizia Panizza. Chicago: University of Chicago Press, 2004.
– *Lettere familiari e di complimento*. Edited by Meredith Ray and Lynn Westwater. Turin: Rosenberg and Sellier, 2005.
– *La semplicità ingannata*. Edited by Simona Bortot. Padua: Il Poligrafo, 2007.
Tasso, Bernardo. *Li due libre delle lettere* ... Venice: Vincenzo Valgrisi, 1557.
Textor, Ravisus. *Officinae Ioannis Ravisii Textoris epitome*. Ludguni: Seb. Gryphium, 1551.
Toscanella, Orazio. *Concetti et forme di Cicerone, del Boccaccio, del Bembo*. Venice: L. degli Avanzi, 1560.
– *Madrigali di G.M. Bonardo*. Venice: N.p., 1563.
– *Modo di studiare le Epistole Famigliari di M. Tullio Cicerone*. Venice: Giolito, 1567.
Vives, Juan Luis. *De institutione feminae Christianae*. Edited by C. Fantazzi and C. Matheussen. Translated by C. Fantazzi. New York: E.J. Brill, 1996.
– *Education of a Christian Woman*. Edited and translated by Charles Fantazzi. Chicago: University of Chicago Press, 2000.
Xenophon. *Oeconomicus: A Social and Historical Commentary*. Edited and translated by Sarah B. Pomeroy. Oxford: Clarendon Press, 1994.
Zenophonte da Ugubio, Andrea. *Formulario nuovo da dittar lettere amorose messive et responsive*. Venice: Francesco Bindoni e Mapheo Pasini, 1544.

II. Secondary Sources

Adams, H.M. *Catalogue of Books Printed on the Continent of Europe 1501–1600.* Cambridge: Cambridge Libraries, 1967.
Ademollo, Alesandro. 'Il brigantaggio e la corte di Roma nella prima metà del secolo decimosettimo.' *Nuova antologia* 1 (December 1880): 454–72.
– *I primi fasti della musica italiana a Parigi (1645–1662).* Milan: Ricordi, 1884.
– *I teatri di Roma nel secolo decimosettimo.* Bologna: Forni, 1969.
Adler, Sara Maria. 'Veronica Franco's Petrarchan *Terze Rime:* Subverting the Master's Plan.' *Italica* 65, no. 3 (1988): 213–33.
Adorni Braccesi, Simonetta. *Una città infetta. La repubblica di Lucca nella crisi religiosa del Cinquecento.* Florence: L. Olschki, 1994.
Affò, Ireneo. *Memorie di tre celebri principesse della famiglia Gonzaga.* Parma: Carmignani, 1786.
– *Memorie degli scrittori e letterati parmigiani.* Vol. 4. Bologna: Forni, 1793.
Ageno, Brambilla. 'Raccolte di lettere ed epistolari.' In *L'edizione critica dei testi volgari,* 228–33. Padua: Antenore, 1975.
Allacci, L. *Drammaturgia, accresciuta e continuata fino all'anno 1754.* Venice: Pasquali, 1755.
Altman, Janet Gurkin. *Epistolarity: Approaches to a Form.* Columbus: Ohio State University Press, 1982.
– 'The Letter-Book as Literary Institution 1539–1789: Toward a Cultural History of Published Correspondences in France.' *Yale French Studies* 71 (1986): 17–62.
Amadei, A. *Cronaca universale della città di Mantova.* Vol. 2. Mantua: C.I.T.E.M., 1955.
Anderson, Michael. 'Making Room: *Commedia* and the Privatisation of the Theatre.' In *The Commedia dell'Arte from the Renaissance to Dario Fo.* Edited by Christopher Cairns, 74–98. Lampeter: Edwin Mellen Press, 1989.
Andrews, Richard. 'Isabella Andreini and Others: Women on Stage in the Late Cinquecento.' In *Women in Italian Renaissance Culture and Society.* Edited by Letizia Panizza, 316–33. London: Legenda, 2005.
Apollonio, M. *Storia della Commedia dell'Arte.* Rome-Milan, 1930; facsimile edition, Florence: Sansoni, 1982.
Aromatico, Andrea. *Alchemy: The Great Secret.* New York: Harry Abrams, 2000.
Arlìa, C. 'Un bandito e una cortigiana letterati.' *Il Bibliofilo,* Anno II agosto-settembre, nos. 8–9 (1881): 164–66.
Bainton, R.H. *Donne della Riforma.* Turin: Claudiana, 1992.
Bareggi, Claudia Di Filippo. *Il mestiere di scrivere. Lavoro intellettuale e mercato librario a Venezia nel Cinquecento.* Rome: Bulzoni, 1988.

Bartoli, F.S. *Notizie istoriche de' comici italiani che fiorirono intorno all'anno MDC fino ai giorni presenti.* 2 vols. Padua, 1782; facsimile edition, Bologna: Arnaldo Forni, 1978.

Barucci, Guglielmo. 'Silenzio epistolare e dovere amicale. I percorsi di un topos dalla teoria greca al Cinquecento.' *Critica letteraria* 126, no. 2 (2005): 211–52.

Barzaghi, Antonio. *Donne o cortigiane? La prostituzione a Venezia: Documenti di costume dal XVI al XVIII secolo.* Verona: Bertani, 1980.

Baschet, Armand. *Les comédiens italiens à la cour de France.* Paris: E. Plon, 1882.

Bassanese, Fiora A. 'Private Lives and Public Lies: Texts by Courtesans of the Italian Renaissance.' *Texas Studies in Literature and Language* 30, no. 1 (1988): 295–319.

Basso, Janine. 'La lettera "familiare" nella retorica epistolare del XVI e del XVII secolo in Italia.' *Quaderni di retorica e poetica* 1 (1985): 57–65.

– *La genre épistolaire en langue italienne (1538–1662).* 2 vols. Rome: Bulzoni, 1990.

Battistini, Andrea. 'Gli epistolari.' In *L'io e la memoria.* Vol. 2, *Manuale di letteratura italiana. Storia per generi e problemi.* Edited by F. Brioschi and C. DiGirolamo, 435–48. Turin: Bolleti Boringhieri, 1994.

Bausi, Francesco. 'Le rime di e per Tullia D'Aragona.' In *Les femmes écrivains en Italie au moyen âge et à la renaissance.* Edited by G. Ulysse, 275–92. Aix en Provence: Publications de l'Université de Provence, 1994.

Beebee, Thomas. *Epistolary Fiction in Europe 1500–1850.* Cambridge: Cambridge University Press, 1999.

Bell, Rudolph. *How to Do It: Guides to Good Living for Renaissance Italians.* Chicago: University of Chicago Press, 1999.

Bellucci, Novella. 'Lettere di molte valorose donne ... e di alcune petegolette, ovvero: di un libro di lettere di Ortensio Lando.' In *Le carte messaggieri.* Edited by Amedeo Quondam, 255–76. Rome: Bulzoni, 1981.

Benhabib, Seyla. 'Models of Public Space: Hannah Arendt, the Liberal Tradition, and Jürgen Habermas.' In *Feminism, the Public and the Private.* Edited by Joan Landes, 65–99. Oxford: Oxford University Press, 1998.

Bensen, Pamela. *The Invention of the Renaissance Woman: The Challenge of Female Independence in the Literature and Thought of Italy and England.* University Park: Pennsylvania State University Press, 1992.

Bergamaschi, Domenico. *Storia di Gazuolo e suo marchesato.* Casalmaggiore: Tipografia Libreria Contini Carlo, 1883.

Berger, Harry Jr. *The Absence of Grace: Sprezzatura and Suspicion in Two Renaissance Courtesy Books.* Stanford, CA: Stanford University Press, 2000.

Bianchi, Dante. 'Una cortigiana rimatrice del Seicento: Margherita Costa.' *Rassegna critica della letteratura italiana* 29 (1924): 1–31.

- 'Una cortigiana rimatrice del Seicento: Margherita Costa.' *Rassegna critica della letteratura italiana* 29 (1924): 187–203.
- 'Trattati d'epistolografia nei XVI e XVII secolo.' *Giornale storico della letteratura italiana* 89 (1927): 111–26.

Bianconi, L., and T. Walker. 'Dalla Finta Pazza alla Veremonda.' In *Rivista italiana di Musicologia* 10 (1975): 379–454.

Biga, Emilia. *Una polemica antifemminista del '600. La 'Maschera scoperta' di Angelico Aprosio*. Ventimiglia: Civica Biblioteca Aprosiana, 1989.

Bochi, Giulia. *Donne e madonne: L'educazione femminile nel primo Rinascimento italiano*. Turin: Loescher, 1982.

Bongi, Salvatore. *Introduzione alle novelle di M. Ortensio Lando* ... Lucca: Baccelli, 1851.
- *Annali di Gabriel Giolito de' Ferrari*. Vol. I. Rome: Bibliopola, 1965.

Bowd, Stephen D. *Reform before the Reformation: Vincenzo Querini and the Religious Renaissance in Italy*. Leiden: Brill, 2002.

Branca, Vittore. *Boccaccio medievale*. Florence: Sansoni, 1956.

Brewer, John. 'This, That, and the Other: Public, Social, and Private in the Seventeenth and Eighteenth Centuries.' In *Shifting the Boundaries: Transformation of the Languages of Public and Private in the Eighteenth Century*. Edited by Dario Castiglione and Lesley Sharpe, 1–21. Exeter: University of Exeter Press, 1995.

Brown, Judith C. 'Gender.' In *Palgrave Advances in Renaissance Historiography*. Edited by Jonathan Woolfson, 177–92. New York: Palgrave, 2005.

Bullock, Allan, and Gabriella Palange. 'Per una edizione critica delle opere di Chiara Matraini.' In *Studi in onore di Raffaelle Spongano*, 235–62. Bologna: Massimiliano Boni Editore.

Bullough, Vern L., and Bonnie Bullough. *Cross Dressing, Sex, and Gender*. Philadelphia: University of Pennsylvania Press, 1993.

Burke, Peter. *The Fortunes of the Courtier*. University Park: Pennsylvania State University Press, 1995.

Butler, Judith. *Gender Trouble: Feminism and the Subversion of Identity*. New York: Routledge, 1990.

Butler, K.T. *The 'Gentlest Art' in Renaissance Italy*. Cambridge: Cambridge University Press, 1954.

Calabrese, Michael A. 'Feminism and the Packaging of Boccaccio's *Fiammetta*.' *Italica* 74, no. 1 (Spring 1997): 20–42.

Calhoun, Craig. *Habermas and the Public Sphere*. Cambridge, MA: MIT Press, 1992.

Calvi, Giulia, ed. *Barocco al femminile*. Bari: Laterza, 1992.

Camargo, Martin. *Ars Dictaminis, Ars Dictandi*. Turnhout, Belgium: Brepols, 1991.

Camillocci, Daniela Soffaroli. 'La monaca esemplare: Lettere spirituali di madre Battistina Vernazza.' *Per Lettera: La scrittura epistolare femminile tra archivio e tipografia secoli XV–XVII*. Edited by Gabriella Zarri, 235–61. Rome: Viella, 1999.

Campbell, Julie. *Literary Circles and Gender in Early Modern Europe*. Aldershot, UK: Ashgate, 2006.

Canosa, Romano. *Il velo e il cappuccio: monacazioni forzate e sessualità nei conventi femminili in Italia tra Quattrocento e Settecento*. Rome: Sapere, 2000.

Cantimori, Delio. *Eretici italiani del Cinquecento*. Florence: Sansoni, 1939.

– *Prospettive di storia ereticale italiana del Cinquecento*. Bari: LaTerza, 1960.

Caponetto, Salvatore. *La riforma protestante nell'Italia del Cinquecento*. Turin: Claudiana, 1992.

Capucci, M. 'Margherita Costa.' In *Dizionario biografico degli italiani*. Vol. 30. Rome: Istituto della enciclopedia italiana, 1960–.

Casagrande di Villaviera, Rita. *Le cortigiane veneziane del Cinquecento*. Milan: Longanesi, 1968.

Case, Ellen. *Feminism and Theater*. New York: Methuen, 1988.

Chartier, Roger, Alan Boreau, and Cecile Dauphin, eds. *Correspondence: Models of Letter Writing from the Middle Ages to the Nineteenth Century*. Translated by Christopher Woodall. Princeton: Princeton University Press, 1997.

Chemello, Adriana, ed. *Alla lettera: Teorie e pratiche epistolari dai Greci al Novecento*. Milan: Angelo Guerini, 1998.

– 'Il codice epistolare femminile.' In *Per lettera: La scrittura epistolare femminile tra archivio e tipografia, secoli xv-xvii*. Edited by Gabriella Zarri, 3–42. Rome: Viella, 1999.

– 'Literary Critics and Scholars, 1700–1850.' Translated by Peter Brand. In *A History of Women's Writing in Italy*. Edited by L. Panizza and S. Wood. Translated by Jennifer Lorch, 135–49. Cambridge: Cambridge University Press, 2001.

Cherchi, Paolo. 'La fonte dei *Cataloghi* di O. L.' *Studi e problemi di critica testuale* 18 (1979): 142–8.

– 'L'*Officina* del Testore e alcune opere di Ortensio Lando.' In *Enciclopedismo e politica della riscrittura: Tommaso Garzoni*. Edited by P. Cherchi. Pisa: Pacini, 1980.

– 'Plagio e/o riscrittura nel Secondo Cinquecento.' In *Furto e plagio nella letteratura del classicism*. Edited by R. Gigliucci, 283–99. Rome: Bulzoni, 1998.

– *Polimatia di riuso: Mezzo secolo di plagio (1539–1589)*. Rome: Bulzoni, 1998.

Cherewatuk, Karen, and Ulrike Wiethaus, eds. *Dear Sister: Medieval Women and the Epistolary Genre*. Philadelphia: University of Pennsylvania Press, 1993.

Chojnacka, Monica. 'Women, Charity and Community in Early Modern Venice: The Casa delle Zitelle.' *Renaissance Quarterly* 51 (1998): 68–91.

- *Working Women of Early Modern Venice*. Baltimore: Johns Hopkins University Press, 2001.
Chojnacki, Stanley. 'Measuring Adulthood: Adolescence and Gender in Renaissance Venice.' *Journal of Family History* 17 (1992): 371–95.
- 'Daughters and Oligarchs: Gender and the Early Renaissance State.' In *Gender and Society in Early Renaissance Italy*. Edited by Judith Brown and Robert C. Davis, 63–86. London: Longman, 1998.
Clough, Cecil H. 'The Cult of Antiquity: Letters and Letter Colletions.' In *Cultural Aspects of the Renaissance: Essays in Honor of Paul Oskar Kristeller*. Edited by Cecil H. Clough, 31–67. Manchester: Manchester University Press, 1976.
Clubb, Louise George. 'The State of the *Arte* in the Andreini's Time.' In *Studies in the Italian Renaissance: Essays in Memory of Arnolfo B. Ferruolo*. Edited by Gian Paolo Biasin et al., 263–81. Naples: Società editrice napoletana, 1985.
- *Italian Drama in Shakespeare's Time*. New Haven, CT: Yale University Press, 1989.
Collina, Beatrice. 'L'esemplarità delle donne illustri fra Umanesimo e Controriforma.' In *Donna, disciplina, creanza cristiana dal XV al XVII secolo*. Edited by G. Zarri, 103–19. Rome: Edizioni di storia e letteratura, 1996.
Constable, Giles. *Letters and Letter-Collections*. Belgium: Editions Brepolis, 1976.
Conti Odorisio, Ginevra. *Donna e società nel Seicento*. Rome: Bulzoni, 1979.
Cortigiane de secolo XVI. Florence: Il 'Giornale di Erudizione,' 1892.
Costa-Zalessow, Natalia. 'Tarabotti's *La semplicità ingannata* and its Twentieth-Century Interpreters, with Unpublished Documents Regarding Its Condemnation to the *Index*.' *Italica* 78, no. 3 (2001): 314–25.
Couchman, Jane, and Ann Crabb, eds. *Women's Letters across Europe, 1400–1700: Form and Persuasion*. Aldershot, UK: Ashgate, 2005.
Coudert, Alison. *Alchemy: The Philosopher's Stone*. Boulder, CO: Shambhala, 1980.
Cox, Virginia. *The Renaissance Dialogue: Literary Dialogue in its Social and Political Contexts, Castiglione to Galileo*. Cambridge: Cambridge University Press, 1992.
- *Women's Writing in Italy 1400–1650*. Baltimore: Johns Hopkins University Press, 2008.
Crabb, Ann. *The Strozzi of Florence: Widowhood and Family Solidarity in the Renaissance*. Ann Arbor: University of Michigan Press, 2000.
- 'How to Influence Your Children: Form and Persuasion in Alessandra Macinghi Strozzi's Letters to Her Sons.' In *Women's Letters across Europe, 1400–1700: Form and Persuasion*. Edited by J. Couchman and A. Crabb, 21–42. Aldershot, UK: Ashgate, 2005.
Crescimbeni, Giovanni Maria. *Commentarij ... intorno alla sua istoria della vulgar poesia*. Rome: Antonio de' Rossi, 1710.

Croce, Benedetto. 'Intorno alla Commedia dell'Arte.' In *Poesia popolare e poesia d'arte*. Bari: LaTerza, 1933.
- *Nuovi saggi sulla letteratura italiana del Seicento*. Bari: La Terza, 1968.

Cyr, Miriam. *Letters of a Portuguese Nun: Uncovering the Mystery behind a Seventeenth-Century Forbidden Love*. New York: Hyperion, 2006.

Daenens, Francine. 'Donne valorose, eretiche, finte sante: note sull'antologia giolitina del 1548.' In *Per lettera: La scrittura epistolare femminile*. Edited by G. Zarri, 181–207. Rome: Viella, 1999.
- 'Isabella Sforza: Beyond the Stereotype.' In *Women in Italian Renaissance Culture and Society*. Edited by Letizia Panizza, 35–55. Oxford: European Humanities Research Center, 2000.

Daybell, James. 'Women's Letters and Letter-Writing in England, 1540–1603: An Introduction to Issues of Authorship and Construction.' *Shakespeare Studies* 27 (September 1999): 161–86.
- ed. *Early Modern Women's Letter-Writing, 1450–1700*. New York: Palgrave, 2001.
- '"I wold whshe my doings myght be ... secret": Privacy and the Social Practices of Reading Women's Letters in Sixteenth-century England.' In *Women's Letters across Europe, 1400–1700: Form and Persuasion*. Edited by Jane Couchman and Ann Crabb, 143–61. Aldershot, UK: Ashgate, 2005.
- 'Scripting a Female Voice: Women's Epistolary Rhetoric in Sixteenth-Century Letters of Petition.' *Women's Writing* 13, no. 1 (March 2006): 3–22.

Davis, Natalie Zemon. 'Beyond the Market: Books as Gifts in Sixteenth-Century France.' *Transactions of the Royal Historical Society* 33 (1983): 69–88.

Dazzi, Manlio. *Il fiore della lirica veneziana*. Vol. 2, *Il libro segreto (chiuso)*. Vicenza: Neri Pozza, 1956.

de' Angelis, Francesca Romana. *La divina Isabella*. Florence: Sansoni, 1991.

De Nichilo, Adriana. 'La lettera e il comico.' In *Le carte messaggiere. Retorica e modelli di comunicazione epistolare: per un indice dei libri di lettere del Cinquecento*. Edited by Amedeo Quondam, 213–17. Rome: Bulzoni, 1981.

Dersofi, Nancy. 'Isabella Andreini (1562–1604).' In *Italian Women Writers: A Bio-Bibliographic Sourcebook*. Edited by Rinaldina Russell, 18–25. Westport, CT: Greenwood Press, 1994.

Di Maio, Romeo. *Donna e rinascimento*. Milan: Il Saggiatore, 1987.

Dionisotti, Carlo. 'Letteratura italiana all'epoca del Concilio di Trento.' In *Geografia e storia della letteratura italiana*. Turin: Einaudi, 1967.

Dixon, Laurinda S. *Perilous Chastity: Women and Illness in Pre-Enlightenment Art and Medicine*. Ithaca, NY: Cornell University Press, 1995.

Doglio, Maria Luisa, ed. *Della eccellenza e dignità delle donne di Galeazzo Flavio Capra*. Rome: Bulzoni, 1988.
– 'Scrittura e "offizio di parole" nelle *Lettere familiari* di Veronica Franco.' In *Lettera e donna. Scrittura epistolare al femminile tra Quattro e Cinquecento*. Rome: Bulzoni, 1993.
– *L'arte delle lettere. Idea e pratica della scrittura epistolare tra Quattro e Seicento*. Bologna: Il Mulino, 2000.
– 'Letter-Writing, 1350–1650.' In *A History of Women's Writing in Italy*. Edited by L. Panizza and S. Wood, 13–24. Translated by Jennifer Lorch. Cambridge: Cambridge University Press, 2001.
Dunn, Marilynn. 'Spaces Shaped for Spiritual Perfection.' In *Architecture and the Politics of Gender*. Edited by Helen Hills, 151–76. Aldershot, UK: Ashgate, 2003.
Eamon, William. *Science and the Secrets of Nature: Books of Secrets in Medieval and Early Modern Culture*. Princeton: Princeton University Press, 1994.
– 'Alchemy in Popular Culture: Leonardo Fioravanti and the Search for the Philosopher's Stone.' *Early Science and Medicine* 5 (2000): 196–214.
Eamon, William, and Francoise Peheau. 'The Accademia Segreta of Girolamo Ruscelli. A Sixteenth-Century Italian Scientific Society.' *Isis* 75 (1984): 327–42.
Earle, Rebecca, ed. *Epistolary Selves: Letters and Letter Writers 1600–1945*. Aldershot, UK: Ashgate, 1999.
Eger, Elizabeth, et al., eds. *Women, Writing, and the Public Sphere 1700–1830*. Cambridge: Cambridge University Press, 2001.
Eisenstein, Elizabeth L. *The Printing Press as an Agent of Change: Communications and Cultural Transformations in Early Modern Europe*. Cambridge: Cambridge University Press, 1997.
Erenstein, Robert L. 'Isabella Andreini: A Lady of Virtue and High Renown.' In *Essays on Drama and Theater: Liber amicorum Benjamin Hunnigher*, 37–49. Amsterdam: Moussalt's Uitgeverij, 1973.
Evangelisti, Silvia. *Nuns. A History of Convent Life 1450–1700*. Oxford: Oxford University Press, 2007.
Fahy, Conor. 'Three Early Renaissance Treatises on Women.' *Italian Studies* 11 (1956): 30–55.
– 'Un trattato di Vincenzo Maggi sulle donne e un'opera sconosciuta di Ortensio Lando.' *Giornale storico della letteratura italiana* 138 (1961): 254–72.
Favretti, Elvira. 'Rime e lettere di Veronica Franco.' *Giornale storico della letteratura italiana* 163 (1986): 344–82.
– *Figure e fatti del Cinquecento veneto*. Alessandria: Edizioni dell'Orso, 1992.

Feldman, Martha. 'The Academy of Domenico Venier, Music's Literary Muse in Mid-Cinquecento Venice.' *Renaissance Quarterly* 44, no. 3 (1991): 476–512.
- *City Culture and the Madrigal at Venice*. Berkeley: University of California Press, 1995.

Feldman, Martha, and Bonnie Gordon, eds. *The Courtesan's Arts: Cross-Cultural Perspectives*. Oxford: Oxford University Press, 2006.

Ferguson, Margaret. 'Renaissance Concepts of the "Woman Writer."' *Women and Literature in Britain 1500–1700*. Edited by Helen Wilcox, 143–68. Cambridge: Cambridge University Press, 1996.

Ferguson, Margaret, Maureen Quilligan, and Nancy Vickers, eds. *Rewriting the Renaissance: The Discourse of Sexual Difference in Early Modern Europe*. Chicago: University of Chicago Press, 1986.

Ferri, Pietro. *Biblioteca femminile italiana*. Padua: Crescini, 1842.

Ferrone, Siro. 'Dalle parti "scannate" al testo scritto. La Commedia dell'Arte all'inizio del sec. XVII.' *Paragone/Letteratura* 34, no. 398 (1983): 53–61.
- 'Arlecchino rapito. Sulla drammaturgia italiana all'inizio del Seicento.' In *Studi di filologia e critica offerti dagli allievi a Lanfranco Caretti*, Vol. 1, 319–53. Rome: Salerno, 1985.
- ed. *Commedie dell'arte*. Milan: Mursia, 1985–6.
- 'Margherita Costa, *Li Buffoni*.' In *Commedie dell'Arte*. Edited by Siro Ferrone. Vol. 2, 245–359. Milan: Mursia, 1986.
- *Attori mercanti corsari. La Commedia dell'Arte in Europa tra Cinque e Seicento*. Turin: Einaudi, 1993.

Findlen, Paula. 'Humanism, Politics and Pornography in Renaissance Italy.' In *The Invention of Pornography: Obscenity and the Origins of Modernity, 1500–1800*. Edited by Lynn Hunt, 49–108. New York: Zone Books, 1993.
- 'Masculine Prerogatives: Gender, Space, and Knowledge in the Early Modern Musueum.' In *The Architecture of Science*. Edited by Peter Galison and Emily Thompson, 29–57. Cambridge, MA: MIT Press, 1999.

Fiocco, Achille. 'Isabella Andreini.' In *Enciclopedia dello spettacolo* Vol. 1, 555–8. Rome: Casa Editrice Le Maschere, 1954.

Firpo, Luigi. 'Thomas More e la sua fortuna in Italia.' *Occidente. Rivista bimestrale di studi politici* 7, nos. 3–4 (1952): 225–41.

Fitzmaurice, Susan. *The Familiar Letter in Early Modern English: A Pragmatic Approach*. Philadelphia: John Benjamins Publishing , 2002.

Fleischer, Manfred P. '"Are Women Human?" The Debate of 1595 between Valens Acidalius and Simon Gediccus.' *Sixteenth Century Journal* 12, no. 2 (Summer 1981): 107–20.

Floris, Gonoria, and Luisa Mulas, eds. *Lettere a Aretino*. Rome: Bulzoni, 1997.

Folena, G. 'Premessa.' *Quaderni di storia e poetica* 1 (1985): 5–9.

- 'L'espressionismo epistolare di Paolo Giovio.' In *Il linguaggio del caos. Studi sul plurilinguismo rinascimentale*, 200–41. Torino: Bollati Boringhieri, 1991.
Fondi, Giovanni Malquori. 'De la "lettre-canevas" à la "pièce de cabinet: les Lettere d'Isabella Andreini, tràduites par Francois de Grenaille.' In *Contacts culturels et échanges linguistiques au XVIIe siècle en France: actes du 3e Colloque du Centre international de rencotres sur le XViie siècle, Université de Fribourg (Suisse) 1996,* 125–45. Paris: Papers on French Seventeenth-Century Literature, 1997.
Fontanini, Giusto. *Biblioteca dell'eloquenza italiana.* Annotated by Apostolo Zeno. Parma: Fratelli Gozzi, 1883.
Franco, Veronica. *Rime.* Edited by Stefano Bianchi. Milan: Mursia, 1995.
Fraser, Nancy. 'Rethinking the Public Sphere: A Contribution to the Critique of Actually Existing Democracy.' In *Postmodernism and the Re-reading of Modernity.* Edited by Francis Barker et al., 197–231. Manchester: Manchester University Press, 1992.
Fumaroli, M. 'Genèse de l'épistolographie classique: rhétorique humaniste de la lettere, de Petrarche à Juste Lipse.' *Revue d'histoire littéraire de la France* 78 (1978): 886–905.
Furey, Constance. 'Intellects Inflamed in Christ: Women and Spiritualized Scholarship in Renaissance Christianity.' *Journal of Religion* 84 (2004): 1–22.
- *Erasmus, Contarini, and the Religious Republic of Letters.* Cambridge: Cambridge University Press, 2006.
Gamba, Bartolommeo. *Lettere di donne italiane del secolo decimosesto.* Venice: Alvisopoli, 1832.
Gambelli, Delia. *Arlecchino a Parigi: Dall'Inferno alla corte del Re Sole.* Rome: Bulzoni, 1993.
Gigliucci, Roberto, ed. *Furto e plagio nella letteratura del classicismo.* Rome: Bulzoni, 1998.
Gilchrist, Roberta. *Gender and Material Culture: The Archaeology of Religious Women.* London: Routledge, 1994.
Gilmore, Leigh. *Autobiographics: A Feminist Theory of Women's Self-Representation.* Ithaca, NY: Cornell University Press, 1994.
Gilroy, Amanda, and W.M. Verhoeven, eds. *Epistolary Histories: Letters, Fiction, Culture.* Charlottesville: University of Virginia Press, 2000.
Ginzburg, Carlo. *Il nicodemismo: Simulazione e dissimulazione religiosa nell'Europa del '500.* Turin: Einaudi, 1970.
Giustiniani, Vito R. 'La communication érudite: Les lettres humanistes et l'article moderne de revue.' In *La correspondance de Erasme et l'épistolographie humaniste: Colloque international tenu en novembre 1983,* 109–33. Bruxelles: Editions de l'Université de Bruxelles, 1985.

- 'Lo scrittore e l'uomo nell'epistolare di Francesco Filelfo.' In *Francesco Filelfo nel quinto centenario della morte. Atti del XVII convegno di studi maceratesi* (Tolentino, 27–30 settembre 1981), 249–74. Padua: Editrice Antenore, 1986.
Goldsmith, Elizabeth C., ed. *Writing the Female Voice: Essays on Women's Epistolary Literature*. Boston: Northeastern University Press, 1989.
Goldsmith, Elizabeth, and Dena Goodman, eds. *Going Public: Women and Publishing in Early Modern France*. Ithaca, NY: Cornell University Press, 1995.
Goodman, Dena. *The Republic of Letters: A Cultural History of the French Enlightenment*. Ithaca, NY: Cornell University Press, 1996.
Gordon, Bonnie. 'The Courtesan's Singing Body as Cultural Capital in Seventeenth-Century Italy.' In *The Courtesan's Arts: Cross-Cultural Perspectives*. Edited by Martha Feldman and Bonnie Gordon, 182–98. Oxford: Oxford University Press, 2006.
Graziosi, Elisabetta. 'Arcipelago sommerso: Le rime delle monache tra obbedienza e trasgressione.' In *I monasteri femminili come centri di cultura fra rinascimento e barocco, atti del convegno internazionale Bologna, 8–10 dicembre 2000*. Edited by Zarri and Gianna Pomata, 146–81. Rome: Edizioni di Storia e Letteratura, 2005.
Greenblatt, Stephen. *Renaissance Self-Fashioning: From More to Shakespeare*. Chicago: University of Chicago Press, 1980.
- 'Fiction and Friction.' In *Reconstructing Individualism: Autonomy, Individualism and the Self in Western Thought*. Edited by Thomas C. Heller et al., 30–52. Stanford: Stanford University Press, 1986.
Grendler, Paul. *Critics of the Italian World*. Madison: University of Wisconsin Press, 1969.
- *Schooling in Renaissance Italy: Literacy and Learning, 1300–1600*. Baltimore: Johns Hopkins University Press, 1989.
Griguolo, Primo. 'Giovanni Maria Bonardo e l'ambiente culturale di Fratta nel '500.' In *Palladio e palladianesimo in Polesine*. Edited by Luciano Alberti et al., 79–85. Rovigo: Associazione Culturale Minelliana, 1984.
- *Una villa al confine: Documenti storico-letterari su Fratta nel '500*. Padua: Bertoncello Artigrafiche, 1988.
Gualtierotti, Piero. *Matteo Bandello alla corte di Luigi Gonzaga*. Mantua: Edizioni Vitam, 1978.
Guardenti, R. *Gli italiani a Parigi. La Comedie Italienne (1660–1697). Storia, pratica scenica, iconografia*. 2 vols. Rome: Bulzoni, 1990.
Guillén, Claudio. 'Notes toward the Study of the Renaissance Letter.' In *Renaissance Genres: Essays on Theory, History, and Interpretation*. Edited by Barbara Keifer Lewalski, 70–101. Cambridge, MA: Harvard University Press, 1986.

Günsberg, Maggie. *Gender and the Italian Stage: From the Renaissance to the Present Day.* Cambridge: Cambridge University Press, 1997.

Habermas, Jürgen. *The Structural Transformation of the Public Sphere: An Inquiry into a Category of Bourgeois Society.* Translated by Thomas Burger with Frederick Lawrence. Cambridge, MA: MIT Press, 1989.

Hagedorn, Suzanne C. *Abandoned Women: Rewriting the Classics in Dante, Boccaccio, and Chaucer.* Ann Arbor: University of Michigan Press, 2004.

Harth, Helene. 'L'épistolographie humaniste entre professionalisme et souci littéraire: L'exemple de Poggio Bracciolini.' In *La correspondance de Erasme et l'épistolographie humaniste: Colloque international tenu en novembre 1983*, 135–44. Bruxelles: Editions de l'Université de Bruxelles, 1985.

Harvey, Elizabeth D. *Ventriloquized Voices: Feminist Theory and English Renaissance Texts.* London: Routledge, 1992.

Henderson, Judith Rice. 'Defining the Genre of the Letter in Juan Luis Vives' *De conscribendi epistolis.*' *Renaissance and Reformation* 7 (1983): 89–105.

– 'The Enigma of Erasmus' *Conficiendarum epistolarum formula.*' *Renaissance and Reformation* 13 (1989): 313–30.

– 'On Reading the Rhetoric of the Renaissance Letter.' In *Renaissance Rhetoric.* Edited by Heinrich F. Plett, 143-62. Berlin: Walter de Gruyter, 1993.

Henke, Robert. *Performance and Literature in the Commedia dell'Arte.* Cambridge: Cambridge University Press, 2002.

Herlihy, David, and Christiane Klapisch-Zuber. *Les Toscans e leurs familles: Une étude du cataste Florentine de 1427.* Paris: Presse de la Fondation nationale des sciences politiques, 1978.

Hills, Helen. *Invisible City: The Architecture of Devotion in Seventeenth-Century Neapolitan Convents.* Oxford: Oxford University Press, 2004.

Hollander, Robert. *Boccaccio's Two Venuses.* New York: Columbia University Press, 1977.

Howe, Elizabeth. *The First English Actresses: Women and Drama 1660–1700.* Cambridge: Cambridge University Press, 1992.

Hughes, Diane Owen. 'Sumptuary Laws and Social Relations in Renaissance Italy.' In *Disputes and Settlements: Law and Human Relations in the West.* Edited by John Bossy, 343–55. Cambridge: Cambridge University Press, 1983.

Hull, Suzanne W. *Women According to Men: The World of Tudor-Stuart Women.* Walnut Creek, CA: Altamira Press, 1996.

Iliffe, Robert. 'Author-Mongering: The "Editor" between Producer and Consumer.' In *The Consumption of Culture 1600–1800: Image, Object, Text.* Edited by Ann Bermingham and John Brewer, 166–92. London: Routledge, 1995.

Infelise, Mario. 'Libri e politica nella Venezia di Arcangela Tarabotti.' *Annali di storia moderna e contemporanea* 8 (2002): 31–45.

– 'Books and Politics in Arcangela Tarabotti's Venice.' In *Arcangela Tarabotti: A Literary Nun in Baroque Venice*. Edited by Elissa Weaver, 57–72. Ravenna: Longo, 2006.

Irigaray, Luce. *This Sex Which Is Not One*. Translated by Catherine Porter with Carolyn Burke. Ithaca, NY: Cornell University Press, 1985.

Jacobs, Federica. 'Aretino and Michelangelo, Dolce and Titian: Femmina, Masculo, Grazia.' *Art Bulletin* 82, no. 1 (March 2000): 51–67.

Jacobus, Mary. 'Intimate Connections: Scandalous Memoires and Epistolary Indiscretion.' In *Women, Writing, and the Public Sphere*. Edited by Elizabeth Eger, 274–89. Cambridge: Cambridge University Press, 2001.

Jannaco, C. 'Stesura e tendeneza letteraria della commedia improvvisa in due prologhi di Flaminio Scala.' *Studi secenteschi* I (1960): 195–207.

Jardine, Lisa. *Still Harping on Daughters: Women and Drama in the Age of Shakespeare*. Sussex: The Harvester Press, 1983.

– *Erasmus: Man of Letters*. Princeton: Princeton University Press, 1993.

Jed, Stephanie. *Chaste Thinking: The Rape of Lucretia and the Birth of Humanism*. Bloomington: Indiana University Press, 1989.

– 'Arcangela Tarabotti and Gabriel Naudé: Libraries, Taxonomies and *Ragion di Stato*.' In *Arcangela Tarabotti: A Literary Nun in Baroque Venice*. Edited by Elissa Weaver, 129–40. Ravenna: Longo, 1995.

Jensen, Katherine Ann. 'Male Models of Feminine Epistolarity, or, How to Write Like a Woman in Seventeenth-Century France.' In *Writing the Female Voice: Essays on Women's Epistolary Literature*. Edited by E. Goldsmith, 25–45. Boston: Northeastern University Press, 1989.

– *Writing Love: Letters, Women, and the Novel in France, 1605–1776*. Carbondale: Southern Illinois University Press, 1995.

Jones, Ann Rosalind. *The Currency of Eros: Women's Love Lyric in Europe 1540–1620*. Bloomington: Indiana University Press, 1990.

– 'Designing Women: The Self as Spectacle in Mary Wroth and Veronica Franco.' *Reading Mary Wroth: Representing Alternatives in Early Modern England*. Edited by Naomi J. Miller and Gary Waller, 135–53. Knoxville: University of Tennessee Press, 1991.

– 'Bad Press: Modern Editors versus Early Modern Women Poets (Tullia d'Aragona, Gaspara Stampa, Veronica Franco).' In *Strong Voices, Weak History*. Edited by Pamela Benson and Victoria Kirkham, 287–313. Ann Arbor: University of Michigan Press, 2005.

Jones, Verina, and Claire Honess, eds. *Le donne delle minoranze.* Turin: Claudiana, 1999.

Jordan, Constance. 'Boccaccio's In-famous Women: Gender and Civic Virtue in the *De claris mulieribus*.' In *Ambiguous Realities: Women in the Middle Ages*

and Renaissance. Edited by Carole Levin and Jeannie Watson, 25–47. Detroit: Wayne State University Press, 1987.
– *Renaissance Feminism: Literary Texts and Political Models.* Ithaca, NY: Cornell University Press, 1990.
Kamuf, Peggy. 'Writing Like a Woman.' In *Women and Language in Literature and Society.* Edited by Sally McConnell-Ginet et al., 284–99. New York: Praeger, 1980.
Kauffman, Linda S. *Discourses of Desire: Gender, Genre and Epistolary Fictions.* Ithaca, NY: Cornell University Press, 1990.
Kavey, Allison. *Books of Secrets: Natural Philosophy in England, 1550–1600.* Champaign: University of Illinois Press, 2007.
Kelly, Joan. *Women, History and Theory: The Essays of Joan Kelly.* Chicago: University of Chicago Press, 1984.
Kelso, R. *Doctrine for the Lady of the Renaissance.* Urbana: University of Illinois Press, 1956.
Kendrick, Robert. *Celestial Sirens: Nuns and Their Music in Early Modern Milan.* Oxford: Clarendon Press, 1996.
Kenney, Theresa M. *'Women Are Not Human': An Anonymous Treatise and Responses.* New York: Crossroad Publishing, 1998.
Kerr, Rosalind. 'Isabella Andreini, Comica Gelosa 1562-1604: Petrarchism for the Theatre Public.' *Quaderni d'Italianistica* 27, no. 2 (2006): 71–92.
King, Margaret L. 'Book-Lined Cells: Women and Humanism in the Early Renaissance.' In *Beyond Their Sex: Learned Women of the European Past.* Edited by Patricia Labalme, 6–90. New York: New York University Press, 1980.
– *Venetian Humanism in an Age of Patrician Dominance.* Princeton: Princeton University Press, 1986.
King, Margaret, and Albert Rabil Jr., eds. *Her Immaculate Hand: Selected Works by and about the Women Humanists of Quattrocento Italy.* 2nd rev. ed. Binghamton, NY: Medieval and Renaissance Texts and Studies, 1991.
Kirkham, Victoria. 'Creative Partners: The Marriage of Laura Battiferra and Bartolomeo Ammannati.' *Renaissance Quarterly* 55, no. 2 (2002): 498–558.
LaBalme, Patricia, ed. *Beyond Their Sex: Learned Women and the European Past.* New York: New York University Press, 1980.
– 'Venetian Women on Women: Three Early Modern Feminists.' *Archivio veneto* 5, no. 117 (1981): 81–108.
Landes, Joan. *Women and the Public Sphere in the Age of the French Revolution.* Ithaca, NY: Cornell University Press, 1988.
– ed. *Feminism: The Public and the Private.* Oxford: Oxford University Press, 1998.
Larivaille, Paul. *La vita quotidiana delle cortigiane nell'Italia del Rinascimento. Roma e Venezia nei secoli XV e XVI.* Translated by M. Pizzorno. Milan: Rizzoli, 1983.

- *Pietro Aretino*. Rome: Salerno Editrice, 1997.
Laven, Mary. *Virgins of Venice: Broken Vows and Cloistered Lives in the Renaissance Convent*. New York: Penguin, 2002.
- 'Cast Out and Shut In: The Experience of Nuns in Counter-Reformation Venice.' In *At the Margins: Minority Groups in Premodern Italy*. Edited by Stephen J. Milner, 72–93. Mineapolis: University of Minnesota Press, 2005.
Lawner, Lynn. *Lives of the Courtesans*. New York: Rizzoli, 1987.
Lea, K.M. *Italian Popular Comedy: A Study in the Commedia dell'Arte, 1520–1620. With special reference to the English stage*. 2 vols. Oxford: Clarendon Press, 1934.
Leigh, M. Diberti. *Veronica Franco. Donna poetessa e cortigiana del Rinascimento*. Ivrea: Priuli and Verucca, 1988.
Lenzi, Maria Ludovica. *Donne e madonne: l'educazione femminile nel primo Rinascimento italiano*. Turin: Loescher Editore, 1982.
Longo, Nicola. *Del 'buon inchiostro': il sistema letterario nelle* Lettere familiari *di Gerolamo Parabosco*. Urbino: Quattro Venti, 1984.
- *Letteratura e lettere: Indagine nell'epistolografia cinquecentesca*. Rome: Bulzoni, 1999.
Lowe, Kate. *Nuns' Chronicles and Convent Culture in Renaissance and Counter-Reformation Italy*. Cambridge: Cambridge University Press, 2003.
MacKenzie, Allan T. *Sent as a Gift: Eight Correspondences from the Eighteenth Century*. Athens: University of Georgia Press, 1993.
MacNeil, Anne. 'The Divine Madness of Isabella Andreini.' *Journal of the Royal Music Association* 120 (1995): 195–215.
- 'The Virtue of Gender.' In *La femme lettrée à la Renaissance*. Edited by Michel Bastianesen, 147–64. Louvain, Belgium: Poetas, 1997.
- *Music and Women of the Commedia dell'Arte in the Late Sixteenth Century*. Oxford: Oxford University Press, 2003.
- ed. *Selected Poems of Isabella Andreini*. Translated by James Wyatt Cook. Lantham, MA: The Scarecrow Press, 2005.
Malavasi, Stefania. *Giovanni Maria Bonardo agronomo polesano del Cinquecento*. Venice: Deputazione Editrice, 1988.
- 'Lucrezia Gonzaga e la vita culturale a Fratta nella prima metà del '500.' In *Vespasiano Gonzaga e il ducato di Sabbioneta*. Atti del Convegno Sabbioneta Mantova 12–13 ott. 1991. Edited by Ugo Bazzotti, Daniela Ferrari, and Cesare Mozzarelli, 301–14. Mantua: Academia Nazionale Virgiliana di Scienze, Lettere Arti, 1993.
Marotti, F. 'Il *Teatro delle Favole Rappresentative*: un progetto utopico.' In *Biblioteca Teatrale*, nos. 15–16 (1976): 191–215.

Marotti, F., and G. Romei, eds. *La Commedia dell'Arte e la società barocca. La professione del teatro.* Rome: Bulzoni, 1991.

Marti, M. 'L'epistolario come 'genere' e un problema editoriale.' *Studi e problemi di critica testuale* (1961): 203–08.

Martin, John. *Venice's Hidden Enemies: Italian Heretics in a Renaissance City.* Berkeley: University of California Press, 1993.

Martin, Ruth. *Witchcraft and the Inquisition in Venice 1550–1650.* New York: Basil Blackwell, 1989.

Masson, Georgina. *The Courtesans of the Italian Renaissance.* London: Secker and Warburg, 1975.

Matt, Luigi. *Teoria e prassi dell'epistolografia italiana tra Cinquecento e primo Seicento.* Rome: Bonacci, 2005.

Maylender, Michele. *Storia delle accademie d'Italia.* 5 vols. Bologna: Licinio Cappelli, 1926–30.

McAlpin, Mary. 'Poststructuralist Feminism and the Imaginary Woman Writer: The *Lettres portugaises.*' *The Romanic Review* 90, no. 1 (1999): 27–44.

McClure, George W. *Sorrow and Consolation in Italian Humanism.* Princeton: Princeton University Press, 1991.

Medioli, Francesca. 'Monacazioni forzate: Donne ribelle al proprio destino.' In *Clio: Trimestral di studi storici* 30 (1994): 431–54.

– 'Alcune lettere autografe di Arcangela Tarabotti: autocensura e immagine di sé.' *Rivista di Storia e Letteratura Religiosa* 32, no.1 (1996): 133–42.

– 'Monache e monacazioni nel Seicento.' In G. Zarri, F. Medioli, and P. Chiappa, 'De monialibus.' *Rivista di storia e letteratura religiosa* 33, no. 3 (1997): 670–93.

– 'The Dimensions of the Cloister: Enclosure, Constraint, and Protection in Seventeenth Century Italy.' In *Time, Space, and Women's Lives in Early Modern Italy.* Edited by Anne Jacobson Schutte, Thomas Kuehn, and Silvana Seidel Menchi, 165–80. Kirksville, MO: Truman State University Press, 2001.

– 'Arcangela Tarabotti's Reliability about Herself: Publication and Self-Representation (Together with a Small Collection of Previously Unpublished Letters).' *The Italianist* 23, no. 1 (2003): 54–101.

Medioli, Francesca, and Flavia de Rubeis. 'La scrittura forzata: Le lettere autografe di Arcangela Tarabotti.' *Rivista di Storia e Letteratura Religiosa* 32, no.1 (1996): 142–55.

Megale, Teresa. 'Una cantratrice, un buffone, una commedia del Seicento: "Li Buffoni" di Margherita Costa.' PhD diss., University of Florence, 1987–8.

– 'La commedia decifrata: metamorfosi e rispecchiamenti in *Li Buffoni* di Margherita Costa.' *Il Castello di Elsinore* 2 (1988): 64–76.

- *Il Tedeschino overo Difesa dell'arte del cavalier del piacere. Con l'epistolario e altri documenti.* Edited by B. Ricci. Florence: Le Lettere, 2003.
Melzi, Gaetano. *Dizionario di opere anonime e pseudonime di scrittori italiani.* Vol. 1. Milan: L. di Giacomo Pirola, 1848.
Migiel, Marilyn. 'Gender Studies and the Italian Renaissance.' In *Interpreting the Italian Renaissance: Literary Perspectives.* Edited by Antonio Toscano, 29–41. Stony Brook, NY: Forum Italicum, 1991.
Migiel, Marilyn, and Juliana Schiesari, eds. *Refiguring Women: Perspectives on Gender and the Italian Renaissance.* Ithaca, NY: Cornell University Press, 1991.
Milani, Marisa. 'L' 'incanto' di Veronica Franco.' *Giornale Storico della letteratura italiana* 262, no. 518 (1985): 250–63.
Miller, Nancy K. '"I's in Drag": The Sex of Recollection.' *The 18th Century: Theory and Interpretation* 22 (1981): 47–57.
Milligan, Gerry. 'The Politics of Effeminacy in *Il Cortegiano.*' *Italica* (2006): 345–66.
Molho, Anthony. 'Deception and Marriage Strategy in Renaissance Florence: The Case of Women's Ages.' *Renaissance Quarterly* 41 (1988): 193–217.
- *Marriage Alliance in Late Medieval Florence.* Cambridge: Cambridge University Press, 1994.
Molinari, Cesare. 'L'altra faccia del 1589: Isabella Andreini e la sua 'pazzia.' In *Firenze e la Toscana dei Medici nell'Europa del Cinquecento.* Vol. 2, *Musica e Spettacolo,* 565–73. Florence: Olschki, 1983.
- *La Commedia dell'Arte.* Milan: Mondadori, 1985.
Morabito, Raffaele. *Lettere e letteratura: Studi sull'epistolografia volgare in Italia.* Turin: Edizioni dell'Orso, 2001.
Moro, Giacomo. 'Selezione, autocensura, e progetto letterario: sulla formazione e la pubblicazione dei libri di lettere familiari nel periodo 1542–1552.' *Quaderni di storia e poetica* 1 (1985): 67–90.
Muir, Edward. *Civic Ritual in Renaissance Venice.* Princeton: Princeton University Press, 1986.
Murphy, James. *Rhetoric in the Middle Ages.* Berkeley: University of California Press, 1974.
Najemy, John. *Between Friends: The Machiavelli-Vettori Correspondence.* Princeton: Princeton University Press, 1993.
Newman, William R., and Anthony Grafton, eds. *Secrets of Nature: Astrology and Alchemy in Early Modern Europe.* Cambridge, MA: The MIT Press, 2001.
Niccoli, Gabriel. 'Autobiography and Fiction in Veronica Franco's Epistolary Narrative.' *Canadian Journal of Italian Studies* 16, no. 47 (1993): 129–42.

Niccoli, Ottavia, ed. *Rinascimento al femminile*. Rome: Laterza, 1991.
Nicoll, Allardyce. *Il mondo di Arlecchino*. Milan: Bompiani, 1965.
Nummedal, Tara. 'Alchemical Reproduction and the Career of Anna Maria Zieglerin.' *Ambix* 48 (2001): 56–68.
– *Alchemy and Authority in the Holy Roman Empire*. Chicago: University of Chicago Press, 2007.
Orgel, Stephen. 'Nobody's Perfect, Or, Why Did the English Stage Take Boys for Girls?' In *Displacing Homophobia: Gay Male Perspectives in Literature and Culture*. Edited by Ronald R. Butters, John M. Clum, and Michael Moon, 7–30. Durham, NC: Duke University Press, 1989.
– *Impersonations: The Performance of Gender in Shakespeare's England*. Cambridge: Cambridge University Press, 1996.
Osteen, Mark. 'Gift or Commodity?' *The Question of the Gift: Essays across Disciplines*. Edited by Mark Osteen, 172–90. London: Routledge, 2002.
Ottaviani, Maria Grazia. '*Mi son missa a scriver questa lettera...*': *Lettere e altre scritture femminili tra Umbria, Toscana e Marche nei secoli X–XVI*. Naples: Liguori, 2006.
Padoan, G. *Il mondo delle cortigiane nella letteratura rinascimentale*. In AA.VV., *Le cortigiane di Venezia dal Trecento al Settecento*, Catalogo della Mostra. Venezia, Casino Municipale, Ca' Vendramin Calergi, 2 febbr.–16 apr. 1990. Milan: Berenice, 1990.
Pagano, Sergio. *Il processo di Endimio Calandra e l'Inquisizione a Mantova nel 1567–1568*. Vatican City: Studi e Testi, 1991.
Palma, M. 'Laura Cereto.' In *Dizionario Biografico degli Italiani*. Vol. 23, 729–30. Rome: Istituto della enciclopedia italiana, 1960–.
Pancrazi, Pietro. *Nel giardino di Candido*. Florence: LeMonnier, 1961.
Pandolfi, V., ed. *La Commedia dell'Arte. Storia e Testi*. 5 vols. Florence: Sansoni Antiquariato 1957–60; facsimile edition, Florence: Sansoni, 1988.
– *Il teatro del Rinascimento e la Commedia dell'Arte*. Rome: Lerici, 1969.
Panella, L. 'Isabella Canali.' In *Dizionario Biografico degli Italiani*. Vol. 30, 704–5. Rome: Istituto della Enciclopedia Italiana, 1960–.
Panizza, Letizia, and Sharon Wood, eds. *Women in Italian Renaissance Culture and Society*. London: Legenda, 2005.
Paolin, Giovanna. 'Monache e donne nel Friuli del Cinquecento.' In *Società e cultura del Cinquecento nel Friuli occidentale. Studi*. Edited by Andrea del Col, 201–28. Pordenone: Edizioni della Provincia di Pordenone, 1984.
– *Lo spazio del silenzio: Monacazioni forzate, clausura e proposte di vita religiosa femminile nell'eta moderna*. Pordenone: Biblioteca dell'Immagine, 1996.
Parati, Gabriella. *Public History, Private Stories: Italian Women's Autobiography*. Minneapolis: University of Minnesota Press, 1996.

Park, Katherine. *Secrets of Women: Gender, Generation, and the Origins of Human Dissection*. Cambridge, MA: Zone, 2006.
Pateman, Carol. *The Sexual Contract*. Stanford: Stanford University Press, 1988.
Pennacini, Andrea. 'Situazione e struttura dell'epistola familiare nella teoria classica.' *Quaderni di retorica e poetica* 1 (1985): 11–15.
Perocco, Daria. 'Prose Production in Venice in the Early Seicento.' In *Arcangela Tarabotti: A Literary Nun in Seicento Venice*. Edited by Elissa Weaver, 73–87. Ravenna: Longo, 2006.
Petraccone, E. *La Commedia dell'Arte. Storia, tecnica, scenari*. Naples: Ricciardi, 1927.
Pettinelli, Rosanna Alhaique. 'Un tempio/una città: Venezia in un poema cavalleresco alla metà del Cinqucento.' *La Rassegna della Letteratura Italiana* 95 (1991): 60–70.
Petrucci, Armando, ed. *Libri, editori e pubblico nell'Europa moderna*. Bari: Laterza, 1977.
Pezzini, Serena. 'Dissimulazione e paradosso nelle *Lettere di molte valorose donne (1548) a cura di Ortensio Lando*.' *Italianistica* 31, no. 1 (1991): 67–83.
Picquet, Thea. 'Profession: Courtisane.' In *Les femmes écrivains en Italie au Moyen Age et à la Renaissance*. Edited by G. Ulysse, Actes du colloque internationale Aix-en-Provence, 12, 13, 14 novembre 1992, 119–37. Provence: Publications de l'Université de Provence, 1994.
Pireddu, Nicoletta. *Antropologie alla corte della bellezza. Decadenza ed economia simbolica nell'Europa fin de siècle*. Verona: Edizioni Fiorni, 2002.
– 'Gabriele D'Annuzio: The Art of Squandering and the Economy of Sacrifice.' *The Question of the Gift: Essays across Disciplines*. Edited by Mark Osteen, 172–90. London: Routledge, 2002.
Portigliotti, Giuseppe. *Penombre claustrali*. Milan: Fratelli Treves Editori, 1930.
Prada, Massimo. *La lingua dell'epistolario di Pietro Bembo*. Genoa: Name, 2000.
Preto, Paolo. *Peste e società a Venezia, 1576*. Vicenza: Neri Pozza, 1978.
– *Venezia e i turchi*. Florence: Sansoni, 1975.
Price, Paola Malpezzi. '*Venetia Figurata* and Women in Sixteenth-Century Venice: Moderata Fonte's Writings.' In *Italian Women and the City*. Edited by Janet Levarie Smarr and Daria Valentini, 18–34. Madison: Fairleigh Dickinson University Press, 1993.
Procaccioli, Paolo, ed. *Anton Francesco Doni contra Aretinum*. Rome: Vecchiarelli, 1998.
Quadrio, Francesco Saverio. *Della storia, e della ragione d'ogni poesia*. Bologna: F. Pisarri, 1739–49
Quaintance, Courtney. 'Veronica Franco's Poems in Terza Rima.' In *Italian Literature and its Times*. Edited by Joyce Moss, 351–9. Detroit: Thomson Gale, 2005.

- 'Defaming the Courtesan: Satire and Invective in Sixteenth Century Italy.' In *The Courtesan's Arts: Cross-Cultural Perspectives*. Edited by Martha Feldman and Bonnie Gordon, 199–208. Oxford: Oxford University Press, 2006.
Quondam, Amedeo. *Le carte messaggiere. Retorica e modelli di comunicazione epistolare: per un indice dei libri di lettere del Cinquecento*. Rome: Bulzoni, 1981.
- ed. *Stefano Guazzo e la Civil Conversazione*. Ferrara: Istituto di studi rinacimentali, 1993.
- 'Note su imitazione, furto e plagio nel Classicismo.' In *Sondaggi sulla riscrittura del Cinquecento*. Edited by Paolo Cherchi, 373–400. Ravenna: Longo, 1998.
Rabil, Albert. *Laura Cereta: Quattrocento Humanist*, Binghamton, NY: Center for Medieval and Early Renaissance Studies, 1981.
Rabitti, Giovanna. 'Chiara Matraini.' In *Italian Women Writers: A Bio-Bibliographical Sourcebook*. Edited by Rinaldina Russell, 269–78. Westport, CT: Greenwood Press, 1994.
Rambaldi, Susanna Peyronel. 'Mogli, madri, figlie: donne nei gruppi eterodossi italiani del Cinquecento.' In *Le donne delle minoranze*. Edited by Claire E. Honess and Verina R. Jones, 45–66. Turin: Claudiana, 1999.
Rasi, Luigi. *I comici italiani*. Florence: Fratelli Bocca, 1897.
Rattansi, Piyo, and Antonio Clericuzio. *Alchemy and Chemistry in the Sixteenth and Seventeenth Centuries*. Dodrecht: Kluwer, 1994.
Ray, Meredith K. 'Settling the Debt: Veronica Franco's Literary Economics.' *RLA: Romance Languages Annual*, 8th ed., 303–10. West Lafeyette, IN: Purdue University Research Foundation, 1996.
- 'La castità conquistata: The Function of the Satyr in Pastoral Drama.' *Romance Languages Annual*. 9th ed., 312–21. West Lafayette, IN: Purdue University Research Foundation, 1998.
- 'Un'officina di lettere: le *Lettere di molte valorose donne* e la fonte della "dottrina femminile."' *Esperienze letterarie* 26, no. 3 (2001): 69–91.
- 'Letters From the Cloister: Defending the Literary Self in Arcangela Tarabotti's *Lettere familiari e di complimento*.' *Italica* 81, no. 1 (2004): 24–43.
- 'Making the Private Public: Arcangela Tarabotti and the *Lettere familiari e di complimento*.' In *Arcangela Tarabotti: A Literary Nun in Baroque Venice*. Edited by Elissa B. Weaver, 173–89. Ravenna: Longo, 2006.
- 'Letters and Lace: Arcangela Tarabotti and Convent Culture in Seicento Venice.' In *Early Modern Women and Transnational Communities of Women*. Edited by Julie Campbell and Anne Larsen. Aldershot, UK: Ashgate, 2009.
- 'Textual Collaboration and Spiritual Partnership in Sixteenth-Century Italy: The Case of Ortensio Lando and Lucrezia Gonzaga.' *Renaissance Quarterly* 62, no. 3 (2009). Forthcoming.

Rebaudengo, Maurizio. *Giovan Battista Andreini, tra poetica e drammaturgia*. Turin: Rosenberg and Sellier, 1994.
Reulens, Charles. *Eryicius Puteanus et Isabelle Andreini: Lecture faite à l'Académie d'Archéologie le 3 Février 1889*. Antwerp: N.p., 1889.
Rice, James V. *Gabriel Naudé (1600–1653)*. Baltimore: Johns Hopkins University Press, 1939.
Richardson, Brian. *Print Culture in Renaissance Italy*. Cambridge: Cambridge University Press, 1994.
– *Printing, Writers, and Readers in Renaissance Italy*. Cambridge: Cambridge University Press, 1999.
Rigolot, François. 'Montaigne and Veronica Franco.' *Montaigne Studies* 15, nos. 1–2 (2003): 117–30.
Rivoletti, Christian. *Le metamorfosi dell'Utopia: Anton Francesco Doni e l'immaginario utopico di metà Cinquecento*. Lucca: Maria Pacini Fazzi Editore, 2003.
Roberts, Gareth. *The Mirror of Alchemy: Alchemical Ideas and Images in Manuscripts and Books From Antiquity to the Seventeenth Century*. London: The British Library, 1994.
Robin, Diana. *Filelfo in Milan: Writings 1451–1477*. Princeton, NJ: Princeton University Press, 1991.
– 'Courtesans, Celebrity, and Print Culture in Renaissance Venice: Tullia D'Aragona, Gaspara Stampa, and Veronica Franco.' In *Italian Women and the City*. Edited by Janet Levarie Smarr and Daria Valentini, 35–59. Madison: Fairleigh Dickinson University Press, 1993.
– 'Cassandra Fedele's *Epistolae* (1488–1521): Biography as Ef-facement.' In *The Rhetorics of Life-Writing in Early Modern Europe: Forms of Biography from Cassandra Fedele to Louis XIV*. Edited by Thomas F. Mayer and D.R. Woolf, 187–19. Ann Arbor: University of Michigan Press, 1995.
– *Publishing Women: Salons, the Presses, and the Counter Reformation in Sixteenth-Century Italy*. Chicago: University of Chicago Press, 2007.
Rogers, Mary. *Fashioning Identities in Renaissance Art*. Aldershot, UK: Ashgate, 2000.
Romano, Angelo. *Lettere di cortigiane del Rinascimento*. Rome: Salerno, 1990.
Rosa, Mario. 'La religiosa.' In *L'uomo barocco*. Edited by Rosario Villari, 219–67. Rome: LaTerza, 1991
Rosenthal, Margaret. 'A Courtesan's Voice: Epistolary Self-portraiture in Veronica Franco's *Terze Rime*.' In *Writing the Female Voice: Essays on Women's Epistolary Literature*. Edited by Elizabeth C. Goldsmith, 3–24. Boston: Northeastern University Press, 1989.

- 'Veronica Franco's *Terze rime*: The Venetian Courtesan's Defense.' *Renaissance Quarterly* 42, no. 2 (1989): 227–57.
- *The Honest Courtesan: Veronica Franco Citizen and Writer in Sixteenth-Century Venice*. Chicago: University of Chicago Press, 1992.
- 'Cutting a Good Figure: The Fashions of Venetian Courtesans in the Illustrated Albums of Early Modern Travelers.' In *The Courtesan's Arts: Cross-Cultural Perspectives*. Edited by Martha Feldman and Bonnie Gordon, 52–74. Oxford: Oxford University Press, 2006.

Rubin, Gayle. 'The Traffic in Women: Notes on the Political Economy of Sex.' In *Toward an Anthropology of Women*. Edited by Rayna R. Reiter, 157–210. New York: Monthly Review Press, 1975.

Ruggiero, Guido. *Binding Passions: Tales of Magic, Marriage, and Power at the End of the Renaissance*. New York: Oxford University Press, 1993.
- 'Who's Afraid of Giulia Napolitana? Pleasure, Fear, and Imagining the Arts of the Renaissance Courtesan.' In *The Courtesan's Arts: Cross-Cultural Perspectives*. Edited by Martha Feldman and Bonnie Gordon, 280–92. Oxford: Oxford University Press, 2006.

Rummel, Erika. 'Eramus' Manual of Letter-Writing.' *Renaissance and Reformation*, new series, vol. 13, no. 3 (1989): 299–312.
- *Erasmus on Women*. Toronto: University of Toronto Press, 1996.

Russell, Rinaldina, ed. *Italian Women Writers. A Bio-Bibliographic Sourcebook*. Westport, CT: Greenwood Press, 1994.

Sanesi, Ireneo. *Il cinquecentista Ortensio Lando*. Pistoia: Fratelli Bracali, 1893.
- 'Tre epistolari del Cinquecento.' *Giornale storico della letteratura italiana* 24 (1894): 1–32.

Schiavon, Alessandra. 'Per la biografia di Veronica Franco. Nuovi documenti.' *Atti dell'Istituto Veneto di Scienze, Lettere ed Arti* 137 (1978–9): 243–56.

Schneider, Gary. *The Culture of Epistolarity: Vernacular Letters and Letter Writing in Early Modern England, 1500–1700*. Newark: University of Delaware Press, 2005.

Schoysman Zambrini, Anne, ed. *Giovanni Maria Filelfo, Consolatoria*. Bologna: Commissione per i testi di lingua, 1991.

Schutte, Anne Jacobson. 'The *lettera volgare* and the Crisis of Evangelism.' *Renaissance Quarterly* 28 (1975): 639–88.
- 'The Permeable Cloister?' In *Arcangela Tarabotti: A Literary Nun in Baroque Venice*. Edited by Elissa Weaver, 19–33. Ravenna: Longo, 2006.

Schutte, Anne Jacobson, Thomas Kuehn, and Silvana Seidel Menchi, eds. *Time, Space, and Women's Lives in Early Modern Europe*. Kirksville, MO: Truman State University Press, 2001.

Scott, Joan Wallach. *Gender and the Politics of History*. New York: Columbia University Press, 1988.

Scrivano, Riccardo. 'Ortensio Lando traduttore di Thomas More.' In AAVV, *Studi sulla cultura lombarda in memoria di Mario Apollonio.* Vol. 1, 99–107. Milan: Vita e pensiero, 1972.
– *La norma e lo scarto.* Rome: Bonacci, 1980.
Seidel Menchi, Silvana. 'Sulla fortuna di Erasmo in Italia: Ortensio Lando e altri eterodossi.' *Rivista storica svizzera* 24 (1974): 537–634.
– 'La circolazione clandestina di Erasmo in Italia.' *Annali della Scuola Normale Superiore di Pisa* 9, no. 2 (1979): 573–601.
– *Erasmo in Italia 1520–1580.* Turin: Bollati Boringhieri, 1987.
– 'Chi fu Ortensio Lando?' *Rivista storica italiana* 106, no. 3 (1994): 501–64.
Selmi, Elisabetta. 'Per l'epistolario di Veronica Gambara.' In *Veronica Gambara e la poesia del suo tempo nell'Italia settentrionale. Atti del convegno, Brescia-Correggio, 17–19 ottobre, 1985.* Edited by C. Bozzetti et al., 143–81. Florence: Olschki, 1989.
Simoncelli, Paolo. *Evangelismo italiano del Cinquecento: Questione religiosa e nicodemismo politico.* Rome: Istituto Storico Italiano per l'Età Moderna e Contemporanea, 1979.
Smarr, Janet Levarie. *Boccaccio and Fiammetta: The Narrator as Lover.* Urbana: University of Illinois Press, 1986.
– *Joining the Conversation: Dialogues by Renaissance Women.* Ann Arbor: University of Michigan Press, 2005.
Sobel, Dava. *Galileo's Daughter: A Historical Memoir of Science, Faith, and Love.* New York: Walker and Company, 2001.
– *Letters to Father: Sister Maria Celeste to Galileo, 1623–1630.* New York: Walker and Company, 2001.
Sommer, Doris. 'Not Just a Personal Story: Women's Testimonies and the Plural Self.' In *Life/Lines: Theorizing Women's Autobiography.* Edited by Bella Brodzki and Celeste Schenck, 107–30. Ithaca, NY: Cornell University Press, 1988.
Sperling, Jutta. *Convents and the Body Politic in Late Renaissance Venice.* Chicago: University of Chicago Press, 1999.
Spini, Giorgio. *Ricerca dei libertini: la teoria dell'impostura delle religioni nel Seicento italiano.* Florence: La Nuova Italia, 1983.
Stallybrass, Peter. 'The Body Enclosed.' In *Rewriting the Renaissance: Discourses of Difference in Early Modern Europe.* Edited by Margaret Ferguson, Maureen Quilligan, and Nancy Vickers, 123–42. Chicago: University of Chicago Press, 1986.
– 'Transvestitism and the "Body Beneath": Speculating on the Boy Actor.' In *Erotic Politics: Desire on the Renaissance Stage.* Edited by Susan Zimmerman, 64–83. New York: Routledge, 1992.

Stampino, Maria Galli. 'Publish or Perish: An Early Seventeenth-Century Paradox.' *RLA: Romance Languages Annual* 10 (1998): 373–9.

Steland, Dieter. 'Ortensio Landos *Lettere di Lucretia Gonzaga* und Girolamo Garimbertos *Concetti:* Plagiat, *Imitatio,* Parodie?' *Italienisch* 30 (2006): 3–19.

Strocchia, Sharon. 'Taken Into Custody: Girls and Convent Guardianship in Renaissance Florence.' *Renaissance Studies* 17, no. 2 (2003): 177–200.

Tanskanen, Sanna-Kaisa. 'Best Patterns for Your Imitation: Early Modern Letter-Writing and Real Correspondence.' In *Discourse Perspectives in English*. Edited by Janne Skaffari, 167–95. Amsterdam: John Benjamins Publishing Company, 2004.

Taviani, Ferdinando, ed. *La Commedia dell'Arte e la società barocca I. La fascinazione del teatro.* 2 vols. Rome: Bulzoni, 1969.

– 'Bella d'Asia. Torquato Tasso, gli attori e l'immortalita.' In *Paragone/Letteratura* XXXV (1984): 3–76.

Taviani, Ferdinando, and M. Schino. *Il segreto della Commedia dell'Arte. La memoria delle compagnie italiane del XVI, XVII e XVIII secolo.* Florence: La Casa Usher, 1982.

Tessari, Roberto. *La Commedia dell'Arte nel Seicento. 'Industria' e 'arte giocosa' della civiltà barocca.* Florence: Oslchki, 1969.

– *Le bravure del Capitano Spavento.* Pisa: Giardini, 1987.

– 'Sotto il segno di Giano: La Commedia dell'Arte di Isabella e Francesco Andreini.' In *The Commedia dell'Arte from the Renaissance to Dario Fo.* Edited by Christopher Cairns, 1–33. Lampeter: Edwin Mellen Press, 1989.

Thompson, Ann. '"Woman/Women" and the Stage.' In *Women and Literature in Britain, 1500–1700.* Edited by Helen Wilcox, 100–16. Cambridge: Cambridge University Press, 1996.

Thouar, Pietro. *Lucrezia Gonzaga.* Biblioteca Archiginnasio di Bologna, Landoni 232.

Tiraboschi, G. *Storia della letteratura italiana.* Vol. 7. Modena: Società tipografica, 1791.

Trexler, Richard. *Public Life in Renaissance Florence.* Ithaca, NY: Cornell University Press, 1991.

Trovato, Paolo. *Con ogni diligenza corretto.* Bologna: Il Mulino, 1991.

Tylus, Jane. 'Women at the Windows: Commedia dell'arte and Theatrical Practice in Early Modern Italy.' *Theatre Journal* 49, no. 3 (1997): 323–42.

Ulysse, George. *Les femmes écrivains en Italie en Moyen Age et à la Renaissance.* Aix-en-Provence: Centre de Recherches Italiennes, 1994.

Vescovo, Piermario. *Da Ruzante a Calmo. Tra 'Signore Comedie' e 'Onorandissime stampe.'* Padua: Editrice Antenore, 1996.

Vickery, Amanda. 'Golden Age to Separate Spheres? A Review of the Categories and Chronology of English Women's History.' *The Historical Journal* 36, no. 2 (June 1993): 383–414.

Weaver, Elissa. *Convent Theatre in Early Modern Italy: Spiritual Fun and Learning for Women*. Cambridge: Cambridge University Press, 2002.

– ed. *Arcangela Tarabotti: A Literary Nun in Baroque Venice*. Ravenna: Longo, 2006.

Westwater, Lynn. 'The Disquieting Voice: Women's Writing and Antifeminism in Italy.' PhD diss., University of Chicago, 2003.

Whitehead, Barbara. *Women's Education in Early Modern Europe*. New York: Garland, 1999.

Wigley, Mark. 'Untitled: The Housing of Gender.' In *Sexuality and Space*. Edited by Beatriz Colomina, 327–89. Princeton Papers on Architecture, vol. 1. Princeton, NJ: Princeton Architectural Press, 1997.

Woodbridge, Linda. *Women and the English Renaissance: Literature and the Nature of Womankind*. Urbana: University of Illinois Press, 1984.

Zancan. *Nel cerchio della luna: figure di donne in alcuni testi del XVI secolo*. Venice: Marsilio, 1983.

Zanette, Emilio. *Suor Arcangela: Monaca del Seicento Veneziano*. Rome-Venice: Istituto per la collaborazione culturale, 1960.

Zanré, Domenico. *Cultural Non-Conformity in Early Modern Florence*. Aldershot, UK: Ashgate, 2004.

Zarri, Gabriella. 'Monasteri femminili e città (secoli xv-xviii).' In *Storia d'Italia. Annali 9. La chiesa e il potere politico*. Edited by G. Chittolini and G. Miccoli, 359–429. Turin: Einaudi, 1986.

– *Sante vive: Profezie di corte e devozione femminile tra '400 e '500*. Turin: Rosenberg and Sellier, 1990.

– et al. 'De monialibus.' *Rivista di storia e letteratura religiosa* 33, no. 3 (1997): 643–715.

– ed. *Per lettera: La scrittura epistolare femminile tra archivio e tipografia, secoli xv-xvii*. Rome: Viella, 1999.

– *Recinti: Donne, clausura, e matrimonio nella prima età moderna*. Bologna: Il Mulino, 2000.

Zarri, Gabriella, and G. Pomata, eds. *I monasteri femminili come centri di cultura fra rinascimento e barocco, atti del convegno storico e internazionale Bologna, 8–10 dicembre 2000*. Rome: Edizioni di Storia e Letteratura, 2005.

Zorzi, Alvise. *Cortigiana veneziana: Veronica Franco e i suoi poeti 1546–1591*. Milan: Camunia, 1986.

Zorzi, Ludovico. *L'attore, la commedia, il drammaturgo*. Turin: Einaudi, 1990.

Index

academies: Addormentati, 86; Incogniti, 188, 189, 196, 209, 309n24, 310nn26, 27, 313n35; Intenti, 164; Pastori frattegiani, 86, 87, 106, 107, 218, 267n27
Acidalius, Valens, 188, 309n24
Agrippa, Henricus Cornelius, 8, 10, 54, 71, 75
Alberti, Leon Battista, 25, 138, 179, 227n25, 228n28
Altman, Janet Gurkin, 6
Andreini, Francesco, 157, 160, 161, 178; *Le bravure di Capitano Spavento*, 162–4; *Ragionamenti*, 176, 179; role in publishing *Fragmenti*, 166; role in publishing *Lettere*, 161–5, 180
Andreini, Giovanni Battista, 303n87
Andreini, Isabella, 4, 9, 12, 80, 120, 131, 184, 215, 216, 217, 220; *Fragmenti*, 166–9; *La Mirtilla*, 4, 157, 159, 162, 175, 177, 296n18; *La pazzia di Isabella*, 156–7; *Lettere*, 4, 16, 17, 42, 157–83, and debate over women, 176–80, hermaphroditic voice in, 157–61, 172–3, 292nn5, 6, 295n11, and humanist themes, 175, and love, 172–5; *Rime*, 158–9, 175; and *commedia dell'arte*, 17, 156–61, 166–70, 216; praise for, 229n33, 293n6, 298n31
anthologies, epistolary. *See* letters and letter collections
Aprosio, Angelico, 189, 194, 205, 201, 203, 206, 208, 209, 211, 310n27; *La maschera scoperta*, 188, 208, 209
Aretino, Pietro, 5, 19, 25, 41, 42, 45, 73, 158, 184, 124, 125, 126, 158, 184, 213; *Lettere*, 4, 8, 15, 17, 20, 21, 24, 28–35, 119, 138, 139, and female interlocutors, 32–4, 35; and prostitutes/courtesans, 130–2, 134, 144, 145; *Lettere a Aretino*, 24, 237n23; *Sei giornate*, 130, 152
Arrivabene, Andrea, 86
Atanagi, Dionigi, 37

Badoer, Federico, 36
Baffo, Franceschina, 124, 133
Bairo, Pietro, 67, 68
Bandello, Matteo, 83, 84, 105, 264n12, 265n15
Barbaro, Ermolao, 26
Barbaro, Francesco, 8
Bassanese, Fiora, 124

Battistini, Andrea, 8
Bell, Rudolph, 73
Bellucci, Novella, 75
Bembo, Pietro, 3, 19, 21, 24, 30, 35, 35, 139, 233n1, 287n66, 300n54; correspondence with Maria Savorgnan, 5; *Prose della volgar lingua*, 29
Bembo, Torquato, 107
Bentivoglio, Camilla, 84
Bergalli, Luisa, 220
Bevilacqua, Niccolò, 112, 278n123
Bissari, Pietro Paolo, 189, 211, 310n27, 313n35, 321n109
Boccaccio, Giovanni, 39; *Fiammetta*, 13, 40–1, 47, 51, 169, 172, 232n49; and illustrious women tradition, 26, 180
Bonardo, Giovanni Maria, 86, 87, 94, 102, 105, 114, 264n12
Bonfadio, Iacopo, 39
Bongi, Salvatore, 89–90
books of secrets, 10, 14, 67–8, 71–5, 215, 255n75
Braccesi, Simonetta Adorni, 56
Bruni, Domenico, 169
Brusantino, Vicenzo, 84
Brusoni, Girolamo, 201, 202, 203, 309n22, 313n35, 314n46, 318nn70, 75, 319n93
Buoninsegni, Francesco, 187, 207, 209, 211, 309n20, 320n99
Butler, Judith, 13

Calmo, Andrea: and courtesans, 130, 132–3, 134, 144, 145; and Pantalone, 169, 170
Campbell, Julie, 154
Capella, Galeazzo Flavio, 54
Caro, Annibal, 35
Casa delle Zitelle, 153

Castiglione, Baldassare, 14, 78, 171; donna di palazzo, 9; *Libro del cortegiano*, 8, 26, 173, 227n26, 229n32; sprezzatura, 3, 222n3
Catherine of Siena, 5, 190, 312n33
Ceci, Battista, 14, 24, 140, 222n3
'Celia Romana.' See *Lettere amorose di madonna Celia Romana*
Cereta, Laura, 5, 9, 15, 20, 22–3, 24–5, 26, 27–8, 233nn3, 4, 237n20
Cicero, 6, 9, 20, 21, 142, 226n15, 234n6
clausura, 17, 185–6. *See also* convents
Colombi, Marchesa, 220
Colonna, Vittoria, 24, 35, 94, 106, 108, 118, 245n1, 272n65; correspondence with Michelangelo, 5; spiritual letters, 5, 245n1
commedia dell'arte: characters, 157, 165–6; commonalities with letterbooks, 160–1; Pantalone, 132, 169, 170; sources, 169; themes, 166, 179, 299n43; universality of, 160, 296n15; women and, 172, 294n7. *See also* Andreini, Isabella
convents: 17, 24, 25, 183, 185–6, 218; coerced monachization, 184, 187, 191, 201, 306n5, 307n6; dowry for, 306n5; *educande*, 203, 308nn12, 13, 318n73; in Isabella Andreini, 180; in Lando, 67–9; number of women in, 306n4. *See also* clausura; Gonzaga, Lucrezia; letters and letter collections, restrictions on; Tarabotti, Arcangela
Cortese, Isabella 74
Coryat, Thomas 127, 129
Costa, Margherita, 4, 131, 303n88; *Lettere amorose*, 4, 181–2, 183, 300n52, 302n62

Council of Trent, 94, 114, 115, 185
courtesans, 123, 124–30, 151–4;
  anxieties regarding, 127–8, 130,
  131–2, 133; as epistolary category,
  130–4
Croce, Benedetto, 180

Daenens, Francine, 56, 58, 60
da Mantova, Osanna, 190, 312n33
Dandolo, Giovanni, 189, 199, 200,
  212, 310n27
D'Aragona, Tullia, 124, 125, 128
da Ostiglia, Pier Francesco Bertioli,
  263n6, 265n17
da Udine, Federico Luigini, 109
da Ugubio, Andrea Zenofonte, 171
Davis, Natalie Zemon, 149
d'Este, Ercole II, 82, 89, 97, 98
d'Este, Luigi (Cardinal). *See* Franco,
  Veronica
de Cardona, Maria (marchesa di
  Padulla), 108
de Grémonville, Nicolas Bretel, 22,
  200, 203, 211, 212, 236n19, 318n72;
  and family, 318n73
de Guevara, Antonio, 223n5
della Rovere, Vittoria, 194, 196, 200,
  209, 211, 263n9, 320nn100, 108
Demetrius, 6, 225n15
de Pizan, Christine, 26
Dionisotti, Carlo, 28, 94
Doglio, Maria Luisia, 126
Dolce, Lodovico, 35, 86, 107; *De la
  istitution de le donne*, 10, 71, 138;
  *Lettere di diversi eccellentissimi
  uomini*, 24, 37, 38
Domenichi, Lodovico, 86
Donà, Regina, 191–3, 195, 313n37
Doni, Anton Francesco, 47, 66, 83,
  94, 222n5

Eamon, William, 74
Erasmus, 6, 9, 59, 67, 75, 92, 115,
  130, 251n25; on the familiar letter,
  221n2, 222n3
Erizzo, Doge Francesco, 200, 317n66
Erspamer, Francesco, 30
evangelism, 115–18, 279nn130, 134

Fahy, Conor, 55
familiar letter, definitions of, 3, 3n2
Fedele, Cassandra, 5, 15, 20, 22, 23,
  24, 26, 27, 28, 233nn3, 4, 237n20
Ferri, Pietro, 94
Filelfo, Francesco, 22, 241n58
Findlen, Paula, 125
Fioravanti, Leonardo, 67
Firenzuola, Agnolo, 26, 67
Fonte, Moderata, 128, 143, 176, 177,
  255n65, 288n85, 316n60
Franco, Nicolò, 30, 32, 130, 133, 134,
  222n5
Franco, Veronica, 3, 4, 9, 80, 123–55,
  158, 160, 175, 215, 216, 217, 218,
  220, 316n60; and Cardinal Luigi
  d'Este, 134, 136, 148–9; and Henri
  III of Valois, 128, 134, 135–7, 140;
  and Inquisition trial, 129; and
  Lettere familiari, 16, 32, 120, 123–7,
  128, 129, 130, 132, 134–55, advice
  to courtesans in, 151–4, as literary
  exchange, 147–50, counsel and
  consolation in, 138–44, economic
  imagery in, 144–9, influence of
  epistolary manuals and repertories on, 135–8, as response to
  detractors, 150–1, self-identifica-
  tion with Venice in, 143–4; and
  Montaigne, 129; *Terze rime*, 124,
  126, 128, 129, 135, 150, 283n26;
  and Tintoretto, 134, 136

358 Index

Galilei, Suor Maria Celeste, 5
Gambara, Veronica, 5, 24, 35, 106, 108, 224n10
Garimberto, Ieronimo: *Concetti*, 91, 135, 151, 171, 215, 258n93, 270n49, 272n62, 287n66, 301n70
Gedik, Simon, 188
Goethe, 158, 294n8
Goldsmith, Elizabeth, 11, 14, 76
Gonzaga, Camilla, 103, 117, 265n14
Gonzaga, Carlo, 114, 265n14, 273n67
Gonzaga, Giulia, 75
Gonzaga, Isabella, 54, 57, 85, 96, 101, 107, 265n14, 275n89, 277n114
Gonzaga, Lucrezia, 3, 4, 9, 10, 11, 17, 57, 80, 81–120, 135, 158, 160, 216, 217, 218, 220; biography, 84–7, 264n14, 273n78; and convent, 85, 87, 103, 104; and heterodoxy, 85, 86, 114–18, 155–6, 218, 267n31, 271nn53, 55; and Inquisition, 85, 266n21; *Lettere*, 16, 32, 81–4, 86, 127, 171, 214–15, and authorship debate, 83-4, 87–94, 267n32, 272n62, and narrative frame, 94–104, and repertories, 91, 93, 272nn61, 62, vice and virtue in, 113–14, 278nn126, 127, 128; manuscript letters of, 85, 88–9, 91, 94, 103, 263n11, 268n39, 269nn40, 41, 272n57; and Ortensio Lando, 16, 54, 83, 106, 109, 111, 112, 118–19, 164, 268n33; as poet, 266n23; praise for, 84, 93, 102, 264n12; as reader, 105–8
Gonzaga, Luigi (of Castelgoffredo), 84
Gonzaga, Luigi, 106
Gonzaga, Pirro, 84
Gonzaga, Vespasiano, 85

Grendler, Paul, 62, 66, 78
Groto, Luigi, 86
Guarini, Battista, 222n3, 236n13
Guazzo, Stefano, 8, 14, 37, 136, 139, 171, 222n3, 227n25
Guillén, Claudio, 9

Habermas, Jürgen, 227n25
Henke, Robert, 165, 169, 170
Heroides. *See* Ovid
heterodoxy. *See* Gonzaga, Lucrezia; Lando, Ortensio
humanists, and letter-writing. *See* letters and letter collections
humanists, women, 15, 19, 22–8; 233n3. *See also individual names of women*

impersonation, epistolary, 4, 10, 13, 47. *See also* Lando, Ortensio, *Lettere di molte valorose donne*; ventriloquism

Jensen, Katherine, 12
Jones, Ann Rosalind, 26, 125, 141, 152

Kauffman, Linda S., 13, 78
King, Margaret L., 9, 139

LaBalme, Patricia, 9
Lando, Ortensio, 3, 14, 84, 86, 161; *Brieve essortatione agli huomini*, 55–6, 65; *Confutazione del libro de' Paradossi*, 53; *Consolatorie*, 56, 91; and defence of women, 52-6; *Dialogo della . . . sacra scrittura*, 57, 87, 115, 116, 118; *Due panegirici*, 83, 85, 87, 88, 93, 102, 108, 109, 118; and female patrons, 57, 79,

93; *Forcinaes quaestiones,* 54; and Isabella Sforza, 56; *Lettere di molte valorose donne,* 13, 15, 16, 26, 45–80, 81, 83, 87, 105, 116, 118, 119, 127, 133, 138, 139, 180, 214, 216, and alchemy, 74–5, and authorship of, 46–52, and cosmetics and beauty, 73–4, and gossip, 76–7, and household management, 73, and marriage vs. convent, 68–71, and play on names in, 258n89, and pregnancy and child-rearing, 71–3, and religious heterodoxy, 58–61, and women's learning, 61–4, and women's virtue, 64–6, play on names in, 258n89; and the literary market, 53; and Lucrezia Gonzaga, 87-94, 106, 107, 109, 118–19, 164, 215, 272n62 (*see also* Gonzaga, Lucrezia); *Oracoli de' moderni ingegni,* 57, 91; *Paradossi,* 48, 53, 54, 73; *Quesiti amorosi,* 48, 169; *Ragionamenti familiari,* 47, 57; *Sette libri de' cataloghi,* 48, 54, 93; *Sferza de' scrittori antichi e moderni,* 54–5, 63, 79; and use of paradox, 52–3, 251n25; and use of repertories, 48–52, 78; *Vari componimenti,* 57
Lauro, Pietro 87, 91
Lawner, Lynn, 128
lettera familiare. See familiar letter
Lettere amorose di madonna Celia Romana, 49, 123, 135, 172, 174; attribution to Parabosco, 13, 231n47
Lettere a Pietro Aretino, 24, 237n23
letters and letter collections: and anonymous publication, 14; anthologies, 5, 14, 37, 39, 40, 41, 115, 223n5, 237n23, 243n83, 244n96, 245n1, 322n7; as communal documents, 6; and dialogue, 22, 236n13; epistolary persona, 7, 10, 230n38; as feminine genre, 10–12, 15; humanists and, 5, 15, 19–24, 213; impact of print culture on, 28–9, 239nn46, 47; and literary market, 14; manuals and repertories, 14, 17, 24, 29, 41, 127, 135, 154, 170–1; private correspondence, 5; and *questione della lingua,* 14; registers, linguistic and stylistic, 7; and religious dissent, 7, 115; restrictions on in convent, 189–90, 311n29, 312n30; revision of, 3, 5, 11, 40, 41, 216; role of editor, 14, 322n3; role of reader, 6; and social critique, 7; tensions between public and private in, 4, 194; typologies: 41, 239n48, consolatory, 22–3, 139–40, 236n17, familiar, 3, 221n2, 222n3, 225n15, 226n16, love letters, 14, 123, 171–5; women humanists and, 20–8, 333n3
Lettres portuguaises, 13, 232n48
libri di segreti. See books of secrets
libro d'autore, 37, 38, 41–2, 243n83
Loredano, Giovan Francesco, 189, 196–9, 200, 204, 205, 208, 309n24, 310n26, 313nn35, 38, 316nn58, 62, 319n92
Luther, Martin, 59, 92, 115, 267n31

MacNeil, Anne, 176
Maggi, Vincenzo, 55
Malaspina, Fiammetta, 124
Malipieri, Andriana, 191
Manfrone, Giampaolo, 82, 84, 87, 88, 89, 95–104, 105, 108, 112, 113, 118, 119, 217, 262n3, 265nn16, 18, 269n42, 273n68, 274n88

Manfrone, Pietro Paulo, 81, 91, 101, 274n88
Manuzio, Paolo, 15, *Lettere volgari di diversi nobilissimi huomini et eccellentissimi ingegni*, 24, 30, 35–41, 70, 79, 113
Marinella, Lucrezia, 176, 177, 237n20, 316n60
Marinello, Giovanni, 67, 68
Marino, Giovan Battista, 4
marriage: ages at, 257n86; in Isabella Andreini,178–80; in Lando, 68–70; in Lucrezia Gonzaga, 102–24; versus celibacy, 256n76
Matraini, Chiara, 4, 42, 140, 175, 302n65
Matt, Luigi, 35
Mazarin, Cardinal Jules (Giulio Mazzarini), 189, 196, 200–1, 311n28, 317n68
Miller, Nancy, 56
Miniatore, Bartolommeo, 14, 24, 135
Minutolo, Ceccarella (Francesca), 5
Molza, Francesco Maria, 38–9
Morata, Olimpia, 5
More, Thomas, 66
Moro, Giacomo, 40, 41
Muzio, Girolamo, 106, 108

Naudé, Gabriel, 189, 200–1
Nogarola, Isotta, 5, 8, 15, 20, 22, 23, 24, 26, 27, 28, 233nn3, 4
Nunnez, Alfonso, 109

Orsi, Guid'Ascania, 191, 192, 193, 201, 211, 313n38
Osteen, Mark, 150
Ovid, 13, 47, 78, 172, 232n49

Palmieri, Matteo, 71

Parabosco, Girolamo, 3, 10, 11, 14, 86, 106, 107, 108; *Lettere amorose*, 13, 123, 133, 135, 231n46. See also *Lettere amorose di madonna Celia Romana*
Paracelsus, 75
Parati, Graziella, 195
Petrarch, 4, 20–1, 22, 39
Piemontese, Alessio, 67, 74
Pighetti, Giacomo, 189, 201, 204, 208, 209, 210, 211, 310n27
Pireddu, Nicoletta, 150
Pisana, Camilla, 124
Polani, Betta, 191, 201
Polani, Giovanni, 204, 206, 207
Pona, Francesco, 189, 310n27
public sphere, 6, 8, 25, 26, 35, 218, 226n25

querelle des femmes, 4, 8, 15, 26, 61, 64, 71, 178, 180, 181, 215, 252n3
questione della donna, 10, 52, 84, 86, 177, 215
questione della lingua, 29, 35

Ramberti, Benedetto, 40
reader, external, 6, 7, 58, 185, 204, 208, 219
reader, internal, 6, 7, 38, 58, 185, 208, 219
Ricci, Bartolommeo, 82
Richardson, Samuel, 13
Rime in lode dell'illustrissima signora ... Lucrezia Gonzaga, 84, 264n12, 272n65
Robin, Diana, 22, 125
Robortello, Francesco, 105, 108
Rodi, Filippo, 82
Roncalli, Giovanni, 110, 111, 112
Rosa, Mario, 190

Rosenthal, Margaret, 152
Rossello, Timotheo, 74
Ruggiero, Guido, 127
Ruscelli, Girolamo, 84, 86, 102, 109, 110, 136, 275n94, 276n104, 277n118

Salutati, Coluccio, 21
Sanesi, Ireneo, 87–8, 91, 95
Sansovino, Francesco, 6, 14; *Del secretario*, 42, 135, 136, 137, 140, 148, 171, 172
Savorgnan, Maria, 5
Scala, Flaminio, 160
Scaligero, Giulio Cesare, 84
Schneider, Gary, 6
Schutte, Anne Jacobson, 115
Seidel Menchi, Silvana, 92
Serao, Matilde, 220
Sesti, Lodovico, 188
Sforza, Bona, 58, 61
Sforza, Isabella, 54, 56, 58, 59, 61, 73–4, 75
Smarr, Janet Levarie, 51
Speroni, Sperone, 10, 35, 38, 39, 40, 54, 130, 152
Stampa, Gaspara, 105, 106, 108
Steland, Dieter, 91
Strozzi, Alessandra Macinghi, 5

Taglienti, Giovanni Antonio, 24, 36, 136
Tarabotti, Arcangela, 3, 9, 10, 17, 22–3, 80, 120, 180, 215–20; *Antisatira*, 187, 188, 199, 201–4, controversy regarding, 207–12; autograph letters, 194; *Che le donne siano della spetie degli huomini*, 188; and forced enclosure, 17, 183, 184–6, 187, 201, 307n10; *Inferno monacale*, 18, 199; *La semplicità ingannata*, 186, 308n15 (see also *La tirannia paterna*); *La tirannia paterna*, 186, 187, 194, 201, 202, 317nn67, 68, 321n111; *Le lagrime*, 191–5, 198, 313n40; *Lettere familiari e di complimento*, 4, 16, 32, 134, 183, 184–5, 188, epistolary network in, 195–201, as defence of other works, 202–13; *Paradiso monacale*, 187, 194, 197, 199, 200, 309nn18, 19, controversy regarding, 201–7, 210, 218; *Purgatorio delle malmaritate*, 199, 309n23
Tasso, Bernardo, 37, 106, 108, 222n3
Tasso, Torquato, 164, 177, 181, 295n9
Terracina, Laura, 106, 108, 277n106
Textor, Ravisius: *Officina*, 48–52, 60, 71, 78, 79, 82, 91, 215, 249nn17, 18. *See also* Lando, Ortensio, use of repertories
Tintoretto. *See* Franco, Veronica
Tolomei, Claudio, 24, 35, 40, 41
Toscanella, Orazio, 86, 87, 135, 142

Valdés, Juan de, 115
Valier, Andrea, 211, 320n108
Vecellio, Cesare, 132
Venier, Domenico, 36, 128, 217; and Veronica Franco, 17, 124, 135, 148
Venier, Lorenzo: *Il trentuno della Zaffetta*, 128, 131, 134
Venier, Maffio, 129, 145, 150, 217, 284n31
Venier, Marco, 148, 150
ventriloquism, 10, 13, 15, 45, 72, 83, 133, 215, 245n3
Vernazza, Battistina, 190, 312n33
Veronese, Guarino, 26
Vives, Juan Luis, 8, 138, 179, 229n31

Weaver, Elissa, 317n69

Women: and chastity, 8, 9, 61–2; education of, 5, 8-9, 61-4, 228nn29, 30, 31; and silence, 8, 9, 11, 61–2; and speech, 92, 227n26. *See also individual names of women*; letters and letter collections

Xenophon, 226n25

Zanette, Emilio, 194
Zeno, Apostolo, 94